*Knowledge to Support
the Teaching of Reading*

Knowledge to Support the Teaching of Reading

Preparing Teachers for a Changing World

Catherine E. Snow
Peg Griffin
M. Susan Burns

Editors

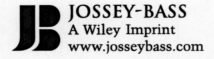

JOSSEY-BASS
A Wiley Imprint
www.josseybass.com

Published by Jossey-Bass
A Wiley Imprint
989 Market Street, San Francisco, CA 94103-1741   www.josseybass.com

Jossey-Bass books and products are available through most bookstores. To contact Jossey-Bass directly call our Customer Care Department within the U.S. at 800-956-7739, outside the U.S. at 317-572-3986, or fax 317-572-4002.

Jossey-Bass also publishes its books in a variety of electronic formats. Some content that appears in print may not be available in electronic books.

Library of Congress Cataloging-in-Publication Data

Knowledge to support the teaching of reading: preparing teachers for a changing world / Catherine Snow, Peg Griffin, M. Susan Burns, editors.
p. cm.—(The Jossey-Bass education series)
Includes bibliographical references and index.
ISBN-13 978-0-7879-7465-7 (alk. paper)
ISBN-13 978-0-7879-9633-8 (paperback)

1. Reading teachers—Training of. I. Snow, Catherine E. II. Griffin, Peg. III. Burns, M. Susan (Marie Susan) IV. Series.
LB2844.1.R4K58 2005
428.4'71—dc22
2005021190

PB Printing   10 9 8 7 6 5 4 3 2

The Jossey-Bass Education Series

CONTENTS

PREFACE

Virtually every teacher finds a need to teach reading as part and parcel of teaching students from kindergarten to grade twelve. We conceive of this teaching as instruction, not intervention. In other words, it is designed not to remediate the teaching and learning missed in a putatively inadequate "reading class" but to address the varying demands that learning to read presents as students encounter different topics and tasks. The question here is what this means for teacher education and professional development. The National Academy of Education, through its Committee on Teacher Education (CTE), devoted several years to analyzing effective initial teacher preparation. *Preparing Teachers for a Changing World: What Teachers Should Learn and Be Able to Do* (Darling-Hammond, Bransford, LePage, Hammerness, and Duffy, Jossey-Bass, 2005) was the result. *Knowledge to Support the Teaching of Reading* is a companion volume to that work; it is based on deliberations by a committee concerned with the teaching of reading by multisubject teachers from kindergarten through the elementary grades and by teachers specializing in the different departments that operate in high schools and some middle schools. Like the main volume, this book is intended for those charged with the preparation of teachers, in colleges and universities as well as in education agencies at the federal, state, district, and school levels.

The learning and teaching of reading has been the subject of detailed recent research, and considerable consensus has been achieved about effective practice; hence, reading is a good topic to start with to complement the broader scope of the main CTE volume. With so much information already available, though, one might wonder why we need another book about reading. Chapter One addresses this question head-on, outlining how rejecting the status-shift view of teacher preparation allows an escape from artificial and unrealistic limits on definitions of the knowledge base for teaching reading. A quite elaborate, specific, and detailed knowledge base can become useable knowledge when teacher preparation is seen as a developmental process of progressive differentiation emerging from recurring cycles of learning, enactment, assessment, and reflection. Chapter Two details the declarative knowledge about language, literacy, and their development that can be progressively differentiated as teachers develop through these cycles. In Chapter Three, the knowledge is depicted as it is enacted, and Chapter Four extends the enactment to the even more challenging situations that most teachers meet. Chapter Five focuses on assessment. Finally, Chapter Six, addressing the contexts of teacher education, provides for reflection on the changing nature of teachers' expertise and of useable knowledge as the cycles recur.

The authoring committee is a group with many differences in education, occupation, location, and practical and theoretical perspectives. One of our first decisions was to recognize two limits to our work. First, we do not attempt to address the preparation of reading specialists. We are concerned with teachers communicating and coordinating with specialists but not with the preparation of specialists themselves. Second, we could not duplicate the scope of the work of the main CTE. Instead, we would take for granted that the work of teaching reading includes matters that apply regardless of the subject being taught, and that each of the chapters in *Preparing Teachers for a Changing World* brought up issues important for planning and enacting teacher preparation regarding reading.

We link evidence about student accomplishments and effective instructional practices to teacher knowledge and teacher preparation. We place our work in one of the early cycles of learning, enactment, assessment, and reflection that should be undertaken by teacher educators. We stake out some grounds that can be enacted, evaluated, and reflected upon and, hence, could nurture further effective cycles of teacher preparation regarding reading.

The essential vision exemplified in this book is that literacy represents a domain every teacher, of any subject and at any grade, needs to know about. Adding literacy to the long list of items teachers must master may seem unrealistic. However, this problem disappears if we acknowledge that teacher knowledge is incomplete at the end of the preservice preparation, that teacher knowledge must be nurtured during inservice programs to ensure continued growth, and that teacher knowledge can become more reflective, analytical, and usable even as it grows. In the following chapters we sketch out the starting points for that growth and some of the steps along the way to expertise.

MEMBERS OF THE NATIONAL ACADEMY OF EDUCATION'S READING SUB-COMMITTEE

Committee chair:

Catherine E. Snow
Harvard University

Committee members:

M. Susan Burns
George Mason University

Claude Goldenberg
California State University,
Long Beach

Louisa C. Moats
Sopris West Educational Services

P. David Pearson
University of California, Berkeley

MaryEllen Vogt
California State University,
Long Beach

Gina Cervetti
University of California, Berkeley

Peg Griffin
Laboratory of Comparative
Human Cognition

Annemarie Sullivan Palincsar
University of Michigan

Dorothy S. Strickland
Rutgers University

Staff:

Helen Duffy, Pamela LePage

ACKNOWLEDGMENTS

Like all community efforts, this work owes a great deal to many individuals and organizations. The Committee would like to recognize Joan Baratz Snowden of the American Federation of Teachers, who conceived the initial idea for this effort and developed a proposal to move it forward. Ellen Condliffe Lagemann, then president of the National Academy of Education (NAE), worked to get the project launched, and Nel Noddings, her successor as president, provided ongoing support and assistance to bring it successfully to its conclusion. Key staff members at the Academy, especially NAE directors Kerith Gardner and Amy Swauger, supported the Committee's work in innumerable ways.

In addition, the Committee was ably assisted in its early stages by Ed Miech and subsequently Pamela LePage, who kept the Committee organized, arranged meetings, reminded us of deadlines, and thought with us about the issues of teacher knowledge of literacy. Helen Duffy contributed invaluably during the later stages of the project. She provided advice about substance and rhetoric as well as coordinated the production of the manuscript, dealing with reviewers, publishers, references, and many other such details until the work was complete.

The fairly lengthy process that produced this volume was highly collaborative. Much of the thinking that enriched all parts of the volume emerged from discussions within the literacy committee and the process of exchanging and revising drafts. It is thus difficult to assign authorship to specific parts of this volume. The entire original committee (Richard Anderson, M. Susan Burns, Claude Goldenberg, Peg Griffin, Louisa C. Moats, Annemarie Sullivan Palincsar, P. David Pearson, Joan Baratz Snowden, Dorothy S. Strickland, and Catherine E. Snow as chair) met once to develop a first outline for the volume. Other responsibilities subsequently made it impossible for Anderson and Snowden to continue working with the committee. We found we needed to bring in the expertise of MaryEllen Vogt and Gina Cervetti to supplement our own capacities at subsequent committee meetings and to assist with drafting chapters. We also profited from the advice of Tom Scruggs on the faculty at George Mason University and Judy Ericksen, a doctoral candidate at George Mason. Specific material was drafted by Snow for the introductory chapter; by Griffin, Moats, Goldenberg, and Vogt for the language base and reading development chapter; by Burns, Palincsar, Griffin, Snow, Goldenberg, and Vogt for the varying student vignettes; by Burns, Palincsar, Snow, and Goldenberg for the special challenges chapter; by Strickland and Snow for the assessment chapter; and by Pearson and Cervetti for the final chapter reflecting on teacher education. After various reorganizations of the available material, Snow, Griffin, and Burns edited the entire volume.

The Committee is grateful to Courtney Cazden, John T. Guthrie, Walter Kintsch, and Carole D. Lee for helpful reviews, and to George Hillocks, the moderator for the revision process on behalf of the Academy. The meeting expenses of the Committee and the staff support for it were funded by the U.S. Department of Education, under grant number R215U000018, and by the Ford Foundation, under grant number 1030-0468, through project officers Thelma Leenhouts of the Department of Education and Joe Aguerreberre of the Ford Foundation. While we are grateful for the support of these funders, the product of this work does not represent the policy of either agency, and readers should not assume endorsement by the federal government.

Finally, all the committee members wish to express gratitude to colleagues concerned with education who have provided information, example, debate, and encouragement. We hope the dialogue continues and the yield for children's learning improves.

ABOUT THE AUTHORS

COMMITTEE CHAIR:

Catherine E. Snow

Harvard University

Catherine E. Snow, Henry Lee Shattuck Professor at the Harvard Graduate School of Education, carries out research on first- and second-language acquisition and literacy development in monolingual and bilingual children. She chaired the committee that produced the National Research Council Report *Preventing Reading Difficulties in Young Children* and the study group that produced *Reading for Understanding: Toward an R&D Program in Reading Comprehension.* She is a former president of the American Educational Research Association and a member of the National Academy of Education. Her research focuses on the social-interactive origins of language and literacy skills, the ways in which oral-language skills relate to literacy learning, the literacy development of English-language learners, and implications of research on language and literacy development for teacher preparation.

COMMITTEE MEMBERS:

M. Susan Burns

George Mason University

M. Susan Burns, Ph.D., is co-coordinator of the Early Childhood Education Program in the College of Education and Human Development at George Mason

University. She has been active in national education policy on young children's early language and literacy development and the preparation of teachers for effective literacy instruction. Prior to her employment at George Mason University, she served as study director at the National Academy of Sciences/National Research Council for the Committee on the Prevention of Reading Difficulties in Young Children and the Committee for Early Childhood Pedagogy. Reports produced under her guidance and editorship during this time included *Preventing Reading Difficulties in Young Children, Starting Out Right: A Guide to Promoting Children's Reading Success,* and *Eager to Learn: Educating Our Preschoolers.* Most recently she is coauthor of *Preparing Our Teachers: Opportunities for Better Reading Instruction.*

Gina Cervetti

University of California, Berkeley
Gina Cervetti is a postdoctoral scholar at the University of California, Berkeley, Graduate School of Education. Her current research agenda concerns the role of text in learning science and the potential of science-literacy integration to support students' development of academic literacy. Before coming to UC Berkeley, Cervetti completed her doctoral work in educational psychology at Michigan State University, where she was a researcher at the Center for the Improvement of Early Reading Achievement.

Claude Goldenberg

California State University, Long Beach
Claude Goldenberg is professor of teacher education and associate dean of the College of Education, California State University, Long Beach. He received his Ph.D. degree in 1984 from the Graduate School of Education, UCLA. Prior to that he taught junior high school in San Antonio, Texas, and first grade in Los Angeles. His research interests include home and school factors in Latino children's achievement and the processes and dynamics of school change. He was a National Academy of Education Spencer Fellow and received the Albert J. Harris Award from the International Reading Association. His 1997 video *Settings for Change* described a five-year school-improvement project in a largely Latino, bilingual elementary school in the Los Angeles area. A book based on this project, *Successful School Change: Creating Settings to Improve Teaching and Learning,* was published in 2004 by Teachers College Press.

Peg Griffin

Laboratory of Comparative Human Cognition
Peg Griffin, holder of a Ph.D. degree in linguistics from Georgetown University, is a research affiliate of the Laboratory of Comparative Human Cognition of the University of California at San Diego. She studies language in education, both

as the topic of reading and writing instruction and as the medium for early education in mathematics and the social and natural sciences. She has collaborated on a variety of books: *Preventing Reading Difficulties in Young Children, Starting Out Right, Preparing Our Teachers: Opportunities for Better Reading Instruction,* and *The Construction Zone: Working for Cognitive Change in School.* Her theoretical interests are best represented in a coauthored book on model systems, *Socialno-istoricheskii Podhod V Psychologii Obuchenia,* and the more recent article "Collaboration in School: 'I (Don't) Know' Answers and Questions." She is currently collaborating on a study about the language, literacy, mathematics, and science content in preschools.

Louisa C. Moats

Sopris West Educational Services
Louisa C. Moats, Ed.D., recently completed four years as site director of the National Institute for Child Health and Human Development Early Interventions Project in Washington, D.C. This longitudinal, large-scale project was conducted through the University of Texas, Houston. It investigated the causes and remedies for reading failure in high-poverty urban schools. Moats spent the previous fifteen years in private practice as a licensed psychologist in Vermont, specializing in evaluation and consultation with individuals of all ages who experienced learning problems in reading and language. She has authored several books, including *Speech to Print: Language Essentials for Teachers*; *Spelling: Development, Disability, and Instruction*; *Straight Talk About Reading* (with Susan Hall); and *Parenting a Struggling Reader* (with Susan Hall). She has also written numerous journal articles, chapters, and policy papers. She is currently collaborating with Sopris West Educational Services on the development of LETRS (Language Essentials for Teachers of Reading and Spelling), a series of modules for teachers.

Annemarie Sullivan Palincsar

University of Michigan
Annemarie Sullivan Palincsar is the Jean and Charles Walgreen Jr. Chair of Reading and Literacy and a teacher educator at the University of Michigan. Her research focuses on the design of learning environments that support self-regulation in learning activity, especially for children who experience difficulty learning in school. She studies how children use literacy in the context of guided-inquiry science instruction, what types of text support children's inquiry, and what support students who are identified as atypical learners require to be successful in this instruction. Palincsar has served as a member of the National Academy's Research Council on the Prevention of Reading Difficulty in Young Children; the OERI/RAND Reading Study Group, The National Education Goals Panel, and the National Advisory Board to Children's Television Workshop. She is coeditor of the journal

Cognition and Instruction. She completed her doctorate at the Center for the Study of Reading at the University of Illinois, Champaign-Urbana.

P. David Pearson

University of California, Berkeley

P. David Pearson serves as dean of the Graduate School of Education at the University of California, Berkeley, and as a faculty member in its Language and Literacy program. His current research focuses on issues of reading instruction and reading assessment policies and practices at all levels—local, state, and national. Prior to coming to Berkeley in 2001, he served as the John A. Hannah Distinguished Professor of Education in the College of Education at Michigan State and as codirector of the Center for the Improvement of Early Reading Achievement. Even earlier, he was dean of the College of Education, codirector of the Center for the Study of Reading, and professor of curriculum and instruction at the University of Illinois. His initial professorial appointment was at the University of Minnesota in Minneapolis. The author of numerous books and articles, Pearson is a member of the National Academy of Education, the recipient of the International Reading Association's William S. Gray Award and its Albert J. Harris Award, and founding editor of the *Handbook of Reading Research.*

Dorothy S. Strickland

Rutgers University

Dorothy S. Strickland is the Samuel DeWitt Proctor Professor of Education at Rutgers University, The State University of New Jersey. A former classroom teacher, reading consultant, and learning disabilities specialist, she is a past president of both the International Reading Association (IRA) and the IRA Reading Hall of Fame. She received the IRA's Outstanding Teacher Educator of Reading Award. She was the recipient of the National Council of Teachers of English (NCTE) Award as Outstanding Educator in the Language Arts and the 1994 NCTE Rewey Belle Inglis Award as Outstanding Woman in the Teaching of English. She has numerous publications in the field of reading/language arts. She has recently authored or edited (alone or jointly) *Learning About Print in Preschool Settings; Bridging the Literacy Achievement Gap, Grades 4–12: Improving Reading Achievement Through Professional Development; Language Arts: Learning and Teaching; Preparing Our Teachers: Opportunities for Better Reading Instruction; The Administration and Supervision of Reading Programs;* and *Teaching Phonics Today.*

MaryEllen Vogt

California State University, Long Beach

MaryEllen Vogt is Professor Emerita of Education at California State University, Long Beach. A former reading specialist and special education teacher, she received her doctorate from the University of California, Berkeley. A coauthor of five books, including *Reading Specialists in the* Real *World: A Sociocultural View* and *Making Content Comprehensible for English Learners: The SIOP Model*, her research interests include improving comprehension in the content areas, teacher change and development, and content literacy and language acquisition for English language learners. She was inducted into the California Reading Hall of Fame and received her university's Distinguished Faculty Teaching Award. She is a former president of the International Reading Association.

STAFF:

Helen Duffy

Helen Duffy has served as the director of the Committee on Teacher Education (CTE) since August 2003. Before joining the CTE, she earned her Ph.D. from the University of California, Berkeley, where she received a UC All-Campus Consortium on Research for Diversity fellowship to study a University of California outreach effort called the High School Puente Project. She has taught English and composition at the high school and university levels and served as academic coordinator for UC Berkeley's English-teacher-education program. In addition to working for the CTE, she has been engaged in a three-year study of an elementary school literacy-reform effort in California's Silicon Valley. Her research interests include preservice and inservice teacher education, school reforms that promote equity and access to higher education, and adolescent literacy.

Pamela LePage

Pamela LePage is assistant professor of special education and co-coordinator of the program in special education for those with mild-to-moderate needs at San Francisco State University. Before working as the director of the Committee on Teacher Education at Stanford University from August 2001 to August 2003, she taught at George Mason University in an innovative and interdisciplinary master's program for practicing teachers. LePage earned a Ph.D. degree in special education from the joint University of California, Berkeley/San Francisco State program after teaching in special education for eleven years. She has coauthored or coedited three books, including *Transforming Teacher Education: Lessons in Professional Development* and *Educational Controversies: Toward a Discourse of Reconciliation.*

Knowledge to Support
the Teaching of Reading

CHAPTER ONE

Yet Another Report About Teacher Education?

In *Preventing Reading Difficulties in Young Children,*[1] enhanced teacher education was identified as a key strategy in improving reading instruction and thus reading outcomes. *Preventing Reading Difficulties* was based on an extensive review and synthesis of a rich research base on reading development. Writing an equivalent report that might be called *Preventing Instructional Disasters in Novice Teachers' Classrooms* would have a much less rich basis in directly relevant research. Many of the claims in such a report would have to be inferred from evidence about children's literacy development, such as that reviewed in *Preventing Reading Difficulties* and in the *Report of the National Reading Panel* (National Reading Panel, 2000). The link from evidence about child accomplishments and effective instructional practices to required teacher knowledge and effective teacher education requires a fairly high level of inference.

Of course, the fictive *Preventing Instructional Disasters* could draw on information such as that reviewed in the National Research Council report *How People Learn* (Bransford, Brown, and Cocking, 1999) about how real, transferable, usable knowledge is acquired, both by adults and by children. It could also draw from the growing body of information about effective and ineffective strategies in teacher education and professional development that is based both

---

[1] A National Research Council report (Snow, Burns, and Griffin, 1998).

in the wisdom of practice and in systematic reviews of successful preservice and inservice teacher-education programs.

Unfortunately, though, all these sources of information add up to less clarity than we might wish to have about the optimal design of teacher education to ensure adequate preparation for all teachers in literacy. We simply do not have the research base we need—a convergent program of research in which content and method in teacher preparation or professional development programs have been manipulated, and accompanying changes in teacher knowledge, teacher behavior, and child outcomes charted. Nor can we wait for that research base. Teachers are being prepared in their thousands every year, and the projected need for new teachers is enormous. Thus, we are impelled to take the relevant information available to us as a basis for recommendations about how to prepare teachers to teach reading more effectively. We offer these recommendations as working hypotheses, with the full recognition that they will need to be constantly evaluated along the way. In other words, teacher educators must start working the way excellent teachers work, by imposing on their own profession a recurrent cycle of *learning, enactment, assessment,* and *reflection.*

Nor should the lack of a fully specified research base discourage us regarding the value of what we do know or the appropriateness of much current practice in teacher education. Medical education, in which professionalization and high standards were introduced in a rather draconian fashion as a result of the Flexner report (Flexner and Pritchett, 1910) and which is often cited as a model for reform in teacher education, has never been subjected to systematic assessment. The content of what is taught in medical schools is defined by "science-based medicine," but medical faculties are experimenting all the time with variations in how to make the learning more efficient and more connected to clinical practice, at the same time preparing M.D.s to function as doctors and to engage in continued informal and formal learning (Tosteson, Adelstein, and Carver, 1994).

We take as a central process in any educational effort the learning, enactment, assessment, and reflection cycle—a cycle of activities in which learners start with what they know, but are committed to assessing efficacy of the enactment of that knowledge in recognition that what they know is insufficient. This cycle applies as much to those of us educating teachers or providing guidelines for teacher education as to those learners starting on the road to certification as teachers. What would this cycle look like for teacher education? It would mean enacting a form of teacher education that is based as firmly as possible on what has been learned from research, assessing systematically the effectiveness of that education, reflecting on where it has fallen short and how it could be improved, thus generating new learning which in turn starts the next cycle at a higher level. In this book we offer a set of recommendations for the design and enactment of teacher education based on what is currently known from research about literacy development, literacy instruction, and student and teacher learning. Needless to say, we accompany this sketch of enactment with an exhortation to attend to the assessment and reflection components of the cycle in enacting these recommendations.

The urgency of our recommendations is enhanced by the consensus among national organizations focusing on education that a new design for teacher education is needed. Commissions, committees, and reports focused on teacher education have been launched by the American Educational Research Association (AERA), the International Reading Association (IRA), the American Association of Colleges for Teacher Education (AACTE), and by the National Academy of Education (NAE). The NAE established a Committee on Teacher Education (CTE), chaired by Linda Darling-Hammond and John Bransford, to prepare a report providing a comprehensive picture of the requirements for improved teacher education. That report, *Preparing Teachers for a Changing World: What Teachers Should Learn and Be Able to Do* (Darling-Hammond, Bransford, LePage, Hammerness, and Duffy, 2005), constitutes the context for this book, which focuses specifically on the knowledge about literacy that all teachers need to have. This report builds on the advanced degree of consensus within the field of education concerning the characteristics of good literacy instruction. The content specifications for this literacy report can build on a broader base of research than would be the case for fields such as math, social studies, or science.[2]

Writing a report like this is not, of course, a novel undertaking. A number of attempts have been made to sketch the teacher's required knowledge base for teaching reading—several with participation by members of this very committee. As one member put it at a planning meeting, "I can't stand the thought of producing another list of things teachers should know and don't"—a sentiment all of us recognized we shared as soon as it was uttered.

How is this report, then, different from its predecessors? It is, first of all, emphatically not a list. It grows out of a developmental view of adult learning that specifies various stages or levels of knowledge, and that presupposes the development of structures to support the learning of teachers across their careers, comparable to the developmental view of child learning endorsed in *Preventing Reading Difficulties*. Second, it focuses on usable knowledge—thinking about how to ensure that teachers develop real, practice-based, useful knowledge rather than the sort of knowledge that is easy to assess but hard to use. Third, it tries to represent the required knowledge systemically, in a way that makes

---

[2] With the release in 2002 of the RAND report on mathematics, which focuses on issues of teacher education for teaching math, one might think that math teaching falls into the same category as literacy teaching (Ball and RAND Mathematics Study Panel, 2002). The RAND report recommendations, though, mostly specify the research agenda needed to figure out what kinds of preparation math teachers need and profit from, rather than specifying what they need to know.

Exhibit 1.1. Previous Reports on Preparation of Literacy Teachers

Teaching Reading Is Rocket Science (Moats, 1999)

Teaching Teachers to Teach Reading: Paradigm Shifts, Persistent Problems, and Challenges (Anders, Hoffman, and Duffy, 2000)

Reading Teacher Education in the Next Millennium: What Your Grandmother's Teacher Didn't Know That Your Granddaughter's Teacher Should (Hoffman and Pearson, 2000)

Features of Excellence of Reading Teacher Preparation Programs (Harmon, Hedrick, Martinez, Perez, Keehn, Fine, and others, 2001)

What Teachers Need to Know About Language (Fillmore and Snow, 2002)

Preparing Our Teachers: Opportunities for Better Reading Instruction (Strickland, Snow, Griffin, Burns, and McNamara, 2002)

Standards for Reading Professionals (Revised). (International Reading Association, 2003)

---

clear how disciplinary knowledge (in this case, drawn both from the various hyphenated-linguistics disciplines and from the cognitive psychology of reading) does and does not shape and dictate teacher knowledge. In this chapter, we describe the structure of our thinking about the following things: adult development; the characteristics of and prerequisites to usable knowledge; and the contributions of cognitive psychology and linguistics, which we take to include psycho-, socio-, and discourse-linguistics, to the definition of the knowledge teachers need to teach literacy effectively.

For each of those three areas we also discuss the warrants for arguing that they are worth attending to. As noted earlier, those warrants do not typically derive from experimental studies demonstrating impact or effectiveness. They often derive from somewhat more indirect arguments. Thus, we are proposing two linked activities: changes in teacher education and professional development, and evaluation of those changes through assessment of teacher and student learning at every stage of the change. Like improving reading instruction, improving teacher education is an inherently empirical undertaking.

ADULT DEVELOPMENT AND TEACHER CAREERS

In *Preventing Reading Difficulties in Young Children,* a contrast was drawn between traditional readiness models of reading and current emergent literacy models. Readiness models see reading as a product of instruction that should only be introduced after certain maturational milestones have been reached. Emergent literacy approaches, however, emphasize the many accomplishments of very young children that are directly related to literacy development—learning about the functions of print, learning about how language is used differently in written and in spoken language, starting to enact writing with scribbling and reading with recitation of the text of familiar picture books, and learning to recognize some letters and some printed words. Whether one wants to identify these accomplishments as "literacy" or not, it is clear that they represent knowledge and capabilities that the maturationist, readiness view would render invisible.

Similarly, we argue that the traditional, and still widely accepted, view of teacher education is one that is too dominated by the identification of sharp shifts in status and hypothesized accompanying shifts in capacity. Young men and women are certified as teachers after a certain number of courses in education and some prescribed number of hours of supervised classroom experience. As soon as certification requirements are achieved, these women and men are given the full list of responsibilities associated with being a teacher—a classroom full of students, considerable choice (in some places) among curricula, partial to complete control over the scheduling of the students' learning activities, accountability for classroom management and for student progress, freedom to refer children for evaluation for special services, and a very high level of autonomy. Such teachers are very unlikely to receive much supervision or, unless they are good at seeking it out for themselves, much consultation or advice. Having achieved the status of certified teacher, they may well then continue in that status for forty years, with no systematic opportunity to move toward a higher degree of qualification, to fill in areas of knowledge that might have been skimped on in their preservice programs, or to become acquainted with newly emerging research findings.

We argue that this *status-shift* view of teacher development accords poorly with what we know about adult development, human learning, and the description of the knowledge domains teachers need to acquire. Compare the teacher-education model to other forms of professional preparation. An aspirant barber in Massachusetts studies for a thousand credit hours over seven to ten months, engaging in supervised practice for up to fifteen hours a week during the "preservice" phase of training, then must operate for a full year in a shop under the supervision of an experienced barber before being allowed to open an independent business. An aspirant medical doctor in the United States is required to cover many hours of premedical, basic science training and pass an exam to qualify for entry into medical school, then to engage in three years of full-time study including increasingly challenging tasks involving patient contact, then to fulfill a full year's internship, before even being allowed to treat a patient without supervision; M.D.s seeking specialization may experience another several years of supervised practice and practice-based learning.

It is striking that teacher preparation resembles barber preparation more than medical preparation—and even then falls short in the amount of supervised practice required before independent action! The aspirant M.D. goes through at least three, and often five, developmental stages, whereas the average aspirant teacher has only two—precertified and certified. Of course, induction-year programs are widely recommended, but they have been effectively implemented for only a tiny proportion of new teachers—far fewer than the number that enters teaching without even having completed a preservice certification program! The single status-shift model for teacher career development places an enormous burden on the preservice program, requiring that it provide far more knowledge and practical skills than anyone could reasonably acquire within a few short years. It also rests on the myth that what teachers need to know is a fixed body of knowledge—that a systematic procedure for ensuring access to new evidence and new conceptions is unnecessary. Most devastatingly, though, it conflicts with the conception of the teacher as a lifelong learner who could be motivated and should be rewarded by recognition of status changes throughout the length of a career—from novice teacher to collaborating teacher to master teacher to coach, for example—especially if those status shifts are accompanied by increases in remuneration and responsibility.

The incentive structure of a career-long developmental pathway for teachers is not the most important reason to propose this model. More compellingly, a model like this fits with our presupposition of *progressive differentiation* as a general framework for thinking about teacher education. *Progressive differentiation* refers to a process of development in which the capacities being used at any point are analyzed and elaborated, in response to evidence that they fall short. Thus, for example, a novice teacher's skillful use of a prescribed, well-structured literacy curriculum represents a developmental accomplishment; the teacher's recognition that the curriculum is not being effective with a subset of the children in her or his first-grade classroom (for example, the English-language learners, or ELLs) generates an opportunity to analyze the curriculum, to think about the skills it presupposes, and to design supplementary or alternative teaching models for the ELL children. The teacher's skill in using the curriculum is not superceded, but rather analyzed and elaborated, leading eventually to a reorganization of her or his enacted knowledge into reflective knowledge.

We distinguish five levels of increasing progressive differentiation roughly correlated with five points in the teacher's career progression: preservice, apprentice, novice, experienced, and master teacher. Teachers at each of these points on their developmental and career trajectories should be engaged in cycles of learning, enactment, assessment, and reflection, though the weight placed on each of these activities shifts with experience. Clearly, preservice, apprentice, and novice teachers are most heavily involved in new learning, whereas experienced and master teachers are placing more emphasis on assessment and reflection. But each of the steps in the cycle is crucial for all. We can describe five points in a teacher's development by characterizing the type of knowing that dominates at each point. Figure 1.1 is a representation of how those different types of knowledge might be distributed at various points in a teacher's career. Remember, though, that the total knowledge available grows.

Declarative Knowledge The student pursuing an education major or certification program is primarily engaged in acquiring declarative knowledge (learning, from books or lectures, about child development, about instructional approaches, about text analysis, and so on) and in acquiring a declarative version of procedural knowledge—the capacity to answer questions about what one should do in various situations. This stage of knowledge development is when a solid foundation of disciplinary knowledge relevant to success as a teacher will typically be acquired; given constraints of time and energy, that

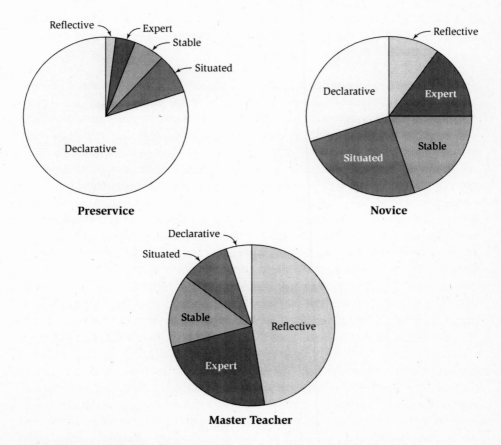

Figure 1.1. Knowledge Representation at Three Points of a Teacher's Career

places on teacher educators the burden of being analytical about precisely what that knowledge must be.

Situated, Can-Do Procedural Knowledge. It is a commonplace observation that declarative knowledge is an inadequate basis for good practice. Having successfully answered a test question about what to do when one's car starts to skid does not ensure that we avoid slamming on the brakes and remember to steer into the skid the first time we hit black ice at sixty miles per hour. Similarly, having studied the normative progression of children from prereading to conventional reading does not ensure that a first-grade teacher can identify precisely where on that developmental progression the children in his or her class are or can know how to arrive at the best instructional response to each of their needs. Procedural knowledge is complex, and we distinguish between the level of procedural knowledge required to function effectively in a relatively simple situation, for example, as a teacher of a small homogeneous group of children or in a highly scaffolded situation (for example, with support from an excellent mentor teacher) and the level needed for independent functioning in a typical U.S. classroom.

Stable Procedural Knowledge. The well-prepared first-year teacher should have a level of declarative and procedural knowledge stable enough to support functioning under "normal circumstances"—she or he can plan instruction that will work for the majority of the class, can maintain order and implement the planned instruction, can assess child progress, and can adapt instruction within the limits of "normal practice." Such a beginning teacher might well be expected, though, to need help in designing and delivering instruction for some percentage of children in the class—those who come from an unfamiliar linguistic or cultural background, those who don't respond to the standard instruction, and those encountering particular difficulties learning to read. The "well-started novice teacher" needs a well-structured, reliable set of supports to deal effectively with such children—supports not only for the benefit of the children, but also supports to student learning that build in opportunities for teacher learning. Think of the analogy with the resident confronting his or her first case of diphtheria or beri-beri, who is expected to request help in diagnosing and treating it and to learn from that experience how to treat the next case.

Expert, Adaptive Knowledge. The experienced teacher is expected to be able to deal with a full array of instructional challenges, to identify problems for which the current knowledge base offers inadequate guidance, to seek new relevant research-based knowledge, and to incorporate that knowledge into his or her knowledge structures. The experienced teacher should have a role in the school that acknowledges and uses his or her experience—supervising student teachers, of course, but also mentoring novice teachers, taking a leadership role in teacher learning groups, and serving as a consultant for students who present particular challenges.

Reflective, Organized, Analyzed Knowledge. The master teacher has enough experience to analyze what she or he has learned in courses, read in books, or heard at professional conferences and evaluate it as useful or not, well-founded or not. The master teacher is, ideally, responsible for leading professional development activities within a school or department, is available as a consultant teacher to less experienced colleagues, and is, perhaps, even collaborating with faculty members in preservice programs to design and deliver teacher-education courses.

We argue that the quantity and complexity of the declarative and practical knowledge teachers need to be successful teachers of reading is so great that it simply cannot be mastered adequately in the brief time available during a preservice program. At the same time, preservice teachers can learn enough about teaching reading to do it adequately for many child learners, if provided with a decent curriculum and a reasonable level of support. With the help and consultation of a more experienced teacher, novices should be able to address the needs of most of the children in any classroom.

We argue, in short, that it is crucial to conceptualize what teachers need to know to teach reading within a developmental framework: How much is needed so that novice teachers at a bare minimum do no harm? How much is needed for a teacher to be in charge of selecting curriculum, and individualizing instruction, independently? How much is needed for a teacher to be a reliable resource for one's colleagues, or to be the person who evaluates teacher performance and designs professional development?

For this report, we specify only a couple of these levels—novice and expert. Of course, these five levels should not be thought of as "stages" separated from one another by sharp discontinuities in knowledge. Rather, they represent points on a trajectory during which knowledge becomes increasingly differentiated and subject to analysis.

DISCIPLINARY BASES

Reading is, at its basis, about language and about thinking. We read language; orthographic systems are ways of representing the spoken language, and characteristics of languages determine to a significant degree how they will be written down. Thus, we start with the claim that prospective teachers of reading need to know something about language structure—systems and subsystems. We recognize as well that courses in linguistics are not typically well-suited to the needs of teachers, precisely because they do not, in general, present knowledge about language in a form that is directly usable.

The linguistic knowledge base for teaching reading is often scanted in teacher education, perhaps because it is seen as too complex and technical. Linguists distinguish a variety of language systems—separate rule systems, each with its own unit of analysis, constraints, and criteria for correctness. These are, for the formal linguist, phonology, morphology, syntax, and semantics. Sociolinguists or anthropological linguists might add pragmatics, which encompasses the expression of communicative intents, conversational rules, and discourse rules. Historical linguists would certainly add etymology to the list. Descriptive linguists would include orthography. (Chapter Two gives a more extended description of each of these domains.)

Cognitive psychologists and psycholinguists would chime in at this point that understanding the language system requires understanding something about how it is used. Language use encompasses many topics—how normal speakers acquire language; process oral and written language for comprehension; generate spoken language in real time; remember information presented linguistically; and segment, identify, formulate, and retrieve meaning for words, expressions, syntactic structures, and texts. In addition, understanding language use requires attention to the ways congenital or adventitious language disorders disrupt various aspects of linguistic functioning. Language is used, furthermore, in somewhat different ways in different fields—historical texts differ in predictable ways from literary or scientific texts, and the discourse rules for various disciplines are clearly distinct. In fact, to some extent the discipline-appropriate use of language functions to define the ways of thinking appropriate to those disciplines and to define the language user as a qualified historian, literary analyst, or scientist.

Psycholinguists would also point out that many speakers progress beyond knowing how to use language as a system of communication, achieving the metacognitive capacity to reflect on language. The capacity to be meta-analytic about phonological structure is directly relevant to understanding alphabetic writing systems and producing puns. The capacity to be meta-analytic about grammatical structure is helpful in comprehending text, understanding structural ambiguities, analyzing style, and revising written texts. The capacity to be meta-analytic about discourse structure is key in literary analysis, in learning from text, and in appreciating differences in text associated with genre and with culture.

Developmental psychologists, furthermore, would emphasize the need to understand the development of these various language systems and functions, as well as the development of knowledge specific to literacy, such as characteristics of the orthographic system and of written language. Indeed, for teachers engaged in the learning, enactment, assessment, and reflection cycle, having acquired a conceptualization of the larger developmental trajectory along which their students are progressing is key to their capacity to enact instruction, to assess appropriately, and to reflect productively.

So are we proposing that future teachers need to study language divided up into these many subcategories of linguistic, hyphenated-linguistic, and cognitive analysis? No, that would violate our commitment to building teacher education on *usable knowledge*—knowledge that is embedded in practice rather than being isolated from it. But we are suggesting that having a sense of the full range of options within a systemic and systematic view of language will help teachers start on their journey to fully differentiated and fully implementable knowledge.

USABLE KNOWLEDGE

There are years' worth of fascinating things one could learn about the cognitive psychology of learning, about linguistics, about social and motivational development, and about other topics relevant to teaching children to read. Indeed, some people devote their entire lives to these disciplines. But considerable work is needed to make the knowledge they generate usable for practitioners. The challenge of sifting the usable from the merely interesting is huge and constitutes one of the reasons that teacher education is so hard to do well. Those best equipped to define what is usable, namely experienced and reflective practitioners, are typically not the best steeped in the disciplinary knowledge base. Those most knowledgeable about the disciplines are ill-equipped to decide what aspects of it are usable (see Burling, 1971, for a linguist's reflections on teaching linguistics to teachers).

The traditional, rather strict, criterion for usability is "Will it help on Monday morning?" This is, of course, short-sightedly restrictive. Next Monday morning is only one point on a teacher's trajectory toward expertise; the usability of knowledge provided in teacher education should not expire so quickly.

We argue that a crucial criterion for usability is contribution to the ongoing differentiation of teachers' understanding—a process that will occur through conversations with other teachers and with researchers throughout their teaching careers. Thus, one crucial role for technical knowledge about reading (and control over the associated technical vocabulary, that is, words like *phoneme, morpheme, orthography, onset, rime,* and so on) is to enable teachers to communicate with one another effectively about their professional experiences. Stigler and Hiebert (1999) note that one of the key outcomes of intensive lesson study among Japanese teachers is their increasing convergence on a shared language for talking about teaching and learning. Another source of such a convergence is learning how certain phenomena are talked about within their source disciplines. Anyone who has not studied reading development, educational linguistics, and literacy methods is likely to be genuinely confused about whether phonological awareness and phonics are the same thing, how phonological awareness relates to phonemic awareness, how cognates are different from loan words, whether using loan words is the same as code-switching, and exactly what constitutes a writers' workshop. If teachers are confused about these questions, that constitutes an indictment of their preservice preparation, because such knowledge is crucial for professional communication (see Fillmore and Snow, 2002). Furthermore, if a group of teachers all use the same terms but each with a slightly idiosyncratic definition, then the possibilities for collaboration and mutual learning are invisibly undermined.

Quite abstruse knowledge is potentially usable—but making it usable is, at least for preservice and apprentice teachers, the role of the teacher educator. We cannot assume that teacher-education students will draw inferences about how and when their newly acquired knowledge should be used, any more than we can assume that fourth-graders will know without instruction how to draw inferences from text.

One way to make knowledge about language usable is to connect it directly to topics of burning interest to teachers: How do I plan instruction? How do I know in general what my students know and need to know? What do I do about the students who seem to be falling behind? The chapters that follow in this book attempt to present the answers to these questions in ways that reveal how knowledge from these disciplinary domains is crucial, and also ultimately highly usable. We have organized those chapters following the learning, enactment, assessment, and reflection cycle, and whenever possible, we describe the implications for the progressive differentiation of teacher knowledge.

Chapter Two focuses on the *learning* stage of the cycle—it defines the declarative knowledge about language, literacy, and their development that teachers need to learn. The topics dealt with in Chapter Two, phonology, orthography, morphology, syntax, semantics, pragmatics, etymology, and metacognition, are related explicitly to key elements of good reading instruction for teachers of students in kindergarten through secondary school. Chapter Two presents a description of reading development that abstracts from the complexities of individual and group differences. It is designed to make clear what usable knowledge about reading development would look like, not just for teachers in the primary grades for whom teaching reading is a well-defined task, but also for content-area teachers whose tasks include teaching students to read for learning in their subjects. Although there is considerable variability in the sophistication with which teachers might know the material presented in Chapter Two, an initial familiarity with it would constitute the stable, procedural knowledge any teacher of reading should have.

Chapter Three bridges from learning to *enactment,* showing declarative knowledge being enacted in a situated, procedural way in typical classrooms; we select kindergarten, fourth grade, and ninth grade to focus on, in order to be able to exemplify instructional approaches to the two major challenges children learning to read face: word reading and comprehension. Chapter Four extends the treatment of *enactment,* introducing the challenge of students who are not acquiring language or literacy skills in the typical, expected way; such students require of teachers expert, adaptive knowledge if they are to thrive, and a considerable research basis exists for recommending intervention with struggling readers, at least in the early elementary grades. While less definitive guidelines can be offered for intervention with middle- and secondary-school students, we summarize the scant available relevant literature as well.

Chapter Five focuses on *assessment,* and in particular on the array of tools teachers could use to chart the developmental progress of their students and to identify particular obstacles the students are facing. It outlines the usable knowledge base for engaging in instructional assessment. Assessment is a key move in the learning, enactment, assessment, and reflection cycle, and thus having knowledge about assessments is crucial for teachers at all points in their development.

Finally, Chapter Six addresses the context of teacher education—the conditions that need to be in place to ensure teachers the opportunities for *reflection* they need. In Chapter Six, we turn to the issue of how the vision for teacher education that is developed here might actually be implemented—what structures in universities, in teacher-education colleges, in school systems, and in professional societies would need to be changed. This is the chapter in which we sketch what is necessary to ensure that this book does more than gather dust on bookshelves next to its predecessors.

Of course, we must acknowledge that the state of knowledge about supporting literacy development, and thus about preparing teachers, is far from complete. In particular, there is need for more evidence about middle and secondary students' literacy learning. Research literature provides only limited answers to questions such as how to support the literacy development of English-language learners who arrive in late elementary or secondary grades, especially those with limited first-language literacy skills, or how best to deliver education to older students with special needs because of dyslexia, language disorders, or other learning disabilities. The limitations on research-based answers to such questions suggest the value of greater attention to the distilled wisdom of successful practitioners as at least a place to start in formulating directions for practice.

THE LIMITS OF TEACHER EDUCATION

Knowledge about language systems is not enough, of course, for a full understanding of reading. Reading with comprehension requires forming a mental representation of the message conveyed—an enormously complex process that is dependent on attentional processes, short- and long-term memory, prior knowledge, and the reader's preexisting theories or cognitive structures, as well as on the accurate conversion of orthographic to phonological representations.

If teachers do not know something of the cognitive bases for successful comprehension, they are unable to support continued growth in reading or use of reading in the content areas optimally. Issues of cognitive development, learning principles, and content-specific teaching knowledge are dealt with in *Preparing Teachers for a Changing World* (Darling-Hammond, Bransford, LePage, Hammerness, and Duffy, 2005).

Furthermore, successful reading instruction requires recruiting student motivation and interest; children learn to read, after all, in order to use that system to read about topics of interest to them, to learn about history and biology and literature, and to participate in a literate society. Unless teachers have some understanding of student motivation, wide knowledge of reading materials that might appeal to students with varying interests, and appreciation for the role of literacy in the lives of their students, they are likely to fall short in preparing their students.

Even expert-level knowledge of language and literacy as abstract systems will not help the teacher who has insufficient knowledge of developmentally appropriate practice for students across the K–12 age span, who do not understand curriculum and its uses, who lack classroom-management skills, and who cannot operate in the complex organizational structure of schools. These topics are addressed in *Preparing Teachers for a Changing World* and so we do not dwell on them here. But we cannot overemphasize their importance.

Improvements in teacher education and professional development hold great promise for improving the quality of teaching and learning in U.S. schools. We must be realistic, though, about the limits of schooling as an agent of reform. As Richard Rothstein points out in *Class and Schools: Using Social, Economic, and Educational Reform to Close the Black-White Achievement Gap* (2004), children arrive at school with vastly different stores of experience, knowledge, and expectations about learning. Schools can be asked to help all children optimize their potential, but they cannot credibly be asked to eliminate all differences among children of different social classes, with their immensely varying familial resources and drastically contrasting expectations for their futures. Eliminating class differences in academic outcomes will require economic and social as well as educational reform. A key aspect of the needed educational reform is to ensure that teachers are well prepared for their challenging tasks.

CHAPTER TWO

Students Change

What Are Teachers to Learn About Reading Development?

"What are you reading that for?" In February, midway through the school year, students in effective schools might offer these answers:

KINDERGARTENERS: "I can read it all by myself. Want to hear me?" "It's about Sponge Bob, see?"

GRADE FOUR STUDENTS: "It's the new Lemony Snicket book." "I want to show my Dad I know how to take care of a Doberman."

GRADE NINE STUDENTS: "I want to do my science project on that DNA that's in murder trials." "It's for a book report. But Marco says it's cool."

They read for information, enjoyment, pride, and curiosity. They read because they have to and because they want to. They read to be grown up, to grapple with ideas and emotions, to solve problems, to make a better way in the world, and to pass the time of day.

All these students are reading in some sense and learning to read in another sense. As students progress, they need teachers in different ways. Sometimes with the youngest children, teachers serve as surrogate readers. The teacher encodes into speech what an author wrote and collaborates with the children so they can integrate information, infer and interpret meaning, use and appreciate the text, and accomplish at least some part of their purposes for reading in the first place. When students do more of the reading "all by themselves," the teacher fills in only when needed and prepares for more progress. There are lessons introducing decoding and comprehension skills, strategies, and problem-solving routines. There are activities designed to ensure that students practice these skills, strategies, and routines. The teacher orchestrates motivation and occasions for application to ever-more-challenging texts. The students begin to succeed on their own, even with texts and words they have never seen before. They rely on the written words to figure out the writer's intended meaning and arrive at interpretations that suit their own purposes.

Students leaving the primary grades take advantage of their growing fluency, quickly and accurately integrating decoding and comprehension. In the middle grades, teachers guide students through encounters with structures and features of written language so they can grapple with more intricate texts and literacy tasks. Lessons focus on texts with harder words—how to pronounce written multisyllabic words and ones with rare spelling patterns, and how to find the meaning of more-specialized words. Students learn to take responsibility for continued learning: self-teaching for automatic recognition of words encountered in texts but not explicitly on the syllabus; refining cognitive and metacognitive strategies and applying them to comprehend passages; using motivational tactics to engage and persist even when the reading is hard; and exercising practical social and intellectual skills to find and use resources needed to understand a word or a text, to pursue ideas, and to answer questions and formulate new ones.

By high school, students in effective educational systems are reading and learning while teachers are teaching everything but reading as it has been conventionally envisioned. Instead, for example, the students' history teacher works on improving their reading of certain kinds of texts read for certain types of purposes, the science teacher for others, and the literature teacher for still more. Different subject matters call for learning specific vocabularies, styles of writing, formats, graphic and numerical representations, canons of reasoning and interpretation, or standards of quality in expression, argument, and proof. Although students are reading and writing and learning to read and write better, the teachers and students think of themselves as doing, for example, physics, African geography, or nineteenth-century American literature.

In this chapter we focus on how students' reading changes from kindergarten to high school and what underlies teacher ability to foster student growth. We define and illustrate the knowledge about language and about literacy development and instruction that effective teachers need, and by implication the kinds of professional preparation and support they should have. It should be clear, though, that preparing to teach students to read well also calls on teacher educators to provide teachers with opportunities to gain pedagogical expertise based on a much wider range of psychological, social, and cultural knowledge, dispositions, and practical skills for working effectively in the classroom (see Darling-Hammond, Bransford, LePage, Hammerness, and Duffy, 2005).

LANGUAGE AND LITERACY: INTEGRATED SYSTEMS AND SUB-SYSTEMS

Literacy is a secondary system, dependent on language as the primary system, so effective teachers of reading know a good deal about language. Part of what they know is how to talk about language using the appropriate technical terms (see Exhibit 2.1). Effective teachers of reading also know about the complexity involved in skilled reading. Figure 2.1 is one psychologist's depiction of the strands that compose skilled reading (Scarborough, 2001). The figure highlights the important distinction between word identification, which becomes increasingly rapid, automatic, and "out of awareness" as it develops, and comprehension, which becomes increasingly strategic, requiring metacognition and resource allocation, as it develops.

Language and Literacy Before School

Development in the preschool years that is relevant to the later teaching of reading is the subject of a good deal of research.[1] In the beginning, a baby's vocalizations are natural (rather than conventional) expressions that are interpreted and responded to by the baby's caretakers. Some baby vocalizations are coordinated with the discourse units of the social group; adults are charmed to interpret babies' turns in conversations. Skeletal pragmatic and semantic acts are encouraged. Adults try to understand babies' utterances as meaningful versions of their language, and babies appropriate what they notice in the adult language addressed to them and used around them. Soon, the structure of the child's sound system migrates toward the phonology of the language used in the community. The child begins to comprehend words and expressions from the language. As the child acquires and uses conventional vocabulary items, the semantic and pragmatic systems also flourish. When a child has between fifty and two hundred words to use, morphological classes (such as nouns and verbs) and processes (for instance, suffix for plural) appear in their repertoire and syntactical structures (for example, subject-predicate sequences) organize words, phrases, and clauses for conventional semantic interpretation and pragmatic function.

The child's metacognition grows in several ways that nourish both further language and literacy learning. First, communicative breakdowns lead children to request clarifications and to repair their own utterances spontaneously. This involves the same kind of comprehension monitoring that will later be a

Exhibit 2.1. A Brief Glossary of Technical Terms About Language and Literacy Systems

Phonology: the sound system of a language. At the subword level, three segmental phonemes make up the word *man.* Change one phoneme and the word changes to, for example, *ran, men,* or *map.* Phoneme ordering matters, too: *stop* is different from *spot.* Suprasegmental phonology includes the pitch and duration patterns that we recognize as sentence intonation and word stress.

Morphology: the system of the smallest units of meaning in a language, words and parts of words. The word *reddened* has three morphemes: the root or base adjective, *red;* the morpheme that indicates the verb class, *-en;* and the morpheme that indicates past tense, *-ed.*

Syntax: the system of phrases, clauses, and sentences. Take the example "What the world needs now is love." It is a sentence with a noun phrase as the subject ("what the world needs now") and a predicate made of a verb ("is") with a very much simpler noun phrase ("love"). The subject of the sentence is an embedded clause, itself having a subject and predicate. Notice the subtle syntactic and morphological differences between the embedded clause and the interrogative sentence, "What does the world need now?"

Semantics: the system of propositions and references. The semantics of a proposition such as "Some parents danced with all the children" is meaningful and can be judged for truth when the parents, children, and dancing referred to can be specified and when the reciprocal relations and scope of the quantifiers ("some," "all") are factored in to sort out who has been asserted to dance with whom.

Pragmatics: the use of language in different situations to accomplish the speaker's intentions. Pragmatics includes systems of conventions and constraints related to interpersonal and institutional relations and purposes (for example, polite and effective requests for action or information, adequate references, deference to elders or superiors, wording and participant structures of legal ceremonies). Discourse pragmatics encompasses variations of genres (such as news accounts, poems, tests), styles (for instance, casual, formal), and specific academic domains (for example, history journal article, biology laboratory report).

Orthography: conventional word spellings; patterns linking graphemes (letters, in a language like English) to sounds (in a language like English, phonemes); includes a set of widely applicable grapheme-phoneme conventions (GPCs) as well as regularities that apply to larger parts of words, some based on morphology, etymology, and the history of the language.

Etymology: the origins of and relations among words.

Metacognition: thinking about thinking, in particular for this discussion, awareness of language systems, including phonological, morphological, grammatical, and pragmatic awareness; pragmatic awareness includes metacognitive monitoring of comprehension in progress.

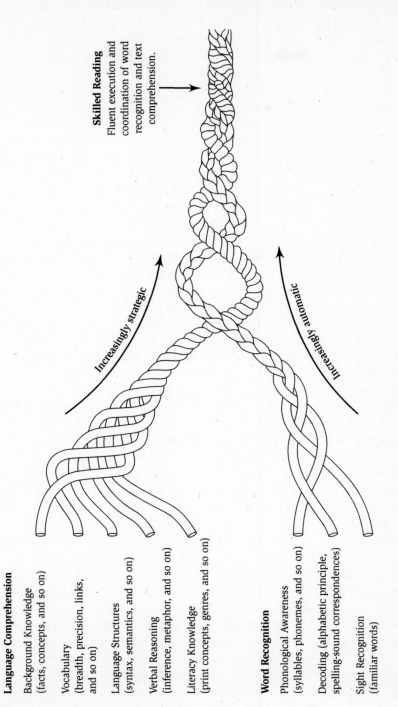

Language Comprehension

Background Knowledge
(facts, concepts, and so on)

Vocabulary
(breadth, precision, links,
and so on)

Language Structures
(syntax, semantics, and so on)

Verbal Reasoning
(inference, metaphor, and so on)

Literacy Knowledge
(print concepts, genres, and so on)

Word Recognition

Phonological Awareness
(syllables, phonemes, and so on)

Decoding (alphabetic principle,
spelling-sound correspondences)

Sight Recognition
(familiar words)

Skilled Reading
Fluent execution and
coordination of word
recognition and text
comprehension.

Increasingly strategic

Increasingly automatic

Figure 2.1. The Many Strands That Are Woven into Skilled Reading

Source: Scarborough, 2001.

metacognitive strategy for effective and successful reading. Second, children start to notice the structure or form of language, not just its effectiveness in communicating. (Bilingual children notice this earlier than monolinguals!) Early on, many toddlers love language events that highlight phonological patterns: songs, nursery rhymes, and games emphasize rhyming segments and alliterative patterns within and between words. As children participate in these language events, they start to exhibit phonological sensitivity, which can be a base for the phonemic awareness that is implicated in early alphabetic reading success.

By the beginning of kindergarten, the child's phonology, morphology, and syntax resemble those of the community to a large degree. A few sounds are still pronounced in an odd way; some more formal or less regular morphological forms may be missing or misused; sentences are still on average syntactically less complex than those that adults use. Semantics, pragmatics, and vocabulary are also well started, but continue to grow into adulthood. Metacognitive systems for literacy comprehension and alphabetic reading have a staging area. Children with the advantage of growing up as bilinguals typically seem like monolinguals for phonology, morphology, and syntax, but may appear somewhat delayed in vocabulary in both languages (see Chapter Three, for more discussion).

Meanwhile, from infancy, babies are surrounded by literacy in the community. Signs, books, labels, magazines, and alphabet cookies are there for them to see, to feel, and even to taste and smell. Babies witness and begin to take part in adults' mundane literacy—scanning the landscape for a restaurant sign, laughing at a comic strip, seeking consolation from a religious or philosophical text, getting good news on the sports page and bad news from the bill in the mail. Some participate in community and church literacy that relies on a different alphabet or another type of writing system altogether. Preschoolers are the key participants in "read-alouds" as family and friends contribute the orthographic and phonological expertise that allows the children to engage in collaborative literacy. The children are exposed to aspects of vocabulary, morphology, syntax, semantics, and pragmatics specialized for (or more frequently in) written language.

Preschoolers learn concepts of print—knowledge of which side of a book is up, which side opens, and which page to turn to next. They find that print is arranged and interpreted differently from pictures: for English, it starts at the top of the page, moves from left to right, sweeps back a row lower and so on. They expect different formats for titles and see the signals for the end of a story or little essay. Preschoolers experience storybooks and informational texts (for example, alphabet and number books, nature and hobby books, menus, directions for games, signs).

Letters, crucial for reading and writing in a language such as English, become important for preschoolers. They chant or sing letter names in alphabetical order. They play with letter blocks and magnets. They recognize letters by name, often beginning with the ones in their own names. They make letters as a part of their early attempts at writing. They recognize the roles of letters and spaces in making up and separating words on a page. Sometimes the children match voice to print and follow with their fingertips what is being read aloud to them. As a few letter-sound correspondences at the beginnings of words are learned, some words are recognized (though sometimes incorrectly) based on the first letter and some general properties such as length and whether there are descenders or ascenders among the other letter features. Some whole words are reliably recognized quite early. High-interest words in special surroundings with certain font designs and colors are recognized on signs, advertisements, and containers for products: Trix, Domino's, bodega. Perhaps the child's names and those of his or her friends are recognized regardless of the surroundings or the design or color of the letters. Some high-frequency words (such as *I, the,* and *is*) are recognized.

Conversations with peers and grownups before, during, and after read-alouds can nurture literacy, as the child stretches his or her syntax, morphology, vocabulary, and semantics by trying out more literacy-specific structures. On their own, as they play at reading, preschoolers may use literate language ("Come in," said grandmother). Their early attempts at independent reading are often more like telling stories, sometimes guided by pictures, sometimes verbatim recitations remembered from earlier read-alouds.

Preschoolers expect to comprehend what is read by them or to them. They ask what a word means, why a character said or did something. They laugh, are surprised, anticipate developments, and express sympathy. They remember titles, authors, characters, and settings. Sometimes they summarize main points and other times object to omitted details of a well-known text. They deeply appreciate some texts, asking for repeated readings and remembering them verbatim. Sometimes, what they understand is different from an adult's understanding of a text. Their comprehension develops as the reading is repeated, as they puzzle over apparent inconsistencies, as conversations about the text unfold, or as they gain more background knowledge.

The language and literacy achievements of the preschool years are complex. Teachers can recognize them as foundations on which future learning can build and to which teachers must attend as they undertake to support the core accomplishments of developing readers.

THE CORE ACCOMPLISHMENTS OF
LEARNING AND TEACHING READING

A fourth-grader is a more developed reader than is a kindergartner. A high school reader is more developed still. What goes on in school so that development occurs without trouble? There are two developments teachers need to make possible—comprehension and the word identification it entails. Fluent readers have learned to integrate these tasks so that reading as an act fades and the purpose for the reading emerges as central. Fluent readers are "finished reading" when they have gotten what they need from the written material, not when they have reached the end of the last word. After a discussion of each core accomplishment, this section concludes with a discussion about sequencing instruction on the two core tasks and about the special relevance of motivating engagement for reading instruction. The final section focuses on examples of reading instruction and the knowledge of language that underlies them.

Comprehension

What Is Comprehension? "To understand a proposition is to know what the world would be like for it to be true" (Johnson-Laird, 1983, p. 155). Take the following as an example:

This page has no print on it.

To understand the example sentence, the reader must envision a possible world that differs from the actual one in which this page *does* have print on it. In some uses, the full paragraph or chapter might invoke some other context so that "this page" does not refer to the page full of print that we are now reading. The proposition may be used for a complex purpose; it may not be intended to inform about the state of the page. It might be an instance of the writer lying, or, as in this case, not a reference in the ordinary sense but a mention in the context of an illustrative example. The reader or listener has to read between, above, and beyond the line to comprehend. What linguists, philosophers, and psychologists have found is that language does not provide enough material to specify fully the knowledge of the world that a reader or listener uses to comprehend even such a simple text as "This page has no print on it."

Because the reader or listener cannot simply receive meaning held in the language someone else uses—their words and sentences—comprehending is said to be an *active and constructive* process. The reader or listener contributes personal knowledge and dispositions to provide background knowledge for the comprehension process. What the speaker or writer indicates in the text is processed by the listener or reader so that it adds to background knowledge, questions it, confirms it, revises it, or transforms it in some other way (compare Graesser, Millis, and Zwan, 1997; Kintsch, 1998).

Background knowledge is acquired through experience in action in the real world. Psychologists study background knowledge as a mental representation that many call a "schema." Experiences and schemata about them are not neatly contained like words in a written sentence, so how they are brought to bear on comprehending written material is not a simple matching exercise. Schemas have fuzzy borders, open slots, and different degrees of surety, guided (or interfered with) by emotional responses, hunches, intuitions, or instincts, and formed in the midst of social and cultural wisdom and biases. Because it entails this kind of unlimited problem space, comprehension brings up special issues for teachers, learners, and testers of reading (see Chapter Five). Recent work on background experience uses the term "funds of knowledge" (Moll, Amanti, Neff, and Gonzalez, 1992). This term highlights the use of schemas as cultural capital for intellectual investment and payoff. Some funds of knowledge are not an easily convertible currency in school—notably the funds gained in communities disparaged by the mainstream community as different in language, ethnicity, ancestors' nation of origin, and socioeconomic status. Promoting the reading comprehension of students whose knowledge schemas conflict with those of school requires creating a "third space," neither home nor school.[2]

Background knowledge includes one's own experiences and vicarious experiences learned during communication with others, especially with those considered more expert. Works by Griffin (2000) and Harris (2002) are examples of analyses of background knowledge built during conversation with those who are more expert. This rather amorphous background knowledge figures at the start of comprehension when the reader or listener's mental model fills in gaps to make sense of the information provided by speakers and writers.[3] It appears again as the outcome of comprehension, carried forward as updated background knowledge ready for new experiences of listening or reading.

Bransford and Johnson (1972) dramatically show the influence from background knowledge on reading comprehension. They created passages that were difficult to understand and tested what happened if the reader did or did not have a cue to use background knowledge to construct the proper mental model. For example, one passage is about doing laundry. When there is no title or other cue that it is about laundry, it is a reflection on procedures, requirements, and repetitions that seems quite exotic, demanding, even hopeless. But when a title or picture indicates it is about doing laundry, the text becomes simple, familiar, and humorous. Readers rely on their mental models of the cultural norms for doing laundry. Studies indicate that with a title or a picture to cue the use of background knowledge, recall of the passage and judgments about comprehensibility change for the better. Researchers have also studied comprehension by using the comprehension analogue of nonsense words: a background world made up for the purpose of the experiment. For example, Cain, Oakhill, Barnes, and Bryant (2001) invented and introduced students to a fictional planet (in which, for example, bears have blue fur and orange juice is a natural resource) in order to study how recall of background knowledge affects the making of inferences needed for comprehension.

Comprehension of spoken language is a well-developed capacity by the time children enter kindergarten. Technically, any written language can be rendered as spoken language, but that is no guarantee that proficient comprehension in spoken-language contexts will transfer to even adequate processing of written language. A reader is usually first a listener, but reading often requires processing vocabulary, syntax, semantics, and pragmatics rarely encountered in spoken language. (See Table 2.4 and Exhibit 2.11 for examples of features associated with spoken compared to written language.)

We expect written texts to be understood outside of the cultural and temporal setting of the writer; they are, in that sense, somewhat context independent. But the activity of comprehending is bound to the reader's specific context and the purposes and pragmatic systems operating therein. The author's intended meaning plays an important role in what a reader comprehends, but it may be muted by more influential elements of the reader's activity context. At advanced levels, readers—even book club members—can be found disagreeing about which of several proposed accounts of the meaning of a text could be correct, while agreeing that some accounts are simply wrong. In some activity contexts, including those associated with different academic disciplines, there are specific routines and rubrics for deciding among competing accounts of the meaning of a text, and there are standards for judging the adequacy and proper use of various claims about the meaning and value of the material. (See the section in this chapter on content area reading and domain-specific learning.)

Teaching the comprehension and use of written language spans the period from kindergarten through high school. Even if a kindergarten lesson is about a small set of short rhyming words (such as *man, can, fan, pan*), it usually goes beyond associating a written form with a spoken word and uses objects, actions, pictures, and use in sentences or books to ensure comprehension. In high school history courses, many teachers' lessons focus on comprehending accounts by primary sources (participants in the historical events) and secondary sources (historians and other remote commentators). There is no consensus on a specific model of reading comprehension development, but age-related contrasts are evident, as the following two examples show:

> In kindergarten, students listen and ask questions as the teacher reads a science book about dinosaurs. It is a favorite topic; there is extensive background knowledge in the group. Some children have brought models and books, reciting for the class the complicated names for dinosaurs. Even children who are not specialists know about dinosaurs from comics and cartoons. Most of the children are surprised to find that the teacher and the book say that people never have had dinosaurs as pets, not even in the "olden days." At first they do not believe the book could mean that. The experienced teacher is not surprised. The lesson builds knowledge, not just about dinosaurs, but also about the differences between fiction and nonfiction and about ways to evaluate the claims made in different sources and ways to use and update background knowledge (compare Smolkin and Donovan, 2001, 2003).

In a high school history class, the students groan as the teacher announces that the Gulf of Tonkin resolution project will use three sources in addition to the brief mention of it in their text book. One source is a letter from a government official written on the day of the vote, explaining his position to a colleague; another source is a chapter from a popular memoir by the same person but written twenty-five years later; and the third source is an article by a respected contemporary historian about U.S. foreign policy developments, using the Gulf of Tonkin resolution as one of three contrasting cases. The teacher also mentions video material in the library that shows more about the historical period but warns that the video source still has to be analyzed carefully. She reminds the students about the work they did on how to analyze and evaluate primary and secondary sources and points out that a memoir written so long after the fact may have to be considered a hybrid. She assigns working groups to identify the questions each piece addresses and ignores. She circulates among the groups offering to help with other strategies for managing the group work and with advice about how to find out more about the geography, history, and sociopolitical facts each source presupposes. The teacher is thrilled when one group sends a member to search the Internet to check on the exact wording of the resolution from government archives and another group asks to borrow a tape recorder for interviews of people in their family and community. A week from Friday, the students know, each one will write an in-class essay about the Gulf of Tonkin resolution and its consequences, highlighting what the different sources contribute as evidence and warrant for the conclusions they draw (compare Stahl, Hynd, Britton, McNish, and Bosquet, 1996).

There are two senses of the phrase "teaching reading comprehension." Unavoidably, it is triage work: a unit or lesson calls for students to understand a particular piece of written material, but some students need teacher intervention to understand the material. In this sense of teaching comprehension, the teacher's main purpose is the content; the reading comprehension instruction he or she provides is a means to the end. In the second sense, teaching reading comprehension is for prevention, transfer, and generalization (see Darling-Hammond, Bransford, LePage, Hammerness, and Duffy, 2005, Chapter Six). The instruction is designed (and written material is designed or chosen) to introduce, practice, and apply specific approaches to comprehending written materials. The purpose is to improve students' comprehension proficiency in current and future reading tasks.

What Do We Know About Influences on Comprehension? The RAND Reading Study Group, composed of experts from various disciplines and schools of thought about the teaching of reading, recently reviewed the available professional literatures on comprehension to point out what can be relied on and what more needs to be learned about it. The group discussed in detail ten major points about the knowledge base currently available for teacher preparation and professional development (Snow, 2002, pp. 31–44):

1. Instruction that is designed to enhance reading fluency leads to fairly significant gains in word recognition and fluency and to moderate gains in comprehension.

2. Instruction can be effective in providing students with a repertoire of strategies that promote comprehension monitoring and foster comprehension.

3. The explicitness with which teachers teach comprehension strategies makes a difference in learner outcomes, especially for low-achieving students.

4. There are a number of working hypotheses about the role of instruction in explaining and addressing the problems of poor comprehenders.

5. The role of vocabulary instruction in enhancing comprehension is complex.

6. Teachers who provide comprehension strategy instruction that is deeply connected to learning subject matter, such as history and science, foster comprehension development.

7. Using various genres of text (for example, narrative and informational text) diversifies instructional opportunities, as assessed by teacher and student discourse.

8. Teachers who give students choices, challenging tasks, and collaborative learning structures increase their motivation to read and comprehend text.

9. Effective teachers enact a wide range of instructional practices that they use thoughtfully and dynamically.

10. Despite the well-developed knowledge base supporting the value of instruction designed to enhance comprehension, comprehension instruction continues to receive inadequate time and attention in typical classroom instruction.[4]

The same report describes four sources of variability in reading comprehension that teachers can learn about and consider when picking texts and curricula, designing instruction, or seeking to understand why progress is not being made with a class or individual student. The sources are the reader, the text, the activity, and the context (Snow, 2002, Chapter Two).[5] *Readers* vary in cognition (for instance, memory stores and cognitive processes), motivation (for example, interest in content or purpose for learning), knowledge (such as concepts, vocabulary, and language) and background experiences. Any single reader also reads differently from time to time, depending on the text, the activity, and the context. *Texts* differ not only in their surface properties but also in terms of underlying ideas and the mental models they invoke. Texts for early-grade reading lessons have been investigated in detail,[6] but, unfortunately, most information about text variation related to comprehension is about the surface properties, a simple quantitative summary about words and sentences that readability formulas measure. A mechanical adjustment (shorter sentences and fewer rare or long words) can lead to a text being rated easier according to the readability formula, but the revised text may not be easier for most readers. For example, longer sentences with subordinate clauses explicitly indicate causal or temporal relations; rewriting the text with shorter sentences to get a "better" readability formula score may make more demands on the reader to "read between the lines" in order to infer causal or temporal relations between the sentences.

Activity differences mentioned by the RAND group include the following: purposes for reading (which can change during the activity, from, say, following a teacher's instructions to information gathering to argument formation); operations (for example, decoding, linguistic and semantic processing, and comprehension monitoring); and outcomes (such as knowledge accretion, problem solving, or engagement with the text as an end in itself). The RAND group's *context* dimension covers the social and cultural factors that support different activities, dependent on how communities transmit information and promote learning and reading in and out of school. For some students, the activities and contexts that school literacy take for granted are just what the students expect and are well practiced in. For other students, the school-preferred activities and contexts are not familiar, or, even worse, are seen as oppositional to beliefs, practices, and values at home and in the community. For some, home activities and contexts may involve languages and literacies in addition to (or in place of) English. The community language and culture may be supported by institutions (churches, shops, banks, clubs, newspapers) and may occasion family and peer group activities and contexts quite different from those presupposed by the written materials and practices of literacy in school. Schools, teachers, and their literacy materials and practices vary too, some providing reading comprehension instruction linked to home and community literacy while at the same time ensuring that students are prepared for the reading comprehension tasks of the communities they desire to enter in the future. How a student comprehends and how (or even if) he or she learns to improve reading comprehension can be affected by these variations.[7]

The RAND report indicates seven areas, beyond proficient word identification, in which differential development can produce differences among readers with respect to comprehension (Snow, 2002, p. 22). Teachers can be made aware that these are the matters that can be influenced by instruction and that mediate the effectiveness of instruction. Each area is described briefly in the following text with footnoted pointers to overviews and other reports that also address it:

1. Readers' *purposes and goals* prime them to bring background knowledge to bear. The purpose can change or can be elaborated with subgoals in the course of reading. Good readers learn how to set a purpose and to rely on it to guide strategies such as comprehension monitoring. Reading may be for peer status (for example, to find information about a cartoon character or athletic events), bureaucratic demands (library card application, driver license test manual), entertainment, problem solving, career purposes, for learning content in various subject areas, and so on. Advanced readers know what not to read as well as what to read, when to skim, and when to study carefully. Reading drives skilled readers to do more—to talk, to listen, to observe, to experiment, to write. One text may lead to another in order to adjudicate conflicts raised by the first, to answer new questions, or to synthesize potentially related information.[8]

2. *Nonlinguistic abilities and processes* such as perception, attention, and memory ease or interfere with comprehension. Memory studies show that ideas from a text are remembered longer than the specific words and sentences of it are. Memory processing appears to go on during reading, not after it, since time spent on reading a passage increases relative to the density of ideas. Recall of propositions differentiates between skilled and less skilled comprehenders. Working memory processes and capacity are crucial for integrating information within a text and coordinating it with background knowledge. Skilled and less skilled comprehenders differ little in most memory-span measures and serial recall of words. The picture changes, though, when the items to be recalled are abstract words, or when specific reading-span tasks are used, supporting the notion that poor comprehenders suffer from a bottleneck due to inefficient word identification and word meaning processes.[9]

3. Learning requires *engagement and motivation,* and success with reading is no exception. Unfortunately, in middle school, interest in both recreational and academic reading declines, and most adolescents spend little time reading outside of school: only one of three reports reading voluntarily at thirteen years of age, only one of four at seventeen. In high school, even skilled readers avoid reading that they do not prize as useful or interesting. Rewards for reading, such as prizes and points, may lead to the opposite of the intended effect: reading avoidance and the use of weak strategies. Conversely, when a reader is invested and deeply engaged in an effort to comprehend, there is a most effective application of cognitive and metacognitive comprehension strategies.[10] There are mutually supportive links among skilled comprehension practices, knowledge of the topic being read, and engagement in reading. What motivates students to be engaged is often tied to their interests and to topics of importance to their

out-of-school communities. (See the later section of this chapter titled "Motivating Engagement for Reading.")

4. *Domain knowledge* can be about broad domains (current events, popular culture) or narrow domains (baseball, World War II history). Not all domain knowledge pays off for reading in school; the funds of knowledge gained in some activities and some communities are rarely taken advantage of for school learning. When domain knowledge is engaged, however, it matters for good comprehension. Skilled comprehenders have complex domain knowledge— enough to, as Wineburg puts it, "create inside their own heads an 'executive board,' where the members clamor, shout, and wrangle over controversial points. Texts are not processed as much as they are resurrected" (1991, p. 506). Skilled comprehenders with sufficient background domain knowledge can analyze what they read and react critically to new viewpoints, taking away adjudicated information as an update of their domain knowledge. Less skilled comprehenders, even if they have some relevant domain knowledge, have more trouble capitalizing on it. When a reader accesses domain knowledge, inferences are routinely generated during reading, resulting in deeper processing of the text. Inference making is inhibited when domain knowledge is scanty, but processing can be enhanced if the written passages have connectives (*therefore, so*), topic sentences, headings, and subheadings. These text features help readers to recall material, but, actually, skilled and domain-knowledgeable comprehenders engage in deeper processing when challenged by texts that do not have such coherency aids. Working out solutions for comprehension problems from texts that are difficult compel the reader to exercise cognitive and metacognitive strategies that otherwise may be unused.[11]

5. *Discourse knowledge* allows one to exploit the features and functions of different styles and genres. Knowledge of discourse associated with school is a special case. As they grow up, people learn and practice patterns of asking questions, giving information, showing that attention is being paid, proving a point, entertaining others, telling stories, indicating respect and fealty to social norms, and so on. For some students, discourse patterns at home and in their community differ greatly from those used in school. To those who have more familiarity with the school discourse, the patterns become almost invisible so the academics come to the front; those less familiar have two tasks—school discourse and academic topics—sometimes at a cost to academic success.

Patterns of written discourse matter a great deal for reading comprehension. Sentence and discourse factors have been shown to contribute more to sixth-graders' comprehension performance than word factors do. Skilled readers are more sensitive to discourse structure than less skilled readers are, particularly on tasks requiring inferences. Explicit instruction on how to analyze text types affects comprehension. Skilled readers can analyze and critique discourse in various media, distinguishing, for example between introductions that are summaries and ones that supply details that merely set the stage for the main point. They interpret the patterns for humor, metaphor, and irony. They recognize persuasive techniques, explanatory models, and logical fallacies hidden in the context. They know how to use supplementary texts: formal reference works, newspapers, and journals. They can access information stored on computers and can search the Internet. Skilled comprehenders can use external representations of the discourse structure—the table of contents, document maps and hyperlinks, outlines, and other graphic organizers. Those who know the discourse patterns of standardized tests have one less hurdle while taking a test. Knowing the way textbooks are structured makes it easier to read them and report on main points. (See Exhibits 2.2, 2.3, and 2.4 for examples of special patterns in content area reading in academic subjects.)[12]

6. *Vocabulary* and *linguistic knowledge* start before school does. Early spoken-language experiences have an effect on later vocabulary learning and on reading comprehension. Books read to children expose them to vocabulary nuances rarely encountered in ordinary conversations. Estimates are that by five or six years of age, children control between twenty-five hundred and five thousand words. They learn about seven words a day in elementary school, have about seventy-five hundred root words by sixth grade, eleven thousand by eighth grade, and fifteen thousand or more at the end of high school. While reading the textbooks typically used in kindergarten and grade one, students with less extensive vocabulary may not have problems but, by the end of grade three, vocabulary limits take a toll on reading comprehension. Vocabulary development involves more than the quantity of words, though,[13] including (a) generative principles related to the roots and affixes in some polysyllabic words that create networks of related words; (b) words specific to certain domains (for example, to literature, physics, or geography); (c) use and explanation of figures of speech and idioms; (d) explicit and efficient word definitions, even for abstract terms such as *justice;* and (e) the extent and limits of a word's syntactic, semantic, and pragmatic relations.

Vocabulary instruction may improve reading comprehension, but there are no guarantees, nor is comprehension failure guaranteed by a poor vocabulary (overall for age or with respect to a particular text). Word learning is influenced by the amount and variety of reading a person does. Building vocabulary is a gradual process, with most words learned from use in context rather than in formal study. When some words are first encountered, they may not be completely understood, but still make sense. Something is retained from these early encounters; to get a meaning that works in most contexts, between four and twelve encounters have been found to be enough depending on the words, the texts, and the readers. A reader's working definition for a word is an accretion of the aspects that overlap from repeated incomplete learning attempts. Teaching

---

Exhibit 2.2. Literary Understanding in English Class

When reading primarily to engage in the literary experience, the sense of the whole
changes . . . emerging out of the developing envisionment of the human situation as
reflected in the characters, events, and relationships portrayed in the text. In literary
readings, readers clarify their ideas as they read and relate them to the growing and
changing horizon. . . . readers continually explore possibilities, see many sides, and
go beyond their envisionments; they focus on the human situation and the complex
meanings embedded in it [Langer, 1991].

A compliant student may read pages assigned by an English teacher but still
miss the point and meaning of the literature assigned. Teachers commonly find
students who read words adequately but pay insufficient attention to purpose,
to author intent, to integrating new with old knowledge, and so on (see Rex and
McEachen, 1999). It is easy to assume that the student has no liking for literature
or that the student need only learn about literary devices, style, and conventions
of different genres or eras; but experienced teachers and contemporary research
indicate that the problem is about more than student preferences or technical tools.

As teachers plan and enact lessons, interpreting student responses and leading them toward more adequate comprehension, they can be aided by analyses of
comprehension (see, for example, Wilhelm, Baker, and Dube, 2001; Buehl, 2001;
Montgomery, 2000; Ericson, 2001; and Mellor and Patterson, 2000). The teacher's
knowledge about the comprehension of literature can enrich the discussion-
based approach to teaching that, along with high academic demand, has been
statistically related to student achievement in English classes (Applebee, Langer,
Nystrand, and Gamoran, 2003). Nystrand (1997) demonstrates the relationship
between student achievement and extended discussions in which students are
active participants, but also notes that such discussions are rare overall and particularly so in classes with many students who are not high achievers. Active
classroom discussions are spurred when teacher questions and follow-up moves
indicate value for the students' interpretations and when student questions occur
in clusters (Nystrand, Wu, Gamoran, Zeiser, and Long, 2003).

The Center on English Learning and Achievement (CELA) developed a series
of studies and an overarching analysis of them that provide details about the
discussions that occur in excellent classrooms that "beat the odds" compared
to similar ones where expected difficulties are not avoided (Langer, 2001, 2002;
and, for example, Agee, 2000; Christoph and Nystrand, 2001; and Ostrowski,
2000). Ninth-graders can discuss Greek epics to arrive at a comprehension of

Exhibit 2.2. Literary Understanding in English Class, *Cont'd*

them when the teacher knows and uses strategies that, among other things, help the students to access and build on prior relevant knowledge (Agee, 2000). In another ninth-grade English class, Ostrowski (2000) observes and analyzes a teacher working with an icon of American literature, the short story "The Secret Life of Walter Mitty" by James Thurber, first published in 1939:

> Gropper [the teacher] began the study and discussion by asking her students to write a brief prediction of what they thought the story would be about based solely on the title. [Students volunteered to read] a fairly wide range of predictions, and in each case Gropper was careful to ask the student to articulate the relationship between the title and his or her prediction. In that way, even in this fairly informal context, students had to defend their responses with careful thinking and reasoning. The students then went on to read the first paragraph and make another prediction in writing about what the story was about, which was again discussed. Finally they read the entire first page, and then followed the same procedure of writing a prediction and then discussing it. By the time they were ready to discontinue making formal predictions about the story, the students appeared keen to discover whether or not their predictions would be accurate or not. That is, they were motivated to read. Thus, in the course of 20 or 25 minutes, Gropper had them reading, writing, and talking about "The Secret Life of Walter Mitty."

Langer and Close (2001) summarize lessons learned from the CELA studies in a practical booklet. On page 15, they describe four ways that teachers scaffold discussions by asking questions that get students actively involved in the class discourse: tapping understanding, seeking clarification, inviting participation, and orchestrating discussion (how to converse, agree, disagree, and connect and extend ideas). They also describe four ways that teachers scaffold student thinking about the literature so that students develop interpretations in and from the class discussions: focusing ideas, shaping arguments, linking concerns (from the discussion, the text, and other readings), and upping the ante (bringing up new ways to think about ideas students express). The following example (Langer and Close, 2001, p. 18) from a high school class reading Fitzgerald's *The Great Gatsby* demonstrates that, as a class matures into a reading collaborative, students provide some of the scaffolding for each other:

TEACHER: Christie, why don't you start us off? (inviting)

CHRISTIE: One thing I wrote down was I wasn't exactly sure why he was invited to Gatsby's party. Why was he invited?

TEACHER: Not why Gatsby, why Nick? (clarifying)

CHRISTIE: Right.

Exhibit 2.2. Literary Understanding in English Class, *Cont'd*

TEACHER: Okay. Do you have any guesses? Any ideas at all? (tapping understandings)

PETAL: They said that Miss Baker, she didn't know Gatsby, right? 'Cause it seemed weird that out of that crowd, that Gatsby like took her aside and told her some secret. I didn't think she knew him at all, only knew who he was.

AUDRA: When he met her, and he met Miss Baker at Daisy's, I thought she said something about Gatsby, and he was curious because he didn't know anything about it but he never got a chance to ask her about it.

PETAL: So he did.

TEACHER: She did. We don't know what the connection is, but she first mentioned Gatsby at Daisy's house. Has your question been answered Christie? Why [was Nick invited]? There are two possibilities. One is that everybody goes to the Gatsby mansion. (orchestrating, shaping)

CHRISTIE: But he got invited by invitation.

TEACHER: Aha. That's your question. Okay, your suggestion is that he is a next-door neighbor. (focusing)

PABLO: Yeah, and maybe that Gatsby just wanted another acquaintance, a different kind of acquaintance. Now all of a sudden he wants to tell him something.

TEACHER: Yeah, we get the sense that these other folks are regulars. What is it that amazes you? This is a word I've heard come out of your mouths. What is it that amazes you? (shaping, upping the ante)

AUDRA: It seems so elaborate that he goes, that these parties are regular parties, but they seem so elaborate and so huge, and so like things that you have to dress up for. People drunk and running all over the place, and people don't even know him.

TEACHER: Jess?

JESS: In a way though, what Audra said about everybody doing it. Because when he finally meets Gatsby and asks, Gatsby is like, "You don't know who I am." It was, you know, everybody should know who he was. (linking)

PABLO: They knew who he was, but they never really met him . . . (clarifying)

RON: Yeah, it seems like these people were in a fog.

The teacher's knowledge and use of techniques to build an understanding of a literary text is apparent in many of the active discussions in the CELA studies. It is also the foundation for procedures and guides that teachers use to implement

---

Exhibit 2.2. Literary Understanding in English Class, *Cont'd*

---

independent reading, paired reading, and literature circle groups. Teachers cue and prompt students to develop their own "dense" questions about a piece of literature and ultimately develop an adequate, even rewarding, understanding of it. Writing responses—from annotations to journals, essays, and research papers—all help with comprehension, and each calls upon a teacher's knowledge of literary reading if they are to be planned, enacted, and evaluated adequately. Even the seemingly casual text marking and annotations in margins or on sticky notes (Porter-O'Donnell, 2004) are fruitful when a student learns from teacher models and guides about prereading and postreading comprehension acts and the prediction, summarizing, questioning, and connections among texts that good comprehenders do during reading, as well as about attention to the meanings derived through literary devices such as metaphor, personification, rhythm, symbols, and other stylistic, rhetorical devices.

---

vocabulary skillfully can yield multiple results: improving the ability to figure out meanings of new words from context, improving reading comprehension overall, and increasing vocabulary knowledge itself. Knowledge of some types of words continues to develop even past high school (for example, verbs of cognition such as *presuppose* and connectives such as *consequently*).

The effect on reading comprehension of linguistic knowledge beyond word knowledge is not studied as much. Syntax, semantic, and pragmatic systems support comprehension; miscommunications can often be attributed to specific structures in these systems. There are, however, mixed results in studies of the relation between measures of syntax and skill at comprehension. Facility with unusual syntax may be as much a result as a cause of extensive reading and proficient comprehension. Certain syntactical structures can slow down if not hinder comprehension, for example, post-modified subjects—the italicized modifier clause in "Entertainment *creating a common culture across class differences* is important to teenage life." Some linguistic structures trigger inferences that a reader must make, for example, anaphoric inference between nouns and pronouns in different sentences in a passage—the items italicized in "*A boy in a red hat* was touching the jewelry. I turned to answer the phone, and then *he* grabbed something and ran away." These are among the more reliably made inferences. Inference making grows during and beyond the primary grades, affected by the memory capacity for sentences as well as by the accessibility of background knowledge relevant to the passage. Less skilled comprehenders (whether young or those with specific comprehension difficulties) have difficulty with inferences that rely on background knowledge to fill gaps. For example, background knowledge about cooking lets a reader know that "Take the pork from the stovetop. Pour off the oil and add it to the sauce" calls for the oil to be discarded and the pork to be added. (Note that a similar sentence can yield a different outcome also dependent on background information: In "Pour off the broth and add it to the sauce" it is the broth that is saved and added to the sauce.) Readers with specific difficulty comprehending also have trouble making inferences that depend on connecting material between sentences in texts; since their performance improves when they are directed back to the passage, it appears that the problem is knowing *when* to infer rather than how to. When training to draw inferences was compared with training to generate questions and training for rapid decoding, the inference training worked best for the students with specific comprehension difficulty, and the gap between their general comprehension scores and those of their age matches decreased somewhat.[14]

7. *Cognitive and metacognitive strategy* development is specifically about improving comprehension. Skilled comprehenders report text-level strategies for remembering what they read (for example, thinking about the main points) and for repairing comprehension problems (for example, by rereading a specific section cued by passage content or a remembered lapse in concentration); their less skilled peers describe approaches at the word level and ones more dependent on help from others than from their own reading practices. Less skilled comprehenders have difficulty noting the contradictions and inconsistencies that would call for repair, and they do not alter their reading speed or style in response to different texts and tasks. The National Reading Panel report includes a lengthy list of strategies that have been shown, across various studies, to improve comprehension. There is no evidence that any one strategy or some subset of them is necessary and sufficient for skilled comprehenders to know and use. It is clear, though, that instruction in strategies is possible and useful. Consider the strategy of generating clear questions. Few students spontaneously ask questions, and it is difficult for teachers to promote student questions during class discussions. Questions that students ask are often details of fact or procedure, not the kind of deeper questions that get at the meat of the text—the central topic, the moral of the story, what the case is an exemplar of, the basic argument, the validity of the explanation, the punch line, and so on. When strategy instruction is linked to content learning in a few different academic subjects, students may recognize the value of the strategies as tools for use in future tasks with different texts. Effective instruction includes modeling the strategy, explanation of the purpose and procedures, and opportunities to apply it with collaboration and guidance and then more widely and independently.

Of the seven topics used in the RAND report to consider differences among readers, *strategies* is mentioned most often. It is inevitably tied to the other six dimensions, though. Strategy use depends on the purposes the reader has, for instance. In turn, learning a strategy (for example, generating questions that the text answers) can assist students in examining and formulating purposes for reading. A student with performance motivation (wanting to avoid the appearance of failure) rather than task motivation (wanting to accomplish the task) would not likely invoke the strategy "recognize and repair comprehension failure." Discourse knowledge figures explicitly in strategies such as prediction. Strategy use can be inhibited if a reader's nonlinguistic processes, linguistic processes, and domain knowledge are insufficient.

A crucial strategy in any reader's repertoire is comprehension monitoring (also called metacognition, executive control, self-regulated comprehension): noticing a problem and having the motive and resources to repair it. Even young children show strategic self-regulation under some circumstances, but experienced readers can fail to monitor and repair their comprehension effectively if they lack the domain, discourse, and vocabulary knowledge the text calls for. Summarizing is another common strategy—including the synthesis of information from several sources. Predicting is a useful strategy as long as it comes with its second half, confirming. Duke and Pearson (2002) describe successful approaches to strategy instruction (including reciprocal teaching and transaction analysis) as routines: sets of, and settings for, strategies that are taught together and function together. Effective readers have a repertoire of strategies and know how to select and use them. Strategies are easy to teach and to learn, but applying them effectively and appropriately is hard. Teaching strategies and how to use them improves student recall and comprehension; students get better at identifying central ideas in passages, understanding relations among them, and providing a gist, summary, and paraphrase.[15]

Types of Texts to Be Read

Primary-grade children mostly read narratives. Recently, concerns have been raised about this narrative bias—or expository gap—in lessons intended to improve comprehension in the early grades. Narratives seem like the easy genre, well practiced in oral language. Children are familiar with formulaic expressions announcing narratives: "The funniest thing happened to me on the way here," "Have I ever told you about the time when . . ." Spoken-language narratives are remarkably well-ordered, with distinct parts: abstract, orientation, complicating action, evaluation, and coda. Written narratives have a somewhat similar pattern when the bare skeletal form is considered: exposition, complication, climax, and denouement. Formulaic expressions are frequently found in narratives read to children, from "Once upon a time," to "They lived happily ever after."

Observations and information gathered from teachers show that throughout the classroom and throughout the class day, early primary-grade students are very unlikely to work with expository text. Trade books in libraries or at book fairs are much more likely to narrate stories than to expose information; even reading textbooks provided by school districts ignore the expository. Yet, in the upper elementary grades students are expected to read expository texts.

Some scholars claim that a narrative bias serves young children well, allowing them more readily to learn content as well as to learn how to read. Many teachers and parents also believe that expository texts should be held off until the students are older and more skilled readers. Recent studies analyze these and similar beliefs and argue that the absence of expository text in the primary grade is neither necessary nor desirable.[16]

Reasons for introducing more informational texts early are many: students' vocabulary and syntax flourish as a benefit of expository text read-alouds; kindergarteners are as able to deal with information-book language as with narrative-book language; first-graders who work with expository texts learn to evaluate the truthfulness of written texts and to read selectively in order to accomplish purposes and achieve goals; and some students are more engaged by expository text than by narratives on topics important to them. Some students may respond to expository material with a narrative, but this does not necessarily mean that they are unable to deal with reading the expository genre. It may just mean that they are following the lead of children's books that mix the expository and narrative genres (for example, the Magic School Bus series of books about science topics). Personification and narrative sequencing as a strategy for understanding and recalling information is not an unusual tactic for people of any age, and not at all unexpected for students whose literacy experience has been essentially narrative.

It may well be that familiarity with one genre, such as narrative, will ease the learning of another one, such as expository, but it is unlikely that the transfer of reading skills to a new genre will be smooth and automatic. Table 2.1 describes some of the ways that expository and narrative texts differ. There are enough complicated differences to suggest a rocky start to understanding expository text if it is rarely encountered until fourth grade.

Expository Texts in Different Subject Domains. Expository materials are almost always used in schools as a part of teaching a specific academic subject. It is not commonly recognized that written materials in an academic content area have special characteristics—and not just specialized vocabulary—that materials from another academic domain do not have. Ways to read the material also differ among academic disciplines. Being able to read well in one domain does not guarantee that one will be good at comprehending the written materials in another one.

The knowledge base about comprehension development includes information about tasks and practices that is discipline specific and that matters for student success in the content domain as well as in reading.[17] A secondary school teacher may have extensive experience with the types and features of written

Table 2.1. Narrative and Expository Genres: Some Comparisons

Narrative	Expository
Has characters with whom students can form an identity	Gives general statements about characteristics of and relations among objects and events
Employs predictable sequencing along a time line; conveys beginning, middle, and end of events presented in chronological order unless marked for devices such as flashbacks or multiple restricted points of view	Uses a variety of text patterns, often in the same text: for example, enumeration, compare and contrast, question and answer, cause and effect, problem and solution, and chronological sequencing
Stands alone; even in a series of books, each narrative can stand alone	Supports, refutes, or elaborates other texts in the content domain
Has illustrations that can be fanciful	Has illustrations that are realistic, such as diagrams, figures, visual models of content, or tables
Has chapter titles, quotations	Has chapter titles, subheads, captions, an index, a glossary, and a table of contents
Uses fewer new words; has many vocabulary items common in spoken language	Uses many new words, including technical words; employs technical use of common words
Is often presented in simple past or present progressive tense	Uses generic nouns, timeless verbs
Offers implicit context support for meaning of less common words	Introduces some new words explicitly, often then uses several technical words in close proximity

material in his or her content area as well as a good deal of practice in the ways of thinking while reading in the domain; still, such teachers may have automatized their disciplinary reading so that they cannot slow it down, articulate it, and teach their students how to do it. Multisubject teachers in elementary grades cannot be expected to have extensive implicit knowledge about reading in all the different content areas they teach their students and so need even more assistance in teacher education and professional development. Without it, some teachers who recognize that students have difficulty comprehending content-area written materials design lessons that make the information available by circumventing the need for students to read connected text passages: lectures, lesson conversations, demonstrations, hands-on experiences, audiovisual presentations, graphic organizers (like Venn diagrams or flowcharts), and so on. Instruction that bypasses reading in the content area fails to prepare students for the future. For example, "doing history" in large measure means reading and writing with the canons of historical scholarship in mind—the evidence, analysis, and argument standards to which historians hold each other as they make new discoveries or refute currently accepted ones. For historians, reading is part and parcel of thinking like a historian. Scientists also read and write as a part of practicing the canons of science and use contemporary developments in the methods and results of biology, physics, or other sciences to guide their reading. Specialists in literature read with reliance on knowledge about particular developments in literary criticism and about how discoveries are made, points are examined, and conclusions are supported or refuted in humanities, aesthetics, and social science. In the following sections, we consider history and science as examples before returning to more general issues of content-area reading.

Science as an Example. Problems with reading informational texts have been linked to low science achievement (Bernhardt, Destino, Kamil, and Rodriguez-Munoz, 1995). Even within science reading activities, different purposes (see p. 28) can lead to different comprehension outcomes: an assignment that encourages students to read in order to assemble an argument results in understanding of the content, while an assignment to read in order to provide a description can lead to recall but little in-depth understanding (Wiley and Voss, 1999).

Science may seem to be the domain in which it is most far-fetched to expect progress to be made about the teaching of reading. It has, however, been the focus for a good deal of study about the use, teaching, and learning of domain-specific literacy throughout elementary and high school grades. Scientists, teachers, and literacy researchers collaborate for much of this work. In some states, high school or middle school science teachers are well versed in the ways of scientists, having college degrees in the sciences and having been apprenticed and trained in the laboratory and literature of the sciences. These teachers can double as scientists and educators in research and professional development that combine to inquire into science reading. Such inquiries provide practical assistance for teaching reading in the sciences.

While some questions remain to be studied, important findings emerge from recent work on teaching literacy in the sciences.[18] There is a recurring tension: hands-on science experimentation and reading science each draw on limited time and energy resources. The press is felt in the syllabus, the classroom, teacher preparation, and professional development. Existing and ongoing studies continue to show that these two efforts need not compete but can be mutually supportive. Written language in science is not just for communicating results. Well-used written materials provide models for doing scientific work, opportunities for studying separate aspects of the scientific process and method (data, claims, evidence, argument, description, relation patterns, analysis, and explanations), and practice recognizing relative strengths and weaknesses in a scientific project. In a classroom or a professional laboratory, common reading of a scientific text allows each member of the group to take advantage of others' differing background knowledge. Reading common texts enriches the interpretation and evaluation of the disparate hands-on experiences of the individual scientists (and science students).

Reading can help students, even in elementary school, overcome a big stumbling block in science learning: developing an explanatory model (see Rowell and Ebbers, 2002). When knowledge from science classes looks like a catalogue of descriptions with barely a mention of relations among features, explanatory models are likely to be the missing link. Adhering to procedures and recording accurate observations are not the whole of an experiment, but sometimes they are the whole yield of time spent in science class. Explanatory models highlight the basic and unifying concepts in a domain. Too often, though, basic concepts are just another entry in the catalogue of unlinked descriptions. For scientists, explanatory models of the basic concepts motivate decisions about which experiment should be done, how it should be designed and carried out, what conclusions are in contention during the experiment, and whether the results can be interpreted as relevant and important enough to support or revise the original explanatory model. Science texts can have typographical and organizational features to help students distinguish claims, data, and evidence, and to trace their differential use in arguments. Reading in science class can focus students on explanations of different types (see Unsworth, 2001). When the syllabus involves multiple texts, there are opportunities to study the various entities that make up explanatory models of the basic concepts, as well as to see models in use, sometimes in productive competition. In effect, reading in science can be the hands-on investigation of how to learn and do science, as well as how to read critically and constructively.

Even among science texts, those with different purposes have different characteristics (see, for example, Norris and Phillips, 1994). There are texts for teaching and learning, for popular understanding, for civic action, and for communication within a subset of the community of working scientists. Research reports are highly stylized, following explicit norms published in journals, and with a high proportion of argumentative patterns. Textbooks follow different norms. Purcell-Gates and Duke (2001) identify features in texts used for laboratory science classes, such as a statement of goals, a main question, description of materials, lists of materials in order of use with domain-dependent measurement terms, explicit numbered steps to be taken in a required sequence, details about procedures and practices including graphic depictions of them, and a scientific explanation for the canonical results. Teachers who study these features and ways to use them in planning and enacting instruction can promote opportunities for the development of comprehension.

Students can be taught to call upon structural knowledge of different genres to identify and represent main points, but they may not reliably transfer, generalize, and use the knowledge. Palincsar and her teacher and researcher colleagues, for example, studied teaching that integrated hands-on science with comprehension instruction that was good but general (that is, not specifically related to the features and practices of reading science). While the students made gains regarding a particular (and difficult) topic, the experience did not lead them to approach a new topic with a more scientific frame. The research group then combined the teaching with innovative discourse materials, adapting as teaching texts laboratory notebooks like the ones scientists use. These notebooks helped students to represent data in diverse abstract and concrete forms, to use the norms and conventions of the scientific community, and to incorporate narrative notes. The notebook can be used not only for coming to an understanding of the particular topic but also for modeling scientific reasoning that can be applied to other topics in the domain.

Teachers can learn to apprentice students to discipline-specific reading with good impacts on the students' reading comprehension (Greenleaf, Schoenbach, Cziko, and Mueller, 2001). Professional development can make explicit the implicit knowledge about reading science that science teachers have (Donahue, 2000; Greenleaf, Brown, and Litman, 2004), including the text features common to the content area and the reading practices of experts in the domain. In one such session (based on the work described in Schoenbach, Greenleaf, Cziko, and Hurwitz, 1999, Chapter Nine), science teachers examined their own practices of reading science (see Exhibit 2.3).

History as an Example. Reading like a historian is not a natural result of being a good reader who happens to use that ability on history texts. Experts from different fields read historical material differently (see Exhibit 2.4 for an example). The practices in high school history classes contrast with the practices of professional historians. If teachers show students how historians read, students see a model of (and engage in procedures involved in) thinking historically. Learning to read both primary sources and the secondary sources that are produced by historians is part and parcel of learning to do history well enough that the discipline can guide opinions on historical and current events. Wineburg has identified specific processes to evaluate the source of the document, corroboration and contextualization for it, and its role in historical reconstructions and explanations. He and others point to difficulties students have with learning and using these sorts of history-specific cognitive processes.[19]

Exhibit 2.3. Scientists Read Strategically

"Our group concluded that scientists read with three goals that reflect their way of thinking about the world:

- To create order out of chaos

- To approximate the 'real world,' which is abstract and often unobservable, by creating models or analogies which will eventually be replaced by better models and analogies

- To disprove any claim made to the truth through thorough and systematic thinking

"First they skim the introduction and conclusion, looking for a question, a controversy, or a hypothesis which will be proved or disproved. They will immediately focus on the conclusion, for that is where the hypothesis and proof are usually summarized. They often summarize this themselves, and provide an analogy or related example (this is like) or a counterexample (could the opposite be true?). They sometimes set a purpose by looking for practical application, but are often interested in theoretical discussion that will simply broaden their knowledge or understanding of the universe.

"They then skim the body of the text for data and other information that [either] support the claim or begin to disprove it. This includes a mental list of potential conflicts in the data or research (based on prior knowledge of the concept). In particularly challenging reading, this skimming is a systematic effort [to] organize a framework on which to place information. Scientists will read headings, subheadings, pictures, and captions in order to predict which types of information will be found where. They create a mental model of this organizing framework, which they reference frequently as they read and reread looking for data. This organizing begins with a 'shopping list' of ideas from the claim in the introduction and conclusion. They describe this phase as setting a purpose based on the question 'what am I going to find?' They almost always try to guess the answer to the hypothesis, and often a reason, or set of reasons, why the answer is wrong.

"As they begin to read more deeply, scientists are continuing to build schema about the central claim or question in order to assess the validity of the claim and the proof that may be offered. They never read important parts just once, but they do prioritize reading based on what is important. They immediately dismiss any narrative, attention-getting devices and seek data. They continually ask 'What happened?' and are rarely interested in who did it unless it is a known or notable scientist whose work stands for a set of ideas (like Newton, for example). They are particularly interested in conflicts in the data that might disprove or weaken any claim. They almost gleefully surface these conflicts, and often ask, 'Yes, but what about . . .' and provide counterexamples.

Exhibit 2.3. Scientists Read Strategically, *Cont'd*

"When reading is difficult (marked specifically by a lack of background knowledge on the part of the reader), scientists will begin a search for explanations of fundamental concepts. They identify which words are survival words, and begin to build conceptual understandings of these words. They rely heavily on pictures and captions for this and continually ask the question, 'What is this like?' As they answered this question, they were accessing related prior knowledge, most often in the form of visual and experiential information. Through this process they build analogies or models to help them understand the new information. They are filling in huge amounts of information from a vast and eclectic fund of prior knowledge.

"They often pictured related, but simpler, examples and sometimes built a set of models that successively approximated the concept they were reading about. Some readers reported that they would visualize an example, return to the illustration in the article and mentally compare the two. Often they would add several visual analogies together in their mind to create a semantic web of ideas. All the readers in our group spoke of 'reading and rereading' the pictures many times throughout the article. They marked these with mental and written notations for later reference. At times with very abstract concepts, such as molecular-level mechanics, readers were accessing models they had built, or lab experiments they conducted in school, or lectures, or even pictures from other texts where they initially learned about the concept. They often drew schematics to show abstract concepts such as vectors, and occasionally added mathematical formulae or notations. As they use this prior [knowledge] to construct mental models, they are comparing their models to the reading, asking, 'Is this accurate, is this true?'

"As they read, they expect their knowledge somehow to be inaccurate. They expect that their information will be made obsolete, or incomplete, by new work. In fact, if they are simply reading about what they already know and understand, they are disappointed in the author and bored by the content. They expect that their understanding of words and concepts will be negated, redefined, or expanded through this process. They are continually assimilating new knowledge. They do not expect authors to explain everything. They also do not expect themselves to know everything in the vast field of science, and know that every scientist has areas of specialty and areas of ignorance. There was an implicit assumption of insider talk[;] scientists are rude conversationalists, you either know what is being discussed and participate, or you stand quietly on the sidelines and don't interrupt the great thinkers. Readers of science know that they are expected to come prepared for a rigorous discussion."

Source: Hale, 2000.

Exhibit 2.4. Reading Like and Unlike a Historian

"For more than a decade, I have studied intellectual habits by asking scholars to read documents in my presence and to describe their thoughts as they do so. I have focused on historical texts because the ability to reconstruct the past from fragmented documents requires an expertise that intrigues me, as a cognitive psychologist. I search for clues that reveal how scholars see patterns among apparent contradictions that daunt less skilled readers."

. . .

"Despite the range of documents, periods, and topics represented in my research, nearly all the historians I've studied have approached the primary sources that I give them in the same way. They glance momentarily at the first few words at the top of the page, but then their eyes dart to the bottom, zooming in on the document's provenance: its author, the date and location of its creation, the time and distance separating it from the event it reports, and, if possible, how the document came into their hands. Then the historians mull over that information like a prospector examining a promising rock for ore. Is the document an un-self-conscious diary entry, or a text written to be read by others? Is the author someone noteworthy, or an ordinary person? Did the author write when the events were fresh in his or her mind, or so many years later that memories may no longer be reliable? The answers to questions like those create a framework upon which the historian's subsequent reading rests.

"Few historians have found the pattern of looking first at the attribution worthy of comment when they describe to me how they approach a document. In fact, when I asked one prominent scholar of American industrialization about his initial focus on the document's provenance, he said, 'Why would I mention that? Everyone does it.'

"For as long as I have been interviewing historians, I've also been presenting the same documents to high school and college students. The students' readings follow a different path from the scholars', beginning with the first word at the top of the page and ending with the last word at the bottom. Rarely do students consider the attribution until they get to it; if they do look at it earlier, their goal is often utilitarian—for example, to clear up a fuzzy pronoun reference. Primary documents differ little from textbooks to students, except that documents are harder to understand. For students, the purpose of both kinds of text is the same: to convey information that they can repeat on tests."

. . .

"Not all intelligent people read the same way—not even all people who spend their working lives with written texts. . . . [A] specialist in 19th-century British literature (volunteered to read aloud to an audience of historians) a diary entry from John Barker, a lieutenant in the British army (on the eve of the revolution-

---

Exhibit 2.4. Reading Like and Unlike a Historian, *Cont'd*

---

ary war). In the entry, Barker said he was writing on the same day as the bloody encounter at Lexington and the even bloodier retreat from Concord. Barker blamed his own men for 'rushing in and putting to flight' the minutemen gathered in Lexington, and he explicitly denied giving the order to fire.

"My volunteer gave a dramatic reading, commenting on archaic figures of speech, the density of the prose (the first sentence has more than 150 words), and linguistic mannerisms indicative of social class. As she read, she made many astute comments about the language but seemed at times confused about the narrator's identity. On reaching the attribution at the end, she said, 'Ah, yes. From a British soldier. That's what I thought.'

"The listening historians confessed to me privately afterward that the reading had shocked them. It had cast doubt on their core assumptions about the reading process, for checking the source before reading the text, which was second nature to them, never occurred to our intelligent and careful reader. Indeed, the trajectory of the literature professor's reading—the subjects it touched on, as well as those it never addressed—demonstrated to the historians the complicated truth that there is no such thing as generic critical thinking. We think critically within the bounds of our disciplines, and features of thought considered critical in one field often fail to appear in another.

". . . [History teachers] can show the strategies they use to corroborate evidence and piece together a coherent context. Or professors could refer students to the useful Website History Matters (www.historymatters.gmu.edu), whose section on making sense of evidence includes acclaimed historians' discussions of how they evaluate different genres of primary evidence.

"By sharing their mental habits, historians could teach students skills they would find useful every time they faced a take-home exam or research paper: how to get started when they lack necessary information, how to prepare their minds to deal with new topics, how to develop a hunch. . . .

". . . As teachers, we need to remember what the world looked like before we learned our discipline's ways of seeing it."

Source: Wineburg, 2003.

The demands of reading history are instructive about the development of reading comprehension in general.[20] Reading researchers use the reading of history to study the use and updating of background knowledge, comprehension in the face of conflicting evidence or claims across different documents, processing challenges due to dialect differences in some source documents, and the syntactic, semantic, and pragmatic features of historical writing (including discourse patterns; text features; and figures, tables, or illustrations). Teaching history means conveying information about historical events, concepts, and theories but also nurturing the skills, dispositions, and practices (including reading) necessary to understand and undertake historical study. Research on literacy in history has involved students in elementary, middle, and high schools as well as college students and professional historians. The dual interests show in studies related to the "DBQ," data-based question, which calls for students to analyze primary sources (produced during or close to the event, mostly by participants in it). DBQs appear on nationwide exams and as a cornerstone of effective classroom practice. To answer a DBQ adequately, the student must read and write like a historian, using background knowledge of the historical era and specialized techniques for reading and writing so that causal and temporal organization can be woven with an argument structure that supports claims about evidence and makes a historically valid point.

Comprehending the Content Overall. Besides history and science, other content areas produce reading challenges and opportunities throughout the grades in multisubject classrooms as well as in classrooms of schools organized by academic departments.[21] The teacher's knowledge base should be sufficient to intervene when students need help understanding, whether the subject is a short story or a criticism of short stories as a genre, directions for using a tool or for building a tool shed, a mathematics word problem or an explanation of an approach to a proof, records of rainfall and agricultural production or a discourse on the relation between the two. The teacher's knowledge base should also be sufficient for choosing, planning, and enacting lessons for content-area-specific comprehension that will prevent problems and enable students to transfer new reading abilities to texts they meet in the future.

Classroom written material in many content areas appears in three major types, each with challenges for the student and the teacher. First, there are materials (secondary sources) constructed by domain professionals (for example, published articles, drafts, informal letters, lectures, marginal notes, trade books on particular topics) and expected to be a contribution to the field. Sometimes, for these secondary sources, the teacher acts as coreader or surrogate reader, reading aloud and using a think-aloud procedure to make more explicit the propositions and conclusions in the text, to fill in the unstated (where conventional information, theories, models, themes, and schools or approaches contextualize or bias presentation of information and reasoning about it), to formulate and test alternatives to evaluate the authors' explanations and conclusions, and to update one's own knowledge in the content area. The teacher may focus not just on the particular new information but on some part of the standard professional procedures that the reading brings up—data gathering to safeguard evidence, an analytic technique, the explanatory model, warrants for claims, objections, and exceptions in the argument structure.

Effective teachers identify the patterns in secondary source materials that are characteristic of the discipline, common to several disciplines, or uniquely associated with one academic content area, and that will guide students when they read within the discipline in the future. Introductions to specialized vocabulary and concepts are important but only a part of the picture. Anticipation guides, for example, may be constructed to make explicit the rhetorical patterning that guides readers in skimming, depth reading, and reading in noncanonical order. The reader may, for example, locate the main question of an article without fully reading the introduction, then skip to the conclusion to read about progress made toward answering the question. The reader may use an anticipation guide to search for another pair of sections, one reviewing relevant literature regarding the topics and methods and the responding section that shows how the new work fits into or challenges the conventional wisdom and methods. Teachers may also point out patterns of organizing paragraphs—for example, problem and solution, question and answer, comparison and contrast, and cause and effect. Specific vocabulary and sentence syntax are associated with some of these patterns. For example, comparison and contrast text signals include *however, on the other hand, as well as, not only . . . but also, either . . . or, while, although, but, similarly, yet, unless, nevertheless, otherwise, compared to,* and *despite.* Punctuation, typography, and formatting features for text and graphics may also be puzzling to students, unless teachers introduce them explicitly and use them to improve student content-area comprehension.

The second type of classroom written materials are primary sources created by participants in the events: the citizenry in social sciences or scientists experimenting and observing in natural sciences. Teachers may have to teach students a good deal about the language of these sources and how to use it to comprehend. (See Darling-Hammond, Bransford, LePage, Hammerness, and Duffy, 2005, Chapter Four, about contemporary language varieties that students come to school already adept with and the varieties they meet in school.) In many cases, the syntax, semantics, and pragmatics of a primary source are foreign to students—the dialect from a different time, place, or social class. Students may need to learn that the language is associated with a certain setting and character in order to interpret it. Some primary sources may be students' first encounter with particular genres, for example, formal essays; ship manifestos; survey data; letters; government records of birth, death, and property; personal letters; business letters; diaries; charts and tables of conditions; and outcomes of observed variants. There is specialized vocabulary but also specialized semantics for commonly used words and phrases; for example, *not guilty* may or may not be taken as equivalent to "innocent" depending on the specifics of a legal system and its particular operation; the meaning of *energy* as used in biology or physics overlaps only partially with its use in *Monster Energy Drink.*

The third type of written materials teachers meet is textbooks. Textbooks may share more across disciplines than they should; in other words, a science textbook may be a better example of "textbook-ese" than it is of science writing. The formats may allow students to "learn the textbook" rather than the content area by cueing ways to identify answers to likely questions without reading in full or comprehending what is read. Teachers can improve students' use of the special typographical and layout formats; rhetorical and discourse patterns; and vocabulary, syntactic, and semantic features in textbooks. However, students still need to learn to read primary and secondary sources in the content area.

Many teachers nowadays take on the teaching of domain-specific reading having taken only a single and general course on reading in the content areas. These courses are often designed and taught by specialists in remedial or primary-grade reading and have a student body of candidates for teacher certification in different disciplines and for different grade levels. There is little chance to work out a rich understanding of how the written language specific to a domain can enrich learning in that domain and which teaching practices will yield good results. The best to be hoped for is that there will be practice applying good comprehension-teaching approaches to materials used in different domains. Currently, in many school districts, English teachers are charged with improving middle and high school students' reading achievement overall, but they are given insufficient professional development in reading for literary understanding, never mind for succeeding in all the other academic subjects. The richly developing field of domain-specific reading suggests that more can be accomplished by engaging domain specialists (for example, working biologists or literary theorists) and literacy specialists in collaboration to build teachers' knowledge of content-area reading. Focused on practices within a specific domain, teacher education can show teachers how to make the reading and doing in a domain mutually supportive and jointly valuable for student achievement.

Word Identification

Word identification is the other core accomplishment, in addition to comprehension, of the proficient reader. By word identification, we mean recognizing in print a possible word that can be pronounced in the language; knowing a word's meaning and its contribution to comprehension of a text involves more and is not necessarily a part of identifying it in this sense. Most students start learning to identify words in preschool and become quite speedy and accurate by the end of grade two, though development continues for years thereafter. As one learns to identify more words more automatically, through lessons and self-teaching, one approaches word identification differently. Marsh, Desberg, and Cooper (1977) studied nonwords such as *tepherd* and *faugh* and found that ten-year-olds are likely to read them as "teferd" and "faw," while college students are more likely to read them as if they rhyme with *shepherd* and *laugh*. Ten-year-olds have a more limited set of mental tools for reading novel nonwords: the grapheme-phoneme conventions (GPCs) for English allow them to recode written words phonologically and come up with good pronunciations, even in tricky cases. College students sometimes use that same tool. But they can also use knowledge of the orthography of English that links graphemes together in patterns. With this knowledge base and extensive exposure to print, the college readers have stored in memory a detailed orthographic representation for a word linked to representations of pronunciation and meaning. Identifying the nonword *faugh* by analogy to the word *laugh* exploits this orthographic sophistication.[22]

To read nonwords (also called nonsense words) in experiments, people ignore meaning. But in ordinary reading outside of experiments, meaning is central. If asked what they are doing, people report reading a story, reading about engines, or doing an assignment; although reading words is implicated in each of those activities, it is not typically the reported activity. At bottom, reading is about communicating meaning. Very young children read words as meaning units—remembering what was read earlier by a family member, or assuming that the Chiquita label on the banana says *banana.* To read for meaning in the way their elders do, though, they "let go of meaning" (as Chall, 1983, put it) in order to begin to treat the written word as standing for a spoken form, not just as a unit of meaning in its own right.

Quite a bit is known about the details of word identification and the development, learning, and teaching associated with it. Because the main units for word-identification research (letters and phonemes) are finite and relatively small, designing and conducting research is a manageable task. For studies of meaning or anything outside the bounds of word identification, the essential generative nature of language and its use complicate the research effort. For reading comprehension, for instance, the written input is in the form of word strings that can be parsed as proposition-like units, but the internal mental structures (for example, background knowledge) to be connected to that input do not have obvious units with clear points of correspondence to parts of the written input. To comprehend a sentence such as "Why did the elephant cross the road?" the reader uses episodes in memory, perceptual-spatial information, linguistic structures, mental models with complexity and massive idiosyncrasy, and a disposition to laugh or not. In contrast, the well-defined problem space of word identification provides an opportunity to build, test, and contest detailed models of processing and development.[23] In the appendix to this volume, there is a summary of research findings about word identification during four periods identified in terms of early school grades. These are rough approximations, not goals or limits, and vary across effective schools and for individual students. The table in the appendix compares the different terminology used in word identification studies, and the sections that follow it provide details about each period, including the considerable degree of variability within each.

Teachers of reading should be sufficiently familiar with models of word identification to understand how they can be used and misused in curricula and instruction. Four models of word identification have been most influential: dual route,[24] connectionist,[25] stage,[26] and wave strategy models.[27] *Dual route* models posit one direct link between the written word form and its meaning (syntactic, morphological, semantic, and pragmatic) and a second, indirect route linking the written form through GPCs with the word's phonological form and through that with its meaning. The dual routes are alternate strategies for most readers; there is no claim about an acquisition sequence for the two routes. Dual route models are sometimes misused as a call to divide students and limit instruction to one of the routes they allegedly prefer. Nothing could be further from the research base; dual route theories specify the interplay between the two routes, not their mutual exclusion.

In *connectionist* models, links form between and within units (and there are a range of units including whole words, parts of words, written and spoken forms, whole letters, features within letters, whole phonemes, features within phonemes) whenever the reader reads. Mental representations constantly change and are instantly constructed. Memory stores the strength of connections for links previously encountered. A novice may have few and weak connections that reflect GPCs. Proficiency, always about the particular word and its subparts, changes incrementally; connections that are stronger—more frequently activated—account for convergence on the particular word to be identified. At first a word is identified slowly and often incorrectly. Connections strengthen with more exposures, as links to the word are activated more often and as its subparts are activated (not only in the word at issue but in words that share parts with it). With strong and varied connections, the identification of the word becomes quick and accurate. The more subparts (phonemes, letters, morphemes, rime units) that have varied and strong connections (GPC, orthographic, or meaning based) and the more words with those subparts, the quicker and more certain is word identification. This model easily accommodates findings from recent studies (Laing and Hulme, 1999; Metsala, 1999) showing an effect from word meaning on identifying words with similar GPCs.

Stage models specify successive and qualitatively different stages leading to mastery of word identification. The earliest stage for reading is holistic, during which the letters of the written form and the sounds of the spoken form are irrelevant for identifying the word. Next, one or more stages occur during which the use of knowledge about letters and sounds (GPCs) delimits the application of the holistic strategy, eventually replacing it with sequential and segmental processing of GPCs to arrive at the phonological form of the word. During the final stage, orthographic patterns in written words, syllables, or parts of syllables are linked to the orthographic representation stored in the reader's memory along with phonological and meaning-based representations of the word. Stage theories in reading, unlike classical Piagetian stage models, do not strictly define stages as qualitative changes with little overlap. Frith's early stage model (1985) called for adding processes at successive stages rather than positing qualitatively different ones. Recently, Ehri and Snowling (2004) suggested the term *phase* would be better than *stage*. The practice and policy communities, however, often take stage models in a more strict sense, expecting children to "finish" one stage before allowing them to undertake activities related to a supposed next stage.

Reading development could hardly be expected to follow strict Piagetian-like stages, since, unlike the matters Piaget studied, there is no doubt that reading is not a universal human trait. In some cultures reading is rare or nonexistent. The alphabet, the range of texts to be read, the routines for teaching at home and school: these are *cultural* artifacts. As with most cultural entities, there is considerable variation within subgroups in a society and across individuals with respect to whether, how, or when they are introduced to reading (see, for example, Heath, 1983; Stuart and Coltheart, 1988; and Baron, 1979). Children do not become readers all on their own; patterns observed to change as students grow older may be patterns of what adults do while teaching rather than patterns due to developmental changes. Progress depends on the texts and curricula available and the support and expectations from formal or informal teachers. Instruction matters a great deal in learning to read, but it is not universally available and is neither the same nor equally effective in the different places and times it is available. Different kinds of instruction affect performance in tasks distant from the instructional setting and unintended by the instructional program (see Barr, 1975; Biemiller, 1970; Monaghan, 1983; Chall, 1983; Carnine, Carnine, and Gersten, 1984; and Goswami and East, 2000). Evidence used in claims about reading stages is hard to evaluate precisely because it may reflect adult ideas of proper instruction rather than developmental forces.

Wave models involve strategies that are similar to the processes identified in stage models, but the wave model expects overlapping in two senses. Depending on the situation and the availability of strategies to the reader, the individual's uses of strategies overlap. Holistic strategies, often the only recourse for beginners, overlap with other strategies used by adult proficient readers: for example, "l8r" is read as "later," "Moussouai" is read as the name of a trial defendant with little attention to, or reliable knowledge of, the letters or phonemes that make up the word; and "84" is read "eighty-four." Strategy acquisition overlaps as well. Transitional phenomena are prominent and longer lasting than a stage model would predict. Even young children primarily using a holistic strategy to identify words are influenced by features of the graphemes in the words, the position of graphemes in the word, and the degree to which the phonemes in grapheme names match the phonemes in the word to be identified. The acquisition of a next strategy, in which the influences from GPCs are central rather than supporting (or interfering) factors is gradual, not a remarkable qualitative shift (see details in the appendix). Wave models also make prominent the question of when strategies appear in the spellings of words relative to readings of them, and whether or how spelling facilitates word identification in reading.

Supporting Both Comprehension and Word Identification

Sequential or Simultaneous? No one doubts that the comprehension and use of written language are impeded by poor word identification. The question is whether, developmentally and educationally speaking, comprehension instruction is better provided simultaneously with or sequentially to word identification instruction. Two of the columns in Table A.1 in the appendix concern aspects of reading beyond word identification. Chall's schema (1983) describes a shift from an early focus on print-speech relations to later emphases on relating print to ideas. Spear-Swerling and Sternberg's schema (1997) similarly shifts to comprehension and use issues in the later periods. Some in the practice and policy communities have translated models like these into curriculum sequences that postpone meaning-based reading instruction and assessment until word identification proficiency has been achieved. The rationale often given is that students in the earlier phase are not yet able to learn to comprehend and that trying to teach them would drain resources needed for word identification.

Certainly, given a particular text, comprehension suffers if the reader fails to identify most of the words quickly, accurately, and without effort. The reader allocates so much attention and effort to words that a bottleneck forms, and few if any resources can be allocated for comprehending the text (see Perfetti, 1985). But this is resource allocation in the reading of a passage (five or ten minutes), not resource allocation in the education of a reader (thirteen years from kindergarten through grade twelve). The research base does not support postponing comprehension instruction and practice until later in a student's education. In fact, since it shows that word identification is necessary but not sufficient for comprehending a text, research supports instruction that integrates word identification with comprehension from the very beginning (Snow, Burns, and Griffin, 1998, pp. 68–79, 313–317). Opportunities for improving comprehension can occur in early grades either by using texts that do not frustrate extant word-identification skills or by focusing on comprehension strategies and tasks while adults read aloud for and with children (see Beck and McKeown, 2001; Smolkin and Donovan, 2001, 2003).

The National Research Council study committee that recommended the integrated approach acknowledged the need for more guidance on how to do it (Snow, Burns, and Griffin, 1998, pp. 343–344), asking, for example, "Through what means can word recognition and comprehension development be coordinated so that they develop most efficiently and synergistically?" The National Reading Panel (2000, Chapter Four) found that although grades three through six were the sites of most studies of comprehension instruction, effectiveness of instruction could not be related definitively to grade level. A recent review of comprehension instruction (Duke and Pearson, 2002) finds there is no compelling case for limiting the teaching of any particular comprehension strategies to certain grades or ages.

Some have made a case, though, for putting comprehension to the side during early reading instruction because they believe that reading comprehension is not a significant entity in its own right, that the reader's understanding of spoken language provides what is needed. In studies in which an experimenter (or a tape) reads aloud passages to test students' listening comprehension, the results show that listening comprehension exceeds reading comprehension for beginners; as early as middle school, however, the two are highly correlated (Bell and Perfetti, 1994; Sticht and James, 1984).[28] Many see the early gap as the simple result of less skilled word identification. For scholars who view reading as identifying the spoken forms of written words and then feeding the result into the same comprehension system that serves for listening, early reading (and the teaching of it) can be a comprehensionless effort, essentially word identification, followed by specific reading comprehension instruction in later grades if needed by some students seen as struggling readers (see, for example, Rayner, Foorman, Perfetti, Pesetsky, and Seidenberg, 2001, pp. 42–43). This approach makes three key assumptions: (1) spoken-language comprehension continues to develop while word identification is taught, whether it develops on its own or with instruction; (2) content-area instruction develops the content knowledge needed for later reading comprehension; and (3) integrating comprehension with word-reading skill is something students can figure out on their own.

In contrast, many studies of very young children assume a simultaneous approach, teaching comprehension and the use of reading for learning from the very beginning. Some support teaching comprehension by modeling it during read-aloud sessions, even before children are able to use the alphabetic principle during their solo attempts at reading. Others demonstrate the power of a variety of early activities: improving comprehension during repeated read-alouds of the same text; attuning children as young as five to the language patterns that differentiate author styles; teaching students story grammar for comprehension gains during read-alouds; learning from informational alphabet books; transferring form and content from information text read-alouds to independent activity with books; and using comprehension strategies during interactive read-alouds of informational books.[29]

In spite of this developing knowledge base, the idea persists that younger students learn to read (and to read words, primarily) while older ones read to learn (so comprehension matters). The belief becomes a self-fulfilling prophecy if young students are given few opportunities to read informational texts that they are expected to learn with (even though some children prefer them to storybooks).[30]

Chall, Jacobs, and Baldwin (1990) suspect that a fourth-grade slump in reading ability may be a consequence of too little practice, in the earlier grades, with informational texts that are so important in fourth grade.

Of course, the rich comprehension work some teachers do in the early grades (for example, read-alouds accompanied by discussions about the text) relies on spoken language and may focus on linguistic processes common to comprehension of spoken and written language. However, we argue that it is really about reading comprehension. In the first place, conversations about readings serve as the motives and means for teaching students of all ages to be active readers, a basic component of learning and applying reading comprehension strategies as well as an essential part of understanding each specific text. The spoken language may be the medium in these lessons, but reading comprehension is clearly the goal and the message. Second, the instruction relies on the durable nature of written-language passages: changing the pacing from segment to segment, inserting interruptions for monitoring and clarifying, repeating and repairing processes, and choosing text segments for examination even if they are out of sequence. The printed text provides a publicly available reference point for teachers and students to explain how they construct their understanding and allow others literally to see the words and structures that contradict or support an interpretation. There may well be a reciprocal relation between growth of the student's spoken-language comprehension and the learning resulting from reading-comprehension lessons, particularly if the lessons center on linguistic processes common to spoken and written language.

Besides the benefits of simultaneous instruction in reading comprehension and word identification, the limits of a sequential approach need to be considered. Students who show difficulty with comprehension at the end of the primary grades may well have needed help with comprehension much earlier. A series of studies has focused on the 10 to 15 percent of young students found to have problems specifically on measures of comprehension.[31] The studies contrast these students with peers who are less skilled at word identification, peers who match them at identifying words but surpass them when it comes to comprehension, and younger children who match them at comprehension, in spite of weaker word identification skills. When these poor comprehenders are eleven, their problems can be predicted by performance at younger ages on tasks of story structure, inferencing skills, comprehension monitoring, and overall comprehension (Cain, Oakhill, and Bryant, 2000; Cain and Oakhill, 2004). In contrast, their word-identification skills at eleven are related to earlier performance on phoneme-deletion tasks, word identification, and verbal IQ.

With this disassociation, it is doubtful that holding off on comprehension instruction until after word identification is mastered is a good move. Broad and deep knowledge of research and practices related to both core developmental accomplishments (comprehension and word identification) provide teachers in all grades with a base for evaluating new studies and suggestions about whether instruction on the core tasks should be sequential or simultaneous.

Motivating Engagement for Reading. Engagement and motivation to learn are important for any student's progress (see Darling-Hammond, Bransford, LePage, Hammerness, and Duffy, 2005, Chapter Eight). There are two dimensions of motivation and engagement that assume even more importance in the knowledge base for the teaching of reading.[32]

First, understanding research findings on the sources of engagement can help teachers focusing on comprehension and fluency. Proficient reading comprehension calls on readers to monitor themselves so that they notice and repair errors; teachers teach strategies for comprehension monitoring and help students to apply them in response to difficult textual material. But motivational circumstances may sabotage comprehension monitoring. Some students learn to avoid errors, even the appearance of them; this can obviously undermine a strategy based on learning from errors! Students who are motivated by error avoidance (as in the learned helplessness profile) may fail to persist in reading difficult texts that call for applying (and thereby improving through practice) comprehension strategies. Some students are motivated to finish tasks rather than to master what is being learned; they may become accustomed to undertaking tasks for extrinsic rewards and so may be unlikely to apply a strategy for the intrinsic reward of understanding the material being read. A student who does not believe in the value of effort to improve outcomes may not engage in the extensive practice at reading that allows for the self-teaching of word identification and leads toward automatic word identification and strategic purposeful comprehension.

Second, many recent studies detail how specific approaches to teaching reading can change student motivation as students engage more fully, become invested in the educational work, and achieve proficiency. The knowledge base includes attention to a variety of activities and instructional approaches. Preexisting student interest in a topic being read about or response to certain social conditions (for example, cooperative learning, climate of respect, well-paced lessons, provisions for a high likelihood of success, indications that a student's time is valued, or connection to matters of importance outside of school) may increase even the initially indifferent student's engagement, investment, and achievement. Topics that motivate a student to be interested have a web of benefits: they allow a student to bring more background knowledge to comprehension tasks; they lead to the use of sophisticated protracted strategies for comprehension; they increase the time on task needed for strategic processing; and they are likely venues for success with understanding the text at hand as well as for learning strategies that can lead to more reading achievement in the future.

READING INSTRUCTION AND
KNOWLEDGE OF THE LANGUAGE SYSTEMS

As teachers engage students in reading instruction, they enact their knowledge about language. In this section, we focus on five widely discussed types of instruction to draw attention to different aspects of the language knowledge base used while teaching reading.[33] Phonemic awareness instruction highlights phonology and metacognition; word attack and phonics instruction add morphology, etymology, and orthography; word meaning and vocabulary instruction bring to the fore semantics; and comprehension strategy instruction adds syntax and pragmatics, especially discourse pragmatics. Fluency instruction promotes the integration of all these systems. (There are brief descriptions of the language subsystems involved earlier in this chapter, in the section "Language and Literacy: Integrated Systems and Subsystems" and the accompanying Exhibit 2.1.) We consider four more general issues first, however.

1. *Teachers' knowledge base for reading goes beyond language*. Various organizations have advocated a wider knowledge base among those who teach students to read.[34] The American Federation of Teachers (AFT) advocates four domains: knowledge of the psychology of reading and reading development; knowledge of language; knowledge of and ability to implement validated instructional practices competently and reflectively; and ability to assess children using research-based tools and strategies. The International Reading Association (IRA) identifies five standards for teacher-education programs. The standards do not conflict with the AFT recommendations, but emphasize additional foundation disciplines (for example, sociology) as well as knowledge about literate environments, variations among cultural backgrounds of students, and options for instructional grouping. The standards also call for teacher-education programs to prepare teachers for continuing learning throughout their careers.

While this chapter emphasizes the *language* knowledge base for teaching reading, we recognize that wider frameworks of knowledge are necessary complements to it. The following chapters bring up some of that knowledge in ways specific to the teaching of reading. For other matters that are important to teaching overall, not just reading, we refer the reader to the related volume *Preparing Teachers for a Changing World: What Teachers Should Learn and Be Able to Do* (Darling-Hammond, Bransford, LePage, Hammerness, and Duffy, 2005).

2. *Instruction for reading improvement goes beyond the five types highlighted here.* The types of instruction we use to illustrate the enactment of underlying language knowledge are not an "all and only" list.[35] We consider them an "at least" list. Furthermore, alternative treatments subdivide the types we use while

Exhibit 2.5. What Effective Teachers Know and Do: More General, More Specific

A recent large and multiyear study of middle and high school classes was the basis for identifying six features of sites where effective instruction of reading and writing took place (Langer, Close, Angelis, and Preller, 2000, p. 3):

- Students learn skills and knowledge in multiple lesson types.
- Teachers integrate test preparation into instruction.
- Teachers make connections across instruction, curriculum, and life.
- Students learn strategies for doing the work.
- Students are expected to be generative thinkers.
- Classrooms foster cognitive collaboration.

We see these features as providing a necessary context for making useable the language knowledge that we concentrate on in this book.

We also recognize that a full specification of the knowledge, skills, and dispositions needed for teaching reading would include details depending on grade levels and, sometimes, the school subject that the teacher specializes in. Texas, for example, has nine standards specifically regarding those who hope to teach English language arts and reading in grades eight through twelve. As a part of constructing a teacher examination, the State Board for Educator Certification and National Evaluation Systems (2003, pp. 6–7) identified four domains represented in these standards: integrated language arts, diverse learners, and the study of English; literature, reading processes, and skills for reading literary and nonliterary texts; writing; and oral communication and media literacy. The weighting of the relative importance of each domain reveals that less than half of teacher competency involves reading processes, its development, or its language base. More specifically (pp. 12–17), the Board expects that a beginning English teacher

- Demonstrates knowledge of genres and their characteristics through analysis of literary texts
- Demonstrates knowledge of literary elements and devices, including ways in which they contribute to meaning and style, through analysis of literary texts
- Demonstrates knowledge of major literary movements in American, British, and world literature, including their characteristics, the historical contexts from which they emerged, major authors and their impact on literature, and representative works and their themes
- Demonstrates knowledge of a substantial body of classic and contemporary American literature

---

Exhibit 2.5. What Effective Teachers Know and Do: More General, More Specific, *Cont'd*

- Demonstrates knowledge of a substantial body of classic and contemporary British literature

- Demonstrates knowledge of a substantial body of classic and contemporary world literature

- Demonstrates knowledge of a substantial body of young adult literature

- Demonstrates knowledge of various critical approaches to literature

- Demonstrates knowledge of various types of responses to literary texts (for example, experiential, aesthetic, or pragmatic) and encourages a variety of responses in students

- Applies effective strategies for helping students view literature as a source for exploring and interpreting human experience

- Applies effective strategies for engaging students in exploring and discovering the personal and societal relevance of literature

- Promotes students' understanding of relationships among literary works from various times and cultures

- Understands and promotes the use of technology in all phases of the writing process and in various types of writing, including writing for research and publication

- Applies strategies for helping students develop voice and style in their writing

- Provides instruction about plagiarism, academic honesty, and integrity as applied to students' written work and their presentation of information from different sources, including electronic sources

- Understands and helps students understand the role of cultural factors in oral communication

- Understands and teaches skills for active, purposeful listening in various situations (for example, skills for note taking, for critically evaluating a speaker's message, or for appreciating an oral performance) and provides effective opportunities for practice

- Analyzes and teaches about the influence of the media and the power of visual images

- Applies and teaches skills for responding to, interpreting, analyzing, and critiquing a variety of media (for example, advertising, visual images, propaganda, and documentaries)

others collapse them (for example, alphabetics to subsume phonemic aware-ness and word identification, or separation between cognitive processes and metacognitive processes in comprehension strategies).

Nowadays, reading instruction is influenced by federal programs, state stan-dards, district benchmarks, mandated assessment instruments, and textbook se-ries. A grade-level team or department, a school, or a district may mandate minute details of scope, sequence, and method—even specifying goals, materi-als, and timing for certain lessons. State or federal government initiatives or funding may constrain local education agencies to favor some instructional types. While contemporary frameworks may lay claim to uniqueness, a com-mon denominator for most of the requirements for instruction is a set of in-structional acts derived from the National Reading Panel (2000) report that reviewed experimental studies of reading instruction. This set includes the five instruction types we deal with here: phonemic awareness instruction, word at-tack and phonics instruction, word meaning and vocabulary instruction, com-prehension strategy instruction, and fluency.

These five instructional practices, though, are not seen as the primary hall-marks of effectiveness in recent empirical studies of exemplary practices. The studies range from the early primary grades through high school, and most focus on data about students whose reading achievements "beat the odds," in spite of circumstances or prior experiences that usually augur ill for student achieve-ment.[36] Consistent with earlier studies of effective education (compare Brophy and Good, 1986), these studies show that higher student achievement appears as teachers are active and directly involved in the students' work in a variety of ways: effective teachers lecture or demonstrate to whole groups; they lead dis-cussions or scaffold peer discussions; they monitor recitations or seatwork by small groups or individuals; they manage behavior unobtrusively and maintain high rates of student engagement; and they teach both well-planned curricular units and opportunistic, responsive lessons that meet and then stretch students' capacities. These exemplary classrooms offer explicit instruction as well as learn-ing and practice in the context of reading and writing tasks that capitalize on and serve the students' cultural knowledge and interests. The studies show students asking and answering questions that require conceptual analysis, often breaching boundaries among school subjects and between school and out-of-school life. The students build procedural and metacognitive knowledge, believe in their own agency, have high expectations, and engage in challenging tasks that help them fulfill their expectations. There is frequent feedback from assessment and high-quality personal relations among students and between students and teach-ers. As high-stakes tests enter the scene, test preparation is integrated into the routines of classroom instruction. In sum, the instructional activities we focus on here are likely to be found in exemplary classrooms, but they are by no means the whole story of what makes a classroom exemplary.

3. *Useable knowledge for teaching has several dimensions.* Knowing how to read does not mean that one knows about the procedures that go on during reading nor about the processes of reading development. Knowing how to teach—to promote, instigate, manage, and monitor student reading achievements—does require knowledge of those procedures and processes. When a student hesitates on a word in a text, which teacher response best supports reading that specific text and best promotes the student's overall reading development? A teacher chooses when to say the problem word and let the student get on with the text, when to prompt the use of a word-identification routine, which routine to choose, when to scaffold the use of a comprehension strategy, when to manage a discussion of the meaning of the sentence or passage, when to plan and implement systematic comprehension and word-identification lessons, and when and how to do and use assessments of student mastery and teaching effectiveness. As they make these choices, teachers have underlying knowledge of the language and the content being read, the student's progress as a reader, and the intended contribution of the lesson to the student's progress. Shulman (1986) used the term "pedagogical content knowledge" to identify the sorts of things that teachers know above and beyond knowing how to read: knowledge of how students (with individual and developmental variations) see (mentally represent) the content as well as knowledge of alternate ways that content can be represented and instructional moves can be structured so that children learn.

A large-scale undertaking referred to as The Study of Instructional Improvement (Phelps and Schilling, 2003; Ball, Phelps, Rowan, and Schilling, 2003) examines the knowledge used in the work of teaching reading—in working on materials for use in instruction and assessment; in working with students; and in working with resource teachers, administrators, and parents. It considers knowledge of content (KC) itself; knowledge of students and content (KSC) in order to interpret students' actions, products, responses, and progress; and knowledge of teaching and content (KTC) to inform acts, interactions, assessment, and planning as appropriate given the subject and the students. The Study developed and validated a test with items for all three kinds of pedagogical knowledge, looking both at core tasks for reading (comprehension and word identification) and at a variety of "online" teaching acts as well as the "offline" choices teachers make when evaluating the day's lessons and planning new ones. Early analyses support the claim that teachers use a language knowledge base and one that is specialized for teaching reading, that is, with appropriate KSC and KTC. There does not appear to be an ordering of the three kinds of pedagogical knowledge; for example, it is not the case that KC is mastered first, then KTC, and finally KSC. There are more and less sophisticated aspects of each type of pedagogical knowledge. Critiquing some previously learned part of KTC may lead a teacher to deeper study and understanding of

---

Exhibit 2.6. Examples of Test Items for Teacher Knowledge

Example of *Knowledge of Content* (Word Analysis) item (Ball, Phelps, Rowan, and Schilling, 2003, p. 14):

When Mrs. Schwartz's children proofread their own writing, they sometimes do not notice when they leave off the ending -*ed*. They are especially inattentive when the *ed* sounds like /t/. Mrs. Schwartz wants to give them targeted, short practice listening for -*ed* when it is pronounced as /t/. Which of the following sets of words should she select? (Mark ONE answer.)

(a) wanted, sorted, banded

(b) picked, sipped, pitched

(c) fringed, dodged, hummed

(d) attached, angled, invented.

Example of *Knowledge of Students and Content* (Word Analysis) item (Ball, Phelps, Rowan, and Schilling, 2003, p. 20):

Ms. Reynolds dictated the following story to her class. She plans to use this to assess her students' ability to hear and represent phonemes (i.e., the smallest segments of speech used to build a word).

I got a little white train.

It was my best gift.

I liked running it fast.

One day I will go on a real train.

She looked at her students' papers. Ron's paper looked like this:

I got a lidl wit chrane.

It was my bst gif.

I likt runin it fast.

Won day I wl go on a rele chrane.

Which of the following words from Ron's writing provide evidence that Ron can identify each phoneme heard when saying the word? (Mark Yes, No, or I'm not sure for each word.)

Exhibit 2.6. Examples of Test Items for Teacher Knowledge, *Cont'd*

	Yes	No	I'm not sure
(a) 'wit' for white	1	2	3
(b) 'chrane' for train	1	2	3
(c) 'bst' for best	1	2	3
(d) 'gif' for gift	1	2	3
(e) 'likt' for liked	1	2	3
(f) 'runin' for running	1	2	3
(g) 'wl' for will	1	2	3
(h) 'rele' for real	1	2	3

Example of *knowledge of teaching and content* (comprehension) (Ball, Phelps, Rowan, and Schilling, 2003, p. 26):

[A multi-paragraph passage, "The Marvelous Manatee" is used in several of the test items; test takers are directed to refer to it for this item.]

The Marvelous Manatee

What do manatees and elephants have in common? You might be amazed to find that they have a great deal in common! The elephant is one of the manatee's closest relatives. Elephants and manatees are also both <u>mammals</u>. Like all mammals, manatees are warm-blooded. They breathe air with their lungs and they give birth to live babies. Some mammals live on land while others live in the water. Mammals that live in the water are called <u>aquatic</u>.

Manatees and their relatives are the only <u>marine</u> mammals that are <u>herbivores</u>. They can weigh up to 3,500 pounds and reach 13 feet in length. They are very <u>tactile</u> and are often observed hugging each other and nuzzling snout to snout. These slow-moving, gentle giants are peaceful and unafraid of humans.

Manatees have a colorful place in seafaring legends. Long ago sailors reported seeing mermaids at sea. These wonderful creatures would come to the surface and beckon sailors to come close. Then they would disappear as soon as the boat neared. In fact, manatees probably inspired legends about mermaids. Manatees have a mermaid-like tail and friendly, expressive faces.

Exhibit 2.6. Examples of Test Items for Teacher Knowledge, *Cont'd*

The peaceful manatee, like its cousin the elephant, is an <u>endangered</u> animal. Manatees have few natural enemies, other than humans. Boat collisions are the single greatest reason for manatee <u>mortalities</u>. Ultimately, however, loss of <u>habitat</u> is the most serious threat facing manatees today. There are approximately 3,000 manatees left in the United States. Without our help the manatee could soon be <u>extinct</u>.

Ms. Gomez is preparing to read the first two paragraphs of "The Marvelous Manatee" out loud to the class. Her plan is to pause as she reads and to model for her students what a good reader might do to figure out an unfamiliar vocabulary word. She has been teaching her students to use two strategies to figure out unfamiliar vocabulary words. One strategy is to look for smaller meaning elements, such as a root word, prefix, suffix, compound word, and so on. Her book refers to this as "structural analysis." A second strategy is to use "context clues"—that is, to look for clues or other information in the text to help understand the meaning of the word. Ms. Gomez is reviewing the vocabulary words in the text to decide if she should model structural analysis, use of context clues, both of these strategies, or neither. What should she decide for each of these words? (Mark ONE choice for each word.)

	Context Clues is the best choice	Structural Analysis is the best choice	Both are equally good choices	Neither are good choices	I am not sure
(a) mammals	1	2	3	4	5
(b) aquatic	1	2	3	4	5
(c) marine	1	2	3	4	5
(d) herbivores	1	2	3	4	5
(e) tactile	1	2	3	4	5

KC, and discussion about some previously unsuspected KSC can lead to searching for new KC and KTC.

Instructional materials require modifications based on the teacher's pedagogical knowledge in order to suit the particular classroom reality—even very fully specified (scripted) lessons and even lessons carefully designed, planned, enacted, evaluated, and redesigned until effective for a specific teacher and her students at a specific time and place. For example, a curriculum covering letter names and letter sounds may be designed with similar and equal time activities for each letter, but the teacher, relying on knowledge of the research literature as well as knowledge of the students and activities in the class, rearranges the ordering so that new routines are introduced with letters the students will find easy, reallocating more time for letters likely to bring up more difficulty, and consuming less time overall. Or a history teacher decides to use an essay by a professional historian but, recognizing the difficulties high school sophomores will have with the unfamiliar genre, plans to read it aloud, interrupting herself to summarize and using the summary to guide some rereading or skimming ahead. As the reading progresses, she gradually does less, asking her "listeners" to work more with the text on their own. In addition to planned lessons, the role of practice and application with different topics and genres is crucial for effective reading education, and teachers use their underlying knowledge to interact during incidental, opportunistic instruction. To notice and act requires deep pedagogical content knowledge of all three types.

Knowledge about language and confident use of knowledge related to the various language subsystems can ease communication among teachers about instructional episodes, student success or difficulty, planning and choices, new ideas, old questions—in short about the professional experiences of teaching. It provides a way to see common progress or problems across very different content—for example, Dr. King's sermons in social studies, lab reports in science, and elegies in English class. It spotlights student behaviors that provide information about student progress. It inspires as teachers plan, design, and create materials or choose among available materials (see Donovan and Smolkin, 2001; Tower, 2002). Within the community of teachers, a common knowledge base provides an opening in the isolating classroom walls with terminology and frameworks that ease collaboration among teachers and promote clarity in communication with mentors, mentees, and supervisors. Professional knowledge supports more in-depth use of teacher resource materials that accompany textbooks as well as publications related to state frameworks and standards. Finally, as Stanovich and Stanovich (2003) point out, teachers with a sufficient knowledge base can examine the credibility of instructional innovations in light of their purported causal models to make informed decisions about giving them a trial in classroom practice.

We acknowledge that the directly relevant research basis concerning pedagogical knowledge for the teaching of reading is still inadequate (compare Roller, 2001). We await the development of the kinds of powerful experimental long-term studies that definitively link specific aspects of teacher education and teacher learning to teachers' use of specific practices and then to improvements in students' learning. There are some movements toward this from different starting points, for example, Hoffman, Roller, Maloch, Sailors, Beretvas, and the National Commission on Excellence in Elementary Teacher Preparation for Reading Instruction (2003) and McCutchen, Abbott, Green, Beretvas, Cox, Potter, and others (2002). Given these beginnings, more general work on learning among adults and in domains such as reading (for example, Bransford, Brown, and Cocking, 1999), and a great deal of agreement in the field that comprehension and word recognition are the two core accomplishments of proficient readers, we feel that there is firm enough ground to propose a language knowledge base for the teaching of reading, recognizing that the details of it will benefit from careful ongoing evaluation. A variety of studies show that many teachers have had little opportunity to learn about language and that they do learn a good deal when given the chance (Moats and Foorman, 2003; McCutchen and Berninger, 1999; McCutchen, Harry, Cunningham, Cox, Sidman, and Covill, 2002; and Bos, Mather, Dickson, Podhajski, and Chard, 2001). Uncertainty of the usefulness of a course in reading pedagogy in the content areas led Barry (2002) to poll former students; many reported that after several years they were in fact still using the kinds of comprehension strategy instruction that they learned in the course. Anderson and Roit (1993) argue that teachers do not continue to use a strategy if they only know procedures for it rather than understanding it in depth. A case in point for developing deeper teacher understanding is the Strategic Literacy Network's generative model for middle and high school teacher study (Greenleaf and Schoenbach, 2004; Greenleaf, Schoenbach, Cziko, and Mueller, 2001; and Schoenbach, Greenleaf, Cziko, and Hurwitz, 1999). It is strongly linked to student improvement and is an example of the learning, enactment, assessment, and reflection cycle for teacher learning advocated in Chapter One of this volume.

4. *Two warnings about language and teaching reading should be considered.* First is language variability and different dialects. Second is whether to teach explicitly and separately about language structures (grammar) to students in elementary and secondary schools. Sometimes in casual conversation we mention that someone speaks a dialect as if others did not; technically, though, everyone speaks a dialect.[37] There is no dialect-free version of English or any other language. Some dialects are less noticeable than others, depending on the situation (Table 2.2).

Table 2.2. Noticeable Dialect

Situation	More Noticeable	Less Noticeable
Soccer Match, United States	"Which team is paying you, ref?" (Pronouncing the first phoneme of *which* differently from the way people pronounce the beginning of *witch*)	Pronouncing *which* the same as *witch*
School	"The colonists picked him out as a skinner, right?" (Pronouncing *picked him* the way people pronounce *pick him*]	Pronouncing *picked him* more like *pick Tim*
Schools in the Northeast and Midwest United States	Pronouncing *spoil* with two syllables	Pronouncing *spoil* with one syllable
New England	"The government is too active in education anymore."	"The government is too active in education nowadays."
African American Communities	Unfamiliar with language rules for signifying (see Lee, 1995b)	Familiar with language rules for signifying

Dialect variation may be associated with region, with social class, with rural-urban differences, with gender, and with ethnicity. It is also related to eras: Benjamin Franklin's dialect is no longer found in Philadelphia, to say nothing of Shakespeare's in London. Some dialects are taken for granted in educational materials and by teachers; thus other ones become known as "different dialects." Dialect differences most often mentioned are those involving phonology and vocabulary items. When members of an ethnic or social-class subgroup resettle in a different dialect region, regional dialect features they use may become markers of ethnicity and social class in the new locales. Some dialect features, for example, pronouncing /l/ in ways described as dark, vocalized, or clear, awaken attitude differences but are associated with no communicative or schooling difficulties. Other differences do contribute to miscommunication. In rural South Carolina, *Watts* rhymes with *whites;* in Los Angeles, *Polly* and *Pauly* sound the same; in New England, *four* has two syllables, but *for* has one and *bath* rhymes with *hearth;* and much to the surprise of many an Englishman, many Americans pronounce *waited* and *waded* the same but pronounce *wait again* and *wade again* differently. As the examples in Table 2.2 indicate, not only the sound system varies; morphology, syntax, semantics, discourse, and pragmatics are also at issue. Often, syntactic and morphological variants (and phonological variants that have an impact on morphology) are not recognized as dialect differences; instead they are seen as grammatical errors. Many dialect features are thought to be "all or nothing," but close study has shown that there is variability related to the phonological context (Is there a vowel at the start of the next word?), to the morphology (Does a final /t/ signal a past tense as in *missed* or is it part of the root as in *mist* ?), to the syntax and semantics (Does the clause have a negative element?). Aside from a conditioning language context, many dialect features have been shown to have a probability of use that rejects the idea that they are always or never used.

Some variants are associated with an informal style in one dialect but are in more general use in another. Hence, the form that students use may be familiar to a teacher but sound very casual. The suffix *-ing* in words like *reading* and *writing*, for instance, has two variants: The more formal variant is pronounced with a velar nasal /ŋ/ (the back of the tongue presses the back roof of the mouth); the informal or fast-speech style is pronounced with an alveolar nasal /n/ (the front of the tongue presses the roof of the mouth toward the front).[38] Both variants appear whether the suffix is a separate morpheme (as in *reading*) or just a two-syllable single-morpheme word like *morning*. Some dialects use the alveolar nasal almost exclusively, regardless of the style of speech. Interestingly enough, for single-syllable single-morpheme words, such as *king* or *sing*, the velar nasal appears no matter the dialect or style. Without an adequate knowledge base about dialect variation, a teacher might think that the issue is sloppiness about all final /ŋ/ sounds or G letters, about wrong verb suffixes, or about students' reluctance to use a formal style. With an adequate knowledge base, a teacher can rely on the strength (the appearance of the velar nasal in single-syllable words) to help students handle the verb suffix in more formal styles.

If teachers are aware of the structure of students' dialects, no particular dialect need be an impediment to reading achievement. Students may benefit in other ways from mastering the spoken form of high-status dialects or formal-language varieties, but they need not replace their home and neighborhood dialects in order to learn to read. The language knowledge base about language variation should ensure that the teacher can identify materials that may be inappropriate for some students and can adjust certain examples and rubrics as the language variation demands. Most teacher education or professional development class cohorts include speakers of various dialects; this makes it easy to study dialect differences as the class works through examples of language subsystems and instructional activities. (See the related volume *Preparing Teachers for a Changing World* [Darling-Hammond, Bransford, LePage, Hammerness, and Duffy, 2005], Chapter Four for broader and deeper discussion of the impact of language variation on education, especially given the common social interpretations of dialect differences;

see Chapter Three of this volume for more information about students with dialects and languages likely to be less well represented in the materials available for teachers.)

The second warning is about the formal teaching of language subsystems to elementary and high school students. Essentially, we know that oral language development is important for reading and learning to read, but we have no compelling evidence that reading is improved through formal lessons about language structures in any of the language subsystems. Teachers need explicit knowledge of the language systems for all the professional work of teaching described in the preceding section. Students, though, may not need explicit knowledge to learn to read well. Extensive experience incorporating formal teaching about language into writing instruction suggests its value is limited:[39] teaching students about syntax and morphology so they can parse sentences has been found *not* to lead to improved student writing, not even when the lessons are designed to help students avoid or correct specific errors. In contrast, time spent on other instruction does lead to increases in the students' repertoire of syntactic structures and improvement in the quality of sentences they use in their writing. Systematic practice combining and expanding sentences, for instance, works well to improve writing, especially when the stylistic effects of the changes are explicitly discussed. It works to teach grammar in the context of writing that has a communicative purpose, in mini-lessons and conferences as students are composing, revising, and editing.[40] And reading helps improve writing: close readings of effective examples, including experiments with revisions and discussion of the results; listening to read-alouds of selections with sentence structures the students seldom otherwise encounter; and extensive reading in general.[41] Further research may show that grammar teaching is useful to improve reading, but currently available research does not support its value.[42]

In general in this chapter, we say little about writing beyond spelling. This should not be interpreted as a denial of a strong connection between reading and writing. We cannot fail to note the cognitive strategies that are common to reading and writing, nor the extensive history of research on the relations between reading and writing development and instruction. We are unable to treat the complexities in this limited venue. See, for examples and overviews, Loban, 1963; Barone, 1990; Tierney and Shanahan, 1991; Nelson and Calfee, 1998; and Olson, 2002.

Phonemic Awareness Instruction: Enacting Knowledge of Language

Phonological awareness is awareness that the sound structure of language can be considered separate from meanings and functions. Phonemic awareness is a subtype, an awareness of the smallest units of sound that allow speakers of a language to differentiate among words. Phonological patterns are prominent in songs, nursery rhymes, and games that have rhyming segments and alliterative patterns within and between words. As children enjoy these patterns, appreciate them, learn to recite them, elaborate on them, and invent new ones, they exhibit phonological sensitivity that can be a base for the phonemic awareness that is implicit in early alphabetic reading success.[43]

Noticing, thinking about, or manipulating phonemes in words shows phonemic awareness (PA). Speaking and listening are not at issue; it is a matter of transcending language-as-communication to think language-as-structure. In languages such as English, the writing system depends on grapheme-phoneme conventions that arbitrarily associate letters and letter combinations (graphemes) with sounds (phonemes). When beginners are learning to identify words in written language, phonemic awareness of the spoken-language form of the words anchors the new (reading) to the known (speaking and listening).[44]

Three types of PA can be seen in instruction and assessment:

Identity: The same phoneme occurs in different words or in different positions of a word. In one identity task (the common-unit task), students listen to a set of words such as *me, am, mutt,* and *small* and are expected to say that it is the phoneme /m/ that occurs in all the items. Aural discrimination does not count as PA; identifying *dig* as odd in *big, big, dig* requires only hearing the same versus different syllabic units, not identifying the phoneme that makes the difference. Selecting *dan* in the set *bit, bell, dan* requires recognizing the identity of the phoneme /b/ in two of the word contexts. Other PA-identity tasks require counting how often a target phoneme occurs in a list of words or producing words that contain a target phoneme.

Analysis: A word is made of a sequence of particular phonemes. In a counting task, students listen to a word like *am* and are expected to respond with the number of phonemes—two. Other examples include segmenting words into their constituent phonemes (*man* becomes /m/ and /æ/ and /n/); elision or deletion of a phoneme to create a new syllable (*bold* becomes *old, steak* becomes *sake*); or recognizing a reordered sequence of phonemes (*stop* as *pots* or *sopped*).

Synthesis: A sequence of separate phonemes forms a word. In the blending task, students listen to a sequence of isolated phonemes, blend them, and say or point to a picture or object that indicates the resulting whole word. Another example is an addition task in which a single phoneme is added to a given word (*old* becomes *bold, coal* becomes *cold, soul* becomes *stole*).

Deciphering spoonerisms (metathesis) requires first analysis and then synthesis to recognize, for example, "belly jeans" as "jelly beans," "biting a rook" as "writing a book." A favorite example, usually attributed to the Reverend

Spooner himself, likens a religious figure to "a shoving leopard" instead of "a loving shepherd." Writing with estimated (invented) spelling exemplifies all three types of PA: there is analysis of the word the writer is attempting to spell, identity of the phonemes in it, association of them with graphemes, and (during reading back of the estimated spelling) a synthesis of the word from the letter cues. Estimated spelling can be helpful for developing understanding of phoneme identity, phoneme segmentation, and sound-spelling relationships, and it is not in conflict with the teaching and learning of conventional spelling. In fact, estimating spelling makes it possible to look up conventional spellings in a dictionary!

Although some students come to school with well-developed phonological-analysis skill, others acquire it over a number of years. PA matters most for most students between kindergarten entry and grade two. There is a relationship between a student's understanding of the concept of words in written texts and PA. Phonemic awareness develops gradually in syllables and single-syllable words; children's awareness starts with beginning sounds, then final-sound awareness appears, and medial sounds are the last to be identified and manipulated reliably. A recent study (Anthony, Lonigan, Driscoll, Phillips, and Burgess, 2003) traces complex relations within phonological awareness instruction, relating the complexity of the linguistic unit (word, syllable, onsets or rimes, phonemes) and the complexity of the tasks (blending detection, elision detection, blending, and elision). Gains are found from PA instruction in programs that allocate modest amounts of time and use relatively simple exercises. There is a reciprocal effect between proficiency at reading and proficiency on PA tasks; that is, successful experiences in one enhance the chance of success in the other. For later-grade spelling and vocabulary instruction, teachers who can work with the students' PA have an advantage: for example, students may conflate similar-sounding words (Does the passage describe cars that "career" or ones that "careen"?); as the teacher brings their attention to the distinguishing phonemes, they can discuss the polysemy of *career* and an author's word choices.

It is not necessary for a student to master all three types of PA tasks as a part of learning to read nor to practice PA on all the phonemes of the language. Some task demands are hard to communicate, such that errors on PA tasks may not be due to a lack of PA but to a failure to engage in the task. Across ages and reading ability, certain phonemes are likely to yield more erroneous answers, as are requests for actions on phonemes in certain positions within a syllable. Familiarity with the written form of a word begins to interfere with responses to PA tasks very early. It is not clear that developmental differences exist within or among the different PA tasks, or that any one of them, as a PA task, has a closer relation to successful learning of word-identification strategies.

Sometimes tiles or tokens are used to represent the phonemes in PA tasks; sometimes letters commonly associated with the phonemes are used. Adding the concrete manipulables or the written symbols can help to communicate the task demands and help the respondents to keep track of the task parts. Essentially, though, PA is about sounds. Even when letters are used, PA differs from phonics because the focus is on the sound constituents of words in the spoken language. Teaching PA in conjunction with letters requires particularly well-informed teachers. Otherwise, misinformation can be communicated; for example, that the letter *C* makes the /s/ sound, even though it equally frequently represents /k/ and in various orthographic contexts can even be associated with /š/. Teachers need to know what letter-sound combinations to use as examples and which ones to avoid early in phonological awareness teaching.

Teacher educators can assist teachers in reading some of the professional reviews of the PA literature and can demonstrate lessons, provide video examples of opportunistic instruction, and instigate role-play using prepared materials. Teacher learners can design and critique units and lesson plans, taking into consideration ordering constraints and integrating information about students from formal and informal assessment. In clinical settings, teacher learners can observe, collaborate, enact, and critique PA lessons and assessments.

Phonology: Knowledge Underlying Instruction. Phonological processing is a part of word pronunciation, word memory and retrieval, short-term memory for lists of words and numbers, and reading regularly spelled unknown words, even nonsense words.[45] The phonological system of a language can be seen as having an inventory of units (the smallest being the phoneme) and a series of processes. Languages have different phonologies. For example, in English /b/ and /v/ are contrasting phonemes that distinguish word pairs such as *ban-van* and *dribble-drivel;* in Spanish, however, that phoneme contrast does not exist— asking for *un vino tinto* works just as well when one pronounces *vino* as *bino*! A Spanish speaker learning English may say *berry* when intending *very.* Every language has its own inventory of phonemes. English dialects have more than forty phonemes, Spanish dialects have as few as twenty-five.

If one learns a word meaning but does not master its normative phonological representation, its phoneme sequence, there are consequences when one communicates with other native speakers of the language, and the problems can spread to problems with writing. Richard Lederer's (1987) catalogue of student "bloopers" offers many relevant examples. For example, one student wrote "Abraham Lincoln became America's greatest Precedent and freed the slaves by signing the Emasculation Proclamation!" (p. 13). Learning words includes learning their sound structures, the phonological representations that distinguish among words. People experience difficulty with word recognition or word recall if phonological representations are faulty or degraded so that words such as *incinerator* and *incubator* may collapse into one word in memory, regardless of the rather dramatic semantic differences.

Exhibit 2.7. Does Phonology—The Sound System—Matter for *Written* Language?

Phonology continues to be important long after the reader has stopped "sounding out" most of the words in a text. Phonology plays a role both in long-term memory storage and in working memory processing. Proficient reading as we know it would be nonexistent if memory were like a kitchen junk drawer, if retrieving a word amounted to random rummaging or even rummaging on the basis of a system other than phonology. Each word is stored in memory as a set of linked representations that provide phonological, morphological, syntactic, semantic, and pragmatic essences connected, for those who are literate, to orthographic representations. The more complete, elaborated, and rich the phonological part of the word's memory representation, the better it is for storing and retrieving, even (but certainly not only) when graphemes rather than phonemes are presented as input.[46]

While skilled readers are reading, phonological activity is not noticeable, but it can be detected in response patterns with special tasks. For example, when asked to decide if a word briefly flashed on a screen names a food, people answer "no" easily to *seat* and "yes" to *meat* but often slow down or say "yes" to *meet* (see, for example, Van Orden, 1987). The phonological representations that homophones share account for the confusion. Not everyone agrees on how much skilled readers engage in phonological recoding (applying GPC to convert spellings into blends of sounds) rather than the orthographic mode for direct association between the visual form of words and their meanings (as they might use for words that defy too many GPCs—remember George Bernard Shaw's "ghoti" as a spelling for *fish* or the unpronounceable name sometimes used by the vocal artist Prince). In accounts that differ on other grounds (for example, Perfetti and Zhang, 1995; Harm and Seidenberg, 1999; and Ehri and Snowling, 2004) there is consensus that readers not only learn to associate spellings of individual words to their pronunciations and learn about GPCs but also develop memory for a three-constituent identity for specific words—orthographic, phonological, and meaning constituents. Phonology-based mapping is the best bet as a basis for memory storage and the retrieval processes called on in reading for a variety of reasons:

1. It is more regular than the orthographic-meaning mapping.
2. It plays a role in tricky cases by preserving a literal form while ambiguities and contradictions are being resolved (for example, *read* pronounced like *red* or *reed*).
3. It works on various partial units in addition to the whole word.
4. There are extensive families of related mappings.

Exhibit 2.7. Does Phonology—The Sound System—Matter for *Written* Language? *Cont'd*

---

5. Constraints on sequences in phonology known from spoken language can guide the development of constraints on orthography.

6. It eases self-teaching of word identification based on items 3 through 5 above.

A poor phonological representation for words met in print is traced as the main problem for many disabled readers; for example, Elbro, Nielsen, and Petersen (1994) argue that the problem is not in procedures but in the paucity of the representation the procedures are searching for. Beyond an effect in reading, it may well be that the richness of a phonological representation affects lexical access and working memory for oral language; for example, Rubin, Rotella, Schwartz, and Bernstein (1991) show that phonological awareness instruction increased picture-naming speed for both good and poor readers.

What do teachers learn about phonology to teach reading well? Understanding of phonology and its role in word learning begins with a tour of the consonant and vowel inventories (that is, the phoneme system), deliberately differentiating between the phonemes of English and the letters in the alphabet, and identifying, producing, segmenting, blending, and manipulating consonant and vowel sounds. At a minimum, those preparing to teach should learn to articulate and identify the consonants and vowels of English and to count phonemes in words as well as to manipulate the phoneme sequencing in syllables. It is not necessary or purposeful to count endless sequences of phonemes in long words; it is often rather short words that are more indicative of mastery of the central idea—knowing that *shoe, eight,* and *know* have two phonemes each and that *cheese, ring,* and *sawed* each have three. Further, understanding that consonant clusters (that is, sequences of consonants like those at the beginning of *cry, fly,* and *spry*) are more difficult than single consonants to segment and blend is an important insight for thinking about how to sequence instruction. Comparisons with other languages can be illuminating to those learning about phonology, for example:

- /ž/, the middle consonant in English *measure,* never appears in a word initially in English, as it does in French.

- The phoneme /ŋ/ begins words in Swahili and many languages used in the Philippines but only appears at the end of syllables in English, for example, *king* and *singing.*

- The voiced /đ/ that begins *this* (but not *thin*) does not occur in Romance languages such as French and Spanish.

Learning about the phoneme inventory, dialect differences, and language contrasts, and practicing phoneme manipulation, brings to teachers' attention the kinds of challenges that may occur in lessons with children. Although the phonemes in a word are distinct units, there is coarticulation of phonemes in words that create subphonemic differences; for example, the same phoneme /k/ is pronounced differently in *kill* and *keel* because of the effect of the following vowel. One word may provide a better example than another for a PA task. Similarly, allophonic (systematic or rule-based) variation based on the place of a phoneme in a word may alter the difficulty of a PA task: for example, /t/ is pronounced quite differently in *top, pot,* and *stop,* despite retaining its identity as the phoneme /t/. It is thus not surprising that a Spanish speaker spells *water* as *warer,* since that middle /t/ sounds pretty different from /t/s encountered elsewhere. Finally, there is variation due to development. Some kindergarten children are still acquiring some aspects of the phonology. For example, single phonemes may be used instead of some consonant clusters, such that the word *dress* may be pronounced as if it begins like the word *jest.* With knowledge of the phonological system, teachers are ready to explore the ways in which reading and spelling errors by children reflect their phonological judgments. They have an interpretation of the common substitution of a *j* or *g* in young children's spellings for the first sounds in *dress,* the frequent omission of the nasal phoneme in *went,* or the Spanish speaker's spellings "guen" for *when* and "ironcker" for "I don't care."

Enacting phoneme awareness instruction calls for the teacher to be sure that sounds and letters are understood as separate entities. Working with letters may be useful in phoneme awareness lessons, but it can lead to confusion unless the teacher understands the difference between a phoneme and a grapheme and consciously differentiates and clarifies the identity of phonemes and graphemes during instruction. For example, the effective teacher will refer to the phoneme /f/ not as the "ef sound" but as the "fff sound"; she or he will know that /f/ is the unvoiced counterpart of /v/, which is articulated identically in all respects except voicing; and she or he will associate it with the last *sound* in the words *half* or *have,* not the last letter. The teacher will say, "How do we spell /v/ at the ends of words? That's right, with a -ve!"

At present, very few textbooks for teachers adequately differentiate the phoneme inventory from the inventory of letters. Fewer still present a *system* of phonemes, for example, one organized by place of articulation (how the sounds are made using the mouth, the tongue, and the teeth) and the manner of articulation (using the nose, vocal cords, and the continuation or interruption of the breath stream). A system is important for understanding the details of language development and the relationships between language and literacy acquisition. A systemic view is essential for making relevant distinctions between consonants and vowels, voiced and voiceless consonants, stops and continuants, nasals and non-nasal sounds, and other phonological entities that are useful for describing children's achievements and problems as they are learning print-to-speech correspondences.

Literate adults often experience interference from their knowledge of print when they try to focus on phonemes, and teachers are no exception.[47] For example, consonant clusters represented by a single letter in print (for example, the /ks/ represented by the letter X) are often undercounted: *box* should be counted to have four phonemes, not three. Single phonemes like /ŋ/ represented by a digraph (ng) may be overcounted: *sing* and *sawed* have only three phonemes each, and *boy* has two. Phoneme matching is more difficult when the letter or letters used to represent a sound are not the most obvious associations. For example, the last sound in *nose* is erroneously identified as /s/, not the /z/ it really is, or the last sound in *walked* is called a /d/ instead of /t/. Paradoxically, it is possible that less literate individuals—those for whom experience with print has been less powerful in their lives—might do better on some of these tasks. In fact, young children producing estimated or invented spellings before they learn conventional ones reflect some details of the spoken language better than do older children or adults; their analysis of spoken language has not yet been influenced by print exposure.

Most prospective teachers read very well; we conclude that they achieved phonological awareness as incipient readers and used it to help support their acquisition of reading accuracy and fluency. After one has passed through the stage of sounding out words, though, close attention to phonological structure and to orthographic complexities becomes unnecessary, perhaps even disruptive. Imagine reading a text such as this one and stopping to note every deviation from the simplest GPC, or to think about the etymological sources of words, or to consider alternative spellings and thus pronunciations. Obviously this would not promote comprehension. To help children learn to read, though, prospective teachers need to be reoriented to these issues of concern to incipient readers, issues which they themselves have mastered and probably forgotten.

More advanced knowledge of phonology is important for teachers who wish to acquire a keen diagnostic eye and focus instruction on exactly what is confusing for an individual child. Say, for example, a student is leaving the /n/ out of *quintet* in spelling. The teacher can ask the student to hold his or her nose to notice the change when the nasalization is interfered with; then they can discuss how the nasal /n/ spreads features to the vowel before it and the consonant that follows it, in essence making a memorable case about representing the /n/ with an *n* in the word's spelling. Teachers can investigate phonological processes such as reduction and word accent to see why it is likely for children, even teenagers, to confuse the sound structures of semantically related words such as *aside* and *beside* or *affect* and *effect*. The more expert teacher will also become sensitive to matters like the difference between the print representations and the spoken form of words such as *nature* and *difference*. The teacher who notices the /č/ in *nature* and that *difference* is spoken with only two syllables is less likely to tell students to sound these words out for spelling and more likely to teach morpheme and syllable patterns, informed by the very real differences between surface speech patterns and the underlying structure of the word.

Metacognition: Knowledge Underlying Instruction. Using language as a means for acting on and in the world is different from thinking about it, talking about it, or manipulating it as a system within itself. *Metacognitive* is the cover term that is applied to language actions beyond speaking and listening; it is an analytical approach to the units of language calling for the ability to represent and think about the units separately.[48] *Metalinguistic* is another term used to describe these acts that monitor one's own linguistic knowledge and disassociate form from function, at least temporarily. PA is one example; there is also awareness of morphology, syntax, semantics, pragmatics, or reading written language. During development, language awareness becomes more explicit, and a reorganization of one's mental representations of language units and processes occurs. The advanced level of metacognition about language that we expect teachers to have—with conscious access and verbal reporting—has not been empirically well studied. It is difficult to assess metacognition accurately, but some of the assessment can rely on humor as an indicator of metalinguistic awareness. "Getting" puns and riddles depends on metacognitive manipulations of word level and smaller language units; classic joke series (knock-knock and light-bulb jokes) depend on metacognition of discourse types.

Phonemic awareness is metacognition operating on the phonological subsystem of language. Phonological awareness can also be about suprasegmental units of phonology, for example, the stress and accent patterns in words or the intonation contours for clauses and sentences. Since so much attention has been paid to phonological awareness, it may seem as if everything is known about it and the studies should shed light on other types of metacognition, but there is still much that is not known. We do know that preschoolers can fill in rimes in a poem or make up new words in a chain of alliterations by responding to the implicit patterning in language, without giving attention to the units or having control over manipulating them. This ability has been called phonological sensitivity or a response to the epilinguistic surroundings rather than being a metalinguistic act (Gombert, 1992; Goswami, 1999). Such sensitivity may or may not develop into awareness—explicit attention to syllables within words, onsets and rimes[49] within syllables, the nucleus and coda in a rime, and the crucial bit for alphabetic reading, phonemes within syllables. In spite of a great deal of research, we are not yet sure what the precursors for PA are. We know it does not come from some good preschool activities that do increase oral-language performance and book-handling types of skills (Whitehurst and Lonigan, 1998). Some studies suggest that vocabulary growth results in a press for segmental restructuring of lexical representations, and that process, in turn, promotes PA (Metsala and Walley, 1998). Others find that early vocabulary growth and particular styles of maternal interaction with one-year-olds predict PA performance at ages three and four (Silvén, Niemi, and Voeten, 2002). Relations have been charted among symbolic play, PA, and literacy skills (Bergen and Mauer, 2000). But, in spite of wide interest and many studies, the precursors to PA are not well established. We know instruction can improve PA, but we also know that instruction is not the only route.

Syntactic metacognition appears to be related to some aspects of reading development.[50] A strong case can be made for specific ties between metacognition of syntax and reading comprehension achievement. Another topic that has been studied frequently over a long timespan is awareness about what a word is,[51] within the study of morphological awareness. A recent longitudinal study (Bryant, Nunes, and Bindman, 2000) yielded two particularly interesting results: earlier morphemic metacognition scores can predict differences in learning to use a morphemically-based feature of English orthography (using apostrophes to indicate possession) at a later age. Second, the predictive power is specific to awareness of morphemic distinctions; that is, measures of metacognition in the realms of phonology or syntax and semantics were not good predictors.

In addition to metacognition about the different language subsystems, there can be metacognition about reading.[52] Metacognitive monitoring of comprehension and metacognitive strategies for remembering and repairing while reading are featured in effective instruction for reading comprehension. To cap it off, there can be an awareness of attempts to read or learn to read; for example, a "metacognitive log" has been used to provide adolescents with a way to record information for later analysis about what promotes and what interferes with perseverance at reading, success in comprehension, and fulfilling purposes for reading.

Teachers whose education has provided them with a critical understanding of existing knowledge about metacognition and the tools and disposition to continue their professional learning will be prepared to take advantage of new claims and advice about this topic. Understanding metacognition allows a teacher to adjust lesson plans to suit a class, to tailor instruction for individuals, and to investigate solutions to dilemmas—for example, will engaging a student with a metacognitive viewpoint on a goal or the lesson task solve a comprehension problem and make a procedure or routine more useful or memorable for the student?

Word Attack and Phonics Instruction:
Enacting Knowledge of Language

The words in a text make different demands on a reader. *Sight words* are those already in the reading vocabulary: identification is quick, easy, and automatic. Other words must be identified with effort, some known to the reader as spoken language but not known in written form, others unknown in any way. Instruction helps, but not because a school curriculum teaches, one at a time, each of the thousands of words a literate person knows.[53]

Words with simple and widely applicable GPCs (grapheme-phoneme conventions) are learned early: for example, *see, it, an, get, run,* and *pop.* Other words occur very frequently and serve grammatical functions, but they follow complex or rare GPCs, or even flout the conventions completely for part of the word: for example, *what, who, of, is,* and *the.* A student is likely to learn about a hundred high-frequency words (no matter how usual or unusual the GPCs for them) in the first months of beginning reading instruction. Knowing the words by sight does *not* necessarily mean they have been learned, are stored, or are retrieved as whole words directly connecting full visual form to meaning. GPCs can influence the learning and access processes for high-frequency words, since at least some of the graphemes in them are conventionally linked with the phonemes of their spoken forms. Sight vocabulary is not limited to high-frequency words with problematic GPCs. Words that have very strict adherence to GPCs are in the sight vocabulary of proficient readers once they have been repeatedly encountered and well learned. It is estimated that in the second grade, students can "teach themselves" new words with as few as four to six exposures—that is, they can come to recognize those words on sight, without sequentially sounding them out.

While enough exposure is important for learning to identify words, so is instruction and curriculum in the early grades. Phonics is an instructional approach to developing word-identification proficiency. Phonics instruction is intended to allow a learner to decode printed words relying on GPCs. That part of the goal is apparent to all; it even has its own slogan, "Sound it out." Beyond that, though, and often out of the learner's awareness, phonics practices can lead to more elaborated phonological representations for words in the mental dictionary, a reliable mnemonic system based on GPCs for locating words in memory given their written forms, a preparation for self-teaching new words and for processing larger orthographic units, and an ever-expanding repertoire of instantly recognizable words so the reader's effort can be directed to comprehension and purpose.

No one claims that a phonics curriculum must cover all the GPCs in English. It has been estimated that there are over 500 common GPCs. Simple first-grade material brings up over twenty vowel spellings that are consistent (that is, following rules, not exceptions). In addition, there is the inventory of consistent spellings for each of the twenty-one consonants. This indicates that GPCs in children's books are not all simple cases of unconditional one-to-one letter-to-sound links. Contemporary programs cover different numbers of GPCs, some around 50, some more than 120. Instead of GPCs, some curricula are based on the set of variant phonemes a grapheme can represent. A phonogram program, for instance, is organized around the twenty-six letters of the alphabet plus forty-six multiletter graphemes, each associated with from one to six phonemes. (For example, the phonogram for the letter *A* refers to the different phonemes it represents in words like *man, may,* and *fall.* The phoneme possibilities are to be tried out in the order given, which represents overall frequency differences.) Another approach to organizing curricula is based on families formed by the syllable's rime—the vowel and any ending consonants—exploiting the fact that rimes tend to be units in which both sound and spelling are fairly predictable. Rimes in English, for example, create a word family for *cat, hat,* and *sat,* and another for *ran, van,* and *can.*

Phonics curricula typically include a procedure for decoding a word by associating a phoneme with the leftmost grapheme (a single letter, like *m* in *me,* a consonant digraph like *sh* in *she,* a vowel team like *ea* in *eat*), then successively working on the graphemes to the right and blending the phonemes into a unit to identify as a match for a spoken word in the language. Word-family-based instruction adds an analogy procedure to the student's repertoire for word identification, recognizing *lump* because of the similarity to *jump* by virtue of the shared rime. Some phonics curricula are analytic, starting with the pronunciation of a whole word followed by attention to the GPC units or word families within it.

The National Reading Panel reports best effects from systematic phonics instruction beginning in kindergarten or grade one and lasting for about two years in combination with instruction for comprehension, vocabulary, and fluency. It calls for lessons that model and practice decoding, teach blending and sound-symbol links, promote generalization, integrate skills in context, and aim toward fluent application to reading connected text.

There is wide professional consensus about the usefulness of word-identification instruction. Questions do remain about the scope and sequence for phonics instruction. Sequencing constraints for early instruction are suggested by differences in the ease of recognizing letters and the way that some letter names provide support for some GPCs. Sequencing decisions are also influenced by the relative frequencies of use of different GPCs in text encountered by beginners.

While some instruction may focus on isolated words in games, charts, and worksheets, proficiency at word identification in connected text is the goal and must be practiced. The design and selection of texts to use with beginners is another topic currently being debated. Levels such as "independent" or "instruc-tional" are determined by the percentage of words that can be read accurately by a reader and are good for practice without and with a teacher, respectively; "frustration"-level text is to be avoided. Readability formulas (measures of sen-tence length or complexity and word length or frequency) are often used to as-sess text difficulty and suitability. Another approach involves predictability measures based on expectations from language patterns alone or some combi-nation of text language and illustrations. Another design dimension of texts is "cognitive load." An early reader needs practice with a word if it is to enter the sight vocabulary; cognitive load is a measure of how often a word, a GPC, or a rime pattern is available for practice once it is introduced. Cognitive load is es-pecially important if the success of phonics curricula is judged by outcomes such as automaticity of word identification and generalization of proficiency, such that new words and patterns are self-taught. Some programs call for the use of decodable texts designed to provide practice for lessons about specific GPCs as well as proof for the learner that decoding works. They avoid words with GPC patterns that have not yet been taught in a specific curriculum or use only words with GPCs likely to be taught early in most curricula. They may pro-vide the student with motivation and reward for attending to phonics lessons.

Full fluency calls for the reader to shift from grapheme-by-grapheme and left-to-right decoding toward the processing of larger units for storing and retriev-ing words from the reader's mental dictionary. Word identification instruction that goes beyond GPCs is sometimes not considered phonics, but whatever it is called, some students need it if they have not made the shift to hierarchical de-coding toward the end of the primary grades. Some struggling readers in high school who map graphemes to phonemes successfully still find it difficult to process words using segments that are orthographic (for example, *ight* in *flight*, *light*, and *night*) or morphologic units (inflectional endings such as *-ed* and *-ing* or derivational affixes like *re-*, *-tion*, *-ize*, or *-ate*). As readers progress, more of the new words they encounter are multisyllabic, so students need procedures for segmenting words to arrive at pronunciations. Some of this instruction con-cerns word roots that can be taught most effectively in different content areas. Students who can analyze word structure and have sufficient exposure to print can be successful at word identification with larger units.

For teacher education, there are many professional reviews of the literature that can be studied as well as many detailed studies of classroom work on word identification. Curricula and instructional tactics can be illustrated, compared, and critiqued on the basis of written descriptions, demonstration lessons, video examples, or role-play. Lessons and units can be created to investigate impor-tant principles of different approaches to word identification instruction, but at-tention must also be paid to opportunistic instruction and the administration and use of formal and informal assessments. A practicum or clinical placement will most likely have one approach to word identification in place as the teacher candidate enters; opportunities to analyze it, to make it work successfully for all students, or to supplement it with another approach should be part of the practicum experience.

Morphology: Knowledge Underlying Instruction. To move beyond the limitations of basic phonics in their instruction, teachers must be able to appreciate and explain the morphemic structure of words.[54] Morphemes are the smallest meaningful units in language. They may be whole words with one or more syllables (such as *pot* or *flower)* or parts of words that contribute bits of meaning to the whole (for example, *in + de + struct + able*; *uni + cycle*), or even as small as a single phoneme (for instance, the plural meaning in *pots* comes from the morpheme {s} which is also a single phoneme /s/). No matter the size, morphemes are meaning-bearing units while phonemes are not.[55] Our spelling system preserves or represents morphology, often in the presence of sound-pattern alternations (for example, the shift from a long vowel in the verb *inspire* to a short vowel in the related noun *inspiration,* or from a hard to a soft *g* in the adjective *legal* and the related verb *legislate).* Morphology also provides the basis for reasoning through the doubled *s* in *misspell* or the single *t* before the suffix in *commitment.* Students who think about morphemes may use knowledge of word structure to determine meanings of new words encountered in text and to remember their written form.

Using knowledge of morphology for teaching students often occurs incidentally, in response to student errors or puzzlement; teachers need to have ease with recalling and using basic information about morphemes and morphological processes and how they connect to English spelling. The English adjectival morpheme {ic}, for instance, has different corresponding sounds, even when attached to the same root as in *electric, electricity,* and *electrician,* but spelling highlights the morphemic relations among the words and between those words and others such as *honorific.* In some cases, the pronunciation of a word may be subject to phonological reduction processes that obscure some part of it. The middle vowel in *president* is hard to spell, unless one remembers the related verb *preside.* In some cases, the "hidden" sound reappears if the root takes on inflectional suffixes; for example, *bolder* and *boldest* highlight the final /d/ in the adjective root *bold,* lost in pronunciation in many linguistic contexts. Derivational affixes such as {er} for agent can have a similar effect on other words.

Where does instruction for the novice teacher begin? If a teacher has never studied the history or structure of English or any other language, morphology is foreign territory, and it may be difficult to identify and categorize morpheme units and morphological processes. In textbooks for teachers, if morphology is taught at all, it is often presented as long lists of prefixes, suffixes, and roots whose behavior in words is not explicated. Several important distinctions among types of morphemes are a productive place to begin.

Morphemes may be free or bound. Free morphemes stand alone; bound morphemes must exist in combination with others. Free morphemes can be subdivided into content words and function words. Content words are an expanding category; function words are a closed category. Anglo-Saxon compounds (for example, *cowbarn* or *wheelchair*) are a combination of two free morphemes; they are marked by the stress pattern on the first syllable or word. Bound morphemes include roots and affixes (prefixes and suffixes). English roots may have a Latin origin; a few commonly occurring and widely combined ones are {fer} (*infer, prefer*), {vis} (*visible, vision, visor, envision*), {struct} (*instruct, construct, destruction*), {cred} (*credible, credence*), and {dict} (*dictate, diction, predict, indict*). Some Anglo-Saxon affixes are combined with Anglo Saxon base words, to produce *knighthood* and *neighborhood, kingdom* and *fiefdom,* or *playwright* and *wheelwright.*

Affixes and morphological rules are of two kinds: inflectional and derivational. Inflectional morphology identifies word classes (also called parts of speech, for example, nouns versus verbs), signals agreement among clause parts (for example, the third person singular verb affix in "she teaches" versus the first person "I teach"), and signal grammatical meanings such as plural, possessive, past, and progressive. Inflectional suffixes, including plural and past tense, can be problematic because their spellings do not correspond directly to their sounds. The past tense {ed} has three pronunciations (/d/, /t/, and /ed/) that are all spelled the same way (add *ed*). In words like *picked* and *pulled*, the {ed} morpheme is pronounced /t/ and /d/, respectively, not as separate syllables even though the *-ed* spelling looks as if it should indicate a syllable. The sounds of the past tense and plural morphemes are determined by phonology—the voicing of the final consonant of the word to which they are attached. These complex relationships can spell trouble. Students may confuse the suffixes, fail to notice them in reading, or leave them off in speaking and spelling and may benefit from being taught about the complex correspondences of sound, spelling, and meaning.

Derivational affixes add meaning or change the word class of the root or word to which they are added. Derivational morphemes change the pronunciation in the root in cases like *divide-division, repeat-repetitive,* or *medicine-medical.* The meaningful relationships among words from the same derivational family can be pointed out and discussed in the context of vocabulary study, spelling, and reading, where they are more obvious than in spoken language. English-language learners whose first language has many cognates to English typically see cognate relationships in written-language spelling more easily than they hear them in oral language. Teachers can give students help to notice derivational relations and encouragement to use them to infer meaning. Providing that help requires that the teacher have some sense of what words are likely to be cognates with words from which other language, through some basic study of etymology and language history.

Novices to morphology and to using it in teaching can learn during productive, guided exploration. Taking one productive Latin root, for example, teachers can locate many examples of words derived from that root and then organize a map of their interrelationships. In so doing, they are preparing themselves to teach students that words can be learned in morphological families, and that those families often share a similar alternation pattern, such as *dedicate-dedication, consecrate-consecration,* or *perseverate-perseveration.* They can form new words by combining roots and affixes. It helps, too, to deconstruct words with assimilated prefixes (*illegal, address,* or *immediate*) that may be useful to help a student puzzling over a way to remember a word meaning. The words can be analyzed for the grammatical role they play and for the relative transparency of the word's meaning in relation to its constituent morphemes. Realizing that multisyllabic word division can be accomplished by either syllable division rules or by morphology is helpful for teachers who want to know the "right" way to divide a word. The answer, of course, depends on which level of language organization is being employed; we can divide *in-struction* morphologically, or *in-struc-tion* syllabically.

Expert teachers can develop a working knowledge of the most common Latin, Greek, and Anglo-Saxon morphemes and their meanings. With this knowledge, they have flexibility to identify the base for some student errors; they can plan and enact "word a day" tasks that promote word identification and word-meaning proficiency in reading as well as spelling proficiency. When student work calls for it, they can bring up less common families of words and differentiate between the combining forms borrowed from Greek and the structure of Latin-based words. Most important, they can teach the connections among meaning, form, and use when words are encountered during reading itself.

Etymology: Knowledge Underlying Instruction. A teacher who regards English as a "layer cake" of linguistic influences has knowledge of etymology and a resource for solving problems with word identification and word meaning confidently and logically, and even has the confidence to say "I don't know about that particular word—let's look it up!" The kinship between English and other languages with which students in the classroom are familiar can be more readily appreciated and used as a resource.

Our base language layer, Anglo-Saxon, a cousin of modern German, is to blame for odd or puzzling spellings that endure today, such as *height* and *weight, thought, through* and *though,* and *said* and *does.* Anglo-Saxon words are the most common, often one-syllable content words for everyday things, ideas,

Exhibit 2.8. Spelling Shows Word Relations

"Chomsky and Halle use the English word *muscle* to show how the seemingly arbitrary spelling of many words is actually key to the underlying meaning of a family of related words (see also Carol Chomsky's elegant essay [1970a] on the same topic). The silent *c* in *muscle* immediately and visibly connects the word *muscle* to its origin, the Latin root *musculus*, from which we have such kin words as *muscular* and *musculature*. In the latter, the letter *c* represents a phonemic (minimal sound) unit of language. In contrast, in *muscle*, the silent *c* reflects the morphemic aspect of language, which dictates the rules for word formation and establishes the correspondence between a word or word parts and its underlying meaning.

"Chomsky and Halle used examples like this to argue that English is a 'near optimal system for the lexical representation of English words' (1968, p. 4), one in which the etymological histories of many English words are captured in their spelling. The centrality of this historical-lexical principle in English orthography can make the alphabetic principle appear to be flimsily embodied in some aspects of English, but that is an indictment of neither the alphabetic principle nor the English language. It is simply the case that in English, the writing system reflects both our language's sound system (phonology) and the way that meanings are represented in the formation of words (morphology). Where it becomes complicated is when morphology trumps phonology (as in the *muscle* example).

"There is a similar morphophonemic principle at work in the multiple print-sound correspondences that can be found in many inflectional suffixes. For example, the suffix *-ed* is a morpheme (minimal unit of meaning) that has one spelling (representing the meaning) but three pronunciations based on the speech characteristics of the preceding phoneme. Thus, we say *banned* and *batted* and *pumped*, and we automatically know that each *-ed* bears the same meaning, but is pronounced differently (respectively, as [d], [əd], and [t]). As Jean Berko Gleason showed us in 1958 with her whimsical 'wug test' for young children (Berko, 1958), the pronunciations of different word endings like *-ed* and *-s* invoke absolutely regular, spoken-language sound rules. Try pronouncing the invented word *wugs* for yourself. You will know that *s* signifies plurality, but you will pronounce the *s* after the *g* as a [z], not as an [s]. This same result would regularly occur in the case of any word that ended with a voiced consonant sound (a sound involving vocal cord vibration).

"Inflectional suffixes, therefore, do not represent a flimsy rule at all; rather, they are another example of the way in which our tacit knowledge of oral language is reflected in a written language that conveys both sound and meaning. Together with our previous example, they illustrate a morphophonemic writing

---

Exhibit 2.8. Spelling Shows Word Relations, *Cont'd*

---

system that makes elegant use of multiple levels of linguistic information. Furthermore, the morphophonemic knowledge that young children possess can be exploited to help them learn to read. Explicitly teaching a child that a given meaning is represented by a single orthographic pattern (e.g., the past tense of *-ed*) but is pronounced in predictable ways in our speech (as we saw in *batted*, etc.) can provide a powerful insight for young learners."

Source: Wolf and Kennedy, 2003.

---

emotions, and the function words that glue sentences together. Anglo-Saxon words also tend to be spelled with digraphs, vowel digraphs, silent letters, and irregular patterns. The realization that pronunciation, meaning, and usage of the base language has changed dramatically over centuries will help teachers search for historical answers to language questions such as the similarity of *two, twice, twenty, twin, between, twilight,* and *twelve.*[56]

Celebrating the history of language and exploring the origins of words help to build the word consciousness and the more sophisticated vocabulary that is characteristic of academic language. Less common content words (those that carry most of the important meanings in expository text beyond the fourth grade) are often based on Latin borrowings brought to English a few hundred years after the Norman French invasion. For example, from Anglo Saxon, we *walk*; but from Latin, we *ambulate.* From Anglo Saxon, we *live*; but with Latin, we are *animate.* From Anglo Saxons, there are *mothers*; Latin brings in *maternal* and *paternal* figures.

Renaissance scholars established the convention of using Greek combining forms for scientific, logical, and mathematical vocabulary. Spelling clues to words of Greek origin reside in the *y* spelling for "short i" (gym), the *ch* spelling for /k/ (charisma), and the *ph* spelling for /f/ (physics). Greek combining forms act like compounds, each morpheme adding equal weight to the word's meaning (psychoneurological, neuropsychological, neurochemical, psychopharmacological). Scientists use these forms (which have closely related versions in all widely spoken modern languages) by consensus to facilitate communication even though they speak many different languages natively.

Teacher-preparation programs can engender a way of thinking about and approaching language study. Introductory exercises may start with a word for a common idea; investigate the origin and history of that word in the *Oxford English Dictionary;* search for synonyms in a thesaurus; and compare the origins, history, and contemporary patterns of use for the alternative ways to express a common concept. At the very least, novice teachers should recognize that spellings and pronunciations are directly borrowed from many languages, such as the French spellings *coquette, unique,* and *rouge,* the Spanish spellings for *mesa, quesadilla,* and *Jose,* and direct Latin borrowings for *curriculum, minimum,* and *alumni.* It is extremely helpful if teachers dealing with speakers of Spanish as a first language know what words are likely to be cognates to common Spanish words, and the regular phonological and morphological relationships between Spanish and English. Advanced concepts for more experienced teachers include the various processes of word-coinage and language change, the rapidity with which expressions enter and leave our language, how separate languages evolve over centuries, and the factors that influence the maintenance of separate language systems even in neighboring peoples.

Orthography: Knowledge Underlying Instruction. Users of English orthography spell by both sound and meaning.[57] Proficient readers of our alphabetic orthography appreciate that letters and letter groups (for example, *ea, eau, igh,* and *eigh*) are the units that represent phonemes. They also recognize syllable patterns and divisions between syllables that permit visual "chunking" of long letter sequences and assignment of a vowel sound to specific letter patterns. Expert spellers (such as those who compete in the spelling bees broadcast on ESPN) have typically learned specific orthographic patterns, principles, and rules, and can state them explicitly as well as use them to decide a reasonable spelling for words rarely encountered. Many people, though, even those good at implicitly using the orthographic system for reading and writing, cannot report reliably about quite common orthographic patterns and principles—such as which sounds are represented by *ng* and *ch.* Even experienced teachers may lack explicit knowledge of orthography[58] and sometimes give students misinformation, saying, for instance, that the *o* and *w* in *tower* represent separate sounds.

Orthography matters to reading, learning to read, and teaching reading.[59] Granted, some information about spellings may not help much with reading words, but knowing about, for instance, the *eigh* grapheme is very productive for recognizing quite common words like *eight, weigh, neighborhood,* and so on. The real importance of orthography to a reader, though, is that spelling and reading build and rely on the same mental representation of a word. Knowing the spelling of a word makes the representation of it sturdy and accessible for fluent reading. Early on, in fact, prior to formal instruction, many children build spellings based on their estimations of how the sound of the word could be represented with letters of the alphabet; this early spelling has been seen as a good window into a child's phonemic awareness and realization of the nature of alphabetic writing. Studies of older children progressing in spelling reveal their changing knowledge of the role of syllables and morphemes in spelling English words. Morphology gets pressed into service as a mnemonic aid to spelling words for some older students: wanting to write *allege* but stymied about which letters to use to represent the /ʤ/ sound at the end, a student turns to the morphologically related word *allegation,* concludes that a *g* should be used, and finds *allege* no longer so difficult to spell. In spite of the success, the student may not be able to explicate the principles he or she relied on to spell the word.

The systemic principles underlying sound-symbol correspondence in English are very complex, so it is not surprising that many highly literate adults who use those rules correctly find it difficult to talk about them or answer questions about them. Teachers who have been taught about phonics (and many have not) have typically received information about orthography presented as lists of rules about letter sequence constraints. Such lists are unmotivated, unappealing, and difficult to learn. Lists without a logical framework or set of principles must be learned by rote rather than reason. Consequently, lacking knowledge of either the orthographic system or its specifics, teachers must try to teach with incomplete information, disconnected lists of formidable rules, and superficial strategies that sometimes mislead, such as "when two vowels go walking, the first one does the talking."

Teacher-preparation programs can improve the teacher knowledge base about orthography by starting with activities such as marking the graphemes that correspond to phonemes in regular, one-syllable words. For example, the word *shell* has three graphemes: *sh, e,* and *ll.* To master this task requires an adequate concept of a grapheme. For English, graphemes may consist of one (*e*), two (*oy*), three (*tch*), or four (*augh*) letters. A grapheme is defined as any letter or letter sequence that systematically represents a phoneme. Since English has over forty phonemes and only twenty-six letters, it can be expected that letter combinations play an important role in English orthography. Tiles with graphemes on them can be used to focus on graphemes in familiar words, in order to analyze the relationship between print and speech. Phoneme-grapheme mapping activities can also be the venue for developing firm concepts and adequate operational definitions for terms such as *digraph, blend, vowel team, vowel-r pattern,* and *vowel-consonant-e patterns.*

Teachers can go on to learn additional complexities in English orthography. Morphological relations among words and the etymology of words explain many otherwise puzzling spellings in English. Appeal to language history and the Germanic origin of Anglo-Saxon is productive for discussions about many of the "silent" letters in our modern spellings. Spellings for particular phonemes also vary by the position of a sound in a word. For example, /k/ is represented by *k* at the beginning but by *ck* at the end of words (as in *kick),* and /č/ is represented by *ch* at the beginning of words (*chip, check*) but often by *tch* at the end of words (*pitch, catch*).

Teacher candidates can also explore the orthography of multisyllabic words. Spelling seems more orderly and predictable in English when syllable types are taken into account: consider the difference between words with closed first syllables (for example, *hopping, hotter, bubble,* or *comment*) and those with open first syllables (*hoping, hotel, bible,* or *moment*). The presence of a double versus a single consonant is reliably associated with this distinction—a fact that can be illuminating to students who otherwise believe that such variants just have to be memorized one word at a time.[60] English has six syllable types, and the juncture principles underlying them account for the way to spell words when suffixes are added (for example, *beg-begging, study-studies,* and *slime-slimy*) (see Table 2.3). Armed with this knowledge base, a teacher can take students beyond guesswork to tackle multisyllabic words with logic and confidence.

Word Meaning and Vocabulary Instruction: Enacting Knowledge of Language

Vocabulary instruction is more than a by-product of word identification and passage comprehension instruction. Early phonics instruction and incidental work on word meaning during text comprehension lessons do little to reduce gaps in

Table 2.3. Six Syllable Types in Written English

Syllable Type	Examples	Definition
Closed	*dap*ple *hos*tel *bev*erage	Syllable has a short vowel, ending in a consonant.
Open	*pro*gram *ta*ble *re*cent	Syllable ends with a long vowel sound, spelled with a single vowel letter.
Consonant-l-e	bi*ble* bea*gle* lit*tle*	Unaccented final syllable contains a consonant, /l/, and silent e.
Vowel team and diphthong	*awe*some *train*er con*geal*	Syllables with long or short vowel sounds use a vowel combination for spelling. *Ou-ow* and *oi-oy* are included in this category.
Vowel-r	spu*r*ious con*sort* char*ter*	Syllable has a vowel that is followed by /r/. Vowel pronunciation often changes before /r/.
Vowel-c-consonant-e	com*pete* des*pite* con*flate*	Syllable has a long vowel spelled with a vowel-consonant-silent e.

vocabulary knowledge that students bring to school with them. "Anchored word" instruction, though, can make a difference; in it teachers focus on word form (the GPCs in a word), word meaning, and use in context to build vocabulary along with other resources for reading. "Text talk" is an example of a routine that builds vocabulary and phonological representations useful for word identification. As a routine part of read-aloud sessions, the teacher and students discuss a few words from the text to arrive at working definitions and information on use in various contexts. Students are helped to give additional uses for the words, and later they engage in extensive and active experience with the words in different activities—for example, writing, playing games, designing bulletin boards, charting incidental use in the daily life of the class.

Vocabulary knowledge is not the same as the ability to provide complete and formal definitions of words.[61] That is a specialized skill that most people apply only to words in limited areas of special interest. In general, a word is considered known if one can match it to a picture or scene, a synonym, paraphrase, translation, or gloss, or can provide or recognize appropriate use of it in noncircular contexts. Vocabulary growth is not merely the accretion of items in a mental dictionary, it is also the refined and deeper knowledge that provides for both wider and more accurately restrictive use of an already-learned word. Occasionally a new concept and a new word are learned together. But students also learn new concepts for which familiar words are used as well as new labels that represent familiar concepts. Concepts and words that express them are learned through multiple exposures in varying contexts. A word's meaning is often represented as interconnected webs with central and peripheral features connected to and through hypernyms, hyponyms, compounds, analogies, partial synonyms with different connotations, antonyms, figurative uses, idioms, and so on. Knowing a word also requires knowing about which other words can or must occur with it in sentences. For example, *win, beat, triumph*, and *victory* can all be used to describe a homecoming game, but the words cannot be switched: the team *wins* a game, but *beats* an opposing team, or *triumphs* over them, or achieves a *victory*. Recognizing related terms is another aspect of knowing a word—relating *victory* not just to *victorious* but also to *convince*.

Curriculum for vocabulary is influenced by texts to be read and subjects to be studied and sometimes by word lists in state standards or benchmarks. They may be chosen on the basis of frequency of use or utility for academics in general or for specific subjects. Vocabulary curricula often emphasize relations among words: homonyms and homophones; synonyms and antonyms; literal, figurative, and idiomatic usage; or structure and etymology (for example, Latin origins for roots and affixes). There is no known best set of words or principles for choosing them or grouping them. In many classrooms, the passage, chapter, or book the class is reading determines the content of vocabulary study. The teacher selects a few key vocabulary words. There are routines for vocabulary study before, during, and after the reading of the connected text. This can integrate examples of different uses of a word, analysis of related morphological forms, consideration of connotation, multiple meanings, and formal definition, as well as study of synonyms and antonyms, idioms, and figures of speech.

Much conventional wisdom about vocabulary instruction fluctuates between two poles: read a lot or make a weekly word list for a Friday quiz. Neither pole is the true north magnet for vocabulary growth with a lasting impact on reading achievement. What does work is well-planned instruction that provokes student engagement in different situations so that new words are used, feedback is given, and students make personal connections among new and known vocabulary items. Explicit instruction about word form is a useful approach to expand vocabulary when it includes practice and application of methods for using word parts to make inferences about the meanings of new words met in reading. A different tack involves context clues that allow a reader to learn a word from other parts of the reading. Instruction can help students to find the signals (typographical, syntactic, and punctuation) that indicate that a word's meaning is being explained within the passage being read. Learning to use context clues magnifies the value to vocabulary building of time spent on reading. Some vocabulary instruction directly addresses words grouped together on the basis of meaning and studied by feature analysis, semantic mapping, or other word-schema methods. This type of vocabulary instruction often incorporates procedures for using (and sometimes making) a word reference tool such as a dictionary, glossary, or thesaurus.

The importance of exposing students to rich vocabulary in the context of engaged and productive learning cannot be overemphasized. To be models for their students and effective leaders of instructional conversations, prospective teachers develop their own verbal proficiency. With adequate verbal skill to build on, novice teachers can learn to monitor their own verbal behavior and prompt students to interpret, clarify, and learn meanings for new words in the context of thematically focused discussions. Viewing models of teachers with facilitative verbal habits is important, as is rehearsal of productive classroom talk.

Vocabulary instruction is treated in detail in many textbooks used in teacher-education programs. There is also a good deal of contemporary research on vocabulary teaching and learning. Practicum placements often expose students to a prescribed program for vocabulary instruction. Often the textbook, the research, and the placement call for quite different approaches to vocabulary instruction. Teacher-education programs need to assist their students not only in planning and enacting effective instruction in different circumstances and with different materials, but in learning to assess and reconcile different ideas of best practices for vocabulary instruction and in adapting vocabulary instruction to the needs and the resources of the students, for instance, their nonacademic vocabulary or their first-language vocabulary.

Semantics: Knowledge Underlying Instruction. Semantics is the branch of linguistic analysis that focuses on meaning, in words (lexical semantics) or in syntactic units (propositional semantics).[62] (Meaning is important in the pragmatics system, too; see the earlier section of this chapter titled "Language and Literacy: Integrated Systems and Subsystems" and Exhibit 2.1.) Studies of learning and development show that knowledge of a word's meaning can remain constricted and contextualized or become deep and decontextualized. Over the life span, most of the lexicon is learned indirectly and gradually. Meanings acquired through incidental learning are often adequate or even rich, but sometimes they are incomplete or wrong. School field trips and hands-on experiences provide more controlled incidental vocabulary learning and can make a contribution to the concepts and words needed in reading and different academic subjects. The listener and reader know something about some words, structures, subject matter, and surrounding context in a conversation or passage; they use that as a basis for guesses about the meanings of new words, broad and tentative at first, more definitive and refined eventually. Explicit attention to word meaning is not rare, though, in school and out, from the toddler's "What's that?" to the biology teacher's "What is the mitochondrial type of DNA?"

Study of the semantic structure of a word and of relationships among words can be complex. The notion that word meanings are bundles of semantic properties can be established in teacher education with a semantic feature analysis that compares the meanings of *van* and *truck;* or of *cup, mug,* and *glass;* or of *couch, sofa, davenport,* and *love seat.* Discussions of connotation and denotation and the author's style or word choice can be enriched with reference to semantic features. When students have learned a unique (or distorted) set of features for a word, analyses can show the need for expansion, clarification, or deepening of students' existing knowledge. Grasping the concept of semantic features also helps teachers differentiate between words that overlap in meaning and words that are merely associated with one another through common usage. Teacher candidates may know what a synonym is but still not have thought about how synonymy can be evaluated by the degree of semantic overlap. Most teachers are familiar with the term *antonym* but can develop a more complete understanding by learning that antonyms can be dichotomous (*dead-alive*) or can be gradable points on a continuum (*hot-cold*). Gradable antonyms provide opportunities to place other words on a continuum of meaning (*torrid, tepid, frigid*) and to locate just the right word for a context. The concept of multiple meanings and multiple uses for words is extremely important to explore with teachers. Our most common words often have the most varied meanings. Discovering that *run* has dozens of listings in a dictionary can promote an interest in vocabulary expansion even with seemingly simple words. Language makes extensive use of metaphor and nonliteral meaning. We do not *keep time* in a physical sense, nor need we worry about tired legs as we *run out of luck.*

Teachers must anticipate the metaphorical, idiomatic, and colloquial expressions that may interfere with reading comprehension, especially because metaphorical language is even more common in written language than it is in everyday speech. Abstract concepts add to the challenge. When a report of a trial claims the defendant "kept justice at bay," the interpretation of the concept of justice is assigned to a concrete event; full understanding involves judgments about the suitability of the assignment and an appreciation of the relation between abstract concepts and a speaker or writer's point of view. (N.b.: Understanding the pragmatic system of language is a crucial part of analyzing non-literal meanings.)

Expert teachers also understand about the meaning that arises as words are used in grammatical roles in the language system—propositional semantics. This aspect of semantics is more likely to be new information for teachers. They use language so they know it implicitly, and they can analyze sets of sentences to make that knowledge explicit. For example, they can see that verbs require *arguments* in a sentence structure. *Argument* here refers to a phrase that occurs in conjunction with a verb to express a proposition; the verb *promise,* for instance, requires three arguments: a person who promises, a something that they promise, and a recipient of the promise, but the verb *run* can get by with one argument and *enjoy* requires two. Words are not unto themselves, but must be known as they are employed within propositions expressed as syntactic structures. The semantics of texts, in effect, call upon and create models of the world. The underlying propositions about the states of the world may be the same but (as with lexical synonyms) one text may be more difficult to understand than another.

Take mathematics as a case in point (see, for example, Hudson, 1983; Carraher, Carraher, and Schliemann, 1987; Baranes, Perry, and Stigler, 1989; and Koedinger and Nathan, 2004). While it is easier for us to make the point about the mathematics examples in this short space, the main point holds for different domains of learning and for reading in general: propositional semantics is worth teacher study because the details of it can have an impact on student achievement and teacher assessment of it. The following three problems require the same math knowledge, but the first is easier for eight-year-olds to deal with whether in Brazil (when rendered in Portuguese with local currency) or the United States, whether the child attends school or is a street vendor:

1. Each donut costs $.25. Tasha gets 10 for her party. How much does she pay?

2. Twenty five cents times ten equals what?

3. $.25 \times 10 = ?$

For many teachers, the idea that the "word problem" (in example 1) turns out to be easier for most youngsters is counterintuitive. (The same point has been demonstrated to be true about algebra teachers and algebra students' performance.) The simple proposition standing in a sentence alone (in example 2) or expressed with mathematical symbols (example 3) does not activate the real-world knowledge that facilitates understanding. (By the way, if the donuts cost $.35 cents, a less culturally salient currency amount, the word-problem format gives Americans less of an advantage.) The importance of the details of expression for a proposition is widespread in studies about learning mathematics: when older students' problems are posed with propositions that name actions (for example, *multiply* or *add*), they achieve more than when the propositions are expressed in other ways (for example, using *times* or *plus*). For young students, "There are five birds and three worms. How many more birds are there than worms?" elicits erroneous strategies or blank stares, but most are successful with the functionally equivalent "There are five birds and three worms. How many birds don't get a worm?"

Using the question "How many birds don't get a worm?" with primary-grade children or choosing between *drown* and *inundate* or between *wow* and *marvelous* is a natural process for sociolinguistically sophisticated speakers. But that natural process can usefully be subjected to review—unpackaged, in effect, during a study of semantics. Teachers can learn to take their implicit knowledge about lexical and propositional semantics and make it conscious, subject to analysis and available during instruction and assessment.

Comprehension and Strategy Instruction: Enacting Knowledge of Language

Two questions are implicit in comprehension lessons: What does this mean? How does one understand? Comprehension instruction addresses the understanding of specific texts, and it prepares students to understand more when they are reading in the future.[63] Some texts need no noticeable effort to comprehend. Typical subscribers to a community newspaper, for example, can grasp information about local sports, politics, and social events as soon as they decode it. In contrast, an essay about constitutional rights in time of war, even on a third or fourth reading, might challenge the reader to form an adequate interpretation of it, to make accurate use of it, and to remember what was in it. Two things stand out about successful reading of challenging texts:

- First, proficient readers do not proceed strictly from beginning to end: they scan and skim the whole at the start, get into it and move on prosaically enough but suddenly read a clause and return to a passage on the page before, jump to a section header and back again a few paragraphs, find a bold-faced word and make a note in the margin, move to the very end and then back to the clause that instigated all the activity. The author's compositional choices are not the sole input for the readers' comprehension. Readers enhance the author's organizational structure through their own work, sometimes heavily influenced by specialized practices of certain domains (see Exhibit 2.2 about understanding literature, Exhibit 2.3 about science, and Exhibit 2.4 about understanding history texts).

- Second, the processes of comprehending require effort. They can be consciously controlled and made public for others during instruction.[64] Metacognitive teacher-student conversations conducted while reading challenging texts in school can address both what the text means and how one works at comprehending texts in general, the two main ideas of comprehension instruction.

Some students are not good evaluators of their own comprehension, acting as though reaching the last word of a passage is the goal, hoping that a bluebird of understanding will land on their shoulders. They may not know or believe that effort expended on strategic reading will pay off. Some have few insights into the kinds of preparations and procedures that can enhance comprehension; others lack options to pursue if they fail to understand. With an effective program of instruction, students can learn strategies for accurate monitoring and active comprehension.

Meta-analyses and other reviews in the professional literature point to curricula and instruction that improve comprehension. In general, effective instruction is long-term, integrated instruction focusing on a few specific strategies fostering engagement and motivating effort through appropriate reading content and social situations. The purposes, goals, steps, and procedures for each strategy introduced are made explicit. Teachers model how and when to apply each strategy, guide and collaborate in initial student practice, and arrange for practice toward independent control by the students. When a new strategy is introduced, special texts may be used to reduce other processing demands. On occasion, teachers might choose texts that force the use of a comprehension resource; for example, background knowledge may be available to a reader (from general experience or a prereading mini-lesson) but not used during reading unless the text requires that inferences for basic sentence interpretation call on that prior knowledge. Instruction is not complete until the students can choose to use the new ability along with other skills and strategies on texts that are challenging and serve purposes beyond being materials for reading lessons. Examples of widely used comprehension instruction include reciprocal teaching, instructional conversation, question-and-answer response, K-W-L (know, want to know, learned), reader's workshop, book club, questioning the author, and transactional strategies instruction.

Particular strategies and approaches are more fitting to use and to teach in certain content areas. The purpose for reading differs with texts and situations between and within content areas; different purposes set up different procedures for monitoring comprehension. Students learn how and when to find and use reference material in libraries or on the Internet, differently for different content areas. Students can be taught to use aids to prompt attention for purposes of reading and to aid in recall and understanding, for example, graphic organizers such as charts, outlines, timelines, story webs, Venn diagrams, and study guides. Students may learn subject-matter-specific reading strategies and academic content as teachers lead interactive read-alouds, explaining central domain concepts and comprehension procedures. These sessions may include note taking and breaks for using other sources or reference material. Teachers can point out intra- and intersentential inferences from syntax, semantics, and pragmatics that are unusual in spoken language. They can also highlight written-language-specific paralinguistic typographical signals (subheadings, boldface print), graphics (charts, illustrations), and book parts (chapters, tables of contents, indexes). When reading aloud expository text, teachers can locate and address misconceptions in students' background knowledge and assist them in using strategies such as mental imagery and analogies to work out what is meant.

For teacher education, professional reviews of the literature can be studied and used as pointers to more specific studies of classroom instruction that can be demonstrated, compared, and critiqued. Student-teachers can design and enact lessons and units as a way to study important principles of comprehension instruction and learn techniques for responsive and effective student-teacher interactions about comprehension. Special attention must be paid to how teachers can stimulate student questions. Teacher educators and those involved in professional development must stop some gaps, too. In professional literature reviews there are pointers to the areas of comprehension instruction that have not been sufficiently researched—for example, teaching when students are at the point of internalizing and automatizing comprehension strategies. Another gap to be filled involves content-area reading (for instance, history or science). Many programs that prepare teachers for a specific content area ignore issues about reading that content; a teacher educator concerned with comprehension instruction must not only provide a student-teacher with an opportunity to learn about teaching reading in the content area but also develop a disposition to do so based on a belief that it is a worthwhile way to spend some of the limited instructional time with elementary and high school students.

Syntax: Knowledge Underlying Instruction. A toddler provides play-by-play commentary of the action she puts her toys through: "Dollies kiss me. I kiss

---

Exhibit 2.9. Teacher Knowledge in a Lesson

Three micro periods, as the RAND reading study group calls them, are a common part of comprehension research and instruction—prereading, during reading, and postreading. Even before the prereading micro period, teachers prepare and plan how to help all students comprehend the assigned text.

To plan a lesson, teachers consider features of the texts to be read and the current abilities of the student readers. They anticipate potential areas of ease and difficulty. They note opportunities and needs for introducing new concepts, skills, or strategies. They plan how and when to check on accomplishments and to prod for the transfer and practice of what was introduced in earlier sessions.

When the lesson begins, teachers and students collaborate on reading, with teachers scaffolding the students attempts—providing advice, help, and repairs just in time and only when needed, looking toward more and more independent expertise by each student. As the lesson goes on, some comprehension strategies span micro periods. Questions, be they self- or other generated, are one example. Analogies are another. The period of prereading is for establishing the purpose (and the accompanying rate and monitoring tolerance parameters) and accessing prior knowledge about the content and discourse type by, for example, brainstorming, questioning the reader's knowledge base to reveal gaps or uncertainty, making predictions, or previewing the text (using headings, graphs, charts, pictures, and vocabulary terms). In the during-reading period, monitoring comprehension is crucial, using tools such as attempts to summarize, to answer prereading questions, or to confirm prereading predictions. During reading, if the reader asks or is asked elaborative questions, prior knowledge of concepts or vocabulary is activated (or the need to remedy gaps in background information is made clear).

The postreading period is for examining the newly updated knowledge base for its consistency with what else the reader knows. If needed, the reader undertakes repairs on comprehension by rereading or more reading or discussions with others. The reader responds to the text as a whole: appreciating it; evaluating it; doing what the text directs; figuring out how to organize and remember new concepts; writing notes, outlines, summaries, or responses; and finding new (or old) texts to test, rebut, or deepen new ideas.

dollies." She uses subjects, verbs, and objects with ease. A preschooler complains, "Johnny's eating the one I brought for you." He uses main and embedded (subordinate) clauses without stumbling, even in the midst of thievery. The acquisition of syntax (the structure of phrases, clauses, and sentences) begins early in life,[65] but facility with some syntactic structures continues to grow throughout the school years and beyond.

Six-year-olds come to school facile with some syntactic structures they were not comfortable with at three years of age (relevant structures are in italics): for example, passives ("Almost everybody saw Sean. *Glenda wasn't seen by anyone.*"); some types of subordinate clauses ("She ran fast *so she wouldn't get caught.* The stairs *she climbed* went to the roof."); participle complements ("He tried *running.*"). Conversely, some structures may appear quite a bit later: for example, appositives ("My dad, *the chief of detectives,* will solve it.") and infinitive adverbials ("They walked slowly *to avoid suspicion.*").

Much of what teachers-to-be can learn about syntactic development comes from in-depth analysis of small numbers of cases. There have been some large-scale studies of the syntax of students from kindergarten through the last year of high school, mostly focusing on language production (rather than comprehension), and some covering both oral and written language. It can be particularly useful to analyze the results of those studies for relevance to the dialects of students the teacher candidates meet in classrooms. Teachers can learn to assess the relevance of studies to work with their students and find ways to use students' background strength while scaffolding their reading of materials that may also assume a different dialect background (for example, Ball and Farr, 2003).

In general, early on, spoken syntax is more complex than written; at about twelve years of age, students' written syntax starts to be more complex than their spoken syntax. The sheer length of sentences increases from about seven to ten words between six and thirteen years of age; at the same time, the number of incomplete clauses decreases. The use of *and,* the ubiquitous clause connector, increases until the students are eleven but begins to decrease among twelve-year-olds. Details of some structures change over time, too. Facility with modifying nouns, for example, keeps increasing in adolescence, using adjectives (the *tiny round green* berry) and prepositional phrases (the tree *without any leaves*), and, at about fourteen years, students begin to vary the order of adjectives suitably for style and pragmatic functions.

Children's syntax for productive use lags behind their comprehension until about eight years of age, when the two are likely to proceed apace. There has been detailed study of the development of comprehension of some structures during the elementary school years. Understanding when the same or a different entity is being referred to within a sentence is tricky for a variety of syntactic structures: While "Marge is anxious to please" and "Harriet is difficult to please," seem similar, Marge is the subject of the infinitive *to please* whereas Harriet is the object of *to please*. Facility with the less widespread structure (the one with *difficult*) is acquired later. Some structures are acquired in a way that seems like a backward step for other structures: In "Leslie promised Chelsea to run fast," Leslie is the subject of *run* as well as of *promise;* but cases like "Harry begged George to run fast," in which Harry is the subject of *beg* but George is the subject of *run* are more common. Children use and understand the *beg* sentences early and erroneously treat sentences with *promise* as if they are the same syntactic structure. As they acquire the *promise* structure, they begin to make errors with *beg*-type sentences. Finally—sometimes as late as ten years of age—both syntactic structures are firmly in place.

There is a long and winding road for many areas of syntactic development that teachers can learn about and expect to deal with as students speak, listen, read, and write. Pronoun reference is another case in point. A listener or reader's inferences about what a pronoun refers to can be (but may not be) constrained by syntactic structure. Who is *she* in the following sentence? "She'll be happy if Fantasia wins the vote." We only know for sure *she* isn't Fantasia—because of the syntax. In some cases, the syntax is not determinate and the reader or listener must use other sources to interpret the pronoun (for example, the *she* can refer to Fantasia or to some other female in "Fantasia will be happy if she wins the vote" or "If Fantasia wins the vote she'll be happy.").

The relationship between a student's facility with syntax and reading is a two-way street (Chomsky, 1972). It appears that students who read more have control of more sophisticated syntax. Students seem to profit most from reading difficult material—with vocabulary and syntax that may seem unlike, even beyond, their everyday language. Readability formulas that are used to indicate the difficulty level of a passage or book rely partly on sentence length. Texts rated for beginners are likely to have single-clause sentences with short and noncomplex noun-phrase and verb-phrase structures. Strangely enough, there is evidence that the comprehension of readers as young as in the second grade can be hindered by texts like this (Brennan, Bridge, and Winograd, 1986; Beck, McKeown, Omanson, and Pople, 1984). When ideas are expressed in a series of short sentences, readers have to infer relations that might otherwise be stated in complex syntactic structures. Consider a paragraph: "How can she win? Fantasia knows. She picks a famous song. She uses her own style. She sings it well." A single sentence can be produced that combines the clauses in those five sentences: "Fantasia knows she can win by picking a famous song and singing it well in her own style." Many other single-sentence versions can be produced, and all would be rated difficult by readability formulae. Students, though, might find some of the single-sentence versions better for comprehension. Teacher knowledge of syntax can apply to assessing books and other texts, to going beyond the rough estimates from readability formulae.

Effective teachers are prepared to help students comprehend sophisticated structures found in written discourse. Teachers can learn to use knowledge of syntax to plan before lessons, examining the written material for structures likely to challenge students. They also rely on syntactic knowledge during lessons to recognize and respond to student difficulties. It may be helpful for teachers to talk about the structures with students, comparing and contrasting them with styles, dialects, and languages more familiar to the students. To recognize student syntactic development and the syntactic demands of texts students are asked to read, teachers can learn to recognize the features of sentences that challenge comprehension: for example, passives; unusual word order ("Surprised, the thief surrendered to the watchman."); negation and modal verbs ("No thief could have failed to notice the open door."). They can also learn to distinguish among simple, compound, and complex sentence structures: compound sentences are two independent clauses joined with a conjunction that signals the relationship between the clauses (for instance, *and, or, but)*. Complex sentences include at least one (and sometimes more) subordinate (embedded) clauses, sometimes introduced with conjunctions and relative or adverbial pronouns (for example, *if, so, because, who, that, when,* or *where*).

Several decades ago, teacher educators could assume that elementary (grammar) schools and high schools would provide technical vocabulary and practice pertinent to syntax, but now many students arrive at colleges and universities without having ways of talking about structures or techniques for analyzing sentences. Some teachers have completed teacher-education programs without having explicit knowledge of syntax (Moats, 1994). For example, when a group of elementary school teachers were given a multiple-choice question on the defining characteristic of a sentence, only one-third chose the response that described a sentence as a structure with a subject and predicate; two-thirds responded to the punctuation characteristics instead of the syntactic ones, identifying a sentence as a group of words with a capital in the beginning and a period at the end. It is true that any adequate grammar of a language allows ellipsis of a subject (for instance, "Take care!"), a predicate (for example, the reply in the following exchange: "Who's missing?" "Mary."), or even both elements of an ellipsed main clause (for example, "Because the metaphor expresses the character's attitude toward women.") It is also true that different linguistic theories may use other terms (for example, *subject*-as-noun phrase, argument, agent or patient, *predicate*-as-verb phrase, function, action or state). Theorists of any ilk and everyday language users, however, are able to use information from surrounding text and context to expand elliptical utterances, retrieving information about their subjects and predicates with ease and accuracy. However, deriving a definition for *sentence* from the rules for representing spoken sentences in print (with capitals and periods) is a slightly more sophisticated version of the error of thinking that *sue* and *sure* start with the same sound. Writing a melange of words with a capitol and period does not make them a sentence (for example, "The expresses than care Mary."), and attempts at ellipsis that cannot be retrieved from text or context are not remedied by using a capital and a period. Teacher education can bring teachers' implicit syntactic knowledge about things such as the defining characteristics of a sentence to the fore so that teachers can use it to understand better their students' development and difficulties presented by reading materials. Occasions for making syntactic knowledge explicit arise during exercises using sentence anagrams (arranging disarranged sentences), sentence combining (making several short sentences into one longer one that preserves the ideas), paraphrasing (saying the same thing in another way), and sentence reduction (taking very long sentences and breaking them into smaller sentences).

Pragmatics and Discourse: Knowledge Underlying Instruction. How language is used, the pragmatics system, differs quite a bit between everyday life situations and school. Academic success requires that students master structures, conventions, and complexities peculiar to academic discourse. It is difficult for many students to adjust to its constraints. Paradoxically, although students need it to read, many learn it from reading. Academic English uses clusters of features that are more common in written than oral language; it conforms to organizational patterns (or genres) tailored to content areas and more common in some cultures than others. Early experiences with certain books read aloud give some youngsters a head start. Many English-language learners and students with language difficulties attain mastery only with expert instruction over a number of years.

Discourse differences are researched as a part of the pragmatics system of language[66]—the system of conventions and constraints that allow one to use language in different situations to accomplish one's intentions. Speech acts, implicatures, and sustaining topics are among the pragmatic issues of particular relevance to education. These are important within different discourse types. *Speech act* and *figure of speech* are technical terms—misnomers, since they are not limited to spoken language. In fact, genres (such as novels or research reports) are seen by some as extended and embedded speech acts that rely on and communicate about the social and linguistic context as part and parcel of communicating the intended meaning of the writer or speaker. Narrative discourse differs substantially from expository discourse in English writing (see Table 2.1), and these in turn differ from genre conventions in other languages. Discourse specific to different academic domains can also be considered collocations of speech acts: teaching students to use the acts that historians, for instance, use as they read, write, and speak is a way to teach them to think like historians.

Success or failure with semantics is often related to pragmatics. Although a language has lexical and propositional near-synonyms, choices among the alternatives are not free and without consequences. Something as simple as using language to get things open, for instance, calls on and communicates a good

Exhibit 2.10. Punctuation and Grammar

Surprisingly little work has been done to study how punctuation marks affect the teaching and learning of reading. Some punctuation is essentially a written-language entity: spaces between words, the use of uppercase letters, and quotation marks (although an iconic curved-fingers gesture to indicate quotation marks can accompany spoken language). Other punctuation is commonly believed to have an elocutionary function, providing signals so the reader fills in the prosody (for example, pauses, stress) they would hear if the author had spoken the sentence.

Beyond the elocutionary, punctuation serves to signify language structure. Just as spelling guides the reader to construct the word being read, punctuation guides the reader to construct the sentence being read. Some punctuation represents boundaries for language structures whether or not the spoken counterpart to a sentence has any overt phonological indicator of the boundary. Morphology is sometimes marked by punctuation. Apostrophes indicate genitive (possessive) case for nouns; in fact, for plurals or other nouns ending in *s*, the apostrophe gives written language a disambiguation that spoken language lacks (for example, *boys* and *boys'*). Other apostrophes indicate contracted elements in verb phrases, affording a marker of a morphological element that disambiguates, for example *he'll* and *heel*, whereas spoken language may have access only to syntactic, semantic, and pragmatic cues. Hyphens are both morphological indicators in compound words and typographical indicators of continued words to accommodate lines' length on a page.

Sentence final punctuation (for example, question marks) can uniquely or redundantly specify syntactic, semantic, and pragmatic information. In Spanish, sentence-level punctuation is available at the beginning of a written sentence, but in English, it is just a confirmation or a call for repairing an interpretation for the reader if the sentence is long and the mark cannot be seen in the typical eye span.

Within sentences, there are commas, colons, and semicolons (and periods, exclamations, and question marks in the case of an embedded quotation). Commas have recently been studied in some detail.[67] Their presence (or absence) has a marked effect on the comprehension processing of certain syntactic structures. When a reader (or listener) starts processing a sentence, its syntactic and semantic structure is being built. There is a tension between the sequential processing of the input and the hierarchical, rather than purely sequential, syntactic structure of the language. Readers may see the words *Some gray dog,* but they process more than that since the three words have grammatical identities, for example, quantifier, adjective, and noun; noun phrase; or subject. A grammatical structure like subject, however, does not stand alone. It carries with it the preparation for a predicate that retrospectively defines the subject. Recognizing a subject as early as possible is good (in fact essential) processing when listening to or reading a

Exhibit 2.10. Punctuation and Grammar, *Cont'd*

sentence. But some sentences invite false parsing: what looks at first like one structure may be retrospectively defined as another, and the reader or listener will have to reparse the sentence so it can be comprehended. For example, compare the following two sentences: (1) When she watched the team scored. (2) When she watched the team the forward scored. Both sentences are usually first parsed as if the subordinate clause ends after "watched," following an efficient processing principal called early closure (EC). When "the team" is encountered, it is expected to belong to the next clause, here the main clause of the sentence. For the second sentence, though, EC processing of the subordinate clause does not work; the predicate of the first clause includes as object the "team." When "the forward" appears, instead of a next clause predicate, it signals that the parsing should be revised if the sentence is to be comprehended.

Consider how commas affect the following sentences:

When she watched, the team scored. [helpful]

When she watched the team, scored. [harmful]

When she watched, the team the forward scored. [harmful]

When she watched the team, the forward scored. [helpful]

Studies show that it is the grammatical importance of the comma that matters, not the use of it to put a pause in the delivery of input to the cognitive language processor. The effect of prior discourse and background knowledge on the processing with or without commas varies according to details of the structures being studied. Even when pragmatic expectations are overridden, however, the syntactic significance of the comma remains strong, especially for EC structures.

While most schools teach punctuation in some way, the common approach to instruction has not been shown to be useful for parsing or reading; in fact, the opposite case has been made (Baldwin and Coady, 1978). Recent work (for example, Steinhauer and Friederici, 2001) suggests that comma habits displayed in writing are related to the use of commas in parsing and comprehension. It appears that teaching punctuation rules or teaching a mechanical response (pausing whenever a comma is recognized) is not helpful. Developing familiarity with grammatical structures more common in written language than spoken language may be helpful. More study is called for to match the advances in basic knowledge about commas with studies of effective work in schools and expanded attention to other aspects of punctuation. Effective instruction might even be designed to ride the wave of student interest in emoticons, the punctuation marks used to symbolize affective dimensions in text messaging, computer chat, and e-mail, for example: :-P (the emoticon for "tongue in cheek").

Exhibit 2.11. Written Language and Spoken Language, Same and Different

A prototype of spoken language has brief utterances and abbreviated grammatical units; it occurs in face-to-face, spontaneous, simultaneous, multiparty interactions; individuals rapidly switch between speaking and listening; topic, domain, audience, and purpose change midstream, contingent on other parties and the shared physical and social context; and the speaker's own intent changes, as does his or her resources and capacities—physical, social, and mental. To measure (in reliable and valid ways) how well an individual comprehends during spoken language encounters is difficult; research that purports to compare the comprehension of spoken and written language usually falls into what Olson (1999) calls the transcription fallacy: for the spoken-language assessment, written language is actually used, but it is read aloud by a tester while the test taker listens.

A prototype for written language has carefully composed (over months, sometimes) long, complex, and grammatically complete units (sentences). The participants act in sequence, writer first, then reader, often at a distance in time and place. Separated readers and writers plan, design, refigure, repair, and finish the complementary acts of processing the language. They are governed by conventions and dispositions, disciplined by topic, content, function, and mental images of the other (reader or writer); they are constrained by and exploit the linguistic and social context by which they assume the other participant is governed. The finished product of a writer is not the complete and sufficient input relied on by the reader for comprehending written language. Much activity goes on during reading comprehension, often using small parts of the written product, not always in the order provided by the writer, not always in solitude by the reader, and best understood as an intersection of contributions from the reader, text, activity, and sociocultural context (Snow and Sweet, 2003).

Actual instances of spoken and written language differ in clusters of features that are more probable or more frequent in one than the other. Some differences can be traced to typical purposes and goals people have when engaging in written or spoken language. Written language, for example, which is less fleeting or more permanent than oral language, is good for record keeping. Pairs of features can be linked across the written and spoken modalities: punctuation, for instance, is present only in written language, but it is related in some ways to the spoken-language prosody (for example, intonation), which is, in turn, largely absent in written language. Consequences of a seemingly innocuous feature can have a surprising effect: the spatial layout of written language, for example, results in line breaks; when line breaks coincide with major syntactic boundaries, comprehension is given a boost (Graf and Torrey, 1966). Table 2.4 contrasts the spoken and the written, mostly from the reader or listener perspective, drawn from the work of scholars from different backgrounds.[68]

Table 2.4. Features Likely Associated with Spoken Versus Written Language

Spoken	Written
Informal, spontaneous	Formal, planned, revised, edited
Fleeting, one-time	Permanent, repeatable
Real time (about 150 words per minute)	Offline, paused and paced by reader (but averages 350 words read per minute)
Time-sequenced	Spatially organized
Working memory limits on availability of surface form of syntax	Syntax can stress readers' working memory
Listener can request repaired input	Reader can repeat, skim, skip, reorder
Listener response is influenced by speaker moves (answers, follows commands, can be checked for attention or comprehension)	Reader response is more under reader control
Linked to a definite shared context, including nonverbal gestures, facial expression, eye contact to support or contradict verbal content	Has indefinite context (reader builds from text), but text is supported by illustrations, graphic models, typographical and layout features, and paragraph structures
Contains hesitations, pauses, fillers, digression, restarts, self-correction, repetitions	Has greater information load per clause
Prosody (for example, pitch change or pause) indicates syntax; stress indicates word differences; voice modulations can indicate emotion	Spaces between words and punctuation marks indicate syntax
Features shorter utterances, more contractions, paratactics for inferring clausal relations, fewer "that-to" complement clauses, more coordination (and, but, so) than subordination, contractions	Features embedded clauses, lengthy prepredicate constructions (clauses, prepositional phrases, qualifiers, dense noun-phrases with adjectives and adverbs), passives, nominalizations, marked relationships between clauses
Indexicals, first and second person and deictic pronouns supported by shared context	More explicit reference and argument structure (premodified phrases, definite descriptions), prepositional phrases instead of deictic pronouns

Table 2.4. Features Likely Associated with Spoken Versus Written Language, *Cont'd*

Spoken	*Written*
Has lower proportion of content words to function words	Has higher proportion of content words to function words
Has lower percentage of unique words to total in a text	Has more unique words in a text
Has shorter words, more quantifiers, onomatopoeia, sound symbolism	Has higher frequency of abstract words

deal about the social and linguistic situation and the participants involved in a spoken or written passage:

1. I hereby open this county fair. [performative speech act, official opening]

2. Open that window. [direct speech act: request for action, to a subordinate or in an urgent situation] Open the window, please. [polite, still direct request]

3. I want you to open the window. [indirect request] Can you open the window? [indirect request] Do you mind opening the window? [more deference, indirect request]

4. I could do with some fresh air. [implicature, flouting maxim of quantity in some contexts]

5. When your brother comes, he always makes sure it isn't too warm in here. [implicature, flouting maxim of relevance in some contexts]

6. I suppose it is too much to ask that you open that stupid window now. [implicature, flouting maxims of quality and manner in some contexts]

Under the right circumstances, each of the final examples (4 through 6) call for an assumption that the cooperative principle of language use, a cornerstone of pragmatics, is in play but that its maxims are blatantly flouted. This calls for a search for a chain of implications leading to the conclusion that the expression conveys the request that a window be opened. While full performative speech acts (example 1) may not be common, even kindergartners use the power of language to effect changes in the world: "You are the daddy" in the play house and "Dibs on the pink crayon" during art. Older students may argue mightily about a jury's pronouncement of innocence based on their understanding of the facts of a criminal case, but at the same time they recognize the institutional constraints that make the pronouncement a performative in the legal system.

Although understanding the sarcasm conveyed by the implicature in example 6 is a late achievement (flowering in adolescence), pragmatic development begins early in life. When babies utter only one word, gestures and intonations allow them to communicate different speech acts—"Mommy" might be, among other things, a request for information, a request for action, a statement of fact, a topic initiation. Very early, children learn alternatives and modulations that indicate deference, politeness, and urgency suitable to the social identities of the people involved in the communicative acts. Between three and six years of age, they become facile with indirect speech acts (example 3). At about five years old, children begin to understand and produce humor that depends on ambiguities and nonliteral meaning (in puns, riddles, and extended joke discourse).

Between nine and thirteen years of age, students are adept at recognizing false statements that are made deliberately and not intended to mislead. This is an advantage for teachers. Not only do the students recognize sarcasm and altruistic lies as such, but they can consciously consider idioms and metaphors. Many figures of speech depend on recognizing the purposeful use of statements that are literally false but still assume the cooperative principle of language use. Idioms often flout a maxim of manner (be brief), since many words are used when a single-word synonym is available ("bought the farm" for "died"). Idioms set or match a style and can express the user's identity and cement social or institutional relations. Metaphoric language may be produced spontaneously by three-year-olds ("smiley line" for a curved line), but the ability to explain it comes later. Explanations, interpretations, and use of culturally important discourse changes as one grows up; proverbs—the epitome of metaphor—are no exception (Nippold, Uhden, and Schwarz, 1997). While teachers may recognize that idioms are specific to certain societies and cultures, they may not know that speech acts (including discourse types and figures of speech) are culture-specific and that instructional power can come from recognizing it. Students about to study the figurative language in a masterpiece of Elizabethan English, for instance, can be prepared in an apprenticeship that includes analyzing figures of speech used in best examples of discourse the students appreciate and have practiced, for example signifying for African American preadolescents and adolescents in Chicago (see Lee, 1995a, 1995b; compare Chapter Three, this volume). For teachers to plan and enact such instruction, they must be prepared to analyze the pragmatics underlying typical school topics (for example, symbolism, irony, satire, the use of unreliable narration in works of literature, emphasis, analogies, allusions, rhetorical questions, asides) and to have facility enough to apply the analysis to examples and discourse from the cultures with which their future students will be most familiar.

As students learn to comprehend, teacher knowledge about cohesion devices—the techniques to tie sentences together in texts—is useful. Cohesion serves topic maintenance, which is still developing during the school years.

When second graders talk, half of their utterances are minimally relevant to the topic, and only about 15 percent are fully relevant; among fifth graders, 75 percent of the utterances are minimally related and 20 percent fully so (Menyuk, 1988, pp. 125–129). It is in middle and high school that students begin to achieve adult conversational levels (about 70 percent fully relevant utterances). There is a good deal of growth in children's use of cohesion devices between three and five years of age, but, during the school years, a wider repertoire of devices appears, and students develop the kind of control over their knowledge that makes it useful for solving problems as they try to comprehend challenging texts. The written material that the students read is *relentlessly* topic relevant; to maintain the topic, authors exploit a full range of cohesion devices, some unfamiliar to the students. Often, it is the cohesion device that cues a reader to use background knowledge to render a text coherent. Cohesion devices that are useful for teachers to know about include the following:

- Ellipsis of a noun, verb, or clause ("Some say teaching is easy. Not I.")
- Conjunctions and discourse particles ("Some say teaching is easy. It is clear, however, that they are ignorant.")
- Lexical relations; for example, hyponyms ("Teaching history is difficult. Social sciences are not lists of facts.") and antonyms ("Teaching is not easy. It is hard.")
- Substantives, including quantifiers ("A teaching career has intellectual and emotional rewards. She wants both.") as well as anaphoric ("Find the proper quadrant. It will have positive X and Y values.") and demonstrative pro-forms ("If Magellan intended to get to the Philippines, he could not have chosen a worse route to get there.")

Of course, cohesion operates over much longer texts than those in the examples above. An exercise that is usually enlightening for novice teachers is the explicit marking of references among nouns and pronouns and between phrases that substitute for one another in a cohesive text. To plan active and critical comprehension instruction, teachers preview the material to be read and prepare to call attention to the cohesive devices that bind parts of the text together and call for the reader to activate background knowledge.

Teacher knowledge about discourse types can also be a resource for planning comprehension lessons, for developing graphic aids for students to use during reading, and for noticing and addressing misconceptions that arise in lessons (for example, Heap, 1991). It is useful for teachers to know about developmental patterns for different discourse types (for example, for narratives, see Hickmann, 2002, Peterson, 1990, and James, 1990). While they may seem less important to serious educational efforts, the discourse of songs and games often sustains focus over a long period of time, allowing practice that might otherwise be difficult to motivate. Several interesting examples that involve new technologies are available for younger students. The Between the Lions Website has several songs and games about grapheme-phoneme correspondences (http://pbskids.org/lions/songs/hung_up_qt.html). A classic jump rope chant ("Miss Mary Mack, Mack, Mack") is another example from a suite of computer activities illustrating phonological sensitivity and letter-sound practice that can be motivating and culturally responsive (www.umich.edu/~medal/ssopmweb/ssop.html; and Pinkard, 2001). For older students, the discourse of text messaging or graphic novels could be useful genres to investigate. Teacher educators can help student teachers to bring knowledge of discourse types to awareness, for example, during practice with identifying the structure and conventions of the texts they will encounter while teaching different subjects—the features of textbooks, and primary and secondary sources—as well as the kinds of motivating discourse types that may not ordinarily appear in the curriculum but can be pressed into service by a prepared teacher.

Style is another matter of pragmatics that appears in teacher preparation. In fact, it has several different uses. One use of the word *style* is particularly for analyzing materials: the style of an author or group of authors involves the collection of syntactic, lexical, and figurative devices that become literary devices identified with the author or type or group of authors. Readers may know that one passage sounds like Henry James and another like Ernest Hemingway (or Roald Dahl and Dr. Seuss, for the younger set). Teachers can learn to analyze the language features that become literary devices in the hands of a master and use that knowledge to prepare students when they first approach work by that writer. Another use of the word *style* refers to the dichotomy between formal and informal (although experts identify not two levels of formality but at least five, involving increasing attention to language use). At about ten years of age, students begin to show evidence of phonological style shifting; younger children have the variants for different styles, but appear not to tie them to the different formality of contexts (see Romaine, 1984). This meaning of style is related to the personal style and identity issues that are central aspects of language use among older students. Membership in a group or opposition to another group can be indicated by features of phonology, syntax, semantics, pragmatics, and discourse. Some of these sorts of language differences involve many features and societywide groups, for example, the gender differences studied by Tannen (1996, 1990) and Maltz and Borker (1982), among others. But there has also been study of small issues and small groups, such as the adolescent reluctance to talk in stepfamilies (Golish and Caughlin, 2002). On a scale in between are recent studies of young people identified as workers, rather than students, that show them using and learning sophisticated language, involving, for example, hypotheses and planning (Heath, 1998, 1999). Teachers who are knowledgeable about and disposed to be sensitive to the issues of style shifting, personal style, and identity may find it a resource for managing relations in classrooms and for striking the right motivational notes that increase student reading engagement.

Fluency Instruction:
Getting Through the Medium for the Message

A proficient reader reads with accuracy and speed, easily comprehending and responding to the material; within the same article or chapter, he or she slows down, makes mistakes, abandons a sentence mid-clause, and retreats to other sentences, paragraphs, or pages to try to understand what just went over his or her head. Proficient readers even know when *not* to be fluent! When the material is at a level considered suitable for late-high-school readers, average adults read silently at about 185 words per minute (wpm); those who are above average (in the 75th percentile of adult readers) make it to 245 wpm. In school a fluent reader is often measured during *oral* reading on grade-level-appropriate passages. Measures take into account three aspects of fluency: the rate (60 to 70 words per minute is a common goal for end of grade one, 110 to 120 for the end of grade three, and up to 145 by the end of grade five), accuracy (90 to 95 percent correct word identification), and "expression" (whether the reader provides appropriate spoken-language prosodic features, such as stress, pitch, timing, intonation, pausing, and text phrasing). It is generally assumed that comprehension occurs if one reads fluently (at least at the 50th percentile for the grade or age group). "Reading with expression" is associated with good comprehension both by intuition (what else but comprehended meaning could it be that is being expressed?) and by research that associates aspects of prosody with syntactic processing, which in turn contributes to the reader constructing a meaning for a passage.

Fluency[69] depends on a reader's knowledge about the topic, vocabulary, and discourse type as well as the reader's purposes and skill with word identification and his or her metacontrol over cognitive and other processes applied in the reading activity. A poignant if not vicious circle is revealed when one examines the relevant scholarship and observes contemporary students: it is easier for fluent readers to become more frequently engaged in reading, but to become fluent calls for more frequent engagement in reading. Survey data highlights the problem: about a quarter of our seventeen-year-olds say they read fewer than five pages a day, in school and out (Education Trust, 2001).

Until recently, fluency was thought best addressed as a fourth step on the way to reading comprehension—first accuracy, then speed, then automaticity, then fluent application to connected text. Achieving fluency meant mastery over words or spelling-sound correspondences within words, essentially just the phonological and orthographical systems. The general idea was to get lower-level processes to occur automatically—without effort and out of awareness—so that attention and other cognitive resources could be freed for comprehending connected text. Some researchers questioned the view, noting that the "expression" part of fluency seemed to be missing from these steps. Clinicians and teachers were aware of students who did not reap the benefits of automaticity—who, even if they appeared to have achieved automaticity while reading connected texts, did not automatically comprehend. In fact, Levy, Abello, and Lysynchuk (1997) took words that students read accurately and taught them to say them faster; they found that this did increase the rate of reading connected text but failed to have the impact on comprehension that fluency improvements usually do.

Newer views of fluency tie it to all of the language subsystems (phonology, morphology, orthography, semantics, syntax, pragmatics, and perhaps even etymology and metacognition), advise integration of all the conventional types of instruction (phonemic awareness, phonics and word identification, word meaning, and comprehension strategies), and emphasize the development of fluency from the very beginning of reading education. As soon as a new aspect of reading enters the learner's purview, it is put into place as a component to be performed accurately and with ease in contexts in which other things matter, too (see, for example, Wolf and Katzir-Cohen, 2001). Readers consolidate abilities with ever-larger units—moving from GPCs to orthographic patterns for word identification and syntactic and semantic contexts to identify the sense meant for a polysemous vocabulary item, the pragmatic discourse or argument structure that a specific claim in a sentence is alleged to support. Teachers connect decoding, spelling, and vocabulary work, aiming for accuracy, richness, and automaticity. It is not enough to identify quickly the pronunciation of -*tion* in words such as *action*. Fluency also involves elaborated vocabulary knowledge, including morphology (-*tion* makes nouns from verbs), syntax (nouns and verbs occur in different structures), and the propositional semantics and pragmatics that define different uses (for example, contrast "Act now" with "Initiate action as soon as possible!"). Some grade-school teachers used to advise their students to "use a word in three different situations and it will be yours." That may not be far off, but teachers need to learn about which uses are important and how much is enough to get the desired impact on fluency and comprehension.

To promote fluency among their students, teachers have essentially three tacks to learn about and learn to do. The new view of fluency advises going beyond instruction for automatic word identification by integrating it with other types of instruction including, as described in this chapter, phonemic awareness, word meaning, and comprehension strategy instruction. The next two instructional tacks toward fluency are different approaches to extensive practice at reading; both the older and the newer views of fluency agree that these approaches are effective. One tack is repeated reading of the same material. The other is extensive reading of many different things.

Repeated readings of the same material work to improve fluency during a brief period in students' reading education: when they have begun to read but are not very advanced, at a late first-grade reading level but not when students are reading at a fourth-grade level. It is a "just in time" practice; to make good use of it, teachers must be aware of and responsive to the different and changing abilities of their students. There are different approaches to repeated readings: students reading on their own while teachers monitor their progress; students reading while another person (or tape) reads along to help; whole-class choral reading and echo reading; or rereading the same text for several days in school and at home and in varying social groupings. Assisted approaches seem to be more effective than unassisted approaches. Although some advise easy materials for fluency practice, it appears that repeated readings of more difficult materials produce more improvement. It is important for teachers to recognize that most uses of listening centers will not reap the desired benefits because there are often no criteria for the amount of repetition, and students are not held responsible for nor given credit for practicing. In the National Reading Panel analysis, repeated reading practices were taken together with other practices such as guided oral reading; some practices that were included, for instance, "round robin" reading (taking turns reading sequential parts of a text), are not repeated readings and have not been shown to increase fluency. Motivation for repeated readings obviously cannot depend on desire for new information or a new emotional response. For some students, charting fluency improvement within a curriculum of repeated reading is motivational; for others, preparing to perform texts in person or on tapes to be heard by others is the motivational spur; still others are motivated by the chance to work with a partner or electronic equipment.

The third tack toward fluency involves more reading through reading widely.[70] Repeated reading approaches do not hold a clear advantage over nonrepetitive approaches, even in the case of tape-assisted readings. It is the sheer volume of reading that is important; to succeed as readers, many students need to read more during the school day, for homework, and in their free time. The National Reading Panel report caused many to question the value of wide, independent, silent reading. In fact, however, there is strong support for wide reading in various reviews of the research (for example, Kuhn and Stahl, 2003; Krashen, 2001), though its implementation in periods (like sustained silent reading) that take time away from working with others to comprehend texts is not always optimal.

Teachers can learn ways to promote more reading of different materials among their students. Teaching students how to set and accomplish purposes for reading and to use metacognitive and cognitive strategies is a start, but helping them to remember to apply what they have learned during independent silent reading is the needed completion to the lessons and a best hope for application during out-of-school reading. Teachers directly or indirectly match students and reading materials. When the teacher does this well, students avoid frustration and boredom and can read enough to get a fluency payoff. It takes teacher knowledge of student capabilities and interests as well as knowledge of materials for students—different levels, different topics, and different styles. Teachers also need to know about summer setbacks in reading achievement and the limited access that some students have to reading material; they need to find out how to ease access to reading materials, working with class, school, and community libraries for reading at school and at home. For adolescents, in particular, limited knowledge about reading as an activity may itself be an impediment to wide independent reading. It can be addressed with discussions about tactics that help a reader to persevere, to know when to skim and when to dig deep, and so on. These discussions can be based on reading logs that record student notes about meta-reading—how an attempt to read proceeded (or ran aground). Even if adult advice is set aside, the message gets through when a peer points out that repeated failures to finish a chapter may not be due to reader ineptitude or text impenetrability, nor to a lack of interest in the topic, but rather to the habit of reading in bad light in bed at midnight. The goal is to identify the topic, time, place, and style that engage students voluntarily in the reading practice that leads to increased fluency.

For teachers, work on fluency integrates all their underlying knowledge of language systems and instructional activities. For students, increased fluency means that reading fades into the background, as communication and thinking take over. This is just what we all want.

Notes

1. For detailed consideration of relations between language and literacy, see Snow (1991); for a sequence of viewpoints on early literacy related to language experience approaches, see Mason and Allen (1986), Stahl and Miller (1989), and McGee and Lomax (1990); for an earlier overview of emergent literacy, see Sulzby and Teale (1991); for a recent synthesis of emergent literacy research, see Gunn, Simmons, and Kameenui (1998); for a recent collection of articles see the handbook on early literacy edited by Neumann and Dickinson (2001).

2. See also Moje, Ciechanowski, Kramer, Ellis, Carrillo, and Collazo (2003); Gutiérrez, Baquedano-López, and Tejeda (1999).

3. Kelter and Kaup (1998) look into a special case in which reading and listening demands on mental models differ: reading requires eye movements that call on mental visual-spatial resources to represent the spatial properties of the text; some text calls on mental models primarily about visual-spatial matters; when such text is read, there is competition for the resources of the visual-spatial systems; therefore, comprehension should suffer. They note relevant experimental results that suggest just such a source of comprehension difficulty.

4. Compare Taylor, Pearson, Clark, and Walpole (1999).

5. Other reviews are compatible with this approach. Curtis (2002) divided the available literature on adolescents into four categories: word identification, other language knowledge and processes, cognition, and situations of engagement. Alexander (2002) describes competent readers in terms of linguistic knowledge, background knowledge, processing strategies, interest, and goal-directed behavior. Sticht (1976, 2002), points to intersecting and variable elements involved in comprehension: (1) content knowledge, (2) procedural knowledge from spoken language as well as GPCs and larger structural patterns, and (3) purposes (read-to-do versus read-to-learn).

6. See, for example, Hoffman, McCarthey, Abbott, Christian, Corman, Curry, and others (1994); Hiebert (2002); Hiebert, Martin, and Menon (2005); Foorman, Perfetti, Seidenberg, and Francis (2001).

7. For study of the context and activity diversity issues in a more general sense, see Au (1997); Baker, Afflerbach, and Reinking (1996); Ball and Farr (2003); Delpit (1986, 1988, 1995); Elliot and Hewison (1994); Gasden and Wagner (1995); Gregory (1997); Jimenez (2000); Lee (1992, 1997); McInerny and Vanetten (2001); Moje, Dillon, and O'Brien (2000); Purcell-Gates (1996); Rueda, MacGillivray, Monzo, and Arzubiaga (2001); Serpell (1997); Strickland and Taylor (1989); and Thompson, Mixon, and Serpell (1996). See also, for more specific situations, Ballenger (1999); Edwards (1994); Goldenberg and Gallimore (1995); Heath (1983); Lee (1995b, 2000); Moje, Ciechanowski, Kramer, Ellis, Carrillo, and Collazo (2003); Neuman and Roskos (1993); Nieto (2000); Schmidt (1995); Taylor (1986); and Volk (1997).

8. See National Reading Panel (2000, Chapter Four, p. 39); Baumann and Kameenui (1991); Brown (2002); Alvermann (2001); Alvermann, Hagood, Heron, Hughes, Williams, and Jun (2000); and Ruddell (2001).

9. See Snow, Burns, and Griffin (1998, pp. 76, 108, 169); Kintsch (1998); Cain, Oakhill, and Bryant (2000); Nation, Allen, and Julme (2001); Daneman and Carpenter (1980, 1983); Yuill, Oakhill, and Parkin (1989); Oakhill, Yuill, and Parkin (1996); Perfetti (1985); and Seigneuric, Ehrlich, Oakhill, and Yuill (2000).

10. See Snow, Burns, and Griffin (1998, pp. 167, 176); National Reading Panel (2000, Chapter Four, p. 26); McKenna, Kear, and Ellsworth (1995); Guthrie, Alao, and Rinehart (1997); McQuillan (1997); Taylor (1999); O'Brien, Dillon, Wellinski, Springs, and Stith (1997); Curtis (2002); Murphy and Alexander (2002); Reeve, Bolt, and Cai (1999); Guthrie and Wigfield (2000); and Moje, Ciechanowski, Kramer, Ellis, Carrillo, and Collazo (2003).

11. See Snow, Burns, and Griffin (1998, pp. 76, 219); National Reading Panel (2000, Chapter Four, pp. 42, 44); Gaultney (1995); Gough, Hoover, and Peterson (1996); Wineburg (1991); Bean (2001); Graesser, Singer, and Trabasso (1994); Cote, Goldman, and Saul (1998); Graesser and Bertus (1998); Singer, Harkness, and Moore (1997); Cain (1999); Cain, Oakhill, Barnes, and Bryant (2001); Graesser, Kassler, Kreuz, and McLain-Allen (1998); Mannes and Kintsch (1987); McNamara, Kintsch, Songer, and Kintsch (1996); Barnes, Dennis, and Haefele-Kalvaitis (1996).

12. See Snow, Burns, and Griffin (1998, pp. 77, 176); National Reading Panel (2000, Chapter Four); Curtis (2002); Armbruster and Anderson (1984); Taylor (1985); Graves and Slater (1996); Vacca and Vacca (1999); Yuill and Oakhill (1991); Alvermann, Young, Weaver, Hinchman, Moore, Phelps, and others (1996); Rowell and Ebbers (2002); Armbruster and Anderson (1985); McKeown and Beck (1994); Spinillo and Pinto (1994); Lee, Rosenfeld, Mendenhall, Rivers, and Tynes (2003); and Dickson, Simmons, and Kameenui (1995).

13. Basic research on vocabulary addresses other sorts of issues. See Williams (1992); Simpson (1995); Marslen-Wilson (1999); and Moss and Gaskell (1999) concerning issues such as the learning and storage of forms (whole lexical forms versus roots and affixes), determining centrality among polysemous words, dominance and contextual bias effect for homonyms, and understanding which aspects of meaning are accessed first.

14. See Snow, Burns, and Griffin (1998, pp. 75–77, 106–111, 122, 169, 216–219) and National Reading Panel (2000, Chapter Four, pp. 15–35). For vocabulary, see Dickinson and Tabors (2001); Hart and Risley (1995); Snow (1983); Nagy and Herman (1987); Curtis (2002); Chall, Jacobs, and Baldwin (1990); Cunningham and Stanovich (1997); Juel (1988); Bear, Invernizzi, Templeton, and Johnston (2003); Baumann and Kameenui (1991); Freebody and Anderson (1983); Pany, Jenkins, and Schreck (1982); Ehrlich and Remond (1997); Oakhill, Cain, and Yuill (1998); Stothard and Hulme (1992); Stahl and Fairbanks (1986); Beck and McKeown (1991); Schwanenflugel, Stahl, and McFalls (1997); Sternberg (1987); Stahl (1991, 2003); McKeown, Beck, Omanson, and Pople (1985); Beck (1981); Bear, Invernizzi, Templeton, and Johnston (2003); and Nagy and Scott (2000). For other linguistic knowledge, see Stothard and Hulme (1996); Yuill and Oakhill (1991); Beal (1990); Chikalanga (1993); Cain and Oakhill (1999); van Oostendorp and Goldman (1999); Gernsbacher (1997); Zwaan and Radvansky (1998); Yuill and Joscelyne (1988); and Yuill and Oakhill (1988).

15. See Snow, Burns, and Griffin (1998, pp. 76–77, 220–223); National Reading Panel (2000, Chapter Four, pp. 39–115); Cain (1999); Ehrlich, Remond, and Tardieu (1999); Oakhill, Hartt, and Samols (1996); Carr and Thompson (1996); Curtis (2002); Alvermann, O'Brien, and Dillon (1990); Alvermann (2004); Guthrie, Van Meter, Hancock, Alao, Anderson, and McCann (1998); Brown (1997); Sperling, Walls, and Hill (2000); Rosenshine and Meister (1994); Duke and Pearson (2002); and Keenan (2002).

16. See Labov (1981) and Labov and Waletzky (1967) for details about spoken narrative structure. Hoffman, McCarthey, Abbott, Christian, Corman, Curry, and others (1994); Moss and Newton (1998); and Smolkin and Donovan (2001) document the disparity in text types used in schools. For a pro-narrative-texts stance, see Egan (1993); for discussion in favor of more expository texts, see Duke, Bennett-Armistead, and Roberts (2003); Purcell-Gates (1988); Pappas (1993); Duthie (1996); Kamil and Lane (1997); Caswell and Duke (1998); Duke and Kays (1998); Duke (2000); Tower (2002); Pressley, Rankin, and Yokoi (1996); and Yopp and Yopp, 2000.

17. See Alvermann and Phelps (1998); Bulgren and Scanlon (1998); Brozo and Simpson (1999); Lenski, Wham, and Johns (1999); Alexander and Jetton (2000); Ruddell (2001); and Greenleaf, Schoenbach, Cziko, and Mueller (2001).

18. See, for example, Kuhn (1993); Palincsar (2001); Hapgood, MacLean, and Palincsar (2000); Ford, Palincsar, and Magnusson (2002); Palincsar and Magnusson (2001); Osborne, Simon, and Erduran (2002); Nesbit and Rogers (1997); Hogan (1999); Van Boxtel, van der Linden, and Kanselaar (2000); King (1994); Spires and Donley (1998).

19. See Wineburg (1999, 1991, 1998, 2003); Barca (1998); Young and Leinhardt (1998).

20. See Afflerbach and VanSledright (2001); Arthur and Phillips, (2000); Beck, McKeown, and Gromoll (1989); Britt, Rouet, Georgi, and Perfetti (1994); Gustafson (1998); Lee (2004); Leinhardt (1994, 2000); McKeown and Beck (1994); Paxton (1999); Rouet, Britt, Mason, and Perfetti (1996); Stahl, Hynd, Britton, McNish, and Bosquet (1996); Stearns, Seixas, and Wineburg (2000); VanSledright (2002); VanSledright and Frankes (2000); Voss and Carretero (2000); Wiley and Voss (1996); Wineburg (1992, 1994); Young and Leinhardt (1998); and Zarnowski (1995).

21. See, for example, Galda and Beach (2001); Harker (1994); Keene and Zimmermann (1997); Langer (1990); Lee (1995b, 1997, 2000); Siegal, Borasi, and Fonzi (1998).

22. About analogy, see Goswami and Mead (1992); Ehri and Robbins (1992); and Nation, Allen, and Hulme (2001).

23. Compare Wolf, Vellutino, and Gleason (1998), for a detailed discussion of models in reading research.

24. See, for example, Coltheart (1978, 2000); Coltheart, Rastle, Perry, Langdon, and Ziegler (2001); Joubert and Lecours (1999); Rastle and Coltheart (2000); Stuart and Coltheart (1988); Visser and Besner (2001).

25. See Harm and Seidenberg (1999); Plaut, McClelland, Seidenberg, and Patterson (1996); Rayner, Foorman, Perfetti, Pesetsky, and Seidenberg (2001); and Seidenberg and McClelland (1989).

26. See Ehri and Snowling (2004); Chall (1983); Ehri (1999, 1994, 1995); Ehri and Sweet (1991); Ehri and Wilce (1985); Frith (1985); Gough and Hillinger (1980); Gough, Juel, and Roper-Schneider (1983); Juel (1991); Marsh, Friedman, Welch, and Desberg (1981); and Spear-Swerling and Sternberg (1997). See also the extensive material referenced in the appendix to this volume that provides details that can be important to both stage and wave models as they apply to preschool through second-grade children.

27. See Bowman and Treiman (2002); Rittle-Johnson and Siegler (1999); and, about wave models in other domains of development, Siegler (1996).

28. Sticht used the term "auding" to distinguish what subjects do in these studies to contrast it with listening in the everyday conversational sense. What is observed

about a person's comprehension from day-to-day contact may be far removed from what is measured in these studies.

29. See, for example, Beck and McKeown (2001); Dennis and Walter (1995); Green (1981); Garner and Bochna (2002); Yopp and Yopp (2000); Tower (2002); and Smolkin and Donovan (2001).

30. See Duke (2000) and Pappas and Barry (1997).

31. See, for example, Yuill and Oakhill (1991); Oakhill and Beard (1999); Oakhill and Cain (2003); Oakhill, Cain, and Bryant (2003); chapters in Cornoldi and Oakhill (1996).

32. See Alexander and Jetton (2000); Murphy and Alexander (2002); Dweck (2000); Guthrie, McGough, Bennett, and Rice (1996); Mitchell (1993); Guthrie, Alao, and Rinehart (1997); Guthrie, VanMeter, McCann, Wigfield, Bennett, Poundstone, and others (1996); Guthrie and Wigfield (2000); Reeve, Bolt, and Cai (1999); Alvermann and Hagood (2000); Moje, Young, Readence, and Moore (2000); Baker and Wigfield (1999); Baker, Dreher, and Guthrie (2000); Deci, Koestner, and Ryan (1999); Gambrell and Almasi (1996); Gambrell, Morrow, Neuman, and Pressley (1999); Pintrich (1999); Guthrie, Wigfield, and Perencevich (2004); Pressley, Dolezal, Raphael, Mohan, Roehrig, and Bogner (2003); Guthrie and Alvermann (1999); Guthrie, Schafer, Wang, and Afflerbach (1995); Jacobs, Lanza, Osgood, Eccles, and Wigfield (2002); Meece and Miller (1999); Pressley (1995); Ryan and Deci (2000a, 2000b); Schiefele (1999); Stipek (2002); Stipek, Feller, Daniels, and Milburn (1995); National Research Council and The Institute of Medicine's Committee on Increasing High School Students' Engagement and Motivation to Learn (2004); Turner (1995); Verhoeven and Snow (2001); and Wigfield and Guthrie (1997).

33. Other books and articles describe the language knowledge base for teaching, for example, Fillmore and Snow (2002); Moats (2000, 1994); and Moats and Lyon (1996). They use different expository frameworks and details but are not in essence making different claims about the content of the knowledge base.

34. See American Federation of Teachers (1999); International Reading Association (2003); and Brady and Moats (1997) for the International Dyslexia Association. There have been no studies that directly test a full set of proposed recommendations or standards. However, support for claims about the effectiveness of teachers educated in programs that reflect the IRA standards is provided in a recent study by Hoffman, Roller, Maloch, Sailors, Beretvas, and the National Commission on Excellence in Elementary Teacher Preparation for Reading Instruction (2003; compare Harmon, Hedrick, Martinez, Perez, Keehn, Fine, and others, 2001), which follows a group of graduates from exemplary programs for the first three years of their teaching careers and contrasts them (and their students' reading achievement) with a group of teachers who did not attend exemplary programs and another group of more experienced teachers.

35. For an example of a more complete picture, but limited to early childhood education, see Strickland, Snow, Griffin, Burns, and McNamara (2002). They call for teachers to learn to provide five opportunities for students so they will avoid reading difficulties. The opportunities were first presented in Snow, Burns, and Griffin

(1998), especially Chapter Nine, in which the set of opportunities is associated with the kinds of academic disciplines or departments that would help teach teachers; see also Burns, Snow, and Griffin (1999) for more information on the opportunities children need.

36. See Cappella and Weinstein (2001); Greenleaf, Schoenbach, Cziko, and Mueller (2001); Langer (2001); Nystrand (1997); Nystrand and Gamoran (1997); Perry and VandeKamp (2000); Perry, VandeKamp, Mercer, and Nordby (2002); Pressley, Allington, Wharton-McDonald, Block, and Morrow (2001); Pressley, Wharton-McDonald, Allington, Block, Morrow, Tracey, and others (2001); Reyes, Scribner, and Paredes Scribner (1999); Taylor and Pearson (2002); Taylor, Pressley, and Pearson (2002); and Wharton-McDonald, Pressley, and Hampston (1998). See also National Literacy Trust and Hertrich (2004) for the summary of a recent study of secondary school literacy in the United Kingdom that includes seventeen features of successful practice.

37. For examples of descriptions of dialect variations, see Leap (1993); Mufwene, Rickford, Bailey, and Baugh (1998); Wolfram and Schilling-Estes (1998); Labov, Ash, and Boberg (2002); and Washington and Craig (2002). For examples of noticeable dialect differences that appear in schooling, see Heath (1983); Hyon and Sulzby (1994); Ball (1995); Gasden and Wagner (1995); Champion (1998); Allen, de Villiers, and François (2002); Ball and Farr (2003); Washington (1996); and Wolfram, Adger and Christian (1999). See also Fillmore and Snow (2002, pp. 26–27) and Strickland, Snow, Griffin, Burns, and McNamara (2002, pp. 88–91). A recent study by Charity, Scarborough, and Griffin (2004) will reawaken debate about the role of dialect differences in early grade reading acheivement.

38. Notice that neither variant is pronounced with a final /g/, the popular expression "dropping g's" and the common spelling strategy of using an apostrophe in place of the letter G aside.

39. See DeBoer (1959); O'Hare (1973); Emig (1981); Hillocks (1986); and Hillocks and Smith (1991). But the obverse works: students learn more grammar if lessons apply it to their own writing (Baker, Gersten, and Graham, 2003).

40. For Writers' Workshop, see Weaver (1996, 1998). Compare Harris (1962); DiStefano and Killion (1984); Anderson, Hiebert, Scott, and Wilkinson (1985, p. 80); and Hiebert, Pearson, Taylor, Richardson, and Paris (1998, Topic 6, p. 4).

41. See Adams (1990, pp. 84–85); Elley (1991); and Krashen (1993).

42. See Hudson (2001). Some research on writing improvement is flawed; in other cases there are hints that sentence combining works for writing because both are production tasks, whereas grammatical parsing tasks may have a closer relation to reading, and so learning to parse may transfer better to reading (compare Tomlinson, 1994).

43. For overviews, see Snow, Burns, and Griffin (1998, 51–57, 107, 111–112, 151–154, 185–188, 248–254); and National Reading Panel (2000, Chapter Two, pp. 9–86). See also Byrne, Fielding-Barnsley, and Ashley (2000); Seymour, Duncan, and Bolik (1999); Ehri, Nunes, Willows, Schuster, Yaghoub-Zadeh, and Shanahan (2001); Wise, Ring, and Olson (1999); Blachman, Tangel, Ball, Black, and McGraw (1999);

Scarborough (1998); Wagner and Torgesen (1987); Liberman, Rubin, Duques, and Carlisle (1985); Moats (1994); Tangel and Blachman (1995); Torgesen, Wagner, Rashotte, Rose, Lindamood, Conway, and Garvan (1999); Treiman (1993); and Read (1971, 1975). See also the appendix and references there to PA development and instruction in the early grades.

44. The reciprocity of reading and PA and the difficulty of measuring PA in expert older readers limit the strength of the claim made here. There is no evidence that PA should or does continue to increase as reading or even word identification ability improves. See also Scarborough, Ehri, Olson, and Fowler (1998).

45. The study of phonological processing is an active field of research; see, for example, Plaut and Kello (1999); Catts (1989); Wolf (2001); Mody, Studdert-Kennedy, and Brady (1997); Rack, Snowling, and Olsen (1992); and Gathercole, Service, Hitch, Adams, and Martin (1999). See also general resources about language development that include phonological development, for example Pinker (1999); MacWhinney (1999); Tomasello and Bates (2001); and Gleason (2001). See Read (1971, 1975) for early work relating phonological development and early literacy. Contemporary studies about the development of phonology cover periods from infancy on and derive from a variety of frameworks, for example, Bloom (1998); Bates, Thal, Finlay, and Clancy (forthcoming); Hulit and Howard (2002); Jusczyk (1997); Ritchie and Bhatia (1998); Nicoladis and Genesee (1997); Archibald (1995); McLeod, van Doorn, and Reed (2001); Bernardt and Stemberger (1997); Hannahs and Young-Scholten (1998); and Zamuner (2003).

46. For recent reviews, see Frost (1998); Harm and Seidenberg (1999); and Rayner, Foorman, Perfetti, Pesetsky, and Seidenberg (2001). Ongoing research into phonological representations indicate they may include units both smaller and larger than phonemes (Marslen-Wilson, 1999; Marslen-Wilson and Warren, 1994; Cutler, 1989; and Mehler, Dommergues, Frauenfelder, and Segui, 1981).

47. See, for example, Moats (1994); McCutchen, Harry, Cunningham, Cox, Sidman, and Covill (2002); and Bos, Mather, Dickson, Podhajski and Chard (2001). See Treiman and Cassar (1997) for an experiment involving the difficulty of phoneme counting for literate adults.

48. Various aspects of the metacognition of language are disucussed in Bialystok (1986a and b); Karmiloff-Smith (1992); Blackmore, Pratt, and Dewsbury (1995); and Ashkenazi and Ravid (1998).

49. The onset is any part of the syllable before the vowel. The rime starts at the vowel nucleus and goes to the coda at the syllable end.

50. See Garton and Pratt (1998, Chapter Seven). Compare Tunmer and Hoover (1992, 1993); Demott and Gombert (1996); and Gaux and Gombert (1999).

51. See Karmiloff-Smith, Grant, Sims, Jones, and Cuckle (1996) for a review, and Papandropoulou and Sinclair (1974) for a seminal study. Other examples include Wysocki and Jenkins (1987); Carlisle and Nomanbhoy (1993); and Lewis and Windsor (1996). Another line of work has studied the evolution of the concept of a written word, for example, Luria (1976–1977); Ferreiro and Teberosky (1982);

Bialystok (1986a); Ferreiro (1991); Roberts (1992); Justice and Ezell (2001); and Yaden and Tardibuono (2004).

52. See the earlier section in this chapter, "What Do We Know About Influences on Comprehension" on cognitive and metacognitive strategy development; also see Paris and Jacobs (1984); Brown, Palincsar, and Armbruster (1984); Yuill and Oakhill (1991, Chapter Eight); and Schoenbach, Greenleaf, Cziko, and Hurwitz (1999).

53. See Snow, Burns, and Griffin (1998, pp. 65–67, 70–75, 188, 204–206); National Reading Panel (2000, Chapter Two, pp. 99–176); Camilli, Vargas, and Yurecko (2003); and, for examples, Ehri (1997a); Juel and Minden-Cupp (2000); Share (1999); Reitsma (1983a and b); Foorman, Francis, Davidson, Harm, and Griffin (2002); Treiman, Tincoff, Rodriguez, Mouzaki, and Francis (1998); Menon and Hiebert (forthcoming); Kessler and Treiman (2001); Venezky (1999); Nagy and Anderson (1984); Cunningham (1998); Just and Carpenter (1987); Perfetti (1985); Shefelbine and Calhoun (1991); Kelly, Morris, and Verrekia (1998); Shankweiler, Lundquist, Dreyer, and Dickinson (1996); and Henry (1988). See also the appendix and references there to GPCs and word identification development and instruction in the early grades.

54. The study of morphology takes place from many perspectives; see the handbook edited by Spencer and Zwicky (1998) and specific studies (for example, Bybee, 1995; and Marslen-Wilson and Tyler, 1998), including those focusing on development (for example, Tyler and Nagy, 1989; Clark, 1993; Marcus, 1996; and Washington and Craig, 2002). Some studies are particularly relevant to literacy (for example, Carlisle, 1995; Carlisle and Nomanbhoy, 1993; Fowler and Liberman, 1995; Derwing, Smith, and Wiebe, 1995; and Bertram, Laine, and Virkkala, 2000) and some involve educational applications (for example, Henry 1993; Moats and Smith, 1992; and Templeton, 1989).

55. The difference between *tent* and *tend*, for example, shows that there is a phonemic distinction in English between voiced and unvoiced alveolar stops—between /t/ and /d/. That phonemic distinction is reflected in the fact that *tent* and *tend* are actually two different words and not simply alternate pronunciations of a single word. However, neither the second /t/ in *tent* nor the /d/ in *tend* contributes at all to the meaning of those words. A tent is not a certain kind of ten, nor is a runt a certain kind of run, a mint a certain kind of min, nor an event somehow related in meaning to even. Thus, those final /t/ phonemes are not morphemes, not tiny meaningful units. One might compare the final phonemes *tens* and *tenth*. The /z/ in tens is a phoneme, of course, but it is also in this particular case an inflectional morpheme {s} signaling plural. It does carry meaning. Similarly, the /θ/ in *tenth* is a phonemic unit but it is also a derivational morpheme {th} that allows the root ten access to the meaning of "ordinal."

56. Gadda (1995) considers the relation between knowing about the history of English and teaching and provides pointers to further information.

57. For reviews and overviews about orthography, see Chomsky (1970b); Templeton and Bear (1992); and Templeton and Morris (2000). See Foorman (1995) about underlying processes. For the structure and organization of English spelling, see

Henderson and Templeton (1986); and Venezky (1999, 2000). For details about student spelling performance and how it changes, see Tolchinsky-Landsmann and Levin (1985); Henderson (1981); Treiman, Cassar, and Zukowski (1994); Treiman, Zukowski, and Richmond-Welty (1995); Treiman and Cassar (1996); Nunes, Bryant, and Bindman (1997); and Seymour (1997). About instructional approaches with different underlying assumptions, see Henry (1996); Hughes and Searle (1997); and Bear, Invernizzi, Templeton, and Johnston (2003). The book edited by Perfetti, Fayol, and Rieben (1997) shows that many contemporary researchers are very interested in studies of orthography.

58. For studies including examination of teacher knowledge of the orthographic system, see McCutchen and Berninger (1999); Moats (2000); Bos, Mather, Dickson, Podhajski, and Chard (2001); Cunningham, Perry, Stanovich, Stanovich, and Chappell (2001); McCutchen, Harry, Cunningham, Cox, Sidman, and Covill (2002); and Moats and Foorman (2003). See also, however, Ravid and Gillis (2002), who raise a question about the link between teacher orthographic knowledge and student performance.

59. See, for example, the arguments and evidence in Henderson (1981); Zutell and Rasinski (1989); Adams (1990, p. 404); Gill (1992); Perfetti (1992); Muter, Snowling, and Taylor (1994); Wimmer and Goswami (1994); Richgels (1995); Ellis (1997); and Ehri (1997b). There are also examples of integrated reading and spelling instruction, for example, Henry (1996); and Bear, Invernizzi, Templeton, and Johnston (2003).

60. Doubled consonants are pronounced as such in other langauges; in Italian, for example, double consonants mark consonant lengthening, so mama and mamma are pronounced differently. Different languages have different orthographic conventions.

61. See Snow, Burns, and Griffin (1998, pp. 47–48, 63, 109–111, 216–219); National Reading Panel (2000, Chapter Four, pp. 15–35); Juel, Biancarosa, Coker, and Deffes (2003); Hart and Risley (1995); Whitehurst and Lonigan (1998); Stahl and Fairbanks (1986); Biemiller (1999); Miller and Gildea (1987); Beck, McKeown, and Kucan (2002); Morrow, Pressley, Smith, and Smith (1997); Blachowicz and Fisher (2000); Henry (1989, 1993); Bear, Invernizzi, Templeton, and Johnston (2003); McKeown, Beck, Omanson, and Pople (1985); Fischer (1994); McKeown (1993); Scott and Nagy (1997); Graves (2000); Laufer and Nation (1999); Anglin (1993); Baumann and Kameenui (1991); Kuhn and Stahl (1998); Johnson and Pearson (1978); Allen (1999); Nagy and Scott (2000); Nagy, Anderson, and Herman (1987); Templeton and Morris (2000); Tinkham (1993); Waring (1997); Stahl and Kapinus (1991); Malone and McLaughlin (1997); Carnicelli (2001); Blachowicz and Ogle (2001); Ruddell and Shearer (2002); Baumann, Edwards, Font, Tereshinski, Kameenui, and Olejnik (2002); Carlo, August, McLaughlin, Snow, Dressler, Lippman, and others (2004).

62. Contemporary research on semantics is undertaken from a variety of perspectives, for example, Lappin (1996); Chierchia and McConnell-Ginet (2000); Löbner (2002); Saeed (2003); Lakoff and Johnson (1980, 1999); Holme (2004);

Hudson (1995); Levin and Pinker (1991); Carpenter (1998); Shibatani and Thompson (1995); Levin and Hovav (1998); Jackendoff (1990); Lehrer and Kittay (1992); and Gee (1999). Some study of semantics is directed specifically toward development and educational applications, for example, Gleitman and Landau (1994); Kuczaj and Barrett (1986); Bloom (2000); Frazier (1995); and Hatch and Brown (1996).

63. For overviews, see, for example, Pearson and Fielding (1991); Snow, Burns, and Griffin (1998, pp. 75–77, 106–111, 122, 167, 169, 176, 216–223; National Reading Panel (2000, Chapter Four, pp. 39–115); Snow (2002); and Duke and Pearson (2002). See also Pearson and Johnson (1978); Alvermann, Qian, and Hynd (1995); Wilhelm, Baker, and Dube (2001); Bean (2001); Beck, McKeown, Hamilton, and Kucan (1997); Beck, McKeown, Sandora, and Worthy (1996); Borasi and Siegel (2000); Brown, Pressley, VanMeter, and Schuder, (1996); Bulgren, Deshler, Schumaker, and Lenz (2000); Clarke, Martell, and Willey (1994); Block and Pressley (2002); Dillon, O'Brien, and Volkman (2001); Gambrell and Almasi (1996); Goldenberg (1993); Guthrie, Wigfield, and Perencevich (2004); Guthrie, Wigfield, and VonSecker (2000); Hacker, Dunlosky, and Graesser (1998); Hoffman and Pearson (2000); Huffman (1998); Kucan and Beck (1997); McKoon and Ratcliff, (1992); McMahon and Raphael (1997); Moje and O'Brien (2001); Ogle (1986); Osborne (2002); Palincsar and Brown (1984, 1986); Pressley (1998, 2000); Pressley, Wood, Woloshyn, Martin, King, and Menke, (1992); Roehler and Cantlon (1997); Rosenshine and Meister (1994); Rosenshine, Meister, and Chapman (1996); Smolkin and Donovan (2002); Taylor and Beach (1984); Taylor and Graves (2000); Vogt and Shearer (2003); Whitehurst, Zevenbergen, Crone, Schultz, Velting, and Fischel (1999); and Whitehurst, Epstein, Angell, Payne, Crone, and Fischel (1994).

64. See Greenleaf (2004) for an example of making public a more expert reading of a novel that can serve as an opportunity for student apprentices to experience the usually private work of a reading "master." See Applebee, Langer, Nystrand, and Gamoran (2003) for an overview of comprehension instruction based on classroom discussion that make public novice and expert reading in the upper grades; see also Nystrand (1997) and Nystrand, Wu, Gamoran, Zeiser, and Long (2003) for an analysis of what leads to productive classroom discussions in general.

65. Information about syntactic development is available in the context of language development in general, for example, Pinker (1999); MacWhinney (1999); Tomasello and Bates (2001); Gleason (2001); and Owens (2001), as well as in reports on studies specifically about the acquisition of syntax, for example, Menyuk (1963, 1964); Chomsky (1969); Hall and Hall (1965); and Schwenk and Danks (1974). See also recent studies of the time lag between children's acquisition of comprehension compared to production of syntactic structures, for example, Smolensky (1996) and Tomasello (2000). Large-scale studies of school-age syntax include Hunt (1965, 1970, 1977); Loban (1963, 1966, 1976); and O'Donnell, Griffin, and Norris (1967). Investigations of the relations between reading and syntactic development, processing, or awareness are not common, but see Chomsky (1972); Gottardo, Stanovich, and Siegel (1996); and Blackmore and Pratt (1997).

66. About the role of pragmatics in stimulating and organizing language development, see Ninio and Snow (1999, 1996); see also publications about language development that highlight pragmatics, sociolinguistics, and communicative competence, for example, Owens (2001, esp. Chapter Eleven); Gleason (2001); James (1990); Menyuk (1988); Reich (1986); and Garvey (1984). For pragmatic developments beyond the early years, see Heath (1999); Hoyle and Adger (1998); Nippold, Uhden, and Schwarz (1997); Hicks (1996); Nippold (1988); and Romaine (1984). Studies of specific aspects of pragmatics development and learning include, for example, Golish and Caughlin (2002); Hickmann and Hendriks (1999); Snow, Pan, Imbens-Bailey, and Herman (1996); Lee (1995a, 1995b); Heap (1991); Peterson (1990); Cacciari and Levorato (1989); Nippold and Sullivan (1987); and Beal and Flavell (1984). About topics and issues in pragmatics and discourse, see, for example, Slobin, Gerhardt, Kyratzis, and Guo (1996); Tannen (1996, 1990); Brown and Levinson (1987); Levinson (1983); Brown and Yule (1983); and Halliday and Hasan (1976).

67. See, for example, Hill and Murray (2000); Scholes and Willis (1990, 1987); and Steinhauer and Friederici (2001).

68. For details, see Biber (1988); Biber, Johansson, Leech, Conrad, and Finegan (1999); Chafe (1982); Cook (2004); Ochs (1979); Poole and Field (1976); Snow (2002); Tannen (1982); and Scholes (1999).

69. See overviews of the research on fluency, for example, Kuhn and Stahl (2003); Snow, Burns, and Griffin (1998, pp. 75, 213–216, 259–262); National Reading Panel (2000, Chapter Three, pp. 5–43); and Snow (2002). See also recent collections about fluency research, for example, Wolf (2001) and Kameenui and Simmons (2001). Research related to fluency includes studies of underlying processes as well as theoretical and empirical investigations of instruction and practices that improve students' fluency, for example, Allington (1983); Allington and McGill-Franzen (2003); Biemiller and Shany (1995); Berninger, Abbott, Billingsley, and Nagy (2001); Berninger, Abbott, Brooksher, Lemos, Ogier, Zook, and Mostafapour (2000); Breznitz (1997); Chomsky (1978); Dahl (1974); Dowhower (1991); Duncan, Seymour, and Hill (2000); Bowers (1993); Carver and Hoffman (1981); Heckelman (1986); Hoffman (1987); Johnston (2000); Krashen (2001); LaBerge and Samuels (1974); McLaughlin and Allen (2002); Meyer and Felton (1999); Pressley and Wharton-McDonald (1997); Rashotte and Torgesen (1985); Reitsma (1988); Samuels (1979, 1985); Samuels, Schermer, and Reinking (1992); Schoenbach, Braunger, Greenleaf, and Litman (2003); Schreiber (1987); Stahl (2002); Stahl, Heubach, and Cramond (1997); Stanovich and Cunningham (1992); Stanovich and Stanovich (2003); Torgesen, Rashotte, and Alexander (2001); Van Bon, Boksebeld, Font Freide, and Van den Hurk (1991); Wolf, Bowers, and Biddle (2000); Wolf and Katzir-Cohen (2001); Wolf, Miller, and Donnelly (2000); Wood and Nichols (2000); and Young, Bowers, and MacKinnon (1996). About fluency as a measure of reading proficiency, see, for example, Fuchs, Fuchs, Hosp, and Jenkins (2001); and Kameenui, Simmons, Good, and Harn (2001).

70. See Cullinan (2000) for a review of independent reading.

CHAPTER THREE

Students Vary

*How Can Teachers
Address All Their Needs?*

In this chapter we introduce Frank and Sara, students whose progress toward success in literacy follows the general course of development described in Chapter Two. Their teachers have provided reasonably good instruction and enough individualized support that Frank and Sara have consistently made the yearly reading progress expected of them. We do not mean to suggest that these teachers are exemplary or universally successful; some of Frank and Sara's classmates are struggling. But these two learners are both getting what they need, in classrooms that in many ways look quite different from one another.

Frank and Sara's teachers have also confronted and overcome adherence to some of the naïve, misleading, but widely held ideas that can interfere with educational effectiveness. These myths pertain to the educational progress of second-language learners and speakers of nonstandard dialects, and to the impact of poverty on literacy development. We list several of these ideas, and the evidence that they are incorrect, after we describe the developmental trajectories for Frank and Sara. We argue that preservice education for all teachers would ideally ensure that even novice teachers understand the arguments against these ubiquitous myths.

We also introduce Rebeca and Krissy, students whose reading instruction has been less responsive to their full array of needs. Rebeca, like Frank, comes from a home where Spanish is used more than English, and Krissy, like Sara, comes from a home where economic and educational resources are limited. In Chapter

Four we present Elena and Henry, students with special needs who have not received the needed levels of adaptation to those needs in their reading instruction. We review in Chapter Four a further set of common myths and misunderstandings that could have interfered with opportunities for students such as Elena and Henry to receive appropriate opportunities to learn.

TWO STUDENTS WHO
DEVELOP AS NOVICE TEACHERS EXPECT

The portraits of Frank and Sara at three points in their school careers reflect composites of students who are progressing well in school and making adequate growth, especially in literacy. The students' report cards and standardized tests show remarkably similar patterns—they always do well and sometimes sparkle. The literacy programs their schools and teachers have selected vary. But the outcomes they are achieving are precisely what their families, their teachers, administrators, policymakers, politicians, and the students themselves like to see.

Sara and Frank live on the same block and see each other at a neighborhood extended day program, but because a school district boundary falls between their homes they attend different schools.

Frank's family speaks Spanish and English at home and in the neighborhood. In fact, his parents and grandparents call him Franco, the name he also used for himself until second grade. Though his grandparents are monolingual Spanish speakers, some of his cousins are much more proficient in English than in Spanish. Frank's parents and two older siblings read with him in Spanish as often as possible, often using church materials and student books handed down from relatives. His father has a factory job in the airline industry, and his mother works part-time at fast food restaurants—more when the father's hours are cut back.

Sara lives with her mother and older sister; her mother's family lives several hundred miles away, in a different state. Sara's mother had dropped out of high school when her older sister was born, but she subsequently studied for and received a high school Graduate Equivalency Diploma (GED), took parenting classes, and got work training through a publicly funded intervention program. Sara's mother currently works as a receptionist in a car repair agency. She plans to start on a degree at the local community college as soon as the girls can spend time without her on evenings and Saturdays.

In fourth grade, Frank's school introduces a departmentalized system: different teachers rotate through the classroom for English, Science, Social Studies, and Mathematics; for computers and PE, the students move to other rooms. Sara continues in self-contained classrooms through eighth grade, with different teachers only for music, PE, and the library—in the years when the school can afford them. In ninth grade, Frank and Sara go to the same consolidated high school with their sights on college.

In Sara's elementary school, fine-grained monthly curriculum goals and the use of mandated materials are closely monitored by the district via student test results and regular supervision of the teacher. In Frank's school, the curriculum standards are year-long goals; teachers in grade-level teams choose materials, and the K–3 teachers share two full-time coaches, one for reading and one for math. Both schools have successful family-involvement programs, with frequent and frank exchanges about students that go well beyond the one-way messages afforded by report cards.

In the high school, community involvement is the norm in competitive extracurricular events, but individual family involvement in classroom matters is not at all common. Department heads and the district curriculum supervisor arrange for materials, but most teachers here and in the earlier grades supplement them at their own expense. The department heads assign mentors for new teachers, and there had been a schoolwide professional development effort to improve literacy in all subjects. State exams and college entrance exams are important not only for the students' careers but also for the school's standing. High scores attract teachers and supplementary funds; low scores may make a school eligible for some extra funding, but they also invite state mandates that replace teacher, department, and school decisions about materials and procedures.

What do teachers know about reading instruction for Frank and Sara? First, we expect that Frank and Sara's teachers have command of the underlying disciplinary knowledge base for literacy instruction (phonology, metacognition, morphology, etymology, orthography, semantics, syntax, discourse, and pragmatics) as well as a respectable complement of teaching practices for using this knowledge. These practices include instruction in phonemic awareness, word attack and phonics, word meaning and vocabulary, comprehension and comprehension strategies, and fluency. In addition, their teachers have understood how reading instruction should be shaped by their knowledge of individual students. The teachers have the expertise to use knowledge about individual learners in their instructional practice to promote student achievement (Block, Oakar, and Hurt, 2002; Darling-Hammond and Youngs, 2002; and Ferguson, 1991).

What aspects of professional development led to teachers' abilities to use knowledge of individual learners in adapting instructional practice? There are a number of findings that speak to the importance of supporting preservice and inservice teachers in dealing with diversity in their classrooms:

- The students of teachers with strong content knowledge, who have learned to work with students who come from different cultures, tested more than one full grade level above their peers who were not assigned such teachers (Wenglinski, 2000)

- Professional development in *cultural diversity* and in *teaching students acquiring English as a second language* is linked with students' high academic performance (Haycock, 1998)

- Teachers who have high expectations of all their students hold their students to high standards, provide more instructional opportunities, and realize higher learning gains (Entwisle and Alexander, 1988).

We present instructional snapshots of Frank and Sara in kindergarten, fourth grade, and ninth grade. These snapshots reflect both the whole-class instruction and adaptations made for these children's individual needs. Their instruction was for the most part effective in content and in use of instructional strategies. We start with scenes from kindergarten. What happens in the kindergarten classrooms, though, is influenced by what the students must be prepared for as they enter first grade. Over the last three years, Frank's school has undergone a change. That makes it differ quite a bit from Sara's (see Table 3.1).

Kindergarten at Mid-Year

Sara: "I Can Read It All by Myself. Want to Hear Me?" Sara's reading group meets right after morning circle, fifteen minutes with the teacher, fifteen minutes of individual and partner work. Sara has been in this group for two weeks;

Table 3.1 Differing Expectations About Students Entering Grade One

Reading	Sara's School	Franco's School
Grasping meaning with written texts intended for primary grade students	*Text type to which students are exposed:* narratives, "how to" and informative trade books, children's literature read by adults, letters, journals, poetry, charts, and tables *Tasks in response to passages read to students:* summarize, ask and answer literal meaning questions, inferences *Vocabulary:* related to literary conventions, figures of speech, concrete and abstract terms from academic domains, and school routines	*Text type to which students are exposed:* primer stories, narratives and expository texts read aloud *Tasks in response to primer passages:* answer literal meaning questions *Tasks in response to passages read to students:* summarize, answer literal meaning questions *Vocabulary:* related to literary conventions and figures of speech; concrete terms from academic domains and school routines

Table 3.1 Differing Expectations About Students Entering Grade One, *Cont'd*

Reading	*Sara's School*	*Franco's School*
Processing to decode written language	*Phonological sensitivity and awareness:* recognize and produce rimes and alliteration, count phonemes (except consonant clusters) in single-syllable words *Grapheme-phoneme conventions (GPCs):* recognize, name, and know the sounds most commonly associated with all letters Independently recognize, with speed and accuracy, words from families with common spelling patterns Independently recognize, with speed and accuracy, some high-frequency words *Write* all letters of the alphabet, show knowledge of GPCs but few conventional spellings except for names	*Phonological awareness:* count and segment phonemes, delete phonemes in initial and final position (except consonant clusters) in single-syllable words *Grapheme-phoneme conventions (GPCs):* know names and sounds associated with letters, including vowel teams and some consonant digraphs Apply GPCs and blend to read words with simple spelling patterns in primer texts Independently recognize, with speed and accuracy, some high-frequency words *Write* all letters of the alphabet, use conventional spelling of many single-syllable words as introduced in primers
Fluency	Finger-point words as books are being read aloud Read highly predictable books after once or twice hearing them read Read short decodable books with primarily CV and CVC words after reading with assistance at least once Emergent reading of illustrated books or books about well-known topics with appropriate pragmatic and syntactic properties and the use of vocabulary and structures that are common to written language	Finger-point words as books are being read aloud Read independently with accuracy short decodable books with primarily CV and CVC words and high-frequency function words

children are regrouped about every six weeks. Today the teacher leads her group in echo reading a new easy-to-decode book. They take the word *can* and find it meaning two different things in the little book. The teacher mentions *homonym* but does not require the students to use the term. They make new sentences and explore near synonyms (*possible, be able to, may*) for the verb *can*. Sara says she is surprised that she knew it and did not know she knew it. They define the other meaning of *can* by describing its function and material form, and develop a semantic web with known and new related words (*jar, tub, pot, container,* and the teacher's favorite that the students decide is for magic, *vessel*). They paste pictures of cans on four-by-six-inch cards and label them in their best printing. Sara volunteers to put her card in the right word-family column on the bulletin board. She stops short, taking time to decide between the column under "-at" and the one headed "-an." As Sara picks, the teacher mouths "Yes," pumping her fist like an athlete. Tomorrow, Sara will teach everyone the new *-an* family word when the class, as a part of opening circle, reads each of the five word-family columns. She is ready to explain that it could be the other word *can,* and to tell when that one is used even if there are no pictures for it. (In a week, Sara will take the card for her word shoebox and use it at the writing table, in the library corner, or for games.) The teacher reminds the students that this book about the cans and the pan is the one to take home to practice with their parents tonight. They find more words in the word families they are working on this week. Then they read the book all together one more time and take turns reading it to partners.

In the afternoon, the whole class settles in for a read-aloud for science. "How frogs grow," the teacher reads, showing them the front cover with a detailed naturalistic drawing of a pond scene. She flips to the table of contents and says, "The first chapter is about tadpoles." They brainstorm about frogs and tadpoles. Sara thinks Kermit is the best frog. Her friend asks about toads, something like frogs and something different, too. Nobody is sure what a tadpole is. Sara thinks there will be frogs in the park they plan to visit tomorrow. The teacher summarizes, writing questions they think the book could answer: What are tadpoles? Are frogs and toads alike? Are frogs and toads different? Do frogs live in parks? Everybody reads the questions with her a second time.

Then the teacher shows the class another book with cartoon frogs dancing in party clothes on the cover and reads its title, "Froggy Went A-Courting." They talk about whether this book will answer their questions. A lively discussion follows about what is real and what is fun and whether fun can be real. The teacher says the book with the dancing, dressed-up frogs is fiction, and they are going to study for a whole month about the differences between fiction books and information books for science.

She puts aside the fiction, promising to read it in the library corner during quiet choice time the next day. They read their questions again, Sara getting a turn on the one about the park. Then the teacher reads the first chapter aloud, showing them the picture and text, keeping track with her fingertips, stopping for comments and questions. She prompts them to recognize when one of their questions is answered. Sara says a tadpole is just a funny-looking fish and everyone agrees, but the teacher says to wait a minute and see what the book says next. The book details the metamorphosis from tadpole to frog, and Sara's friend asks if the teacher is sure this is real. At the end of the reading, the class answers one question, using a sentence from the book ("Tadpoles are baby frogs.") and takes information from various places in the chapter to infer that frogs could live in parks. There is no information about toads, though.

The teacher puts the book and a taped reading of it in the listening center and shows them the other materials they have about ponds, frogs, and tadpoles. Maybe the other chapters or the other books will have information about toads, she says. Finally, the teacher unveils a new aquarium with a few large, swimming tadpoles. Over oohs and ahs, Sara says, "See? Just funny-looking fish." Everyone starts talking: Will they really get legs? What do they eat? When will they be frogs? The teacher pulls out a notebook and says that tomorrow they are going to start to write a new science journal about how the class tadpoles grow. But now it's time for recess. She stifles a smile as the students groan, and she promises she will let them learn more tomorrow.

Many other times during the day Sara deals with the instructional foci introduced in Chapter Two. The class has completed a phonemic awareness program that took about fifteen minutes a day in the whole group; activities in the program included sorting picture cards by first sounds (*bug, bat* in one pile and *pin* in another) and by rimes (*bat, hat* in one pile and *pig* in another), segmenting words made up of a consonant-vowel-consonant (CVC) sequence (mmm-aaa-nnn), and blending to identify words "stretched out" by the teacher. Phonemic awareness tasks continue to be practiced periodically in music class and during writing sessions. By October, most of the students have learned reliably to name all the letters, in both upper- and lowercase, and in any order; before the New Year, they can all give at least one sound for most of the letters and give a list of words that begin with each of them. They have games and worksheets for school and home that call for quick word identification for an ever-increasing list of high-frequency words (about fifty by year's end) and ones that are decodable given the phonics underlying the word families they study. They have collections of vocabulary words and methods for defining them. More of them ask and answer questions, summarize, predict, and confirm, as a part of reading and being read to. They reread books with partners, with assistance from tape recorders, from computer software, and from family members at home. They read and use calendars and daily schedules, monthly menus, charts of the day's helpers, and other information for classroom living. For favorite books, they make posters and mobiles of word networks to hang in the classroom and at home. They now write using letters, not scribbles, sometimes copying from books or word cards, sometimes estimating spelling after segmenting the word into phonemes and figuring out likely letters to use.

Frank: "It's About SpongeBob, See?" After the attendance check and a little more school business, Frank's class has a ninety-minute literacy block, starting with a forty-five-minute whole-group reading lesson. They start with a familiar fast-paced phonemic awareness game, focusing today on the long *a* (/ey/) sound. The teacher says "sail." One student selects a picture of a sailboat, repeats the word, and passes the picture to Frank. He repeats it and segments it into phonemes, with exaggerated pauses: /s/ /ey/ /l/. Frank hands the picture to the next student, who repeats the segments and then blends them back into the word *sail*. The three players bow while the teacher and class clap for them. The group does seven words altogether, three students at a time. Frank asks if they can play the "omit" game, but the teacher says it is not much fun to take vowel sounds out—and shows him by taking the /ey/ out of *tray*. They all laugh. She briefly reviews their lessons on *ay* and *ai* corresponding to the /ey/ sound and says that after their stories, they'll learn a new pattern for the /ey/ sound.

The teacher and students do a choral reading of a story (about one hundred words long) introduced earlier in the week. Sentence by sentence, subgroups read it a second time. The teacher introduces and reads a new story, making sure the students follow with their fingertips in their own books. She asks questions about the characters and events in the story and helps the students to answer by finding phrases in the story.

Finally, the teacher holds up a covered poster board. The students recognize the prop for a word hunt. The teacher uncovers the poster gradually: a picture of a cane; the word *cane;* the grapheme pattern *a_e;* a list of words (*gate, rake, vase, lake, mane, cape*). The students clap and giggle when she shows the grapheme pattern like a television game show hostess. The students repeat as she reads each word a second time. She calls on individuals to read a word as she points to it out of order. Frank, segmenting and blending from left to right, says "man" for *mane* and another student says "cap" for *cape*. Each time, the teacher goes back to the grapheme pattern on the poster and reminds the class of the long *a,* and everyone says the word correctly.

"I get it," says Frank's friend. "That little line between the *a* and the *e*? It means any old letter." The teacher is flabbergasted as the student hones in on the class's first instance of a grapheme convention that is discontinuous. She suspects that the other students will not be ready to talk about it yet. She plans to get into it more deeply only after she introduces the final *e* patterns for long *i* and long *o*.

"Right," she says, "The a and something and then an e is another pattern for /ey/. And today we are going to hunt for words with that pattern. Everybody look at the new story. Who is a hunter? Raise your hand." The word hunt continues. The teacher closes the forty-five-minute lesson by reading the new story again, as the students echo-read each sentence after her.

After the group lesson and a singing parade around the classroom, six students go to a fifteen-minute session with the teacher. Frank's small group meets at the end of the ninety-minute class-literacy block; until then, he is in the library and listening corner. The reading coach is there today. Frank's list of work says free reading, computer vocabulary, and tape reading. He finds his partner and his favorite book, which is not easily decodable. Usually Frank reads this book to his partner by telling about the pictures and a few sayings that he knows by heart; but today, he looks at the name of the cartoon hero, Sponge-Bob SquarePants, and notices that *square* fits the day's word hunt. He and his partner rush to find more words like it in the book; *are* gives them pause, so they agree to ignore it and get back to reading the book anyhow. Later, Frank and three classmates are at a computer with software that introduces new mathematics vocabulary words by morphing shapes and providing audio output: *circle, oval, square, rectangle, cube, sphere.* On the quiz part, they do pretty well but stumble on the pronunciation of *rectangle* and the meaning of *sphere.* Finally, Frank goes to one of the carrels in the listening center, reading out loud along with a tape. It is a decodable book that he has been practicing for a few times at the listening center. When the reading coach comes by, he reads the book out loud, without the tape, for her to time. She gives him another passage with the same kinds of words and times that, too. They celebrate his skill, together noting his progress on a fluency chart. The coach helps him to choose a book to check out for homework and to find the updated word lists for his family to help him with: cumulative reading and spelling word lists according to his reading group and the updated class vocabulary list.

Since September, Frank's literacy block time has been divided pretty much the same. Earlier there was more whole-group time on phonemic awareness and some individual remediation on letter recognition and production. They covered basic consonant graphemes and short-vowel patterns in the fall. Now they are on long-vowel patterns and consonant digraphs. They apply their phonics to new decodable books, but even with such controlled material, their reading is slow enough that it hinders their comprehension. Thus, the fluency work in the listening corner has increased. On different days, the other tasks in the listening and library corner include spelling practice, writing dictated sentences, creative writing with computer software, recognizing high-frequency words, learning vocabulary words from other academic subjects, and work on drawing conclusions and completing deductions for comprehension skill building. After recess and a snack, a math lesson, math small groups, and art and science projects fill out the schedule. Most days, a story is read aloud and discussed just before students go home at noon.

Grade Four at Mid-Year

Sara: "It's the New Lemony Snicket Book." Sara's earlier interest and pride in reading are overshadowed by new hobbies, chores, and worries. Occasionally a fad like Lemony Snicket intervenes. She is not the only fourth-grader going through this change. "Chill time" is part of her teacher's response: twenty minutes to read and work quietly on reading with a friend. The students choose materials and tasks with teacher advice and consent; every other week they report on what, why, or how they have been reading—a brief written paragraph, an interview with the teacher, a letter in the class newspaper, or a panel discussion on an intramural television program. Today, Sara and her friend are using *Miss Alaineus: A Vocabulary Disaster* as the basis for a talent show skit they will do at the Boys' and Girls' Club.

The teacher calls the class to order for a word-study lesson. They review their last unit on pronouncing long words by finding syllables in them, and then the class moves on to the new unit. There is a word table started on the board, with only the column of examples filled in. The teacher calls on students to fill in the next three columns, following the rules of a television quiz show about not repeating part of the word in the meaning. Sara and her friend gleefully answer for the first two rows, hinting about their skit (Table 3.2).

The teacher elicits answers for the rest of the first row, finishes the second row herself, and asks students to raise hands when they have an idea for the rest of the answers and an explanation. A lively discussion follows, and the teacher teaches some new word-study terms, *prefix* and *root*. The teacher points out that the prefix *mis-* is like a word because of the separate meaning it has, but, like a syllable, it is a part of a word at the same time. She shows them dictionary entries for *misbehave* and *misjudge,* pointing out how prefixes are indicated.

The teacher claims that prefixes make it easier to learn more words, and fourth graders have to know a lot of words, so they need all the help they can

Table 3.2. Analyzing Words into Meaningful Parts

Examples	Syllables	Words	Meaning	Meaning Parts	First-Part Meaning
Miss Alaineus	5	2	Woman's name	2	Unmarried
Miscellaneous	5	1	Mixture of things	1	0
Misjudge	2	1	Make a bad conclusion	2	Bad
Misspell	2	1	Use wrong letters	2	Wrong
Misbehave	3	1	Act opposite to good	2	Opposite

get. This week they are to learn forty-eight words with the *mis-* prefix. Before the class rebels, she reminds them of *misjudge:* when the prefix occurs with a well-known root, it is easy to learn. They will study in groups for three fifteen-minute class periods before the test next week, but everyone will have to study at home, too. The teacher passes out a sample worksheet for each student and one copy of the first part of the word list for each group (Tables 3.3 and 3.4). She advises them to start by picking out words they can figure out right away and do not need to study. She warns them to make sure everyone writes down each word; otherwise they could end up in the predicament in the book that Sara and her friend read and have their own vocabulary disaster. For words they don't know right off, they can look in the dictionary or the index or glossary of a book they have. They will get the second part of the list and a practice test they can work on the next time the groups meet. The groups begin their work.

In the afternoon, the reading is in history, a study of Native Americans before European contact. The immediate purpose for the reading is so the students can form and defend opinions about which of five groups they would find it most interesting to live in. The textbook starts them off, later to be supplemented by material from the teacher's collection and by student searches in the school library and on the Internet. Today, the teacher has the class review reading strategies they had worked on in the morning during reading period. They discuss what the teacher did to predict and confirm when she told them what she was thinking while reading a passage on careers in animal care. They pull out the guide sheet for "predict and confirm" that they had practiced using and prepare to use it again.

Table 3.3. Sample Worksheet: The Prefix *Mis-*: Opposite, Bad, Wrong, Negative

Word	Prefix	Root	Meaning
Misspell	mis	spell	Use wrong letters for a word
Misbehave	mis	behave	Act badly
Misalign	mis	align	Not line up correctly

Table 3.4. Word List, Part One: The Prefix *Mis-*

misadventure	misjudge	misappropriate	miscalculate	misreport	mislay
miscarry	misremember	misconceive	misfortune	misalign	misbehave
misgovern	misshapen	misdirect	misfire	misfit	misnomer
misinform	misguide	mishandle	mishap	mishear	misspend

The students have unit partners to read with. The teacher indicates the section of the text to work on today and reminds them to start with predictions. Then she circulates, stopping to compliment Sara and her partner for brainstorming on what they knew about Native Americans. She reminds them what they know about how to read their history book, such as skimming the passage for headings, titles for tables and charts, and bold print for technical terms. Later she tells them to pick a segment to read and then stop to check their predictions—confirm them, or change their ideas, and make new predictions for the next segment. The teacher works extensively with two of the partner groups that are having trouble getting off to a good start. Forty minutes into the lesson, she tells everyone to stop and make summary notes so they can pick up their work the next day. She reminds them what they are aiming for, to explain which group they would find most interesting to live in. She adds an invitation: anyone wanting help checking what they have so far or choosing what to read next should drop a note in the mailbox on her desk.

Ever since September in Sarah's fourth-grade class, there has been specific study of words and comprehension strategies as well as practice and application outside of reading lessons in history, science, and literature. The teacher wants to find ways to encourage more wide reading and, for some students, repeated readings to improve fluency. She is certain that the class is well prepared for eventual word study that is more complex, involving, for example, phonologically conditioned prefixes (for example, *illogical, irretrievable, impatient, inescapable*), other prefixes that express the same meaning but have a different etymology (for instance, *unthinkable*), and prefixes that have the same shapes but express different meanings (such as *import*). She is also confident that the class will soon move from a focus on separate comprehension strategies to more flexible use of a set of strategies, according to the demands of different texts.

Frank: "I Want to Show My Dad I Know How to Take Care of a Doberman." Frank does community service. For ten minutes twice a week and one period once a month, his group in English class makes tapes for people at the senior center who have trouble seeing print. Frank found a report on the Internet about caring for large dogs; he has read it over and over to get fast, error free, and able to really "sell" it. His teacher doubted seniors wanted to know about that topic, but Frank argued they should know about big dogs for protection. The teacher then confessed that her motives for sponsoring the project were not purely for the seniors' sake. She hoped practicing before final taping would help her students to become more fluent readers. She said that was called an ulterior motive. Frank admitted to an ulterior motive for choosing his topic: he hoped his father would listen to a copy of the tape and be convinced about getting a large-breed dog.

The rest of the English class is devoted to a discussion of characters in fiction. The class has read a good set of books to compare and contrast. One Harry Potter book took a few weeks: the teacher read aloud parts every few days and left other parts for students to read, sometimes in class groups, sometimes for homework. After that unit, the class formed book clubs. Two clubs, including Frank's, read *Maniac Magee* by Jerry Spinelli (1990). Frank picked that club because the book jacket mentioned baseball, but he got quite caught up in Jeffrey "Maniac" Magee's troubles, first at his aunt and uncle's house and then in the town of Two Mills. Other clubs read *The Night Journey*. Last week, the clubs led discussions to summarize the books for the people who had not read them. Today the whole-class topic is "muggles"—what it means to be one and to call somebody one. The Harry Potter books use the term to denote those who are not wizards, but the definition has some loose ends, and the general idea about muggles could be used to identify characters and groups of them in other books, too. Frank has more to say than ever before in English class—about the legends *Maniac Magee* started with and a list of events that seemed magical. He says maybe Jeffrey's weird aunt and uncle had kept secrets about Jeffrey's parents and maybe Earl Grayson was not a muggle either, but Spinelli had not written enough about those things. Other students have strong ideas, too, and the class ends with people ready to write and defend their opinions about one or two characters in the book they had read for book club. Meanwhile, the teacher says, next week they are going to talk about the theme of prejudice, so they should keep that in the back of their minds.

After recess, the science teacher is ready to start a new biology unit. The task is to make a presentation at the Arthropod Assembly. At the end of the month, all the fourth- and fifth-grade groups will present their results, explaining why they came to the conclusions that they did about arthropod groups, behaviors, structures, and habitats. They are to work on passages and specimens at their tables, but first they will work on some new key words to add to their personal science dictionaries. For the compound *arthropod,* the teacher asks about the root's meaning in *arthritis;* Frank helps to establish the focus on joints, remembering his grandfather's problems. The teacher introduces the second Greek root, *pous,* for foot, and brings in words the class has some familiarity with— *pod,* used to describe the school division into wings for different age groups, as well as *podium* and *podiatrist.* So, joint-footed is what arthropods are, the teacher says. The second key term is *exoskeleton.* Although the prefix and root look easy, she says, the specialized meaning is something to be on the lookout for and maybe look up in the big science dictionary, too.

Next, the teacher reviews semantic webs, getting students to remember they had used them to observe, read, organize, summarize, and remember science information and to figure out what they should do next in observations, experiments, and research from reading. The class has a set of design conventions for biology webs. At the teacher's prompting, the class recalls that they used black circles to indicate groups and subgroups within them. Frank offers *phylum* as an example; he has liked the term ever since he learned that the Greek root meant *tribe*. The teacher mentions that arthropod is the name of a phylum. Next they identify blue rectangles as the convention to indicate structures, and the teacher reminds them about "joint-footed"; Frank's friend says *exoskeleton* would fit there too, wouldn't it? They finish with recalling that a red oval border indicates a behavior, and a green diamond means habitat.

In addition to erasable paper and colored pencils for making the web, each table gets a box with different reading materials, some marked "homework," and different specimens, some rubber and some real for each table, including an ant colony, butterfly cocoons, hermit crabs, spiders, and beetles. The teacher circulates among the groups, hinting about writing in the phylum and the species they know the names of, helping to develop questions to guide their reading, agreeing with some students about the importance of the number of legs. She reminds them about being ready to explain what they said about their species. Frank says some fifth-graders were on his soccer team, and it would take a lot to convince them of anything fourth-graders said!

Since September, Frank's class has progressed quite a bit with decoding multisyllabic words and ones with complex orthographic patterns. In English class, they worked on word reading and on figurative language, synonyms (to replace what the teacher called "dead words" in their writing), antonyms, homonyms, idioms, and context clues and comprehension strategies for narratives and poetry. Expository reading strategies and specialized vocabulary were brought up in science, history, and geography classes. There was always a tension between finding texts easy enough to understand and to practice fluency but challenging enough to provoke practice with comprehension strategies and the learning of new vocabulary.

Mid-Year of Freshman Year in High School (Grade Nine)

Since September, Sara and Frank have adjusted to high school life with the different teachers, status, and peer groups from class to class. They take advantage of study-hall time to do as much homework as they can because they have so much they want to do outside of school time. Sara has band practice, saxophone lessons, and babysitting, to say nothing of TV shows and phoning her friends. Frank has workouts to get ready for soccer season, and he bags groceries at the supermarket, likes TV, and is interested in a few Internet chat rooms. Beyond assignments, reading is rare for either student—limited to an occasional entertainment or sports magazine or a glance through the local newspaper for comics and stories about school events, sports, entertainment events, and a few high-profile dramatic criminal cases. Reading assignments for school keep them in practice, though: a news magazine each week for social studies, lengthy novels and plays as well as shorter literature pieces in English, and required articles and chapters for other classes.

Neither Sara nor Frank lose track of what they are reading because of word recognition difficulties; they may not be sure how to pronounce a word here and there, but such problems are rare enough that their comprehension does not suffer overall. Word meaning is explicitly taught (and often tested) in all their courses; Sara finds that her foreign-language course gives her new information about English words.

Comprehension is tested, but approaches to comprehending written language are seldom taught except in the context of understanding books or chapters in content-area courses. A study-skills unit in English class did cover ways to look at section headings to locate where the information is likely to be, so that they could choose what to read more carefully in order to answer chapter-end questions or do some other specific assignment.

In literature, social studies, science, and math, coverage of written materials tends to take for granted basic comprehension and focus on how to analyze and evaluate the texts, dealing with figurative language, literary devices, technical words, and the styles of writing used in different subjects. Occasionally, in class, a chapter or passage will be highlighted to show how deliberate use of specific comprehension strategies helps to clear up the meaning. As the teacher defends or explains an analysis, the sophisticated reading processes he or she employs are made public for students to use as models (think-alouds). For Sara, as for Frank, it is a relief to find that sometimes reading is hard even for the best readers and that they are not the only ones who sometimes slow down and reread parts, while at other times they skim and skip over sections hoping they do not really miss anything important.

Frank has decided to take Spanish this year. He has pretty much stopped speaking Spanish at home, responding in English when his grandparents ask him questions, and getting his mother to translate for him when the conversation gets more complicated. He thinks the introductory class should be easy since he still understands a lot of Spanish, though he has never learned to read it. His teacher comments that his accent is very good, but she corrects him when he uses some of the expressions he is familiar with from home, and she clearly expects that his reading will be better than it is. In fact, though Frank learned how to pronounce written Spanish rather easily, he finds it remarkably hard to understand what he is reading. He relies a lot on cognates to make sense of the Spanish newspaper articles he occasionally tries to read at home, and comments to his mother that reading in Spanish is a lot like reading in biology—hard work!

In many of their classes, when students have questions about the readings, their teachers often coach them in methods for reading more deeply to repair misunderstanding or address more complex layers of meaning. Their history-class discussion of the disaster at the World Trade Center was a case in point.

Sara, Frank, and their classmates found opposing viewpoints when they wanted a clear and comforting explanation. In the news magazines and on the Internet, they would find one article showing that Al Qaeda documents made valid complaints about the West, particularly the United States. Then they would find another that showed Al Qaeda members as immune to evidence and argument that would counter irrational grudges. Their teacher helped them to confront the gaps in their background knowledge about religions and political conditions in other countries that accounted for some of their confusion. They also worked on identifying an author's point of view and evaluating how it had an impact on the statements they made. There were no simple single answers, but the problems seemed a bit more approachable.

Sara: "I Want to Do My Science Project on That DNA That's in Murder Trials."
Sara's science class is working on the latest in a series of what the teacher calls the smallest science texts ever written. Each text in the series has two opposing statements in italics, followed by numbered statements and room for the students to add others (Exhibit 3.1). Sara works with a lab partner. First, they decide if there are other kinds of evidence or explanations that they want to add to the numbered list. Next, they consider the usefulness of each numbered statement: if it is true, does it support or contradict one or both or neither of the theories in italics? Finally, they have to research whether the evidence and explanations are true and are strong enough collectively to support one theory and dismiss another. The culmination is a class discussion during which they are expected to defend one of the italicized statements, explaining why it should be believed and answering any questions the other students have. The "reading" takes three science classes in a row and some library research as homework.

By the time they finish reading this small text, Sara and her partner will have made and tested predictions; designed, performed, and interpreted an experiment; read a variety of sources (their ordinary science textbook, an encyclopedia, articles on the Internet); and consulted with their teacher. They will have developed a glossary of terms about light and vision. They will be gaining practice in evaluating and using evidence and theories to make scientifically valid explanations. Sara and her partner now are good at revising their argument as they understand a term or a theory differently or as they see the limited validity or reliability of a piece of evidence. The teacher has to challenge them regularly, though, to make explicit what makes a piece of evidence matter even if it is true. They do these kinds of lessons every six weeks. Some lessons get into critical literacy concerning science and the public interest: one piece involves claims about weight loss and another involves claims about a nuclear power plant in the state.

Sara asks her science teacher for help locating better reading material on her topic of choice: "I want to do my science project on that DNA that's always in murder trials." She had kept getting discouraged trying to read what she found

---

Exhibit 3.1. Small Science Text

Light rays are produced by a source of light and reflect off objects into our eyes so we can see them.

Light rays travel from our eyes onto the objects and enable us to see them.

1. Light travels in straight lines.

2. We can still see at night when there is no sun.

3. Sunglasses are worn to protect our eyes.

4. If there is no light we cannot see a thing.

5. You have to look at something to see it.

6. We "stare at" people, "look daggers," "catch people's eye."

7. _____

8. _____

9. _____

10. _____

Source: Adapted from Simon, Erduran, and Osborne, 2002.

---

on her own. It seemed she was looking up every other word. At the other extreme were overly simple readings that just did not get deep enough to give her any hints about a science project. The teacher says she knows what Sara is going through. She meets her in the library and shows her how to find and sample articles to see if they are readable. They end up with an article about mitochondrial DNA. Sara decides to take it, even though it isn't the kind of DNA used in trials. It seems interesting, and it might give her more background for reading other things on DNA closer to the use in criminal trials.

Frank: "It's for a Book Report. But Marco Says It's Cool." Frank's English class is working on a prize-winning poem by Hetty Hughes:

> txtin iz messin,
> mi 'headn'me englis,
> try2rite essays,
> they all come out txtis.
> gran not plsed w/letters shes getn,
> swears i wrote better
> b4 comin2uni.
> &she's african

The class buzzes when the copies of it first circulate. It is immediately recognized as text messaging, even by students who do not own mobile phones. When the teacher asks what the buzz is about, Frank says, "It's different, you know? It's like not in school." His friend backs him up, saying he is surprised that the teacher even knows about text messaging. The teacher says she worked hard to learn about it and expects to learn more from them. She hopes, she says, with a grin, that the learning will be mutual.

She explains that the class will work on the poem and on two other genres it brings up: first, there are articles from a London newspaper about the text-messaging poetry contests; they will have to find and read them for homework. She gives a Web address for them to start with (www.guardian.co.uk/online/story/0,3605,481985,00.html) but tells them to be sure to look back in time for the beginning and forward for follow-ups to the story. Second, there is a mention in the poem of a personal letter. Next week they will start working on the role of personal letters in biographies, and this will give them a head start for thinking about that genre. In the letter, the newspaper articles, and the poem, she explains, there are cultural differences and author's perspectives that they will have to take into account. She says she will start them off with a freebie: for people in England, "uni" is used in places that "college" would be used in the United States. It comes from the word *university*.

She asks them to listen to what she has learned about text messaging and to correct or add to it if they can. She says a message is limited to 160 characters including spaces; it just cuts off anything you write that goes over the limit. You have to make good word choices, and there are special spelling conventions. Capital letters are pronounced as the names of the letters are; some stand for whole words (*R, B, C, Y, U*). A student adds that you can put two together to make a word like *EZ* or *QT*. Another mentions that whole sentences have only letter name words: *RUOK? BCNU*. The teacher says that she knows there are some repeated spelling patterns. She starts them off with *8, d8,* and *l8,* and the class comes up with more examples: *gr8, l8r, 2, 2day, 2moro, wan2, sk%l, c%l*. Frank mentions that *CUl8r* is an example of combining both the letter name and the *8* pattern. Others bring up *thnQ* and *thX* but agree they aren't as cool as Frank's example. The teacher says that she read about *cub* for "call you back" and wants to know why it isn't "see you something." A chorus calls out that there aren't capital letters in cub. They add abbreviations to her list: *imho* for "in my humble opinion," and *lol* for "laughing out loud." The teacher asks them if they ever use *fyi*, and when they say yes, she says she thought that *fyi, imho,* and *lol* are not to be taken literally, that they express an attitude or tone. They agree and then turn the discussion to the real attitude markers that bypass letters. They come to the board to show the emoticons that you have to look at sideways:

:-)   Happy/Smiley

:-|| Angry

:-))   Very happy

%-)   Confused

:-&   Tongue tied

:'-(Crying

:-D   Laughing

Finally, the teacher challenges them with a reading test: "aQr8 & balNsd RTcL." Frank is among the first to read it accurately.

Then the teacher says they have twenty minutes left for groups to start on their RIFFN routine: Read it; Identify and try to resolve uncertainties; Figure out if the author was speaking for them, against them, or was irrelevant to them; Find the form—characteristics of the genre and some cool and some poor choices the author made; Notice a question or point to take away.

Tomorrow, the teacher says, they will have more group time and another task—contrasting poems, newspaper articles, and letters. She will help them find more information, too. By the end of the week, she says, they will be ready to present as a group to the class and then individually to write two essays. One essay is to persuade readers that their analysis of the poem is sound; the other is to be a description of similarities and differences among the three genres involved. The class groans, but someone says, "Next time, can we do a graphic novel?" And the teacher groans back that she has no idea what a graphic novel is, but maybe she can learn!

Frank is glad when his group gets right into the last line of the poem. He says it was a dig. He thinks that to say that line you have to believe that Africans are dumb and can't notice bad writing. Somebody else says it just means the grandmother usually spoke a different language, an African one, and even though she didn't use English a lot, she noticed the crazy spellings. Someone else says, well if the gran was African so was the author and you wouldn't make a dig at yourself. Others disagree with that altogether. Someone asks what *African* really means in London—does it mean people from Africa or is it used like *African American* is in the United States? They end the group thinking that looking up the newspaper article might help some.

Frank's English teacher tries to encourage students to read outside of class. She has several books on the list for book reports that feature protagonists that Frank could relate to. In *Buried Onions,* for instance a young man, Eddie, struggles to survive in a gang-infested barrio in Fresno. At first, Frank was lukewarm about the book: "It's for a book report. But Marco says it's cool." Fairly soon, he related strongly to Eddie's difficulty developing his uniqueness, given considerable family and peer pressure to conform.

Summary

The teachers in the snapshots presented here have managed to give both Frank and Sara what they needed to keep moving ahead in reading and other subjects. These teachers possessed sufficient content knowledge about common variations in children's language and literacy development to understand Frank's and Sara's needs, and to deploy the right instructional tools and practices to keep them on track. Frank and Sara both thrived under the "default educational practices" of their teachers. Neither of these children showed signs of falling behind, or particular difficulty with aspects of the curriculum. Nonetheless, their teachers did address their individual developmental accomplishments, interests, preferences, and profiles in designing instruction for them.

LEARNING TO ADDRESS ALL STUDENTS' LEARNING NEEDS

Frank and Sara had classmates, though, who did not progress so reliably under their teachers' and their districts' default educational practices. Some of those classmates arrived at school not speaking English, or speaking a nonstandard dialect of English, or from homes with particularly limited educational and financial resources. In some cases, the teachers felt overwhelmed by the presence of such children in their classrooms—they felt unprepared to address their particular needs or to compensate for what they saw as their deficits.

Knowledge about the full range of normal variation in language and literacy development can help teachers with all the students in their classes, not just the Franks and the Saras. Widely held and potentially harmful myths can distract practitioners from successfully meeting the individual learning needs of many of their students. Teachers are subject to the same simplifying beliefs and unsupported stereotypes that muddy the layperson's understanding of various groups of learners.

These myths constitute a major challenge to teacher educators, whose job it is to confront and undermine them. This challenge differentiates teacher education in key ways from other sorts of professional education; preparation for the professions of medicine, law, or engineering can focus primarily on the new learning that is needed, since the students are unlikely to hold robust faulty theories of healing, therapy, or design that might interfere with their practice. Faulty theories about learning and development, about cultural and social differences, and about intelligence and intellectual potential, however, abound. Such misconceptions must be countered with research-based understandings if teachers are to be prepared for the diversity of their future students. The "apprenticeship of experience," unfortunately, might well reinforce these misconceptions (see Chapter Three in Darling-Hammond, Bransford, LePage, Hammerness, and Duffy, 2005), and thus it is particularly crucial to offer preservice teachers alternative ways of understanding linguistic diversity, race, and poverty. If teacher-education programs do not directly address misleading conceptions and stereotypes about cultural and social differences, these misconceptions may constrain how teachers teach, leading to instruction that unwittingly limits some students' opportunities to learn.

There is a large research literature suggesting the difficulty of radically changing, deeply held, often covert beliefs and prejudices (see Wegner and Bargh, 1998, for a review). Just telling people that women are as competent as men, for example, or that blacks are as smart as whites, does not necessarily change their contrary views; in fact, even those who accept such views explicitly may reveal implicit doubts about their correctness (see http://implicit.harvard.edu/implicit/demo). Thus we are not suggesting that a preservice course on multicultural education will by itself eradicate myths and misconceptions from teacher candidates' minds. In fact, struggling with these misconceptions may be a career-long project for most of us.

We begin with myths and knowledge about social, linguistic, or cultural diversity, related to students who speak a language other than English in their homes, to those who speak socially stereotyped varieties of English, and to those living in poverty. These groups are highlighted because research evidence indicates that they have been relatively likely to receive inadequate literacy instruction, reflecting the influence of myths held by teachers, administrators, and members of the general public.

These students are thus disproportionately represented in the population of underachieving readers. It is critical, however, to distinguish group membership from causes of or explanations for reading difficulties. Within every demographic group there is a wide array of reading outcomes, and membership in a particular group neither ensures success nor leads inevitably to failure (West, Denton, and Germino-Hausken, 2000).

The goal of exposing these myths and misconceptions is to make certain that they do not exacerbate the educational risks to which children in lower-achieving demographic groups are subject. We do not suggest that group differences in achievement can be entirely explained by differing teacher expectations or by the failure of teachers to communicate effectively with children from some demographic groups. But these teacher factors might well compound the challenges such students face, and preservice teacher education should have as a goal eliminating those negative influences.

Widely held and potentially dangerous myths are abundant, and we certainly have not been exhaustive either in listing myths or in rebutting them in this chapter or the next. We juxtapose each myth with information based on research or, if insufficient research is available, on the convergent views of experts in the relevant fields.

Students Who Speak a Language Other Than English at Home

Students who come from homes where a language other than English is spoken contribute to the diversity of contemporary U.S. classrooms. These students bring social, linguistic, and cultural backgrounds that enrich the culture of a classroom and that often require specialized teacher knowledge. According to the 2000 U.S. census data, 6.3 million children, or 14 percent of the school-aged population, came from a home where a language other than English was spoken. Of this number, it is estimated that about half are students who would be identified as English-language learners. Fifty-three percent of these students are found in kindergarten through fourth grades. Moreover, 8 percent of all kindergartners are believed to be acquiring English as a second language (August and Hakuta, 1997). Adding to the complexity of this picture is the fact that 77 percent of students learning English as a second language are eligible for free- or reduced-cost lunch, as compared with 33 percent of their monolingual peers attending the same schools. Hence, these students are challenged not only by the language demands of school, but by the fact that their families may be struggling financially.

Second-language acquisition is a complex process in which the speaker must develop vocabulary, learn grammatical rules for sentence production and comprehension, and acquire pragmatic skills, in order to use language for cognitive tasks and interpersonal communication. Despite this complexity, the *best predictor of the success* these students will experience acquiring literacy is their *access to effective instruction*. Access to effective instruction requires teachers who understand the challenges the children are facing. Unfortunately, the overwhelming majority of elementary school teachers in the United States are women of European-American descent who speak only English. These teachers may not have an experience base to question incorrect or oversimplified claims about second-language learners. Thus they may well misunderstand the language and literacy learning of students in families who speak a language other than English. We present the myths about second-language learners in two subgroups—myths about language learning and bilingualism, and then myths about the relation of language to academic achievement.

Myths About Second-Language Learning

MYTH: Younger students acquire a second language faster, with more proficiency, than do older students.

REALITY: "Students who start learning English in English-only educational settings [in kindergarten or preschool] take longer to achieve age-appropriate levels of performance on academic tasks than do students who start in grades 2 through 6" (August and Hakuta, 1997, p. 38). This may be because older students have more highly developed cognitive skills to bring to the tasks. It may be that it is important for students to master the basic grammar of their first language to support second-language learning.

MYTH: The native language of young second-language learners is secure, and exposure to English will make them bilingual.

REALITY: Most immigrants to the United States experience "subtractive" bilingualism, in which they lose proficiency in the home language while gaining proficiency in English. Young and preliterate learners are particularly likely to lose their first language while learning a second. However, in thoughtfully designed programs (such as the prekindergarten program studied by Winsler, Diaz, Espinosa, and Rodriguez, 1999), students can learn English without losing their native language.

MYTH: Exposure to two languages can confuse a student linguistically or cognitively.

REALITY: Studies that carefully select participants, and control for confounding variables, have found bilingual persons to be superior to monolinguals "on a variety of measures of cognitive skills, in particular, metalinguistic abilities." Studies of bilingual individuals report a "positive relationship between degree of bilingualism" and cognitive skills (August and Hakuta, 1997, p. 33).

Myths About Bilingualism and School Achievement

MYTH: Students who converse well in English have adequate command of the language for school tasks.

REALITY: Academic language is different from conversational language. Face-to-face conversation is highly supported by context and is less cognitively challenging. Furthermore, it can proceed satisfactorily with a relatively small inventory of words. Academic language concerns abstract, complex ideas, often experienced with less contextual support, and uses a much wider variety of vocabulary. Experience with performing a particular task in English, rather than overall proficiency in English, predicts the ability to perform that task (in English). Hence, second-language users should be assessed in the context of completing particular school tasks (August and Hakuta, 1997).

MYTH: Students always perform better on assessments in their native language.

REALITY: It is always informative to perform assessments in a student's native language. However, it also may be the case that a student will perform better on particular—seemingly difficult—school tasks using the language of the school (August and Hakuta, 1997). This is especially likely if the student has received no schooling in the native language and if all literacy instruction has taken place in the second language.

MYTH: English-language proficiency testing is the right tool for determining placement in, progress in, and exit from language programs (for example, sheltered English, English as a second language, or bilingual education).

REALITY: English-language proficiency is a complex concept, and its assessment is still relatively underdeveloped. Most proficiency assessments measure command of grammatical structure, not the real-world demands of using language for social interaction, classroom participation, or learning from text. Young English-language learners should have "instructionally embedded assessment," in which teachers make a plan about what, when, and how to assess; collect information from observations, prompted responses, classroom products, and conversations with family; develop a portfolio; write narrative summaries; meet with family and staff; use this information to develop curriculum; then assess again to see if the learning goals have been met (August and Hakuta, 1997). Although under the provisions of No Child Left Behind wide-range English-language proficiency assessments must be developed by the states, most currently available assessments (for example, the Language Assessment Scales-Oral [LAS-O, 2000]) test only very basic proficiency; they are thus not capable of predicting performance on academic tasks.

MYTH: Achievement testing will help determine skills in specific subject-area knowledge.

REALITY: There are several potential problems affecting the reliability and validity of formal testing for English-language learners, leading to underestimates of their aptitude:

- Norming bias—minorities constitute a small proportion of the population with whom the assessment was normed and are likely underrepresented in the sample.

- Content bias—the content and testing procedures reflect the language, norms, and knowledge of the dominant culture.

- Linguistic and cultural bias—adverse factors such as speed—rather than power—assessment and the exclusive use of English vocabulary delimit optimal performance for linguistically and culturally diverse learners (August and Hakuta, 1997).

MYTH: If students do not have sufficient command of English, they should be exempt from formal, statewide assessments.

REALITY: If English-language learners are not tested to determine how they compare with other students, they may not be eligible for federal assistance (Title I) (August and Hakuta, 1997) and their needs may well be underemphasized by school administrators and policymakers. According to an Office of Policy and Planning report (1995), 36 percent of first-grade and 45 percent of third-grade English-language learners were not given achievement tests in English; 27 percent of all English-language learners were not given any achievement test.

Successful Instruction with Students Learning English as a Second Language

What do we know with some confidence about successful instruction with students learning English as a second language? We know that there are school-level variables that are important predictors of these students' success. For example, when the school culture values the linguistic and cultural backgrounds of English-language learners, encourages the enhancement of native-language skills, and communicates high expectations for academic achievement in English, this augurs well for students.

We know that a single label often refers to students who are very different from each other in their English-language proficiencies (see Darling-Hammond, Bransford, LePage, Hammerness, and Duffy, 2005, Chapter Four, for more detail). For example, English-language learners may be newly arrived students who have very little knowledge of English. These students are described in Table 3.5 as Incipient Bilinguals. The term *English-language learner* may also be used to refer to intermediate learners of English who can comprehend quite a bit of English but who are limited in their production of the language. The characteristics of these students are described in this table as Ascendant Bilinguals. The term *English-language learner* is also used to refer to fluent-functional bilinguals who are not identical to native speakers but who are, strictly speaking, beyond the "learner" stage. These individuals, described as Fully Functional Bilinguals, will, like monolingual English-speaking students, continue to develop English, but they have already acquired high levels of proficiency in the language. There are other groups of language learners not easily accommodated in the table. Frank arrived at school already dominant in English, but still showing some influence from Spanish in his English; in high school, when he started studying Spanish formally, he might be described as a "recovering bilingual," though he will probably remain stronger in English than in Spanish skills.

We know that students fare better if the transition from reading in one language to reading in another is a gradual, carefully planned transition that is supported by activities designed to ensure success mastering complex concepts. Consider the demands on the student attempting to learn to read in a language

Table 3.5. English-Language Characteristics of Students Known as English-Language Learners

Incipient Bilinguals	Ascendant Bilinguals	Fully Functional Bilinguals
Comprehend very little oral English.	Generally, comprehend oral English well. May have problems understanding teacher explanations on unknown topics.	Are native-like in their comprehension of oral English.
Comprehend very little written English.	May have trouble comprehending written English in textbooks as well as other materials. Have limitations in academic and technical vocabulary.	When well-prepared, have no problems in comprehending most written English materials. When at-risk (like at-risk monolingual English speakers) and having trouble reading, have reading problems and not language problems.
Produce very little oral English.	Produce English influenced by their first language. May sometimes be difficult to understand. May have trouble expressing opinions, explaining statements, or challenging others.	Produce oral English effortlessly. Can carry out presentations and work effectively in groups. Can challenge, contradict, explain, and so on. Traces of first language may be detected in their accent or word choice.
Produce very little written English.	May produce writing that contains many "errors" that make it difficult for teachers to focus on their ideas. May take longer to complete written assignments and tests.	Depending on previous experience with writing, may produce writing that contains errors typical of monolingual basic readers. Disfluencies reflecting first-language influence may still be present.

Source: Darling-Hammond, Bransford, LePage, Hammerness, and Duffy, 2005, Chapter Four.

other than his or her home language. As the preceding chapters attest (see also Snow, Burns, and Griffin, 1998), students being taught to use the alphabetic code without the language skills to understand and appreciate how the alphabetic code represents meaningful messages are much more likely to fail. Students learning to read in their first language bring to this task a wealth of resources: a well-developed capacity to hear phonological distinctions, phonological awareness derived from exposure to rhymes and song, knowledge of letter shapes and names, the experience of "reading" environmental print, several thousand vocabulary words, and control over the grammatical and discourse rules of the language. These resources position the child to learn how letters represent sounds, to expect meaning from texts, to use context to support the decoding of irregular or complex words, and to bring syntactic and pragmatic linguistic understandings to their reading. Children receiving initial reading instruction in English before they have learned to speak English must operate without most of these resources. For these reasons, the evidence to date suggests that English-language learners have better literacy outcomes in English if they have received bilingual rather than English-only educational programs (Willig, 1985; Thomas and Collier, 2002).

Furthermore, there is evidence that end-of-second-grade Spanish literacy skills (that is, phonemic awareness, letter identification, word recognition, and fluency in letter and word identification) of Spanish-speaking students who have been taught to read only in Spanish predict their performance on the same skills assessed in English at the end of third grade (Greene, 1997). These data support the use of initial native-language instruction in teaching students to read. It is important that teachers understand why initial literacy instruction in the native language is preferable, but also, since teachers often have no control over how students are placed in programs, they need to know how to address the heightened instructional needs of students learning to read in a language they do not yet speak well.

Fortunately, professional groups such as the International Reading Association (IRA) are now active in making policy statements regarding literacy instruction for second-language learners. For example, the IRA published a policy resolution in 1998 that it summarizes as follows:

> The International Reading Association urges that initial literacy instruction be provided in a child's native language whenever possible.
>
> Research in the field of bilingual education and literacy leads to the conclusion that while initial literacy instruction in a second language can be successful, it carries with it a higher risk of reading problems than does beginning with a child's first language. Further, it may compound risks such as those associated with poverty, low levels of parental education, or poor schooling.

The Association believes that policies on initial instruction should support the professional judgment of the teachers and administrators responsible for teaching students whose first language is not English and opposes any restrictive federal, state, or local initiatives. [www.reading.org/resources/issues/positions_second_language.html]

Students Who Did Not Receive Appropriate Instruction in the Early Grades

Consider Rebeca. Rebeca is a nine-year-old girl of South American descent who was born in the United States. She lives with her parents, who use Spanish almost exclusively although they can speak some English, and with her grandparents, who are monolingual Spanish speakers. Rebeca has been able to communicate with her parents and grandparents in their native language, but in the last year she has begun to find it frustrating that she doesn't have the Spanish words to talk about what she is learning in school. While her English-receptive vocabulary is close to age- and grade-appropriate, Rebeca's oral-language production and writing are several years below what would be expected. Rebeca's oral reading is distinguished by the failure to use lexical information in figuring out correct pronunciations (for instance, reading *coming* as if it rhymed with *homing,* or *dictionary* as *dick-tee-on-airy*), a tendency to omit whole words, and a lack of expression. Her comprehension is considerably below grade level.

Contrary to what is known about best instruction and strongly influenced by the myth that younger students learn new languages easily, Rebeca was placed in an all-English kindergarten, even though she knew almost no English at school entry. Though she received some extra supports in English-language learning in first and second grade, her reading instruction was neither adapted to her still-limited oral English skills nor presented at the higher level of intensity needed for her to learn the English phonological distinctions, vocabulary, and literacy-related academic vocabulary that her classmates had already mastered.

Rebeca's third-grade teacher is struggling to become knowledgeable about whether Rebeca's current limited oral language reflects her earlier experiences in learning English or the language models that she hears in her home and community. She recognizes that Rebeca still needs help with word reading—practice in reading and understanding frequently occurring morphemes such as *-tion, -ily, -ate,* and *-ize,* practice in recognizing the relationship of derived words to their roots (*coming* and *come, happily* and *happy, information* and *inform*). If Rebeca's teacher knew Spanish, she could help Rebeca see when knowledge from Spanish might help her with English, in understanding cognates, and in recognizing shared morphological patterns. Unfortunately, she doesn't, and it never occurs to Rebeca that her Spanish might be a resource in English reading. Rebeca's teacher tries to think about the ways in which Rebeca's uses of reading outside of the school context (for example, looking at picture books with her younger siblings) could be used to support in-school reading. She needs to identify ways in which she can use Rebeca's experiences and aspirations to help her make connections with school literacy, and she needs to be knowledgeable about ways she can immerse Rebeca in print-rich environments and use meaningful literature and texts to advance Rebeca's awareness of the purposes of reading and writing and her activity as a reader and writer. She needs to identify curriculum-based assessments (see Chapter Five) that will help her define skills and strategies that need to be addressed.

Rebeca and Frank (presented earlier) are two students of the many at different stages of bilingualism (Rebeca learning English and Frank losing, then regaining, Spanish) who need to be taught to read in U.S. classrooms. These students might be new immigrants to the United States with little English, or fairly advanced in oral English but still struggling with literacy. Some of these students might also have language or learning disabilities, disabilities which tend to be underidentified among English-language learners (Donovan and Cross, 2002; see Chapter Four for a discussion of teaching children with special needs). The ubiquity of children like these argues for the universal preparation of teachers for effective functioning in classrooms that include second-language learners. While no single approach to preparing teachers for these challenges can be recommended, steps to ensure they understand the realities and not the myths about second-language learning represent a beginning. Requiring that all teacher candidates have at least four years of study of a foreign language, or proficiency in a language other than English, would also increase the level of sensitivity to the needs of ELLs.

Dialect Variations of Academic American English

Because the United States is a country of immigrants, varieties of American English reflect features of the language spoken by those immigrants—specific characteristics of the English brought to the continent by immigrants from England and Ireland, as well as traces of other home languages. For example, some persons living in New York City have a dialect that shows influences from Yiddish; Cajun English dialect has influences from French. Aspects of these dialects are incorporated in the regional variation of English spoken by persons who are English-language speakers from birth and who have never even been exposed to the language that lent its particular pronunciations or grammatical structures to the variety. These dialects carry with them indicators of perceived status. Varieties of American English that have high status, in both the media and the academy, are typically not strongly regionally marked, though recent U.S. presidents have been identifiable as New England and southern speakers, respectively. There are many American dialects that are widely disdained or associated with low status and low intelligence outside their own communities: southern American dialects in general, including Cajun English and Appalachian English, the Spanish-influenced English of Miami, and African American English.

Knowledge about these language varieties and their origins can help teachers make specific instructional decisions (for instance, understanding that when southern dialect speakers spell *pen* as *pin* they have simply neutralized this distinction before nasals, not that they cannot hear the difference between short *i* and short *e*). In addition, though, teachers who understand that no language variety is inherently less complex or less sophisticated than any other are less likely to make global judgments about or to hold lower expectations for speakers of regional, social, or ethnic dialects.

In the following section we present more detail on students who speak African American English (AAE). We use AAE as an example of the sorts of things that should be understood about any socially stereotyped dialect for two reasons. First, because among the dialects often judged as "bad English," it has been studied the most. Second, widely held myths about AAE may be related to the high risk of poor reading outcomes experienced by African American students educated in urban schools. Between 1971 and 1988, African American students improved on national assessments of achievement faster than did their white peers; however, this positive trajectory—which has been attributed to the socioeconomic and educational gains spurred by the civil rights movement—has not been sustained over time. Current explanations for the "achievement gap" abound and include factors specific to the contexts in which African American students are educated, as well as factors such as the use of AAE.

Research on the relationship between use of African American English and reading has mostly been conducted with low-socioeconomic-status (SES) students, who typically have more African American English features in their speech than do higher-SES African Americans; hence, low SES and use of African American English are confounded in the research to date (Washington and Craig, 1998). There are a number of myths that surround African American English. The following list is a sampling of these. As with the myths about second-language speakers, we divide these into myths related to the dialect itself, and myths relating the dialect to reading achievement.

Myths About African American English

MYTH: African American English is unique in its status as a nonstandard dialect.

REALITY: Speakers of English all over the world display considerable dialectical variation, and in the United States there are regional dialects as well as English dialects spoken by various immigrant groups, such as Caribbean English, Indian English, Singapore English, and so on. Some of these dialects vary from standard American English as much as or more than does African American English, and of course American academic English differs from standard British English in many ways as well. Speaking American academic English, standard Indian English, or another national standard form is a generally accepted goal because these varieties have come to be associated with high socioeconomic status and high educational achievement within their various countries, not because they differ less from British English than AAE or other socially disparaged dialects do.

MYTH: AAE is a deficient form of speech that oversimplifies standard American English.

REALITY: AAE is a systematic, rule-governed variation of American academic English that is rich in both form and content. In some ways, AAE is more complicated than American academic English; for example, it marks some verb aspect distinctions (inherent versus occasional) that American academic English ignores. Other features of AAE that make it appear "backward" to American academic English speakers, such as copula deletion (he my daddy) or double-marking of negatives, are shared with the standard dialect of many languages, for example, standard Hebrew and standard French respectively. Thus, while AAE is a form of language that can bring its speakers social disadvantage, it certainly is not a deficient language.

MYTH: The use of nonstandard forms is inconsistent with use of standard forms.

REALITY: AAE speakers are often described as bidialectical—capable of switching from African American to American academic English according to the situation or the interlocutor. Bidialecticalism, when it is thought of as like bilingualism, is a useful oversimplification. In fact, use of each of the many features that differentiate any two varieties is probabilistic. Under intimate or informal circumstances, an AAE speaker might use most of those features most of the time, and under more formal circumstances only a few of them infrequently. But none of them is likely to be used all the time, no matter how intimate or informal the situation. So being "bidialectical" is not like being bilingual. Bilinguals really can (though they don't always) speak in either of their languages, and there is not typically a continuum from, say, "all-Spanish" to "all-English" with all points in the middle represented. But the continuum from "very African American" to "very academic American" English does exist, and speakers move along that continuum freely under the influence of situation, topic, interlocutors, and decisions about self-presentation.

Because AAE speakers use AAE in informal, intimate, in-group settings, but shift toward more frequent use of more standard forms in formal settings or when speaking to American academic English speakers, the teacher need not try to stamp out AAE features. Rather, bringing learners' attention to AAE forms and to alternative ways academic English speakers express the same ideas can help students learn to speak appropriately in a wide variety of settings.

MYTH: AAE speakers are just like second-language learners of English.

REALITY: Certainly it is valid to think of AAE speakers as like Spanish or Chinese speakers, in that all have an intact language system. But AAE is, in fact, a form of English, and AAE speakers can by and large understand American academic English speakers. Thus, it is less clear, particularly to young students, why they should change the way they talk, or why American academic English speakers might profess to have so much trouble understanding them.

Myths About AAE and Reading

MYTH: Phonological features of AAE contribute to students' difficulty with learning sound-symbol correspondence.

REALITY: Students' ability to learn sound-symbol correspondence is not predicted by their use of AAE phonological variations (Goodman and Goodman, 2000). Since phonological awareness is a metalinguistic skill, it is unlikely to be affected by the motor patterning of pronunciation of AAE speech. Supporting this claim is the finding that pronunciation of other U.S. regional dialects has not been associated with reading problems.

MYTH: Students need to acquire standard English before they can profit from reading instruction.

REALITY: There is no evidence that students must have access to standard English in order for literacy instruction to be successful. Good teachers use literacy instruction to help teach students how their own language forms differ from the academic standard, rather than assuming a unidirectional relationship between language and literacy.

MYTH: The use of AAE interferes with reading comprehension and fluency.

REALITY: While the morphological and syntactic features of a student's language appear to influence achievement of reading proficiency, this process is not well understood. Some studies have shown greater use of AAE syntax and morphology to be associated with poorer oral reading and comprehension of verbs in American academic English, but other studies have found no cause-and-effect relationship linking dialect use to reading proficiency. These mixed results may reflect the variability among AAE speakers; nonstandard dialect speakers do not show less variability in language use than do standard dialect speakers. Some have hypothesized that it is not the dialect but the teacher's rejection of it that interferes with the process of learning to read (see Banaji and Bhaskar, 2000; Blake and Cutler, 2003; Greenwald and Banaji, 1995; and Greenwald, McGhee, and Schwartz, 1998). Bolstering this hypothesis is Cunningham's (1976/1977) finding that teachers correct dialectical miscues more frequently than nondialectical miscues (78 percent of dialectical versus 27 percent of nondialectical miscues corrected).

In contrast to this rather mixed picture for reading, considerable evidence suggests that quality of writing can be associated with use of AAE features. Rhetorical structures common to African American oral discourse are preferred by some African American high school students and are correlated with high-quality writing in classroom research (Ball, 1992; 1995) and in reanalyses of the National Assessment of Educational Progress writing-assessment data (Smitherman, 1994). These findings have led to successful writing interventions using prompts that promoted the use of AAE discourse features, such as pictures of routine events from African American life (Lee, 1995a). In related work, Lee (2001) has successfully taught struggling adolescent readers metacognitive reasoning strategies to help them understand symbolism, irony, satire, and other nonliteral language forms in literature, by using rhetorical features of AAE as a bridge to literary tropes. Key in the effective teaching of African American students is to see their language as a resource and not an obstacle (Strickland, 1998).

Many questions about AAE remain: What is the full set of specific AAE features? How do those features develop? How does control over dialect variation develop? What do teachers need to know about AAE to determine which students are or are not on track? What are the implications of this emergent knowledge base regarding use of AAE and reading development?

Teachers need to be mindful that correcting oral AAE features may discourage AAE speakers from participating in class discussion, that counting AAE productions during reading as miscues underestimates African American students' reading ability, and features of American academic English needed for comprehension can be explicitly taught. Furthermore, they need to consider the ways in which reading tasks and assessments may be a disadvantage to speakers of AAE. For example, read-aloud tasks that require translating written academic English into AAE oral forms may be more difficult for these students than silent reading tasks. Nonetheless, there is now considerable information available about the nature of African American English (Mufwene, Rickford, Bailey, and Baugh, 1998) and about the language development of African American English-speaking children (for example, Craig and Washington, 1994; Seymour and Roeper, 1999), and tests have been developed to help distinguish normally developing AAE speakers from those with language disabilities (Seymour, Roeper, de Villiers, and de Villiers, 2003; see also www.umass.edu/aae; and Washington, 1996).

Students Living in Poverty

In the sections on English-language learners and dialect, we refer to the central role that poverty plays in these students' access to effective instruction. In many situations the impacts of language and poverty are impossible to disentangle. Quality of education is a significant factor that is related to poverty. Measures of poverty based on individual family socioeconomic status do not predict quality of education or student outcomes as strongly as measures of concentration of poverty within a particular school or community (Snow, Burns, and Griffin, 1998).

Research on students living in poverty has consistently shown that SES predicts cognitive and academic outcomes (Hess and Holloway, 1984; White, 1982; and Pungello, Kupersmidt, Burchinal, and Patterson, 1996). Although reliable, the relationship between poverty and reading achievement is more complex than is generally realized. One example of this complexity is found in the research findings of Alexander and Entwisle (1996), who showed that low-SES students progress at identical rates as middle- and high-SES classmates during the school year, but they lose ground during the summer.

SES includes household income and parents' education and occupation, and is often estimated by whether a student qualifies for federal lunch subsidies. Families rated as living in poverty are not only less affluent but tend to receive less adequate nutrition and health services, including prenatal and pediatric care, and are exposed to a broad array of conditions that may be detrimental to the health, safety, and development of young students (for instance, lead paint or cockroach infestations raising the risk of asthma). In 2000, 16 percent of American students were living in poverty (below $13,861 for a family of three; U.S. Census, 2000). As noted earlier, there is considerable overlap between groups of students living in poverty and the two groups of learners previously discussed, students who have a home language other than English and those speaking AAE.

Myths and realities related to the impact of poverty that are important for examination in preservice education and professional development for teachers are presented below.

MYTH: Poverty is a characteristic of an individual family.

REALITY: Poverty is a family variable to the extent that, among students attending the same schools, youngsters from low-income-status families are more likely to underachieve than are those from high-income-status families. Poverty is also a *group risk factor.* Students from low-income communities are more likely to become underachievers than are students from more affluent communities in part because the former are more likely to attend substandard schools. The correlation between poverty and low achievement is mediated by differences in the quality of school experiences (Bryk and Raudenbush, 2002; White, 1982).

MYTH: Reading achievement is similarly affected for all students living in poverty.

REALITY: Students are more likely to underachieve in reading based on the status of a school or a community or a district, not the status of their families. A student from a low-income family attending a generally moderate or upper-economic-status school is far less at risk than he or she would be in a whole school or community of low-economic-status students.

MYTH: Home literacy environment is the most important family factor influencing reading achievement.

REALITY: The quantity and quality of verbal interaction in families relates to student vocabulary scores (Hart and Risley, 1995; Weizman and Snow, 2001), which in turn are highly related to literacy outcomes. Findings relating home-literacy environments to outcomes are mixed (Walberg and Tsai, 1984). Home environment may influence outcomes differently at different ages, however. In particular, the opportunities provided in the home for literacy acquisition during the preschool years may contribute primarily to the student's acquisition of attitudes toward literacy, of knowledge about the purpose and mechanics of reading, and of skills (such as vocabulary growth and letter knowledge) that may facilitate learning when school instruction begins. Once the student has begun to attend school and has started to learn to read, the contributions of home and parents may be somewhat different; assistance with homework, listening to the student's efforts at reading aloud, the availability of resources such as a dictionary and an encyclopedia, and so forth may be particularly important for fostering high achievement in school.

MYTH: Students who enter kindergarten with weak language and literacy skills will be poor readers.

REALITY: While language and literacy skills at kindergarten entry are associated with later literacy achievements (Snow, Burns, and Griffin, 1998), these relationships are probabilistic, not deterministic. Misleading conclusions can be reached if risk factors are interpreted as controlling destiny. It must always be borne in mind that many students whose language and literacy skills are weak at the outset of schooling can become successful readers, especially if they have access to intensive and high-quality instruction.

MYTH: All schools in neighborhoods of poverty are ineffective, with students underachieving in reading.

REALITY: There are effective schools in poor neighborhoods—the so-called "beat the odds" schools (Taylor, Pearson, Clark, and Walpole, 2000). These schools are likely to have the following characteristics (Langer, 1998; Stringfield, 1994; and Venezky and Winfield, 1979):

- High demands are made of students, reflecting high expectations for their achievement.

- Students are organized and goal-oriented, knowing *why* they are being asked to do a task, how the task builds on prior schoolwork, and how it might be expected to lay a foundation for future work.

- Teachers provide well-paced instruction and optimize opportunities for interaction with students.

- The school schedules maximize use of time for academic tasks.

- Resources such as the library are used effectively.

- Professional development is provided for teachers.

- Principals are involved with the teachers and in their professional development.

- The schools are given public recognition for their success.

Example of a Student Who Lives and Attends School in a Community of Poverty

Krissy, age eight, comes from a poor rural family. She lives in a community predominantly made up of other families living in poverty and attends third grade in an elementary school characterized by chronic underachievement. Though she has been in this school for two years, her family moves quite often, and since kindergarten she has attended four different elementary schools. There are additional familial stresses in her home. In school she is disruptive in class, has difficulty making and retaining friends, and has been known to steal other children's lunches and property. Her academic achievement profile is quite scattered; she has a few areas of significant strength (like mathematical problem solving), but her reading and writing are at end-of-first-grade level, and her contributions to class discussions are often hard to follow. Krissy's teacher has the challenge of addressing Krissy's educational needs with the limited resources available to her at her school. What does this teacher need to know in order to move Krissy to grade level in reading?

First, some command of the underlying knowledge base for literacy instruction described in Chapter Two (phonology, metacognition, morphology, etymology, orthography, semantics, syntax, and pragmatics and discourse) helped Krissy's teacher analyze her domains of weakness. Noting Krissy's problems with oral expression, the teacher seized an opportunity to read to her an Amelia Bedelia story (Parish, 1979) that other children had enjoyed reading themselves and to ask some comprehension questions; she discovered that Krissy didn't know the meanings of many of the words in the book, and thus didn't understand any of the jokes. She also noted that Krissy was completely accurate in letter-sound mapping for word beginnings, but seemed not to attend to the ends of words and often just gave up on trying to pronounce longer words. So the teacher decided to teach her explicitly about "finding little words in big ones," using cards with *in, for, at, able, to,* and other such "easy words" (all, in fact, function words or affixes) printed on them, and a list of longer reading and vocabulary words to work on, such as *information, indefatigable,* and *strategy.* She also designed some word sorts that would force Krissy to attend to word endings, for example, *street, straw, straight, strand, strange, strap, straddle, straggle, strategy, struggle, scrap, scrape, scratch, scrawny, screech, scream, screen, screw, script, scroll, scrub, scrabble, scramble, scribble.* She thought that perhaps these words would serve to expand Krissy's vocabulary as well as her reading accuracy. She was mostly worried about Krissy's comprehension, but decided to focus on teaching her comprehension strategies during read-alouds, since Krissy wasn't yet able to read texts of any complexity with sufficient accuracy or fluency. Mostly, the teacher wished she had someone to help her decide whether these teaching approaches were the most promising ones, and to help her test whether they were working (see Chapter Five).

Attending to Krissy's needs was hard in a classroom with twenty-one other students, many of whom also needed well-structured literacy instruction with a high degree of explicitness, predictability, and clarity regarding expectations. Many of the other students, like Krissy, seemed weak in vocabulary and in the background knowledge presupposed in the social studies and science curriculum; remembering that these children were fully capable of learning, and that they needed alternative ways to learn about the world while they were becoming fluent readers, was a constant struggle for Krissy's teacher, especially since some of her colleagues seemed more inclined to assume that the children were all unmotivated and limited in capacity.

CONCLUSION

All teachers require the knowledge and skills of Krissy's teacher, and of Rebeca's and Frank's and Sara's. With these they can meet the literacy needs of all the students in their classes, as children like Krissy, Rebeca, Frank, and Sara populate classrooms all over the United States.

A particularly helpful resource for educators seeking support for their work with diverse learners is the array of professional organizations that have provided standards for various subsets of learners. These organizations have also published statements about the knowledge and skills teachers need to provide effective instruction for students living in poverty, for those who are English-language learners, or for those from varying cultural backgrounds. Across professional organizations, there is a shared interest in ensuring that diverse learners have access to rigorous curriculum content and are held accountable to high educational standards.

The responsibility of preservice and induction programs is to ensure that the teacher in every classroom has a store of well-integrated declarative knowledge about language and literacy, knowledge sufficient to help them question and reject popular myths and misconceptions about second-language learners, about speakers of nonstandard dialects, and about children growing up in poverty. Connecting that declarative knowledge to well-chosen teaching practices and classroom procedures can optimize the literacy outcomes of every student.

CHAPTER FOUR

Students
Encounter Difficulties

When Teachers
Need Specialized Knowledge

One student in ten in American classrooms qualifies for special education (McDonnell, McLaughlin, and Morison, 1997). Such students may face developmental challenges that go beyond the knowledge base of the average, even the experienced, classroom teacher. Some disabilities that make learning to read difficult—impairments of vision and of hearing, various forms of mental retardation, or severe language disabilities, for example—are relatively rare, and teachers might well need consultation with specialists to deal with these students effectively. Some more frequently occurring diagnoses, such as specific language disability or dyslexia, are much less specific than their names suggest; both these categories include students with a wide array of actual impediments to learning to read. Here again, any teacher might well benefit from the opportunity to work with a reading specialist or a speech-language practitioner in addressing the needs of such students. Nonetheless, all these students, including those with Individual Educational Plans (IEPs), those using assistive technological devices, and those qualified for special services, will probably receive most of their reading instruction in the mainstream classroom, so every teacher does need some basic knowledge about their special needs as well as about the needs they share with all students—for well-designed and well-adapted reading instruction.

It is important to note that the rate at which children were identified as disabled in households at or below poverty increased from 1983 to 1996, while during the same time period the disability rate remained relatively flat for households above the poverty line (Fujiura and Yamaki, 2000). In 1986, 68 percent of students with disabilities lived in families with incomes below $25,000 (Black, Wagner, Cameto, Hebbeler, and Newman, 1993). Thus, some students may be subject to multiple sources of risk; it is especially challenging for teachers to maintain high expectations under such circumstances, but not less important.

There are a number of findings that speak to the importance of increasing preservice and inservice teachers' capacities to deal with disabilities:

- Teachers report that they are prepared to teach the average student but not those with special needs (Lewis, Parsad, Carey, Bartfai, Farris, and Smerdon, 1999).

- Students in classes where teachers have acquired strong content knowledge as well as knowledge about working with students who have special needs performed more than one full grade level above their peers who were not assigned such teachers (Wenglinski, 2000).

- Professional development in *teaching students with special needs* is linked with high student academic performance (Haycock, 1998).

- Literacy skills are particularly important for students with moderate to severe disabilities (for example, to effectively use augmentative communication systems) (Schloss, Alexander, Hornig, Parker, and Wright, 1993), and these students are typically underachievers in the area of literacy (Katims, 2000).

- Many children are being identified as having a learning disability (with the primary problem being identified as a reading disability), where problems could have been avoided with effective early intervention (U.S. Department of Education Office of Special Education and Rehabilitative Services, 2002).

While the preceding paragraphs have cited empirical warrants for attention to students with special needs in teacher education, there are also face-valid warrants that derive from a description of the kinds of challenges teachers typically confront in contemporary classrooms. The following vignettes of two learners have been constructed to illustrate some of these challenges. Each suggests the knowledge a teacher would have to have in order to deal effectively with the full range of learners.

Henry. Henry was adopted at eighteen months and came to this country malnourished and with significant delays in his physical and cognitive development. He is now ten years of age, is in third grade, and is being treated, medically and behaviorally, for attention deficit disorder. Cognitive evaluations indicate that he is performing at or below the 20th percentile on virtually every measure used to determine how he processes information, although it is almost certainly the case that his poor expressive language skills, coupled with his distractibility, may be masking his full potential. He demonstrates fairly well-developed decoding skills; however, given a retelling task, he is unable to recall a single detail, even after reading a short story twice, and his challenges with short-term memory and visual discrimination make it difficult for Henry to recall sight words. Furthermore, the challenges he has with fine-motor skills render handwriting extremely demanding, and frustrating. While he can be very inattentive at times, when given concrete instructions he can also be very focused on the task at hand. In out-of-school contexts, Henry displays a keen memory for routines and places, a great sense of curiosity about how things work, and an uncanny ability to disassemble and reassemble objects.

Henry receives but three thirty-minute sessions a week with a special educator, who is addressing his academic and fine-motor-coordination skills, and two thirty-minute sessions a week with a speech and language clinician who is addressing Henry's articulation and pragmatic use of language. For the remainder of the schoolweek, Henry is the responsibility of the classroom teacher. This teacher is challenged to guard against having lower expectations of Henry than are warranted and to plan instruction that will keep him engaged and on-task, advance his receptive and expressive language skills, parlay his decoding skills into the meaningful use of reading and writing, and recognize how she can use the interests and abilities he has demonstrated to develop a positive sense of himself as a learner.

Elena. Elena is a nine-year-old third-grader from a moderately affluent suburb of a major metropolitan area. In her preschool years she was identified as having a speech/language delay and has received services for this delay ever since. During this time she progressed from largely unintelligible to mostly intelligible speech. Elena has average cognitive abilities with strengths in performance tasks rather than in verbal ones. Although she has received explicit phonics instruction through her classwork in first and second grade and extra support of the school reading specialist, her reading is not fluent and continues to show difficulties in certain areas of phonological awareness (particularly in phoneme deletion; for instance, she is not able to hear a word, say it, and say it again deleting either a syllable or phoneme). Though instructional emphasis has been placed on diphthongs (such as /ou/, /oi/), she seems unable to manipulate diphthong phonemes when tested using individual words and sentences that include them.

Elena's teacher is struggling to plan effective instruction for Elena. Elena spends an hour a week at school with the speech therapist and works with the reading specialist in class five times a week for thirty minutes. For the remainder of the schoolweek, Elena is the responsibility of the classroom teacher. Currently she refuses to read aloud in class and her writing is sparse. Although Elena has a basic grasp of the sound-spelling system, she often cannot apply what she has learned to read connected text. Her spelling seems based on rote memorization of words, and when using this strategy she performs well on spelling tests. Across content areas there is a gap between what she understands and how she writes reports about that information. Her teacher seems confident that Elena will learn further aspects of phonics with her instruction and that of the school specialists. The teacher is challenged to plan instruction that will help Elena apply phonics rules while reading connected text, writing, and spelling.

STUDENTS WHO QUALIFY
FOR SPECIAL EDUCATION SERVICES

Reauthorization of the Individuals with Disabilities Education Act (IDEA) and increased inclusion of students with disabilities in general-education classrooms make it increasingly necessary for general-education teachers to understand how to teach special populations. For example, between 1997 and 1999, 88 percent of children with speech and language difficulties were being served primarily in general-education classrooms (Nathanson, 2001). Not only do fully prepared teachers have in-depth knowledge of subject matter and how to teach it effectively, but they know how to diagnose learning problems, individualize instruction, and provide effective early intervention, thereby avoiding inappropriate referral, unnecessary testing, and misclassification in special education (Council for Exceptional Children's 2002 response to the President's Commission on Excellence in Special Education report, 2002). Such preparation can have a dramatic effect on all students' achievement. Students whose teachers have been prepared to work with special populations outperform their peers by more than one grade level (Wenglinsky, 2000). However, a recent survey conducted by the National Center for Education Statistics (Lewis, Parsad, Carey, Bartfai, Farris, and Smerdon, 1999) indicated that while 71 percent of the teachers surveyed taught students with disabilities, only 21 percent felt well prepared to meet their needs.

Numerous categories are used to classify children with disabilities. Given our focus on teacher professional development for instruction or intervention in reading, we concentrate on the following groups of learners (adapted from U.S. Department of Education Office of Special Education and Rehabilitative Services, 2002 and Snow, Burns, and Griffin, 1998). First we discuss students most often referred to as those with *developmental disabilities*. These are students with specific learning disabilities (SLD), speech and language impairments, emotional disturbance, mild mental retardation, and developmental delay (U.S. Department of Education Office of Special Education and Rehabilitative Services, 2002, page 20); we also include those with related reading disorders (for instance, children with attention deficit hyperactivity disorder [ADHD]). A second group we discuss are those with moderate to severe cognitive deficits. Finally we briefly address students with sensory impairments.

Students with Developmental Disabilities

Students with developmental disabilities constitute 90 percent of those qualifying for special education (Individuals with Disabilities Education Act Amendments of 1997). There are three particular language problems relevant to preparing teachers to understand the instructional needs of these students: challenges with lexical retrieval, poor phonological awareness, and depressed vocabulary knowledge.

Lexical retrieval refers to the speed and accuracy with which one recalls words—for example, when asked to name a series of pictures. This skill is related to reading comprehension. Lexical retrieval difficulties have a particular impact in prekindergarten through grade two, when young children are not yet proficient decoders and still depend upon listening comprehension for understanding written material (Curtis, 1980; Wolf and Segal, 1992).

The second problem area is *metalinguistics,* that is, difficulties with phonological awareness, or the ability to recognize and analyze the sounds in words. The relationship between deficits in phonological ability and depressed reading achievement is well established (Lyon, 1995; Torgesen, Wagner, Rashotte, Rose, Lindamood, Conway, and Garvan, 1999; and Wolf, Bowers, and Biddle, 2000).

A third problem area is *low vocabulary development* in typically developing children. Low vocabulary is highly correlated with poor reading comprehension. For example, Cunningham and Stanovich (1997) reported that vocabulary knowledge assessed in grade one predicts more than 30 percent of reading comprehension achievement in grade eleven, significantly more than predicted by decoding skills.

There are numerous myths that must be confronted in providing reading instruction for students with developmental disabilities.

MYTH: Reading instruction is qualitatively different for students with a specific learning disability (for example, those who demonstrate a disparity between intelligence—as measured by an I.Q. test—and achievement) than for students who are identified as poor readers but do not show any evidence of a learning disability.

REALITY: The instructional needs of poor readers—with and without learning disabilities—are quite similar. A number of studies have found no differences between these two groups on various measures of reading achievement (Stanovich and Siegel, 1994; Fletcher, Shaywitz,

Shankweiler, Katz, Liberman, Stuebing, and others, 1994). A recent meta-analysis of forty-six studies addressing the differences between these groups (Stuebing, Fletcher, LeDoux, Lyon, Shaywitz, and Shaywitz, 2002) found substantial overlap in reading achievement between poor readers and students with learning disabilities. Essentially, reading instruction has to prepare learners to deal with the nature of English orthography and the challenge of making meaning from text; though that challenge is greater for some students than for others, eventually they all have to do it pretty much the same way.

MYTH: Phonological core deficits are the most important instructional variable to consider with poor readers; therefore, instruction should focus on this specific need.

REALITY: A focus on phonological awareness, phonemic awareness, and phonics is essential for poor readers but not enough—instruction must also address key areas such as comprehension, vocabulary, the identification of irregular words, and fluency. Only some learners with reading disabilities have particular problems with phonological awareness.

MYTH: Most students with ADHD have reading problems.

REALITY: The prevalence of reading disability in individuals with ADHD is estimated to be 25 to 40 percent; hence, attention deficit does not constitute a primary cause for reading disability. The majority of children with ADHD have no reading problems (Catts and Kamhi, 1998).

MYTH: The reading problems of poor readers with ADHD are more likely to be based on difficulties with executive functioning as compared to poor readers without ADHD, whose problems are most often based on phonological processing problems.

REALITY: Swanson and colleagues (Swanson, Mink, and Bocian, 1999) administered a battery of verbal IQ, reading, and spelling subtests, as well as measures of memory and attention to task, to ninety first- through fifth-grade students, all of whom were poor readers. On the basis of the test results, this sample was divided and compared across subgroups: reading disabled with IQ greater than 85, slow learners with IQ less than 85, reading disabled with ADHD, and slow learners with ADHD. The findings did not support the intuitive assumption that poor readers without ADHD have more intact executive functioning than do poor readers with ADHD, and that poor readers with ADHD have more intact phonological processing, with executive functioning problems the primary cause of reading failure in ADHD. In fact, the findings generally support the phonological core-difference model (Stanovich and Siegel, 1994) in which phonological processes are assumed to be independent of a central system of executive processing.

MYTH: Children with reading disorders benefit only from specialized interventions to address their difficulties, and more global general-education instruction is not effective.

REALITY: Children with reading disabilities need systematic, explicit instruction to promote reading achievement (such as increasing depth and flexibility with word meanings across multiple contexts, or teaching to enhance decoding and fluency), but the overall teaching practices typically used in general education can contribute to their reading success.

Research that has systematically examined literacy learning in inclusion contexts speaks to the needs of these students to experience frequent, sustained, and consistent opportunities to read, write, listen, and talk about literacy. For example, the *Early Literacy Project* developed and investigated by Englert, Mariage, Garmon, and Tarrant (1998) included (a) teaching with thematic units that contributed to vocabulary and general knowledge development; (b) multiple opportunities to promote decoding and fluency, including the use of Project Read, choral reading, silent reading, and partner reading; and (c) opportunities to attend to comprehension through story response and discussion. In addition, successful students in inclusion classrooms experienced multiple opportunities to write (via journals, morning message, and writing across genres in teacher and peer-supported contexts). Many similar features are found in the Cooperative Integrated Reading and Composition (CIRC) programs investigated by Stevens, Madden, Slavin, and Farnish (1987).

MYTH: Struggling adolescent readers just need phonological awareness and phonics instruction to make gains in reading.

REALITY: Even if poor word-reading skills were the initial unsolved literacy challenge in the lives of struggling adolescent readers, simply addressing those issues in adolescence will not be adequate. Struggling adolescent readers probably lack vocabulary, background knowledge, an understanding of how to read purposefully, knowledge of useful strategies to rely on when reading difficult texts, and motivation to read. Without appropriate individual assessment of adolescents' reading needs and strengths, middle and high school reading teachers simply do not know where to focus their instruction (see Chapter Five for suggestions concerning assessment).

At present, in many middle and high schools throughout the United States, models of reading remediation unchanged since the 1970s are being implemented in a wholesale fashion, with little attention to the needs of individual students (see Anders, 2002). Many of the commercial programs designed for older learners include a heavy emphasis on decoding or fluency. English teachers and other content-area teachers interested in helping students become better readers have been enlisted (or coerced) to teach reading classes with euphemistic names like "Reading Power," "ExCELL," "Reading Improvement," "Basic Reading," and so forth. While these materials and classes may respond appropriately to the needs of some students, they are an unnecessary waste of time for some and insufficient for many. Without an effective diagnostic assessment battery, it is impossible to determine which students need decoding instruction, including phonemic awareness and phonics, which should spend time on learning comprehension strategies, which need help with vocabulary, and which need all these kinds of teaching.

The number of middle- and secondary-school students needing intensive work in reading is staggering. There are several troubling issues related to the efforts to serve these students. They include

1. An absence of individual diagnoses of reading needs and strengths. Frequently, standardized test scores are used to place students in ability groups. Teachers lack the knowledge or time to employ other assessment procedures that would provide better guidance for instruction.

2. Scarcity of reading specialists. The number of reading specialists in secondary schools has declined over the past decade (Bean, Cassidy, Grumet, and Shelton, 2002; Vogt and Shearer, 2003), leaving far too few for the size of the demand. Thus the reading specialists working in middle and high schools may be required to serve hundreds of struggling readers.

3. Students' delayed vocabulary development. With a strong correlation reported between vocabulary development and comprehension (Pressley, 2000), a major focus of reading remediation at the secondary level should be on vocabulary development, and its relationship to comprehension.

4. Too much or too little appropriate decoding instruction. While some secondary students would definitely benefit from explicit, systematic decoding instruction, other students do not need this instruction. Again, a lack of diagnostic information often results in a one-size-fits-all, quick-fix solution in many secondary schools.

5. Lack of appropriate and explicit comprehension skill and strategy instruction. Those who are teaching remedial reading classes at the secondary level may not be cognizant of current research in comprehension that advocates for explicit instruction and modeling in both skill and strategy instruction. Models of remediation from ear-

lier decades focused exclusively on skills instruction. More recent research indicates the need for comprehensive strategy instruction as well (Alfassi, 1998; Dole, Duffy, Roehler, and Pearson, 1991; Peterson, Caverly, Nicholson, O'Neal, and Cusenbary, 2000).

6. Repackaging of scripted and decades-old programs. In 1978, Dolores Durkin's research suggested that the majority of American teachers were testing, rather than teaching, comprehension. With programs from that period currently resurfacing with new covers but little substantive change in content, we may be repeating the mistakes of the past in addressing the needs of struggling secondary readers.

7. Reduction of focus on content teaching. As in previous decades, students who are struggling with reading are being diverted from grade-level-content classes in order to receive reading remediation, despite the insistence that all students meet grade-level-content standards. If struggling readers are denied opportunities to learn the material associated with these standards, how can they be held accountable for meeting them?

8. Too little time and too much to teach. Secondary-content teachers, who typically teach over one hundred students each day, can easily be overwhelmed by the numbers and diversity of reading challenges among their students, leading to feelings of futility.

Vogt (1997) found that adolescents who struggled with literacy at the secondary level had typically experienced difficulty with reading since they began schooling. These students had adopted complex strategies to avoid reading out loud in class, had poor grades, low self-esteem, limited decoding and vocabulary skills, and virtually no (expressed) interest in school or extracurricular activities.

Based initially on the work of Valerie Anderson (Anderson, Chan, and Henne, 1995), a model of intervention for middle and high school students (Vogt, 1999) was designed that incorporated intensive word study, the critical reading of almost-grade-level texts, Reciprocal Teaching (Palincsar and Brown, 1984), and Vocabulary Self-Collection Strategy (Ruddell and Shearer, 2002). This intervention model reflects a growing body of evidence supporting the instruction of strategic reasoning for literacy-delayed adolescents (Shearer, Ruddell, and Vogt, 2001). Post-test findings after ten months of daily instruction indicated an average gain on the Woodcock-Johnson Psycho-Educational Battery-Revised of 5.3 years in Word Identification and 4.4 years in Comprehension for grade eight students and an average gain of 4.8 years in Word Identification and 4.1 years in Comprehension for grade seven students (Shearer,

Ruddell, and Vogt, 2001). A follow-up study one year later found that the previous year's gains had been either maintained or surpassed. This study identifies the following features as supporting development of literacy skills among secondary struggling readers: (1) choice in what they read; (2) choice of and instruction in identifying vocabulary words that are important to learning the content in authentic texts; (3) peer coaching while reading complex texts; (4) at-home reading of at least twenty minutes per day; (5) intense word work with polysyllabic words for brief periods (approximately ten minutes per day) prior to engaging with challenging texts; (6) highly motivating texts that are challenging, rather than leveled texts (for example, Edgar Allen Poe's "The Tell-Tale Heart" was a student-selected text); (7) development of self-efficacy and motivation in students who previously intensely disliked reading; and (8) instruction from a highly qualified reading specialist.

If we truly desire to improve the literacy development of adolescents, we must use research to guide best practice and use knowledge about individual students to guide instruction for them. This requires that teachers abandon the assumption that struggling adolescent readers all just need more primary literacy instruction.

MYTH: Struggling adolescent readers don't want to learn to read.

REALITY: Dismissing adolescents who struggle with reading by assuming they "just aren't interested in reading" is probably wrong and certainly unhelpful. As many have noted, students are often able to use reading and writing for their own specific purposes even if they struggle with school assignments. Vacca (2005) suggests there is a crisis in adolescent literacy due to a benign neglect of adolescents' literacy needs, misunderstandings of their literacy development, and a general disregard for the "hidden" or personal literacies in adolescents' lives. These multiple literacies include those associated with surfing the Web; using CD-ROMS and DVDs; reading contemporary texts (such as teen 'zines); using and exchanging music videos, movies, e-mail, and television; creating hypertext and personal Websites; and manipulating a wide variety of digital images (Vogt and Shearer, 2003). These teen-literacy materials differ strikingly from the dense and often unmotivating textbooks offered to students in school.

During the past decade, traditional secondary reading programs have in a few places been supplanted by contemporary adolescent literacy approaches in which the definition of literacy is broadened, acknowledging the ever-expanding literacy demands of the workplace and the increasingly diverse nature of the society in which we live (Alvermann, 2001; Moore, Bean, Birdyshaw, and Rycik, 1999; Vacca, 2005; and Vogt and

Shearer, 2003). More information is needed about the efficacy of these approaches.

Alvermann (2003) and the RAND Reading Study Group (Snow, 2002) suggest that, to reduce the gap between basic and more advanced levels of reading proficiency among adolescents, the instruction should focus on comprehension of text and vocabulary development. Further, consideration of and attention to students' motivation and development of self-efficacy in learning from text should be paramount concerns (Alvermann, 2001; Guthrie and Wigfield, 2000; and Schunk and Rice, 1993).

Students with Moderate to Severe Cognitive Deficits

There is emerging research supporting the claim that students with moderate to severe cognitive limitations can demonstrate the capacity for cognitive symbolic literacy in appropriate contexts. Kliewer and Biklen (2001) documented literacy learning outcomes for students with severe cognitive deficits when teachers did not assume that literacy skills must emerge in accordance with a predictable, normative sequence of events and did not demand passage through each step of the sequence before moving to the next step. With the assistance of adults who presumed that these students were capable of symbolic activity and worked to create opportunities that allowed for expression of those capacities, many were able to attain sufficient literacy skills to be able to interact meaningfully with others and to engage in reading for communicative and pleasurable purposes.

MYTH: Identifying children with cognitive deficits is straightforward.

REALITY: A far greater percentage of African American boys than of any other demographic group are identified with moderate to severe cognitive deficits (mental retardation). Odds of being identified as mentally retarded are 2.24 times as high for African American as for white children. Such sharp disparities in rates of identification suggest strongly that African American children are overidentified as mentally retarded by the available tests, perhaps because they are more likely to be referred for testing or because the tests used are biased against them (Donovan and Cross, 2002).

MYTH: Children with severe disabilities are less able to make literacy gains and therefore instruction for them should not focus on reading.

REALITY: There are a number of documented case studies suggesting that children with severe disabilities can achieve functional literacy (for example, Blischak, 1995; Erikson and Koppenhaver, 1997). The principal obstacle these learners face appears to be one of instructional opportunity. For example, Koppenhaver and Yoder (1993) documented that children with severe disabilities received only fifteen minutes of literacy instruction per school day. Furthermore, research conducted by Pierce and McWilliam (1993) indicates that children with severe speech and physical disabilities do not typically have control over book selection and pacing of reading sessions.

MYTH: Drill and practice of isolated, decontextualized skills such as knowledge of alphabet letters, sound-symbol correspondence, and single-word decoding must dominate instruction for children with severe deficiencies because they need to have these mastered before moving on to more complex literacy tasks.

REALITY: Children with severe deficiencies benefit from rich, intensive, and extensive literacy experiences (Kliewer and Landis, 1999). Unfortunately, methods of literacy instruction for people with severe cognitive challenges have been dominated by interventions featuring highly sequenced drill and practice of isolated, decontextualized skills such as knowledge of alphabet letters, sound-symbol correspondence, and single-word decoding. Required to master this linear set of mechanical subskills, individuals with severe challenges rarely experience reading well-constructed, connected texts. Katims (2000), among others, has argued that a shift in orientation from defining literacy exclusively as the sequential acquisition of increasingly complex skills to using literacy as a tool for communication, obtaining information, or experiencing pleasure will increase literacy outcomes for these individuals.

The Council for Exceptional Children recently published a monograph on the topic of literacy instruction for students with mental retardation (Katims, 2000). The monograph encourages direct instruction in letter, word, syntactic, phonetic, and semantic analyses in the context of reading literature and reading the writing that students have dictated to others.

Students with Severe Hearing Loss

Seven million (14.9 percent) K–12 students have an educationally significant hearing impairment, which is defined as a high- or low-frequency hearing loss of 16 dB or more (Third National Health and Nutrition Survey, reported in Flexer, 1999). Fortunately, the number of students with severe to profound hearing impairment is decreasing; in fact, it is less than half of what it was ten to thirty years ago and only 4 to 6 percent of children with hearing loss are deaf. Understanding the literacy instructional needs of children with hearing loss demands that all teachers know some basic information about this disability. Hearing loss occurs on a continuum, and students with hearing impairments typically have a certain degree of loss; however, with many types of hearing loss, the level of hearing fluctuates. A student's functioning on this continuum, along with his or her cognitive functioning, is associated with language and literacy outcomes.

MYTH: Students with minimal hearing loss do not have trouble understanding what is going on in reading instruction.

REALITY: The impact of minimal hearing loss, while not readily obvious, is frequently manifested by immature and inattentive behavior due to the fatigue associated with increased effort expended to hear. Students with minimal hearing impairment miss at least 10 percent of classroom instruction and have difficulty detecting subtle conversational cues, keeping up with fast-paced communicative exchanges, and hearing the sounds that signal distinctions for verb tense, plurality, possessives, and other grammatical features.

MYTH: Since students have annual hearing screenings, every teacher receives information identifying the students in his or her classroom who have hearing impairments.

REALITY: School hearing screenings often miss cases of minimal to mild hearing loss because of the (often noisy) conditions under which screening occurs and the lenient criterion for passing (often 25 to 30 dB, rather than the recommended 15 dB). Also, a student who hears well on one day early in the school year may later develop poor hearing as a result of ear infections and fluid in his or her ears.

MYTH: It is difficult to provide the accommodations needed by students with hearing impairments when their hearing loss is fluctuating or not always apparent.

REALITY: Most of the accommodations needed are actually good practice for all learners, all the time. Studies show fewer at-risk readers, regardless of their hearing status, graduating from classrooms in which sound-field amplification systems are used to teach phonemic awareness (Flexer, 2002). Other accommodations such as reducing classroom noise and reducing the distance between speaker and listener are good practices for all classrooms with young children.

MYTH: With a hearing aid or cochlear implant, a student should be able to hear normally.

REALITY: "Hearing aids do not correct the hearing impairment; rather, they function to amplify and shape the incoming sounds to make them audible to the child" (Flexer, 1999, p. 111). Hence, the learner's hearing is unlikely to be normal. Audiotapes available from the American

Academy of Audiology or Self Help for Hard of Hearing People, Inc. can demonstrate to teachers what hearing-impaired students are actually hearing. For a child with a cochlear implant, the experience of hearing is dramatically different from normal hearing, or from hearing with an aid. A cochlear implant is not a hearing aid. It is "a surgically implanted biomedical device designed to provide sound information. . . . The implant bypasses some of the damaged parts of the inner ear; coded electrical signals stimulate different hearing nerve fibers which then send information to the brain" (Flexer, 1999, pp. 143–144).

Students with Visual Impairments

A visual impairment is not—by itself—a predictor of reading disability, although there is a slightly greater percentage of visual deficits among children with reading disabilities than among those without reading disabilities. Furthermore, students with visual difficulties tend, as a group, to read more poorly than those not so encumbered. However, many children with visual deficits learn to read as well as—or better than—children without visual problems (Bond, Tinker, Wasson, and Wasson, 1984). In many cases, augmentative devices are needed to see print. If such devices are not available, or are ineffective for a student, Braille can be taught. Braille is alphabet based and—if taught correctly—can enable visually impaired children to learn to read.

PROMOTING COLLABORATION AMONG PROFESSIONALS IN THE BEST INTEREST OF THE LEARNER

An assumption underlying this chapter is that the most effective preparation of preservice educators and enhancement of inservice educators occurs through engagement in inquiry (learning, enactment, assessment, and reflection) regarding their own practice. We also are aware of the need to attend to the larger contexts in which teacher—and student—learning occur; these contexts are shaped by resources (such as availability of books, of technology, and of support from specialists), the culture of the classroom, practices like (flexible) grouping, the nature of the curriculum, and the assessment system in place.

The reauthorization of the IDEA, together with standards-based reform, has implications for the knowledge bases and roles of general and special educators, as well as support personnel (such as bilingual educators, speech and language clinicians, and reading specialists). The IDEA calls for individualized educational plans for students identified with special needs, designed in the context of the general education curriculum and for the purpose of supporting subject matter learning. The standards-based reforms similarly call for the performance of *all* students to be measured against more uniform—and ambitious—standards. These thrusts have, in fact, led some educational scholars to call for the unification of teacher-education programs across the domains of expertise historically aligned with special education or with curriculum and instruction (see Pugach and Warger, 1996). A case in point is the teacher-education program at Boston College, in which prospective teachers take some courses in common with others who will serve students in the school setting—school nurses and social workers, for example.

Teaching has typically been portrayed as an isolated and solitary activity (Rosenholtz and Simpson, 1990). However, if schools are to meet these new mandates, there will have to be greater cooperation and collaboration between general educators and specialists. Toward this end, prospective teachers will benefit from introduction to the procedures and various service-delivery models that are employed in identifying and educating students with special needs. They can learn how to engage in problem-identification and problem-solving conversations with colleagues. For example, Pugach and Johnson (1989) prepared teachers to use structured dialogues with one another for the purpose of supporting collaborative efforts leading to alternative classroom interventions. Prospective general educators can learn how to complement their subject-matter knowledge and knowledge of the classroom context with the expertise of specialists so that together they can plan, enact, and evaluate modifications to curricula, instruction, or assessment for students with special needs.

While The Council for Exceptional Children and The American Speech-Language-Hearing Association identify standards in the same spirit, they emphasize modification of learning environments and the use of assistive technology to enable independent reading and writing and to support the use of rigorous curriculum and high achievement expectations. In 2003, the International Reading Association published the revised *Standards for Reading Professionals* to address questions about the nature of the desirable preparation for teachers of reading, reading specialists, and literacy coaches. In addition to having the requisite knowledge base, these various practitioners must also learn how to collaborate to ensure optimal reading outcomes for all children.

Standards for the various categories of professionals, including reading specialists, can be consulted at http://www.reading.org/resources/issues/reports/professional_standards.html.

CHAPTER FIVE

Learning to Use
Reading Assessments Wisely

Jill Murray sits at a table in her third-grade classroom. It is the Thursday afternoon of the first full week of school. The children have all gone home. Yet vibrant images of them are summoned as Jill reads through a stack of their writing samples. Most often the samples confirm what she has already observed about them as learners: Ken's strong vocabulary and great sense of humor, Marita's sensitivity and her love of animals, Nisa's struggle to keep up academically, Jesus' hesitancy to write anything at all, though he was assured that it was fine to write in Spanish or a combination of Spanish and English. Now and then, a writing sample belies Jill's expectation. Kyla's writing ability seems extremely limited compared to her oral expression. Malik's writing is poorly constructed and violates many language conventions, yet it suggests he possesses a wealth of background knowledge that had not been revealed to Jill so far.

More than half of the children in her class of twenty-three attended either first or second grade in this school. Most attended both. For these children, Jill has folders containing information forwarded by previous teachers: results from informal reading inventories, two writing samples, and a brief summary statement about each child's academic achievement to date. Jill finds the information useful, but she is careful to withhold judgment about a child based on the folder alone. During the year, Jill will continue to add information to each child's folders. Notes from conferences with resource staff and with parents, informal and formal assessment data, and observational notes will be included, but many of these may be removed when they are no longer useful. Jill sees the folders as living repositories of data that help document and monitor student learning and inform her teaching. The information will be used as a basis for conferences with students, parents, and support staff. At the end of the year, some material will go home with the child. Some key information, previously agreed upon by the faculty, will be forwarded to next year's teacher.

Six of her students are new to this school. Four of these come from outside the district and two, both English-language learners, from outside the country. Several of the other students are relatively new to this country and come from homes where English is rarely spoken. Nevertheless, most of them have gained fairly good oral command of their second language. Later in the week, Jill plans to meet with Jesus' parents to learn more about his background. She has arranged for an interpreter to sit in on the conversation. On Monday, Jill will meet with the learning disabilities specialist to discuss one child who is slated for special intervention within the class-room. So far, one student who had previously been in a special-needs class has been mainstreamed in Jill's class for part of the day, and two others have special medical needs that sometimes affect their academic performance.

The makeup of Jill's class is typical of the classes in this increasingly diverse district. When she began teaching here, Jill was struck by the ethnic and linguistic diversity she encountered. She soon realized that the individual differences among children were even more important. Jill never ceases to be amazed at the unique-ness of each child. She feels fortunate to be in this school where professional devel-opment is considered to be a key part of every teacher's job. During the past year, the school embarked on a three-year professional development effort focused on linking instruction and assessment. To meet the challenges they face, the district has heavily emphasized ongoing classroom assessment. Teachers work together at each grade level and with the reading specialist to set up mechanisms for collecting and examining information they can use to tailor instruction. Emphasis is placed on each learner's strengths and needs in relation to his or her own past performance as well as the performance of the group. The teachers also look at the strengths and needs of the group as a whole in order to guide and evaluate what is taught.

Jill and the other teachers in this school view assessment as a process of infor-mation gathering to inform instruction. In deciding on assessment procedures, they consider (1) the information they have, (2) the information they need, (3) the ways in which the information they need may be acquired, and (4) how they can use that information to improve learning and teaching. They are working through the learning, enactment, assessment, and reflection cycle that we argue is central to learning, with a particular focus because of the professional development activities on improving their capacities to assess and reflect.

WHAT TEACHERS NEED TO KNOW ABOUT ASSESSMENT

We organize our hopes for teacher education and professional development around the learning, enactment, assessment, and reflection cycle. Without knowledge about and skills in assessment, teachers do not have the informa-tion about which they need to reflect. Whether their enactments of their own learnings are working or not can only be revealed through the systematic collection of data about student learning.

An understanding of the principles and uses of assessment is essential for *all* teachers, and in particular for teachers of reading. The Committee on the Prevention of Reading Difficulties in Young Children (Snow, Burns, and Griffin, 1998) made the recommendation that state certification requirements and teacher education curricula incorporate a knowledge base that includes procedures for ongoing, in-class assessment of students' reading abilities as well as information on how to interpret results from district- and state-mandated assessments and modify instruction according to assessment outcomes. Various position statements and standards have taken that challenge and now emphasize the importance of using and interpreting high-quality assessment in reading instruction. For instance, the Interstate New Teacher Assessment and Support Consortium's Standard 8 is

> The teacher understands and uses formal and informal assessment strategies to evaluate and ensure the continuous intellectual, social, and physical development of his/her learners.

National Council for Accreditation of Teacher Education (NCATE) program standards for preparing the specialized reading professional include prescriptions about assessment in Standard 10:

> The reading professional will be able to:
>
> > Develop and conduct assessments that involve multiple indicators of learner progress, and
> >
> > Administer and use information from norm-referenced tests, criterion-referenced tests, formal and informal inventories, constructed response measures, portfolio-based assessments, student self-evaluations, work/performance samples, observations, anecdotal records, journals, and other indicators of student progress to inform instruction and learning.

In addition, the standards presented by the American Federation of Teachers, the National Council on Measurement in Education, and the National Education Association (1990) specifically outline the skills that teachers need to acquire to assess effectively.

The assessment literature and the standards point to four major areas in which teachers need knowledge and skills related to assessment; these apply to all the content areas, but since performance on any test about any topic will require reading skill, it is of particular importance that these domains of knowledge be applied to reading assessments. In the following sections of this chapter, we discuss these four domains:

- *The basic principles underlying quality assessment.* While teachers do not need technical knowledge about assessments, they do need to understand the principles that distinguish good assessments from poor ones. Even informal assessments must follow certain principles if they are to generate usable results.

- *Familiarity with a wide range of assessment tools and practices, including both standardized tests and informal classroom strategies and assessments.* Teachers of reading have to assess many different aspects of student knowledge, working with many different kinds of learners. Having a large repertoire of tools helps them do a good job of evaluating their students' learning.

- *Knowing how to use assessment outcomes to inform instructional decision making.* All too often tests are given or observations made, but then no further use is made of the information collected. Drawing guidance from the results of classroom assessments is the only rationale for taking time to do the assessments—and teachers have no way of knowing how to use assessment results without instruction.

- *Skill in communicating assessment results to students, parents, administrators, and other members of instructional teams.* A key advantage enjoyed by teachers who engage in regular assessment is that they create a language for talking about their ideas. They have examples of scores on particular tests, specific patterns of errors, and well-analyzed pieces of student work to make concrete what they mean by "poor reading" or "excellent writing." Teachers like Jill can present evidence to parents, to fellow teachers, and to students about what performance should look like and what it does look like. In the process, a shared way of talking about teaching and learning emerges.

Research confirms that literacy instruction is affected by the systematic collection and use of information about curriculum standards or student progress. For example, a study of Title 1 schools in Texas that had a higher-than-expected Texas Assessment of Academic Skills (TAAS) pass rate (Klein, Johnson, and Ragland, 1997) noted that teachers were familiar with the Texas standards and the TAAS objectives, and aligned their instruction with those objectives. In a study of seven schools in Chicago that had particularly large reading-achievement gains (Designs for Change, 1998), teachers were seen to use both observations of student work and test data to monitor student progress. The Center for the Improvement of Early Reading Achievement's Beat the Odds study of schools performing better than their demographics would suggest they should (Taylor, Pearson, Clark, and Walpole, 2000) emphasized that teachers in those schools monitored student progress systematically and used student data as a basis for discussion and collaborative planning of instruction. There is considerable research support for the claim that students are more likely to do well in classrooms where teachers systematically collect and use data about their progress.

PRINCIPLES UNDERLYING QUALITY ASSESSMENT

Many of the principles underlying quality assessment are general, not specific to reading assessment. Perhaps the most basic of these is that assessments only ever reflect a small sample of the target domain of knowledge. As a result, assessments can be dangerous, either by leading teachers to concentrate on the inevitably limited definition of the domain reflected in the test, or by leading to misattributions based on insufficient information. Thus, it has been argued that high-stakes decisions, such as retention in grade, should never be made based on only a single test (Heubert and Hauser, 1999).

Another basic principle is that assessments vary widely in quality. Assessments themselves need to be evaluated for validity, reliability, appropriateness, freedom from bias, and utility. Even published and widely used tests are not always of high quality, or are inappropriate for the uses to which they are put. Some tests include items that operate differently for different subgroups of students, thus introducing bias into the score. Assessments also vary in difficulty, even when they purport to assess the same construct. Thus, for example, the TAAS was a fairly easy test with a low passing score (that is, a relatively high pass rate), whereas the Massachusetts Comprehensive Assessment System (MCAS) posed much harder questions. Thus many students who sailed through the TAAS would have failed the MCAS, though in principle both tests were used to define grade-level expectations for literacy skills (Snow, 2003).

It is important in thinking about literacy assessments to distinguish those that reflect "large problem spaces" from those that are targeted at "small problem spaces." Reading comprehension—especially comprehension in the content areas, vocabulary, and writing are large problem spaces; they constitute complex, multifaceted accomplishments. Different adults might define what it means to comprehend well or to write well somewhat differently, and any test of such complex knowledge domains samples it very sparsely. Letter knowledge, word attack, phonological awareness, and spelling are, in contrast, rather constrained domains, easier to sample richly. Furthermore, any two tests of letter knowledge or word attack are likely to be highly correlated, and at least during the first years of school, letter knowledge scores are likely to correlate highly with phonological awareness and word attack (Paris, 2001). These smaller and easier-to-test problem spaces are, as it happens, the domains most likely to be thought of as relevant to early reading instruction, though we would argue that the larger domains are equally important in the primary grades. Thus, we have a relatively rich array of well-designed, highly reliable assessments for the skills associated with the word-reading instructional task.

However, general assessments of reading comprehension (as opposed to assessments of the comprehension of specific texts for specific purposes) are widely acknowledged to be unsatisfactory; they fail to represent the domain adequately, they show low intercorrelations and poor reliability, and they provide little specific information that is helpful in planning instruction (Snow, 2003). Consider, for example, two students who are both having trouble reading their ninth-grade biology text. Their teacher refers them for assessment. One scores at sixth-grade level on the comprehension test, and the other at ninth-grade level. What help do these findings provide for the ninth-grade science teacher? All she now knows is that one of the students is better than the other at reading the test passages, but she still does not know what aspects of the ninth-grade biology text are creating problems—whether the presupposed background knowledge, the disjointed rhetoric, the technical or nontechnical vocabulary, the minimally engaging text, or the complexity of the syntax is the obstacle. Only by moving to more diagnostic testing would the teacher procure the information needed to adapt her instruction.

Many would agree with Koretz (2002) that high-stakes assessments do more harm than good, as they almost always lead to some narrowing of the curriculum and in some cases to investment of considerable time in test preparation, pressures to teach to the test rather than to the standards, and in the worst case even to cheating. Nonetheless, high-stakes assessments are here to stay, and so teachers and students need to learn how to use them most productively. One option is to treat the texts and accompanying questions that are incorporated into reading comprehension assessments as a target of analysis. Test questions are a particular genre, with all the characteristics and specific comprehension demands of any genre. Students can be helped to do better on tests if test questions are dealt with, among many other types of text, in their study of genres.

A final principle is that there is a lot to know about assessments, assessment systems, and the effective use of data collected through assessments. The companion volume *Preparing Teachers for a Changing World: What Teachers Should Know and Be Able to Do* (Darling-Hammond, Bransford, LePage, Hammerness, and Duffy, 2005) describes in considerable detail the promise and challenges of formative, summative, and large-scale assessments. It argues that teacher-education programs should provide teacher candidates opportunities to engage in the analysis of student work and student learning and in assessment design, and to understand the relation of learning and motivation to assessment as well as how standards and accountability relate to assessment. It also provides a useful sketch of a teacher-education program that offers excellent models of assessment in action, applied to student as well as teacher performance.

A WIDE RANGE OF ASSESSMENT TOOLS AND PRACTICES

In this section we describe formative assessments—those designed to help teachers do their work. Teachers need assessments to give them information about their own degree of success with their core instructional tasks, in other words, about which aspects of their instruction are working well and which are not. They also need assessments to guide their work with particular struggling readers, that is, diagnostic tests that identify which particular components of the reading task such students are struggling with. Thus, teachers of reading need to think about two ways of using formative assessments, one focused on the core instructional tasks identified in Chapter Two and the other focused on helping design instruction for students like those described in Chapters Three and Four.

Assessment methods are, of course, dictated by one's analysis of the learning task. In the previous three chapters we have described the progress of students toward success in reading, pointing out that successful readers have learned about several different aspects of the literacy system—how print works, how words can be segmented into phonemes, how letters represent sounds, what words mean, how to read accurately and fluently, and how to construct meaning using print. It is not necessary that all of these components be assessed systematically—if a fourth-grader is reading enthusiastically and at grade level, the teacher can be sure that the component skills are in place! It is important to know, however, which of the components should be assessed systematically at earlier stages of reading development, and how to assess them independently for diagnostic and instructional purposes if a student is not reading at the expected level.

In Table 5.1 we suggest formal and informal assessments for skills related to the two reading instructional tasks, comprehension and word identification, as well as for motivation, one of the key enabling conditions for successful reading development. While Table 5.1 does not present an exhaustive list, it does demonstrate that many possibilities exist for assessing important skills. For each component some of the available assessments are quite brief and simple to administer, and for many of the components standardized assessments in Spanish are also available.

The informal methods we suggest are relatively straightforward—although of course practice in using and interpreting the results of at least some of these assessments should be part of preservice preparation. Equally importantly, future teachers need to be taught how to fit assessment into their daily practice, how to manage the classroom so assessment of individual students is possible, and how to manage the data that regular assessments generate. Perhaps the most effective technique for teaching these management skills to future teachers is

Table 5.1. Some Common Tools and Methods Used to Assess Reading

Elements to Be Assessed	Published Assessments*	Informal Teacher-Assessment Strategies** (includes observations and evaluation during the following activities)
Word Identification		
Phonological awareness	CTOPP; DIBELS phonemic segmentation fluency; GRR; PAT; TOPPS; TPA; YOPP-SINGER; Spanish Phonological Test	Riming instruction, word play, writing, language and word study activities
Orthography or spelling	CAP; Developmental Spelling Inventory; DIBELS letter-naming fluency; GRR; SLA; WRMT letter-identification subtest; Spelling Inventory	Shared reading activities, independent reading, student writing
Word attack	DIBELS nonsense word fluency; GRR; OSELA; RIC; WRMT word-attack subtest; WLPB-R letter-word-identification subtest	Word study activities, reading, writing, running records
Comprehension		
Fluency	DIBELS oral-reading fluency; DFA; TORF	Oral-reading activities, running records
Nonreading comprehension	Narrative Picturebook Comprehension; CELF	
Reading comprehension	BRI; Gates-MacGinitie; QRI; STANFORD; TORC; WLPB-R passage-comprehension subtest	Response to literature or print (talk, writing, art, drama), reading conferences, cloze procedure, retellings, student self-assessment
Vocabulary	PPVT; TVIP; WLPB-R vocabulary subtest	Language and word study activities, response to literature, reading conferences, cloze procedure, retellings

Table 5.1. Some Common Tools and Methods Used to Assess Reading, *Cont'd*

Elements to Be Assessed	Published Assessments*	Informal Teacher-Assessment Strategies** (includes observations and evaluation during the following activities)
	Motivation	
Concepts about print	CAP; Instrumento de Observación de los Logros de Lecto-Escritura Inicial	Read-alouds, free reading time, writing
Interest or attitude	MTRP; RAA; RAAT; Reading Self-Concept Scale	Shared reading, independent reading, teacher read-aloud sessions, general interest in books, teacher interviews, interest and attitude inventories, parent interviews, surveys

*More information about the published assessments is given in the text that follows or in the list at the end of this chapter.

**Makes use of anecdotal records, checklists, portfolios, and rubrics.

to offer opportunities to observe, develop, and practice them in preservice programs. If we expect teachers to develop and use rubrics in their classrooms, then it is useful to develop rubrics collaboratively for their performance in the preservice program. If we expect them to keep records of twenty to twenty-five children's reading progress in the primary grades, then a good place to start is for them to keep records of their own progress—by creating their own data-management system, building a teaching portfolio, maintaining a reflective journal focused on their own learning, or all of the above. In the section that follows, we focus on the array of literacy assessments teachers should be able to deploy to learn about their students. Devising optimal ways to ensure that future teachers know about these types of assessment is a crucial undertaking that we only touch upon here.

For teachers to be able to select assessment methods to match the kinds of information that they want, they need to have articulated clear, specific learning targets that center on what is important and that fit into the big picture described through the curriculum guidelines and standards (McMillan, 2001; Stiggins, 2001). All too often, tests drive instruction rather than supporting it. Armed with an understanding of what students are expected to know, teachers will be able to choose, develop, and implement assessment methods that are appropriate for making instructional decisions (American Federation of Teachers, National Council on Measurement in Education, and National Education Association, 1990). Teachers need to be able to think, talk about, and act on observations of students' reading and responses to reading through talk, writing, and actions (performing a task) in ongoing informal classroom assessment as well as targeted classroom assessment. Sometimes benchmark assessments and high-stakes tests offer this sort of information as well; good teachers figure out when and how to use the information they generate.

Assessing Skills Related to Word Identification

As noted earlier, many reliable tests are available to aid teachers in assessing student skills related to word identification (see Table 5.1). Some of these tests, such as phonological awareness and letter naming, are valuable primarily for emergent and beginning readers. Information about emergent literacy skills is also richly available in children's writing and invented spelling, in their word play, and from careful observations of their spontaneous uses of books.

Assessments of word reading using sight words, real words, and regularly spelled pseudowords are informative until students become independent readers. Teachers of children having trouble with word identification might find it useful to keep track of student performance on different spelling patterns during word-study activities, or even to design an individual diagnostic word reading test to ascertain whether, for example, a student knows digraphic vowel spellings (*ow, ou, ae, ai, ea, oo,* and so on) or reliably recognizes the consonant digraphs *sh, ch,* and *th* distinctively.

Observing students' reading can also provide insight into their levels of skill with word identification. During such observations, teachers need to record actual behaviors and specific comments that children make rather than offer a broad interpretation of what is observed. For example, a teacher may wish to note that particular children pointed out letters in their names, commented on letters that they recognized in a book, or followed along appropriately in a small book as the teacher read in a big book. Children's understanding of concepts of print can also be assessed during such classroom activities, as well as with specific assessments designed for that purpose (Clay, 1993).

Assessing Students' Comprehension

Comprehension and the abilities that are related to comprehension should be tested from the earliest stages of reading instruction and through secondary grades. Before children can themselves read, their ability to understand books read aloud can be tested informally, or by using standardized listening comprehension assessments such as the CELF (see Table 5.1). The ability to identify the story represented by a sequence of pictures can also be tested; Paris and

Paris (2003) have developed and collected norms for a picture-book narrative comprehension measure that can be used with pre- and early readers.

As noted, reading comprehension is hard to test in ways that are specific and diagnostic. Standardized tests can serve to assure us that students can comprehend adequately and to identify students who need special help. In addition, though, careful observation of student talk about texts provides teachers with information about their level of comprehension. Furthermore, observing the reading process in one-to-one conferencing or in small-group or whole-class discussions can be productive. Student think-alouds, retellings, and discussions enable teachers to assess the reading strategies they are using. For effective conferencing, teachers plan independent work for the rest of the class and prepare questions that will allow insights into student understandings (North Carolina State Department of Public Instruction, 1999). The use of one-on-one conferencing about readings and about students' written work requires, of course, that teachers know how to set absorbing tasks for other students and to manage a classroom in which independent work is going on.

Discussions and conferences need to be documented. This can be done through anecdotal records or checklists, which allow teachers to look at specific learning targets. Because there is a tendency for people to hold unintentional biases and to see what they're looking for, teachers need to learn to observe skillfully and record observations systematically. For example, strategies used before reading (book selection, previewing of text, and so on), during reading (predicting and confirming, using chunks within multisyllabic words, checking understanding against prior knowledge, and so on), and after reading (retelling, making comparisons, using information in a book to justify a response, and so on) can be tracked with checklists. Checklists may also prompt teachers to note whether the student uses a given strategy most of the time, is still working on a strategy, or has not yet started using one (Winograd and Arrington, 1999).

Many teachers use informal reading inventories (IRIs) such as the Qualitative Reading Inventory (QRI) to assess comprehension. IRIs are designed to sample a child's reading on passages that are graduated in difficulty from very easy to more difficult. Accuracy in both word identification and comprehension are taken into account. Instruments of this type also yield initial estimates useful for thinking about placement and diagnosis (Cooper and Kiger, 2001). Informal inventories yield information about a student's independent reading level (the level at which he or she can read with ease, meeting few or no challenges); instructional level (students have some challenge; the level at which a teacher instructs toward independence); frustration level (student meets so many challenges that efforts at decoding and comprehension break down). The IRI and similar assessment strategies that include oral reading (such as miscue analysis, running records, and the analysis of tape-recorded oral reading segments) help teachers understand the strategies students rely on and reveal what they need to learn. Oral reading is also used to assess fluency, the ability to read connected text aloud smoothly and accurately.

Comprehension can also be assessed through student responses in essays, reflective writing, answers to open-ended questions, or reading journals. Having students write about the reading that they do can enable them to think critically about the text, respond to the text, and back up their positions with the text. Many standardized tests include open-ended questions to which students must respond with supportive evidence from a passage they have read. In the instructional process, teachers can give students opportunities to practice this type of response, assess their efforts, and give appropriate feedback. Teachers must learn to model responses to questions, provide adequate time for students to respond, provide feedback that gives students specific ways to improve their writing, and teach students how to edit and revise their responses. The comprehension of young students, though, and of those who are not yet fluent writers can be severely underestimated through their writing.

If students score below grade level on listening or reading comprehension measures, then diagnostic testing can be used to discover what aspect of the reading process is blocking comprehension. Some students with poor comprehension, even in middle or secondary grades, have deficits in word identification. Word-attack tests will be helpful in identifying these difficulties. Other students are accurate at word identification but read too slowly, with too much effort. The DIBELS reading fluency subtest is a quickly administered measure, with benchmarks up through grade six, that can help identify such students. Other students have mastered word identification and fluency, but lack the background knowledge or vocabulary necessary for reading their content-area texts and the texts used in many comprehension tests. Targeted vocabulary assessments are very helpful in these cases; below-grade-level performance typically indicates limited stores of background knowledge as well (judicious interviewing can also reveal gaps in background knowledge relevant to particular instructional texts). Second-language readers and children from homes where the adults have low literacy levels often have limited lexical and world knowledge. A teacher who knows this can focus instruction on those areas, rather than wasting the time of such students with instruction in comprehension strategies or inferencing, skills on which they may well be completely competent.

Assessing Motivation and Interest

Some children arrive at kindergarten with very little understanding of the nature of literacy, or of the many reasons one might want to read and write. A teacher has the responsibility to be aware of students' understandings about literacy, to be aware of their interests in particular topics and types of reading, and to document how students feel about themselves as readers. Indeed, students who have experienced reading failures often have motivational blocks to further reading progress (see Guthrie and Knowles, 2001, for a review of the mutual relationship between reading and motivation). Furthermore, students who have particular interests can often overcome reading difficulties if guided toward texts that address those interests. If teachers do not know what their students want to read, they cannot leverage motivation to support reading growth optimally.

Assessments such as concepts about print (see Table 5.1) help teachers estimate kindergartners' previous exposure to literacy artifacts and activities. Surveys of students' reading attitudes (see Table 5.1) help us to find out about students as readers. This kind of information is extremely valuable when combined with observations of students reading, responding to, and discussing books in the classroom. Adding this information to reading conference records and reading journals builds a more complete picture of individual strengths as students read over time in a variety of contexts. It is helpful to discover how students feel about reading, the uses they find for it, the importance it has in their lives, and how they see themselves as readers. All of this is necessary information to plan effective instruction.

In addition, the teacher can assess students' attitudes toward reading by noting how often students choose to read when they have the option; recording instances when they bring books in from home; giving examples of their participation in storybook sessions or literature discussions; or describing a time when they got excited about encountering a familiar letter, word, author, or topic. Anecdotal records of such events contain the concrete information from which patterns can be described and conclusions made (Harp and Brewer, 2000).

Teachers can also use performances such as readers' theatre, oral presentations based on reading, or perhaps the designing of a Web page that presents book reviews written by students, both to assess student interests and to promote motivations for reading. Reading activities can be integrated with larger performance tasks that mirror real-life experiences. In these tasks, students can show how they use literacy to collect information, make connections, solve a problem, do research, or make decisions (North Carolina State Department of Public Instruction, 1999).

Valencia and Pearson (1991) distinguish three types of portfolios for literacy assessment: a showcase portfolio of best work in final form, a documentation portfolio that contains a cumulative record of students' school life and work, and an evaluation portfolio that contains work completed under standardized conditions. Portfolios may include a reader's log or a literary response journal, a taped oral reading, or a collection of responses to reading assignments (García and Pearson, 1991). Glazer (1998) recommends dividing portfolios into sections of comprehension, composition, vocabulary and language study, and independence and self-monitoring. Teachers may want to include various samples over time of one indicator, such as periodic running records, with an evaluation criterion that remains constant (Stiggins, 2001).

Portfolios can become a springboard for students' conversations as they learn to plan, select work, and self-assess with peers, teachers, and parents (Tierney, Clark, Fenner, Herter, Simpson, and Wiser, 1998). The portfolios can also help enable students to take responsibility for their learning as students use them to monitor their own progress and communicate it in student-led conferences (Glazer, 1998; Stiggins, 2001). For portfolios to be successful, teachers need to be able to develop clear guidelines for selecting work and to guide students in the assessment process.

Assessments Particularly Useful for Those Teaching Middle- and Secondary-School Students

How do teachers at the secondary level (grades six through twelve) who teach in departmentalized content courses implement effective assessment when they teach five or six classes each day of thirty to thirty-five (or more) students each period? What is a realistic expectation for assessment in these classrooms? Clearly, these teachers must design an assessment program that can efficiently provide the most critical information about their students, and it is not typically possible to use individually administered assessments or to implement teaching plans unique to each student. Middle-school and secondary-content teachers must learn how to conduct global assessments in a whole-class environment, in order to identify and refer students for whom reading is a particular problem to reading and other specialists for more individualized, one-on-one diagnosis. For example, the following assessments can be administered as whole-class activities at the middle school or secondary level:

- *Interest Inventory:* This is a questionnaire that provides information about students' lives, families, interests, hobbies, reading preferences, reading habits, and so on.

- *Spelling Inventory* (see Bear, Invernizzi, Templeton, and Johnston, 2003): This provides information about students' phonics knowledge and stages of spelling development.

- *Writing Sample:* Students write to a prompt. Their writing provides information about how they develop ideas, their maturity of thought, their sentence and paragraph construction, their background knowledge, and their vocabulary and spelling development.

- *Content Textbook Inventory:* This provides information about how textbooks are organized and how students use textbooks. What is the purpose of the table of contents, the index, the glossary? Why is some text in color, bold print, or italicized? When assigned a chapter to read, how do you begin?

- *Reading Strategies Inventory:* This is a questionnaire designed to provide information about students' strategy use. When you come to a word you don't know, what do you do? After you read a paragraph you don't understand, what do you do? What do you do if you have no prior experience or background about the topic you're to read about? If you have background knowledge, how do you use it to help you understand what you're reading? How do you approach completing a study guide? How do you organize the information you're learning while you're reading?

This limited battery of informal assessments would provide teachers with a basis for initially planning instruction for a group of students. Using the findings from the assessments, teachers may decide to refer some students for additional individual, diagnostic assessment with a reading or special education specialist.

USING ASSESSMENT IN INSTRUCTIONAL DECISION MAKING

To make informed instructional decisions, effective teachers combine their knowledge of a subject area with the information gathered from ongoing classroom assessments. The language arts curriculum encompasses a comprehensive body of knowledge, skills, and strategies that students need to master. Mastery of specific skills may be determined through teacher-made or standardized tests created by publishers of textbooks used to teach the school curriculum. These tests may be norm- or criterion-referenced. Norm-referenced tests show how a student compares with others who took the test. Criterion-referenced tests evaluate student performance against some established standard. Having assessment instruments linked to instructional materials becomes an incentive for teachers to use both aspects of a publisher's products. Understanding the advantages and disadvantages of this is part of what teachers need to be alerted to.

There are two routes by which assessment can enhance the instructional process. One route is teacher use of the information to evaluate effectiveness of instruction. For instance, the Phonological Awareness Literacy Screening (PALS) system (http://pals.virginia.edu) established in the state of Virginia provides, through its Website, a set of early reading assessments and information about how children in various grades and subgroups across the state perform on the various assessments. A teacher can administer the PALS assessments, then upload the information to the Website (this service is free for Virginia teachers, but can be accessed with a fee for teachers in other states) and see immediately how the performance of his or her class stacks up. Then teachers can redesign instruction to focus on areas in which their own students generally score poorly. The PALS Website offers instructional guidance to address weaknesses identified by the classroom profiles. When assessment is integrated with instruction, it can help teachers know which activities are useful, when to give more examples and when to move on, and where to target instruction (American Federation of Teachers, National Council on Measurement in Education, and National Education Association, 1990; McMillan, 2000).

The second route to improved outcomes is feedback to students both during and after activities (Wiggins, 1998). Effective feedback is immediate, frequent, ongoing, and related to specific goals. It compares student work to exemplary work, such as through the use of anchor papers and rubrics. Instead of general-purpose terms like "good job" or "getting better," it describes qualities of performance, using concrete indicators and traits. For example, after analyzing a set of miscues, the teacher might recognize that a student has problems with morphologically complex words; this could then lead the teacher to sit down with the student and explain how to segment and pronounce words that end in *-ate, -tion, -ic,* and so on, telling the student specifically what kinds of words she or he is having trouble with and needs to work on. Feedback is information to the learner about how successful he or she is at what activities, while guidance is information about how to improve one's performance. Teachers need to provide both feedback and guidance; feedback alone is typically not enough for students to know how to improve, but guidance alone can leave them puzzled about what they are doing wrong. Assessment and giving feedback can take place at the same time during scheduled conferences with students or informal conversations; guidance can be communicated through questions that prompt students to think about what they know, to evaluate their own work, and to make decisions about what they need to know next (North Carolina State Department of Public Instruction, 1999).

Giving good feedback requires knowledge of what the learning targets are and what they look like when they are achieved, as well as an information-management system. Teachers need to analyze anecdotal records systematically, looking for evidence that children are moving toward learning targets. They might focus on a few students each day, or they might select a focus, such as reading fluency, comprehension, responses to literature, or students' interests, and look for specific understandings of all the students. Some use a form that includes the date, names of students, and focus of observations while others write directly on stickers which they then place in the student's record where they can be reviewed and evaluated regularly. After observing particular students and taking notes regarding the area of focus, these anecdotal records combined with other gathered evidence can be used to inform instruction and to give feedback to students about their progress (Winograd and Arrington, 1999).

Assessment can be especially powerful as an instructional tool when students learn to assess their own work. Students can take active roles in their own learning as they become trained in self-assessment, and as a result they can understand the main targets of their learning and what it is that they must do to achieve (Black and William, 1998; Stiggins, 2001; and Wiggins, 1998). This is a lesson that is best learned through the lavish use of self-assessment during the preservice and apprentice stages of teacher preparation and that can be effectively reinforced by certain kinds of collaborative mentoring and professional development.

Assessment that supports and informs instruction, then, will be assessment that has positive consequences for children. Quality assessment will foster an understanding of reading processes and purposes and will result in the development of motivated independent readers. Good assessment not only evaluates instruction but will also *be* instructive as it provides ongoing feedback and involves students in the assessment of their own reading. In addition, as teachers gather information to plan their teaching, students will benefit from instruction that is tailored according to their specific understandings and needs.

COMMUNICATING ASSESSMENT RESULTS

As noted earlier, a key use of assessment results is to communicate with students about their work. Here, the hope is to help students gain insight into their own strengths and needs and develop self-monitoring systems that lead to self-improvement—after all, they too can benefit from the learning, assessment, and reflection parts of the improvement cycle. The use of portfolios for student-teacher conferences is a key means of supporting student self-assessment. Unlike more formal self-evaluation procedures, conferences allow teachers to follow the students' leads, offering the feedback necessary to prompt as well as guide reflections. The number of conferences held varies widely among teachers, however; most agree that a minimum of one conference per term or marking period is critical, in addition to those held around individual pieces of work. Tierney, Carter, and Desai (1991) identify three kinds of conferences used in conjunction with portfolios.

- Planning conferences help students pull together their portfolios, including self-evaluative remarks. For example, "I don't know if this is good enough to go in. I did a better job on the story when I did it for the class newspaper. What do you think? Should I keep this draft?"

- In sharing conferences, students share their portfolios with classmates. For example, "This is what I've written about bugs and creepy crawlers. I have some information pieces, some pictures, and some jokes about them."

- Formative conferences involve joint assessment of the portfolios by the teacher and students as they develop goals for the future. For example, "I've learned about descriptive writing, and I think I want to learn about persuasive writing next." "Why don't you think about expository writing, too? That's a natural direction to take after descriptive and persuasive."

Paris (2001) found that although teachers used assessment most frequently for diagnostic purposes, the second most frequently stated use was in parent-teacher conferences. Teachers found that even the most informal conversations about a child were enhanced when actual work samples were available to review and discuss. Documentation of children's written composition, spelling, and oral reading along with a discussion of curriculum goals at a particular point in the year can be very enlightening for parents, who may have little to guide them about the school's expectations. It helps when teachers frame the discussion around both the child's strengths and needs. It also helps to discuss intervention or remedial efforts in place, so that parents get a sense that their child is getting the help he or she needs.

The same kind of conferences described for parents are helpful when discussing assessment results with administrators and other support staff. Obviously, the language used will be more technical than that used with parents. However, the goal is similar. This is an opportunity for others to gain insight into the child's day-by-day approach to learning and academic achievement. The classroom teacher is best suited to provide this kind of information, which is virtually impossible to garner from targeted, one-shot assessments administered by someone outside of the classroom. By looking across both types of results, a richer picture of the child as a learner can be sketched. A discussion of assessments of various types in different settings can yield suggestions for all those responsible for the education of the child, both in and out of school.

Finally, and most important within our view of teachers as career-long learners, communicating about the results of classroom assessment with colleagues can be a rich source of teacher learning. Teacher learning groups, whether informally convened or structured as part of a school's professional development effort, can benefit enormously from spending some time looking collaboratively at student writing, reviewing running records, or sharing observations or videotapes from student conferences or presentations, or from class discussions. Such collaborative use of assessment information generates shared ways of talking about phenomena—ensuring that everyone is defining "good writing" or "fluent reading" in similar ways. If teachers are sharing information across grade levels, it helps each to prepare students for later learning and increases coherence across grades in curricula and in standards. Such collaborative discussions are likely to take place during IEP conferences but may be completely absent from standard classroom practice. Yet we would be appalled if our medical care was delivered by different specialists who failed to check with one another about their diagnosis or about what drugs they were prescribing. Both children and teachers benefit if classroom assessments feed into opportunities for professional teacher learning.

TEACHER PREPARATION AND
SUPPORT FOR EFFECTIVE ASSESSMENT

Both preservice and inservice teachers need strong backgrounds in assessment. Because of the current "culture of assessment," it is safe to say that this topic has greater professional priority than ever before. There are a number of things that instructors at the preservice level can do to ensure that their students enter the profession with the background they need to meet the curricular demands they are sure to face.

As part of their reading-methods courses, and during their supervised practice, prospective teachers of reading should receive a thorough orientation to assessment as described in this chapter. This includes an understanding of the basic principles of assessment, familiarity with various types of assessments for reading and opportunities to administer a selection of them, knowledge about and practice using information from assessments in instructional decision making, and practice communicating assessment results.

A suggested procedure for this follows:

1. Select one or two assessments that you want all of the students to have experience administering. The Informal Reading Inventory or some other type of oral reading observation would be an excellent choice for use as a whole-group experience, as well as the DIBELS or a pseudoword reading task for one-on-one testing.

2. Through the use of videotapes or actual demonstrations, introduce the instrument and show how it is administered and scored. Discuss what the record of the particular student in the demonstration might mean. What strengths does he or she show? What needs are indicated? Encourage students to draw on what they know about reading development to discuss the assessment and insist that they use accurate terminology to describe what has been observed and recorded in the demonstration.

3. Give students an actual record of a student's oral reading based on an oral-reading assessment. Have students work in pairs to write responses to prepared questions about what they see and what it indicates about this student's reading abilities and needs. Present the findings for class critiques.

4. Then provide other assessment information on that same student, from an array of standardized diagnostic tests. Have the students work in pairs to expand or revise their conclusions about the student's abilities and needs.

5. Provide students with the necessary materials and have them administer an IRI to a child or adolescent. Have them provide a written analysis of the results along with suggestions for instruction. Action projects such as these require students to apply what they know about the content of reading instruction and assessment in a way that has practical significance for the classroom. It also requires them to use the language of literacy to make sense of the data they gather and to communicate about it with others.

6. In addition to the scaffolded whole-group experience described above, have each student select one or two additional assessments to administer, analyze, and introduce to the group. In this way, all students will have the benefit of exposure to a range of assessment tools.

Professional development for practicing teachers that is focused on assessment can be highly productive. The growing emphasis on assessment has increased teachers' interest in tools that they can use to monitor and document student progress. This is particularly true when an entire school is working toward the same vision and when teachers view the assessment results as useful for instructional decision making. Often, these efforts are linked to statewide and local curriculum standards and assessments. Following is a model that some districts have found useful.

1. The process starts with a thorough review of the local and statewide standards and assessments, and an analysis of the relation ("alignment") between them. Often, it is assumed that simply because teachers have these documents they are familiar with them. Workshops that involve grade-level meetings to discuss the content of these documents and what they mean for instruction should precede any decisions about planning for schoolwide systematic ongoing assessment. Obviously, the assessments teachers select for periodic administration at the classroom level should be closely tied to day-by-day instruction. However, these should also reflect the content of summative assessments given at the district and statewide levels. *When curriculum links to standards and standards link to both formative and summative assessments, there is no need for targeted test preparation. Experiencing the curriculum is the preparation.*

2. Teachers might want to select one or two measures that they administer periodically (perhaps once each marking period) as a means of gauging individual growth and assessing where each student is in relation to grade-level expectations.

3. Rubrics or checklists to accompany the assessments should be thoroughly discussed by teachers within and across grade levels. For example, if a type of oral reading inventory is used, teachers should be provided with a sample set of raw data from the assessment. The set should include students with varied abilities. These may be scored and analyzed independently by the teachers and then used as the basis for discussion at grade-level meetings. A common understanding about the nature of an instrument, how it is coded and scored, and how it informs instruction is critical.

4. Faculty should agree on a schedule for the collection of reading samples. In many schools, teachers collect an initial sample during the first two weeks of school to use as baseline data. Subsequent samples are collected toward the end of the first marking period and each additional marking period. Often, this is done in conjunction with the collection of writing samples to give a more comprehensive literacy profile.

5. Forms for recording results of the assessments may be developed by the teachers. At least two types of forms are recommended. One form should record the individual child's overall score for each sample taken and, if applicable, the scores for each subcategory of the reading assessment administered. At the bottom of that form there should be room for comments related to each assessment sample taken throughout the year. This form allows the teacher to get a profile of the individual student at a glance. It is an excellent tool for conferences with parents and others, because it shows both how the child is reading and how the teacher has analyzed the information and made notes about possible follow-up. These forms can be placed in each child's folder along with any raw data from the assessment.

A second form should be designed to transfer overall scores and subcategory scores for all students to a single sheet. This form should also be accompanied by teacher notes about the whole group's performance based on each sample. The group form has the potential to yield information about how each child is performing in relation to others in the group. More important, it provides information about the strengths and needs of the entire group, thus informing the teacher about what aspects of the curriculum have been effectively taught and whether any have been slighted. Each type of information has important implications for small and whole-group instruction.

6. Periodic teacher meetings within and across grade level to discuss assessment results and to exchange ideas regarding follow-up instruction turns collecting assessment data into a foundation for professional development. Teachers should be encouraged to exchange materials and ideas for lessons, model for each other, and develop a nonjudgmental study-group atmosphere. Sharing assessment data and interpretation of those data is a key strategy for developing the normative ways of thinking and talking that are characteristic of any profession.

Exhibit 5.1. Assessments Listed in the Text and in Table 5.1

Basic Reading Inventory (BRI)
Dubuque, IA: Kendall/Hunt.

Clinical Evaluation of Language Fundamentals, (4th ed.) (CELF-4)
Semel, E., Wiig, E., and Secord, W. (2003). Sydney, Australia: The Psychological Corporation.

Cloze Procedure
Harp, B. (2002). *The handbook of literacy assessment and evaluation* (2nd ed.). Norwood, MA: Christopher-Gordon.

Comprehensive Test of Phonological Processing (CTOPP)
Wagner, R., Torgesen, J., and Rashotte, C. (1999). Evanston, IL: Cognitive Concepts.

Concepts About Print (CAP)
Clay, M. M. (1993). *An observation survey of early literacy achievement.* Portsmouth, NH: Heinemann.
Escamilla, K., Andrade, A. M., Basurto, A. G., and Ruiz, O. A. (1996). *Spanish reconstruction of an observation survey: A bilingual text; Instrumento de Observación de los Logros de Lecto-Escritura Inicial.* Portsmouth, NH: Heinemann.

Developmental Spelling Inventory
Bear, D. R., Invernizzi, M., Templeton, S., and Johnston, F. (2003). *Words their way* (3rd ed.). Indianapolis: Prentice-Hall.

Diagnostic Fluency Assessment (DFA)
Martinez, M., Roser, N. L., and Strecker, S. K. (1999). *The reading teacher, 52,* 326–334.

Dynamic Indicators of Basic Early Literacy Skills (DIBELS) (see IDEL below)
Eugene: University of Oregon, CBM Network, School Psychology Program, College of Education.

Gates-MacGinitie Reading Tests
Itasca, IL: Riverside Publishing.

Get Ready to Read
New York: National Center for Learning Disabilities.

Indicadores dinamicas del exito en la lectura (IDEL)
Eugene: University of Oregon, CBM Network, School Psychology Program, College of Education.

Motivation to Read Profile (MTRP)
Gambrell, L., Palmer, B. M., Codling, R. M., and Mazzoni, S. (1996). *The Reading Teacher, 49,* 518–533.

Exhibit 5.1. Assessments Listed in the Text and in Table 5.1, *Cont'd*

Narrative Picture Book Comprehension
Paris, A. H., and Paris, S. G. (2003). Assessing narrative comprehension in young children. *Reading Research Quarterly, 38*, 36–76.
Clay, M. M. (1993). *An observation survey of early literacy achievement.* Portsmouth, NH: Heinemann.

Peabody Picture Vocabulary Test-III (PPVT-III) (see TVIP below)
Dunn, L. W., and Dunn, L. M. (1997). Circle Pines, MN: American Guidance Service.

The Phonological Awareness Test (PAT)
Austin,TX: PRO-ED Publishing Company.

Qualitative Reading Inventory (QRI)
Reading, PA: Addison-Wesley Longman.

Reading Attitude Assessment (RAA)
Harp, B. (2002). *The handbook of literacy assessment and evaluation* (2nd ed.). Norwood, MA: Christopher-Gordon.

Reading Attitude Assessment Tool (RAAT)
McKenna, M. C., and Kear, D. J. (1990). Measuring attitude toward reading: A new tool for teachers. *The Reading Teacher, 43*(9), 626–639.

Reading Inventory for the Classroom (RIC)
Upper Saddle River, NJ: Prentice Hall.

Reading Self-Concept Scale
Chapman, J. W., and Tunmer, W. E. (1995). Development of young children's reading self-concepts: An examination of emerging subcomponents and their relationship with reading achievement. *Journal of Educational Psychology, 87*(1), 154–167.

Running Records
Clay, M. M. (1993). *An observation survey of early literacy achievement.* Portsmouth, NH: Heinemann.

Spanish Phonological Test
Wagner, R. K., Torgesen, J. K., and Rashotte, C. (n.d.). Austin, TX: Pro-Ed Publishing Company.

Specific Level Assessment of Print and Sound (SLA)
Pacific Grove, CA: Brooks/Cole Publishing.

Spelling Inventory
Bear, D. R., Invernizzi, M., Templeton, S. R., and Johnston, F. (2003). *Words their way* (3rd ed.). Upper Saddle River, NJ: Prentice Hall.

Exhibit 5.1. Assessments Listed in the Text and in Table 5.1, *Cont'd*

Stanford Diagnostic Reading Test (SDRT)
San Antonio, TX: Psychological Corporation.

Test of Oral Reading Fluency (TORF)
Eden Prairie, MN: Children's Educational Services.

Test of Phonological Awareness (TPA)
East Moline, IL: Lingui Systems.

Test of Phonological Processing in Spanish (TOPPS) (see CTOPP above)
Washington, DC: Language Testing Division, Center for Applied Linguistics.
www.cal.org

Test of Reading Comprehension (TORC)
Austin, TX: PRO-ED Publishing Company.

Test de Vocabulario Imagenes Peabody (TVIP)
Dunn, L. W., Padilla, L., and Dunn, L. M. (1986). Circle Pines, MN: American
Guidance Service.

Woodcock Language Proficiency Battery, Revised (WLPB-R)
Woodcock, R. W. (1991). Itasca, IL: Riverside Publishing.

Woodcock Language Proficiency Battery, Revised: Spanish form (WLPB-R)
Woodcock, R. W., and Muñoz-Sandoval, A. F. (1995). Itasca, IL: Riverside
Publishing.

Woodcock Reading Mastery Test (WRMT)—Revised
Circle Pines, MN: American Guidance Service.

Yopp-Singer Test of Phoneme Segmentation
Newark, DE: International Reading Association.

CHAPTER SIX

A Model of Professional Growth in Reading Education

S pecifying the knowledge that teachers of reading should possess, while a daunting task in its own right, pales in comparison to specifying the course of development of that knowledge. Given that we know what effective, mature teachers should know about teaching reading (which is the explicit purpose of the five chapters preceding this one), the central question addressed in this chapter is how much of that knowledge teachers need at key stages of development on the way to full expertise or mature knowledge. How much do they need to learn in their preservice programs? What part of that corpus is better learned in professional development or graduate degree settings when teachers are "on the job" apprentices? What can wait until they are experienced professionals and ready to stand for some advanced recognition, such as the National Board of Professional Teaching Standards? In answering the question *How much when?* three further questions arise:

- What is it that *develops* over time?
- What are the characteristics of programs, activities, or both that help teachers embrace the full range of professional dispositions that present themselves in different phases of a teaching career?
- How can we measure teachers' knowledge at any of these points of development?

The answers we achieve will require different models of teacher education and different models of professional development than those we have used in the past. As the 1996 report from the National Commission on Teaching and America's Future (NCTAF) documents, our lack of clear standards along with a lack of a clear sense of accountability has led to a default teacher-education curriculum in which an "apprenticeship of practice"—relying on what you remember from being a student—is the dominant model (Lortie, 1975):

> Until recently, most teacher education programs taught theory separately from application. Teachers were taught . . . in lecture halls from texts and [by] teachers who frequently had not themselves ever practiced what they were teaching. Students' courses on subject matter were disconnected from their courses on teaching methods, which were in turn disconnected from their courses on learning and development. They often encountered entirely different ideas in their student teaching, which made up a tiny taste of practice added on, without connections, to the end of their coursework. When they entered their own classrooms, they could remember and apply little of what they had learned by reading in isolation from practice. Thus, they reverted to what they knew best: the way they themselves had been taught. Breaking this cycle requires educating teachers in partnerships with schools that are becoming exemplars of what is possible rather than mired in what has been [p. 31].

Clearly, whatever we provide in the name of improved experiences for reading teacher education, greater articulation among the components of the curriculum (both those components controlled by schools of education and those that are the responsibility of departments in the arts and sciences) is the first requirement of any such reform. Much of what is presented in the five preceding chapters is designed to address the articulation question, at least in terms of the content of the curriculum. But articulation is not the only problem. Other problems include inadequate time; uninspired teaching methods—especially methods that are at odds with the pedagogy advocated in the class (National Commission on Teaching and America's Future, 1996); superficial curriculum— a once-over-lightly treatment of too many topics (National Commission on Teaching and America's Future, 1996); a lack of grounding in subject matter— in the case of reading, subject matter would include language, orthography, learning, and assessment (see, for example, Fillmore and Snow, 2002); and a failure to address the contextual issues of schooling in a highly technological, increasingly multicultural society. And finally there is the biggest obstacle of all—the lack of any plan for well-sequenced continuing education for teachers once they leave the academy, a circumstance in which teacher education largely ends with college graduation. What is offered afterward consists mainly of updates on new techniques and materials or required workshops to meet state mandates. This lack of an intentional model of continuing education is paralleled by a lack of meaningful career paths for teachers, with little opportunity for advancement within the profession. The result is a system in which teachers are provided with neither the knowledge nor the incentives to achieve professional growth.

RESEARCH ON THE EFFECTIVENESS OF TEACHER EDUCATION

In a perfect world, teacher educators would not have to make a case for teacher education. After all, no one asks doctors, lawyers, or engineers whether professional preparation is necessary to become a competent member of their professions. But teachers and teacher educators seem to have to prove the worth of professional education again and again and again. And the attackers of formal teacher education are once again flexing their muscle (U.S. Department of Education, 2002), with the latest claim being that a combination of subject-matter knowledge and verbal ability is all that is required to be an effective teacher. Fortunately, the evidence for the efficacy of teacher education is compelling. Recent studies and reviews of research have shown that there is a consistently positive relationship between teacher preparation and student outcomes (for example, National Reading Panel, 2000; Fuller, 1999; Darling-Hammond, 1999; and Laczko-Kerr and Berliner, 2002). Teacher preparation and certification not only predict student achievement in reading but also are significantly related to teaching practices associated with higher levels of reading achievement (Darling-Hammond, 1999). Moreover, "more teacher education appears to be better than less—particularly when it includes carefully planned clinical experiences that are inter-woven with coursework on learning and teaching" (Darling-Hammond, 1997, p. 10). Darling-Hammond (1999) reports that "measures of teacher preparation and certification are by far the strongest correlates of student achievement in reading and mathematics, both before and after controlling for student poverty and language status" (Darling-Hammond, 1999, p. 4).

In one of the few systematic "natural experiments" on this question, Laczko-Kerr and Berliner (2002) compared the academic achievements of students in grades two through eight taught by undercertified (emergency, temporary, and provisionally certified) teachers and regularly certified primary school teachers (those from accredited universities who met all state requirements for their initial teaching certification). The SAT-9 National Curve Equivalent scores were not statistically different across the three categories of undercertified teachers, but students taught by certified teachers outperformed students taught by undercertified teachers on each of the three SAT-9 subtests—reading, mathematics, and language arts—by about two months on a grade-equivalent scale.

Working with survey data from teachers, Darling-Hammond, Chung, and Frelow (2002) analyzed the responses of beginning teachers in New York to questions regarding their preparedness and personal views about teaching. Compared with teachers who had entered teaching through alternative pathways, graduates of teacher-education programs responded that they felt better prepared to make subject-matter knowledge accessible to students, to plan instruction, to meet the needs of diverse learners, and to construct a positive learning experience.

The 2000 ETS report, *How Teaching Matters,* indicated that what teachers do in classrooms makes a great deal of difference, and that much of what makes that difference is content-specific pedagogy of the sort often gained in teacher-education programs (or in professional development settings) (Wenglinsky, 2000). Specifically, student-achievement gains are associated with being in the presence of teachers who develop higher-order thinking skills, promote hands-on learning experiences, and can work with special populations. These findings suggest that while the *what* of teaching is important, so is the *how* (see also Taylor, Pearson, Peterson, and Rodriguez, 2003; the how of teaching is dealt with extensively in Darling-Hammond, Bransford, LePage, Hammerness, and Duffy, 2005).

It is not just preservice teacher education that matters; so does professional development for inservice teachers. The National Commission on Teaching and America's Future (1996) pointed out the necessity of creating "stable, high-quality sources of professional development" (p. 82). Ultimately, the quality of teaching depends not only on the qualifications of individuals who enter teaching, but also on how schools structure teacher work and teachers' learning opportunities. Teachers who feel they are enabled to succeed with students are more committed and effective than those who feel unsupported in their learning and in their practice.

In summary, other things being equal, teacher education does make a difference. This is an important starting point for this discussion of the characteristics of preservice programs that seem to matter most. It suggests that we can be confident that what we are reforming is a worthy enterprise to begin with, thus rendering any reform efforts all the more important.

WHAT DEVELOPS, AND HOW?

Different views have been offered over time about the nature of development. The earliest conceptualizations of teacher knowledge distinguished between content knowledge (knowing your subject matter well) and pedagogical knowledge (knowing *how* to deliver that subject matter in the classroom—the stuff of which "methods" classes in universities are made). And in the case of education for future elementary teachers, we have traditionally finessed the content-knowledge question by offering a smattering in each subject matter or by suggesting that child development is the real content of elementary school teaching expertise. In the 1960s, due primarily to the widespread use of the National Teachers' Examination (NTE), the tripartite distinction between subject-matter knowledge, professional knowledge, and basic skills (reading, math, and writing mechanics) was introduced (see Porter, Youngs, and Odden, 2001). Gathering momentum through the 1980s, this conceptualization of teacher knowledge (and the multiple-choice assessment tradition accompanying it) prospered until it ran into a brick wall in the late 1980s and early 1990s. Some scholars criticized this approach as portraying too narrow a view of teaching and failing to address the most critical question—can teachers apply their content knowledge in the pedagogical context of a classroom? Shulman (1987) coined the term *pedagogical content knowledge* to capture exactly this complex interplay between subject-matter knowledge and teaching prowess.

From the late 1980s onward, two national innovations—the National Board for Professional Teaching Standards (NBPTS) and the Interstate New Teacher Assessment and Support Consortium (INTASC)—and several state movements have converged to put forward a different model of teacher knowledge, one that is driven by a clear depiction of "content standards" (what teachers should know and be able to do), a heightened sense of professionalism (we are members of professional communities of practice), and assessments that do justice to those standards. The conceptualizations of teaching underlying these new movements emphasize a few key components consistently (see Porter, Youngs, and Odden, 2001): (a) subject-matter knowledge; (b) knowledge of students; (c) the ability to engage students in active learning; (d) reflective practice (the capacity to examine and learn from one's own practice, including clear mistakes); (e) pedagogical content knowledge; and (f) professional commitment (active participation in professional communities). Compared to earlier views of teaching, the more recent views emphasize the application of knowledge in context (both the classroom and the communities of practice in which teachers work) and the interplay among the different types of knowledge.

But these new models did not arise spontaneously or as an isolated event. They really emerged from the intensive work on new models of teacher development from the mid-1980s through the 1990s (Berliner, 1988; Feiman-Nemser, 1983; National Commission on Teaching and America's Future, 1997; and Moir, n.d.). These models tend to fall into two categories—stage models, which are laid out on a continuum of expertise, and phase models, which move along a chronological continuum. Berliner's (1988) five-stage (from novice through competent through expert) model was based on a study of teachers' responses to classroom images at different stages of their careers. He noted that novice and expert teachers differed in their ease in interpreting classroom phenomena, discerning the importance of events, using routines, predicting classroom phenomena, judging typical and atypical events, and evaluating performance. Feiman-Nemser (1983) conceptualized learning to teach as a life-long process, involving four phases: pretraining, preservice, induction, and inservice learning. Feiman-Nemser's model represents an important contribution in its recognition that preparation for teaching begins even before future teachers enter preservice programs.

In yet another attempt to characterize the course of teacher development, the NCTAF document (National Commission on Teaching and America's Future, 1997, p. 67) proposes a fusion of stages and phases. The underlying continuum (see Figure 6.1) has phase-like labels, but four of the phases specify a criterion by which knowledge at that stage can be measured.

These models share important characteristics with the development model we have chosen for this volume. In Chapter One, we suggested that as teachers gain experience (and receive appropriate education), their knowledge base changes along the following path: (a) declarative knowledge; (b) situated, can-do procedural knowledge; (c) stable procedural knowledge; (d) expert, adaptive knowledge; to (e) reflective, organized, analyzed knowledge. All of these models, including ours, recognize that learning to teach is a process in which expertise develops over time and is marked by increasing sophistication of and control over a complex and multifaceted knowledge base.

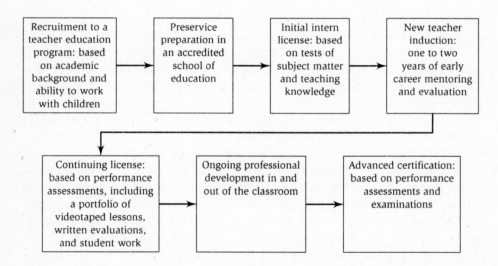

Figure 6.1. A Continuum of Professional Development

Source: Adapted from a document prepared jointly by the National Council for Accreditation of Teacher Education, the Interstate New Teacher Assessment and Support Consortium, and the National Board for Professional Teaching Standards by removing their labels for the various tests and standards.

With respect to models of teacher learning, the question of level of expertise has proved elusive to the profession. This chapter can be regarded as an attempt to create a developmental model of teacher learning by embedding the increasing sophistication of teacher knowledge (teacher knowledge includes all of the concepts and practices appearing in the previous five chapters) within the typical phases encountered by teachers as they move through their careers and refine their craft. A central issue is how the knowledge standards for initial licensure should differ from standards for permanent certification. For example, the NBPTS presents a rich model of what expert teaching looks like once it is in place. However, knowing how much novice teachers should know prior to placing them in classrooms is much more difficult for us to gauge and curiously absent from the National Board's characterization of expert knowledge. Its absence from documents like the NBPTS standards should not surprise us. Our research base for specifying requisite knowledge at different phases in a teaching career is sketchy at best. Wilson, Floden, and Ferrini-Mundy (2001) have characterized just how weak our knowledge base is in this regard, suggesting that "we need more studies that relate specific parts of teachers' preparation (subject matter, pedagogy, clinical experiences) to the effects on their teaching practice, and perhaps on student achievement" (p. iv).

Teaching reading is no exception to this enigma. As far as we can tell, there is a lot yet to learn about what literacy teachers need to know, but even more about what they need to know when. We have some important guideposts, including the other chapters in this book, and work like that of Fillmore and Snow (2002), but many questions remain unanswered. We do not, as we suggested earlier, have a strong research base that can guide us in thinking about what constitutes subject-matter knowledge in literacy or the kinds of knowledge (and skills or abilities) that make the greatest contribution to skillful teaching and student learning. But we do have the makings of professional consensus to get us started as we sort out the relationships between teacher subject-matter knowledge, teacher practices, and student achievement through careful research studies of the sort we have not done in our profession (Snow, 2002; Wilson, Floden, and Ferrini-Mundy, 2001). More important, we possess some very recent evidence suggesting that when it comes to knowledge about teaching reading, preservice programs that promote greater knowledge about and skill in teaching reading are consistently associated with greater gains in student achievement.

Ball (2000) discusses three problems that must be addressed in order to prepare teachers who know content and can use that knowledge to help students learn: (a) identifying content knowledge that matters for teaching, (b) understanding "how" that knowledge needs to be held, and (c) learning what it takes for teachers to put that knowledge into practice. To get started on these tasks, Ball proposes that we conduct job analyses of teaching:

> Instead of beginning solely with the curriculum, our understanding of the content knowledge needed in teaching must start with practice. We must better understand the work that teachers do and analyze the role played by content knowledge in that work . . . To improve our sense of what content knowledge matters in teaching, we would need to identify core activities of teaching, such as figuring out what students know; choosing and managing representations of ideas; appraising, selecting, and modifying textbooks; and deciding among alternative courses of action, and analyze the subject matter knowledge and insight entailed in these activities [Ball, 2000, p. 244].

In the same breath in which we admit that we have little evidence to guide us in answering the question of what knowledge is required when, we must try to fashion as good an answer as our current research-based knowledge, informed generously by experience and professional consensus, will allow. In a sense, that is what this whole book has been about.

We argue that as teachers learn more and gain more experience, their knowledge base changes in two ways. First, the magnitude increases: other things being equal, as teachers gain experience, they know more. Second, the proportion of the knowledge base that is allocated to the five types of knowledge outlined in Chapter One (declarative, situated, stable-procedural, expert-adaptive, and reflective) changes, with more and more knowledge moving to the expert-adaptive-reflective end of the continuum. Figure 6.2 represents these changes graphically in three different phases of a career.

The pie charts in Figure 6.2, as useful as they are in illustrating the dramatic progression of knowledge throughout a teaching career, mask certain subtleties of growth in teacher knowledge and advances in teacher education. For example, the large declarative piece of the pie for novices probably better characterizes traditional teacher-education programs in which students enroll in a number of lecture courses on campus before they set foot in a classroom. Current programs strive for greater integration between college coursework and practicum experiences; some even situate the college courses in school sites. In those programs, the boundary between the declarative and situated pieces of the pie are likely to be more permeable, perhaps even requiring a new name for this partly declarative, partly situated knowledge (see Figure 6.3).

A second characteristic of teacher learning obscured in the pie metaphor is the continuous acquisition of new declarative knowledge by experienced teachers. No matter how expert teachers become, or perhaps precisely because they are experts, they continue to learn new things, and for some period of time—at least until they apply it in their classrooms—that new knowledge is declarative in nature. The size of this piece of declarative knowledge obviously varies greatly from time to time depending on involvement in professional activities and explicit attempts to incorporate new practices into daily classroom routines. A third shortcoming of the pie metaphor is that it seems to suggest that less mature

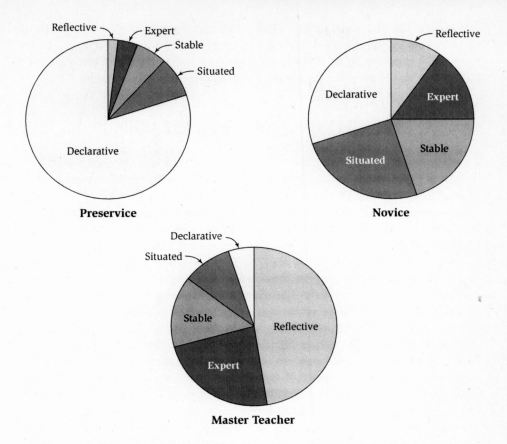

Figure 6.2. Knowledge Representation at Three Points of a Teacher's Career

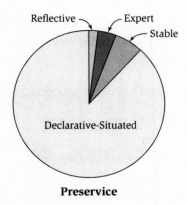

Figure 6.3. Reconsidering the Partitioning of Professional Knowledge

knowledge, like declarative knowledge, disappears once it matures into situated or reflective knowledge. It would be more accurate to say that the declarative knowledge remains a part of the more mature forms, perhaps providing a foundation that lies hidden but accessible beneath the surface (see Figure 6.4).

PRINCIPLES OF PROFESSIONAL LEARNING

As a profession, we have a great deal of experience, if not research, about the nature of experiences and content that prospective teachers encounter at different "programmatic" phases of their careers. By programmatic, we mean the sorts of learning experiences they are likely to encounter and the kinds of standards they are likely to be held accountable to in these various phases. Some phases have clearly delineated boundaries, such as preservice; others, such as master teacher, are more elusive because they depend less on an easily demarcated criterion, such as time, and more on a more opaque standard, such as expertise. Even so, we can take knowledge standards implicit in the various chapters preceding this one to develop a clear path of development to guide us in establishing programmatic efforts across these phases. Our developmental trajectory will be research-based in the sense that it will be based upon the research about the nature of reading acquisition in school settings—the sort of conclusions documented in broad-based research syntheses such as the report of the National Reading Panel (2000), *Preventing Reading Difficulties in Young Children* (Snow, Burns, and Griffin, 1998), and their historical predecessors (for example, Anderson, Hiebert, Scott, and Wilkinson, 1985). We stop to remind ourselves that what is lacking, and the task that remains ahead of us as a profession, is documentation that teachers who possess this sort of knowledge actually teach better and more effectively (where more effectively means students learn more and better) than those who do not (although the recent IRA study is certainly a step in the right direction). We have combed the research literature looking for broad principles to guide us in rethinking what can and should

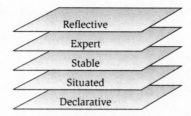

Figure 6.4. Less Mature Levels of Knowledge Underlie More Mature Levels

occur during professional preparation and development across the course of a teaching career. In this section, we use the principles we unearthed to organize our presentation of key findings.

Principle 1: Programs that address the ideas and beliefs about teaching that teachers bring with them are more likely to foster dispositions of openness to new ideas and reflection on their own assumptions about effective teaching and learning.

A great deal has been written about the role that preservice teachers' images and beliefs about teaching play in shaping their experiences in teacher-preparation programs (for example, Lortie, 1975; Holt-Reynolds, 1992), with Lortie's "apprenticeship of observation" looming large in all accounts of teacher's incoming beliefs. These studies suggest that preservice teachers use their pretraining experiences in education as a lens or filter through which they view the information and experiences offered to them in teacher-education programs (Borko and Putnam, 1997). Anderson, Armbruster, and Roe (1989) lament that "[w]hereas formal training often has embarrassingly little influence on how teachers teach, there is no doubting the influence of teachers' prior personal experience as students" (p. 3). Teacher-preparation programs should actively address teachers' pretraining experiences by helping future teachers articulate their experience-based beliefs about teaching and literacy education so these beliefs can be critically examined. Following their review of the research on teacher learning, Borko and Putnam (1997), in summarizing the work on beliefs, use a quote from Holt-Reynolds (1992, p. 681) to epitomize their conclusion that preservice education should "encourage preservice teachers to share the beliefs that guide their thinking and action, identify differences between those beliefs and the principles that teacher educators want them to explore, examine the strengths and limitations of using their personal beliefs as a data source, and respect and utilize their beliefs as standards against which to judge research-based principles." In addition to helping teachers examine their existing conceptions about teaching, preservice programs should ensure that future teachers are exposed to models of good teaching. If teachers' experience-based conceptions about teaching are to change, it must be through exposure to new experiences and images—within teacher-education programs and within K–12 classrooms.

The firm conviction of many teacher educators is that if we are to reverse these strongly held beliefs about the nature of pedagogy, then teacher educators must model teaching that is consistent with the beliefs and practices we are attempting to foster. As Feiman-Nemser (2001) notes, we often fail to provide models of good teaching, especially the sort of teaching we espouse: "The pedagogy of teacher education mirrors the pedagogy of higher education where lectures, discussions, and seat-based learning are the coins of the realm" (p. 1020). There is a certain irony, of course, in *telling* adults not to spend so much time *telling* kids what they should know. In a study of seven exceptional teacher-preparation programs, the National Commission on Teaching and America's Future (1996) found that these programs possess "a common, clear vision of good teaching that is apparent in all coursework and clinical experiences" and "strong relationships, common knowledge, and shared beliefs among school- and university-based faculty" (Darling-Hammond, 1997, p. 30). Of course, even if the pedagogy within teacher-education programs is altered, there is still the question of the models of teaching that candidates encounter in the workplace. And for years, teacher educators have noted the conflict between the models they espouse and the models implicit in the classrooms in which their teacher candidates intern (Hughes, Packard, and Pearson, 2000). This inconsistency is, of course, precisely the motivation for the Holmes Group's call, in the late 1980s and early 1990s, for professional development schools that could serve as an analogue for "teaching hospitals" in medical training, as sites in which the most current research-based practices could be seen at work in everyday classroom life (Holmes Group, 1986). And it has also served as the primary motive for using technology to document and create a living library of video cases of exemplary teaching (see, for example, Teachscape, n.d.; Hughes, Packard, and Pearson, 2000).

It is important to note that while most of the research on this issue has focused on the beliefs of preservice teachers, it applies equally as strongly, perhaps more strongly, to practicing teachers who have developed what we might label "self-apprenticeships of practice" rather than apprenticeships of observation. Practices that are deeply rooted in personal experience are highly resistant to change.

Principle 2: Programs that foster the expectation of and skills required for continuous learning are more likely to support the development of career learning paths.

If we conceptualize teacher development as a lifelong series of developmental stages, each stage must lay the foundation for the next. As such, a primary objective of teacher-preparation programs should be creating a foundation for continued learning about literacy education. This commitment to preparing teachers to "learn how to learn" is necessary because the sheer bulk of information and skills that teachers must possess to be effective in promoting literacy cannot possibly be acquired in the short duration of teacher-preparation programs. Creating this foundation for continual learning requires that we prepare teachers not only to use the knowledge they have acquired in teacher-preparation programs—knowledge about learning, development, motivation, language, culture and so on—but also to analyze novel situations and, perhaps most important, to seek out additional information to solve problems and improve instruction in the classrooms and schools in which they work (National Commission on Teaching and America's Future, 1996).

Programs at every level should help teachers see that part of their professional identity goes beyond the walls of their classrooms and schools, that they are lifelong learners who "continually strive to improve their practice" (International Reading Association, 2000, p. 3). Creating a foundation for continual learning requires that teachers be disposed to keep current about new policies, practices, and research related to the teaching of reading and to read this information critically: "Teacher study should include preparation for keeping abreast of new developments in the field of teaching reading to young children and for separating the wheat from the chaff therein, as well as practice in translating new information about literacy development and difficulties into instructional and assessment activities for children" (Snow, Burns, and Griffin, 1998, p. 288–289).

All programs of professional learning bear the responsibility for promoting these lifelong learning dispositions, but preservice programs bear the initial, and perhaps the primary, burden. They must prepare teachers to use the information they acquire in teacher-education programs, to seek out additional information as needed to solve problems that arise in the daily routines of teaching, and to develop the professional commitment and disposition to staying current with new developments in the professional knowledge base. The pressures of day-to-day life in classrooms will easily bury the best of intentions regarding nurturing one's own personal and professional growth. Early on, teacher-education programs must help teachers understand and accept their professional obligation to acquire new knowledge and then help teachers develop the tools needed to acquire it.

These dispositions are also important in professional development programs. The RAND Reading Study Group (Snow, 2002), for example, suggests that teachers must be front and center in discussions about how to improve comprehension instruction in schools today. Much educational research has failed to capitalize on teachers' capacity to contribute to reform and research efforts. Several new approaches, including Lesson Study (Stigler and Hiebert, 1999) and Video-Sharing (Taylor, Critchley, Paulsen, MacDonald, and Miron, 2003), enact this principle of continuous teacher learning by emphasizing collaboration amongst equals and the application of teacher experience and analysis to problems of practice. These approaches also put a premium on (a) respecting the contribution that teachers can make to the design and refinement of instructional strategies and (b) requiring them to be accountable for their practice and its impact on student learning.

Principle 3: Programs that ensure the development of a comprehensive and usable knowledge base are more likely to sustain successful initial teaching experiences.

Subject-matter preparation, particularly for elementary teachers, has a long and stormy history (see Chapter Six in Darling-Hammond, Bransford, LePage, Hammerness, and Duffy, 2005). In the days of the normal school and two-year programs of preparation (that is, no B.A. degree requirement), it was assumed that elementary school teachers needed to know something (but not a lot) about each of the important subjects taught in the elementary school. After Sputnik's embarrassing indictment of America's public education system in the 1950s, the call for more subject-matter training at all levels of teaching, but particularly for elementary-level teaching, was loud and clear. This was an era in which states began to require specific subject-matter coursework in mathematics, English (including knowledge about language and its development), science, art, music, history, health and physical education. In the past forty years, teacher education has experienced an ebb and flow regarding subject matter, at least in the policy debates about teacher preparation. Some critics of strong teacher-education programs (for instance, Kanstoroom and Finn, 1999; U.S. Department of Education, 2002) have suggested that strong subject-matter backgrounds, along with innate verbal ability, matter a great deal more than any pedagogical or professional preparation. Others have suggested that it is but one of many planks in a truly professional program of preparation (for example, Darling-Hammond, 1996).

LIKELY COMPONENTS OF A
KNOWLEDGE BASE FOR TEACHING READING

Knowing full well just how weak the research base is in this regard, we set out to find at least a starting point for the subject-matter knowledge base for teaching reading, and we did it by consulting several accounts of key elements in that knowledge base. Some of these accounts represent elaborate consensus documents, such as the two documents prepared by the Learning First Alliance, *Teaching Reading Is Rocket Science* (Moats, 1999) and *Every Child Reading: A Professional Development Guide* (Learning First Alliance, 2000); *Prepared to Make a Difference,* the position papers on teacher education prepared by the International Reading Association (National Commission on Excellence in Elementary Teacher Preparation for Reading Instruction, 2003); or standards specified by the National Board for Professional Teaching Standards (n.d.) and the Interstate New Teacher Assessment and Support Consortium (1992). Others represent careful scholarship by individual scholars or small groups of scholars, such as the essay prepared by Fillmore and Snow (2002) or the review of

Anderson, Armbruster, and Roe (1989). And, of course, the single most important resource in subject matter understandings for teaching reading have been the chapters prepared by our colleagues in this volume. Almost fifteen years ago, in trying to characterize the knowledge base for teaching reading, Anderson, Armbruster, and Roe suggested a combination of knowledge sources that contextualizes the role of subject-matter knowledge (the *what* or the knowing *that*) appropriately:

> What do expert teachers know? They possess a rich body of knowledge, including knowledge of curriculum and content; of learners and their characteristics; of the ends, purposes, and values of education; and of educational contexts (Shulman, 1987). In addition, expert teachers have organized problem-solving strategies and routines at various levels of generality. For example, teachers may have a global routine for conducting reading lessons, with specific routines for correcting errors, managing independent seatwork and handling disruptions. Expert teachers negotiate "knowing that" and "knowing how" as they plan, predict, anticipate and solve problems, estimate what students know and don't know, revise teaching plans, and make the most of unexpected opportunities [Anderson, Armbruster, and Roe, 1989, p. 2].

So, for these scholars, writing at a time when constructivist views of teaching and learning were in their ascendancy, subject-matter knowledge, what would have been labeled "declarative knowledge" in those days (and dubbed "knowledge of curriculum and content" by Anderson, Armbruster, and Roe, 1989), was one among many knowledge bases needed by teachers, along with a great deal of procedural knowledge (knowing *how*) and conditional knowledge (the knowledge of *when* and *why* that permits teachers to predict, anticipate, revise, and adapt teaching plans). In the current policy context, after a long period during which student reading achievement (Grigg, Daane, Jin, and Campbell, 2002) has been stagnant, the demands for subject-matter knowledge—especially regarding issues of language, orthography, and the psychological underpinnings of reading development—have been loud and clear (for example, Snow, Burns, and Griffin, 1998; Learning First Alliance, 2000; and International Reading Association, 2000).

What do excellent reading teachers know about reading development? In a position statement on excellence in the teaching of reading, the International Reading Association responded to this question by saying that excellent reading teachers "understand the definition of reading as a complex system of deriving meaning from print that requires all of the following:

- The development and maintenance of a motivation to read
- The development of appropriate active strategies to construct meaning from print

- Sufficient background information and vocabulary to foster reading comprehension
- The ability to read fluently
- The ability to decode unfamiliar words
- The skills and knowledge to understand how phonemes or speech sounds are connected to print (International Reading Association, 2000, p. 2)

To provide a "thought experiment" about what this knowledge base might truly look like across the career span of teaching, we applied the levels rubric outlined in Chapter One (levels of knowledge ranging from declarative through situated to reflective) to two elements that are a part of the knowledge base in our conceptualization, phonemic awareness and the pragmatics of language use—just to see how a model of emerging expertise might begin to take shape. The results of those efforts, detailed in Tables 6.1 and 6.2, suggest that we can begin to think about clear differences in the nature and use of knowledge across these levels.

Principle 4:   Programs that help teachers apply what they have learned in teacher-education programs to particular contexts and students ease the transition to classroom teaching.

In their report *What Matters Most,* The National Commission on Teaching and America's Future (1996) presents a series of recommendations for improving teacher preparation and professional development. Among these recommendations is a call for the creation of mentoring programs for beginning teachers (paired with evaluation of teaching skills). The Commission points out that even high-quality preservice teacher preparation cannot adequately address all of the challenges that teachers will confront in their early years of teaching. Feiman-Nemser agrees that teacher education cannot be solely responsible for preparation, suggesting that "if preservice teacher educators could count on induction programs to build on and extend their work, they could concentrate on laying a foundation for beginning teaching and preparing novices to learn in and from their practice" (2001, p. 1016).

The NCTAF recommends that all beginning teachers be assigned a skilled mentor who can provide ongoing consultation and evaluation: "[R]esearch shows that beginning teachers who have had the continuous support of a skilled mentor are much more likely to stay in the profession and much more likely to get beyond classroom management concerns to focus on student learning" (National Commission on Teaching and America's Future, 1996, pp. 80–81).

Perhaps motivated by such encouraging evidence, many, indeed most, states have enacted statutes mandating induction programs for new teachers along the lines suggested by NCTAF. However, few states have funded those mandates,

Table 6.1. Changes in Teacher Knowledge Across a Career Pathway: Phonemic Awareness

Type of Knowledge	What Phonemic Awareness Knowledge Might Look Like
Declarative knowledge	Teachers would know that a phoneme is a basic unit of sound, that it is different from a syllable, and that in English the match to graphemes is uneven. They would know that phonemic awareness is a subcategory of phonological awareness, and that the capacity to blend phonemes together to make words and to segment words into constituent phonemes is a key understanding for kids to possess early on.
Situated, can-do procedural knowledge	Teachers would possess at least a few routines for assessing phonemic awareness (for instance, blending, segmentation, elision) and a few routines for engaging kids in its application (such as rhyming games, elision tasks, alliteration tasks). As teachers implement the routines, they would likely consult guidelines or a manual regularly. The lessons (or assessment protocols) would appear to be relatively rigid and prepackaged as they are enacted. Teachers would require expert scaffolding from a mentor to make adaptations.
Stable procedural knowledge	At this level, the routines have become more or less automatic for the teachers, and the teachers are beginning to be able to adapt to the performance needs of different groups and individuals. The repertoire of routines for teaching different aspects of phonemic awareness (for example, blending, segmentation, elision) have expanded and some differentiation has occurred. The teacher sees connections between steps in the PA program adopted by the school and the kinds of PA performance exhibited by students when they are asked to spell words "the way they sound" during writing time.
Expert adaptive knowledge	Teachers at this level have come to see the strengths and weaknesses of different PA programs (both formal and informal), they know which programs fit the needs of different sorts of students, and they can reconcile conflicting results from different approaches to PA assessment. They can conduct staff development sessions on how to administer PA tests and how to teach PA in different ways.
Reflective, organized, analyzed knowledge	When teachers possess reflective, organized, and analyzed knowledge, they can examine PA programs and assessments critically, with an eye toward predicting which programs are likely to be successful with different populations of students. They might well be involved in a districtwide committee to develop a professional development program for improving PA instruction.

Table 6.2. Changes in Teacher Knowledge Across a Career Pathway: Pragmatics

Type of Knowledge	What Knowledge About the Pragmatic Dimensions of Language Might Look Like
Declarative knowledge	Teachers at this level understand the fundamental form-function relationship in language use—that writers and speakers use the formal tools and features of text to fulfill different functions and achieve different goals (such as to inform, to persuade, to entertain).
	They have a passing acquaintanceship with key terms related to pragmatics—such as discourse, register, genre, textual devices and conventions, voice, style, persona, stance, perspective—but their knowledge is not well-developed or differentiated.
	They understand the social and cultural functions that texts perform in different contexts (school, work, play, home) and ways in which those contexts shape textual use and interpretation.
Situated, can-do procedural knowledge	Teachers possess at least a few routines for addressing these features of language use, such as Questioning the Author, and teach students about how to use genre and register to achieve particular effects on an audience (for instance, persuasion or entertainment). These lessons would be fairly prescribed and circumscribed—the understandings about text developed therein may or may not be applied to reading and writing activities in other classroom contexts.
	Teachers may be more skilled at teaching students the meaning of terms, such as *genre*, *voice*, and *perspective* than helping students apply these understandings to their reading and writing of texts.
Stable procedural knowledge	At this level, the routines have become more or less automatic for the teachers, and they are beginning to be able to adapt to the performance needs of different groups and individuals. Teachers have acquired additional routines for developing students' understandings of the pragmatic dimensions of text and are beginning to develop approaches for assessing these understandings.
	The teacher's knowledge is becoming increasingly differentiated, as is instruction. Instruction may include more explicit attention to the form-function relationship, may include analysis of more subtle stylistic features (for example, the connotative loading of words and idioms), and may include increasing attention to the ways that societal forces shape authors and texts.
Expert adaptive knowledge	At this level, teachers are less reliant on specific routines and are better able to integrate issues of discourse and pragmatics into students' daily interactions with texts.
	The teacher's own understanding of these issues and their application to reading and writing has become more sophisticated. Whereas in the

Table 6.2. Changes in Teacher Knowledge Across a Career Pathway: Pragmatics, *Cont'd*

Type of Knowledge	What Knowledge About the Pragmatic Dimensions of Language Might Look Like
	declarative stage teachers understood the meaning of terms such as *discourse, register* and *genre,* they are now able to connect these stylistic variations to the pragmatic or social (and political or ideological) functions of text.
	Teachers at this level can anticipate and respond to obstacles that their students will confront in applying these understandings to their interpretation and composition of texts.
Reflective, organized, analyzed knowledge	At this level, teachers can use their understandings about the pragmatic dimensions of text proactively and in larger contexts. They can evaluate the effectiveness of programs, routines, and activities designed to develop students' understandings about the pragmatic dimensions of text and their ability to apply these understandings to their reading and writing.
	These teachers may be involved in developing new approaches to teaching pragmatics at the school or district level.

thus rendering implementation uneven both within and across states. Some districts have chosen to fund their own; others have created voluntary programs in which both the novice and mentor teachers contribute their time to the effort. Like the weather, it remains an effort that everyone talks about but no one does much about. Even so, the principles emerging from the research are clear and deserve our professional attention.

Principle 5: Programs that promote articulation among the key components (standards, coursework, and internship experiences) are more likely to help teachers develop the sense of personal efficacy and professional responsibility they will need to achieve an integrated understanding of theory and practice.

Teacher-preparation programs need to do a better job of building conceptual links between classroom, clinical, and field-based experiences in ways that will prepare future teachers to apply their course work and other preservice experiences to their teaching practice (Snow, Burns, and Griffin, 1998). Ball (2000) notes that the teacher-education programs fragment or isolate elements of the required knowledge, thus leaving the task of integration and articulation, especially between subject-matter knowledge and pedagogy, up to the students in their programs. Feiman-Nemser (2001) suggests also that preservice programs are missing key components designed to promote just the sort of articulation needed, such as ". . . well-designed opportunities to link theory and practice, develop skills and strategies, cultivate habits of analysis and reflection through focused observation, child study, analysis of cases, microteaching, and other laboratory experiences" (p. 1020).

Commenting on a basic "structural" problem in staffing teacher-education programs, the NCTAF suggests that successful teacher preparation includes carefully designed, high-quality clinical and field experiences that are closely connected to the teacher-preparation curriculum (National Commission on Teaching and America's Future, 1996). Unless cooperating teachers in whose classrooms students intern are considered a part of the teacher-education program, discontinuities between theoretical and pedagogical coursework and the practices interns see in their clinical settings are likely to be as powerful as the discontinuities promoted by their long-standing "apprenticeships of observation" that Lortie brought to our attention so long ago.

Just as with principle 4, induction will have to be a central consideration in implementing principle 5. Discontinuity between the content of teacher education and early independent teaching is just as disconcerting as discontinuity between the components of the teacher-education program. We need to reverse the all-too-common observation (such as by Britzman, 2003) that one of the first things new teachers do is set aside everything they have learned in their teacher-education program. Britzman goes on to argue that the primary reasons teachers set aside their earlier learning is that they have difficulty seeing its relevance. Effective induction programs could, if properly structured, help new teachers see the potential connections between the problems they face and the knowledge they have acquired thus far in their development

Principle 6: Programs that "stay the course" are more likely to succeed than those that change foci frequently.

While this principle applies to all programs, it is especially relevant to professional development programs for practicing teachers. Both the National Commission on Teaching and America's Future (1996) and the RAND Reading Study Group (Snow, 2002) express strong reservations about traditional approaches to teacher professional development, suggesting that the traditional "one-shot" approaches are ineffective because they fail to provide enough time or genuine content. The Commission notes that, unlike teachers in countries such as Germany, Japan, and China, U.S. teachers get few opportunities for ongoing learning. A few characteristics of more effective approaches clearly distinguish them from the typical fare of teachers in U.S. schools. First, they are "linked to concrete problems of practice and built into teachers' ongoing work with their colleagues" (National Commission on Teaching and America's Future, 1996, p. 40). Second, they contribute to the development of teachers' everyday practice, rather than focusing on trendy or isolated techniques, methods, or activities. Third, they provide mechanisms for follow-up (for instance, additional assistance with implementation).

Approaches such as Lesson Study (Stigler and Hiebert, 1999; Lewis, 2002) and Video Sharing (Taylor, Critchley, Paulsen, MacDonald, and Miron, 2003) address these concerns through sustained and focused lesson development and analysis. While traditional professional development often involves the sharing of specific tips and favorite activities, a more deliberate, sustained approach involves dedicated study, planning, and reflection related to a specific focus. Lesson Study groups in Japan, as they have been implemented in math and science, may devote three or more years to a content area and may maintain a specific focus (such as introducing subtraction and borrowing) for one to two years. A similar dedication over a substantial time period will be required to make research-based literacy practices a part of daily life in reading classrooms (see Taylor, Pearson, Peterson, and Rodriguez, 2003b).

Principle 7: Programs that are sensitive to local context are more likely to succeed than generic approaches.

When practicing teachers study and plan instruction jointly, they can address issues that arise in the local context. Rather than adopting traditional, popular, or research-based strategies "in principle," teachers can seek out research and other information based on their particular needs. In doing so, they inform their own classroom instruction, and they provide valuable information about the portability of research-based reading practices, the degree to which more generic strategies can be adapted to their own situation. And even if the teachers in a given school, in reading and reflecting upon the research, end up adopting all of the strategies used by another school down the road, on the other side of town, or across the nation, they are likely to exhibit greater commitment to implementation than if someone had handed them the very same curriculum intact, with a mandate to teach it, or else. Local context is not limited to the individual classroom; it also includes school-, community-, even districtwide concerns, such as

- Schoolwide and classroom goals for student learning
- Research that informs collective concerns
- Cultural and linguistic perspectives unique to a school community
- Schoolwide approaches to assessment, curriculum, and instruction

Principle 8: Programs that encourage careful analyses of teaching and the generation of shared knowledge are more likely to nurture a sense of collective responsibility for instruction.

Professional development should encourage teachers to consider the nature of teaching and curriculum as they build specific lessons. Teachers encounter new ideas and confront opposing points of view as they analyze the research, the practice of others, and their own practice. They work not only to build and improve upon existing lessons but also to come to deeper understandings about instruction and the basis for instructional improvement (Hiebert and Stigler, 2000). Through this careful analysis, teachers not only build a shared knowledge base but establish joint ownership of the curriculum and instructional strategies. For example, an approach like Lesson Study encourages teachers to develop a common vision of good practice and of schoolwide learning goals for students (Lewis, 2000). Similar results have been obtained when teachers get together to conduct careful examinations of student work, primarily because questions about variation in the quality of student work invariably devolve to the kinds of instruction that led to the work observed in the samples (Mitchell, 1999).

Principle 9: Programs that achieve a balance between school or program needs and the needs and goals of individual teachers are more likely to support teachers' movement along the developmental continuum toward becoming expert, adaptive practitioners.

It is difficult to document this principle with hard, or even soft, evidence because few if any professional development efforts have concerned themselves with teachers' personal growth trajectories, focusing instead on the needs of schools and districts, often as a part of school-reform efforts. Hence, existing approaches are unlikely to help teachers "view themselves as lifelong learners and continually strive to improve their practice" (International Reading Association, 2000, p. 3). Given the press to improve performance on external assessments in our current reform zeal, it is possible that the failure to address the individual developmental needs and aspirations of teachers may, in the long run, prove to be the Achilles' heel of professional development. One of the shortcomings of most schools is that they have too few "experts" on staff—individuals who possess an extra measure of knowledge and expertise in a particular domain, such as math, reading, assessment, or management. An intentional approach, in which a faculty worried about developing such specialists, could make real the goal of distributed expertise.

CODA

Some critics characterize the reading performance of America's students as a national crisis and point to the teaching profession and schools of education as the most culpable parties in creating that crisis (for example, Sweet, 2004).

While the overall trends in performance over time do not suggest a crisis (in fact, after a just barely detectable increase in the 1970s and 1980s, NAEP reading achievement has been remarkably flat since about 1990), the achievement gap between the rich and poor, the privileged and marginalized, the advantaged and disadvantaged in our society is still unconscionably wide. If for no other reason than getting serious about narrowing that gap, those of us who call ourselves professional educators—both members of the P–12 teaching profession and the teacher educators who offer pre- and inservice experiences—need to engage in a serious self-examination of the challenges of teaching in today's world and the knowledge and skills needed to meet those challenges. We must take seriously our own learning—from the first day one makes a commitment to become a teacher until the day that one decides to retire from the profession—and make it as high a priority as eliminating the achievement gap that robs so many students of the opportunity that, as Americans, they are entitled to. We cannot, we believe, eliminate the achievement gap in our schools without closing the knowledge gap in our profession.

APPENDIX

T able A.1 compares terms used in models of early reading. The sections that follow provide more details on the changes encountered between preschool and grade two. (Only the last two columns of the table go further; for matters beyond word reading, see Chapter Two.)

PRESCHOOL, EARLY KINDERGARTEN [1]

Sample Responses

- Attempts to read "Crest" on a tube of toothpaste, but says "toothpaste"
- Learns to read "three little pigs," then when one word is covered up, reads "two little pigs."

Alternate Names

Prealphabetic, visual cue, selective cue, paired associate, logographic, linguistic guessing, prereading, pseudo-reading

Descriptions

- Acts as if written language directly represents meaning, as if words signify by overall shape, length, type design, or color
- Recognizes words from graphic visual cues

Table A.1. Comparing Views of Strategies Used by Beginning Readers

Approximate Starting Point	Ehri (and Wilce)	Juel	Gough and Hillinger	Gough, Juel, and Roper-Schneider	Frith	Marsh and others	Chall	Spear-Swerling and Sternberg
Preschool through early kindergarten	Prealphabetic, visual cue	Selective cue	Paired associate	Visual cue	Logographic	Linguistic guessing	Prereading Pseudo-reading	Visual cue
Kindergarten through early grade one	Partial alphabetic, rudimentary alphabetic, phonetic cue					Discrimination net guessing		
Grade one	Full alphabetic	Spelling sound	Cipher reading	Cipher reading	Alphabetic	Sequential decoding	Initial reading or decoding	Controlled
Grade two	Consolidated alphabetic				Orthographic	Hierarchical decoding		
Grade three							Confirmation, fluency, ungluing from print	Automatic
Grades four through six							Reading for learning new: single source	Strategic reading
Grades six through eight							Reading for learning new: multiple sources	
High school							Multiple viewpoints	Proficient adult
College and after							Construction reconstruction	

Note: Ehri and Snowling (2004) have a most clear, broad, deep, and critical review of much of the alphabetic system part of this material.

- Associates arbitrarily selected visual features of a word to a spoken form or meaning of a particular word stored in memory
- Guesses words based on contextual, syntactic, or semantic information
- Easily reads own name and some brand names, names of favorite characters (toy, TV, book), or places
- Misled by irrelevant features (such as when a stain on a word card is removed, the word is no longer read)
- Does not identify known words if presented in a neutral form and context
- Limited number of associations can be held in memory, so not many words read
- Cues for known words overlap, so has frequent gaps or inaccurate responses
- Mediates associations word by word (two Os in *look* are eyes), so misreads GPC-related words ("book" or "cook" for "look")
- Does not link graphemes to phonemes
- Does not attend to detailed visual information of written word form
- Does not finger-point read
- Learns words that are taught as wholes but does not generalize patterns to GPC-related words

Other Word-Identification-Related Proficiency

Phonological sensitivity: recognizes, recites, and invents rimes and alliteration

Phonemic awareness: but may be limited to syllable initial phonemes and to certain tasks; recognizes about fifteen letters by name, has a sound correspondence for about five letters; produces some conventional letter shapes (more often in isolation or isolated words than when producing extensive text) (Sulzby, Barnhart, and Hieshima, 1989).

Variability and Transitions

Compared to words with visually distinctive forms (W^{B}C for *giraffe*), words that are phonetically plausible (JRF for *giraffe*) are more difficult for children to learn (Ehri and Wilce, 1985); however, letter and sound knowledge does exert an influence on word learning even at this early point. The visually distinct form advantage gives way (Treiman and Rodriguez, 1999; Treiman, Sotak, and Bowman, 2001; and Bowman and Treiman, 2002) if children know letter names and if the words to be learned use the phonology of letter names (*tm* is a help to learn *team*, but not *tame*) and if the letter name cue is in the initial position (the *l* in *lf* helps for *elf* compared to the final position of *l* for *fell*). The advantage for visually distinct forms was not found in studies using a spelling task, which appears to force a more analytic and less logographic approach to word identification.

Performance on letter-sound correspondence tasks also varies, influenced by the pronunciation of the letter's names and its position in the word: even preschoolers are more likely to match beginning *d* and /d/ in *dear* than in *door* and ending *m* and /m/ in *hem* than in *ham* (Treiman, Tincoff, and Richmond-Welty, 1996).

KINDERGARTEN, EARLY FIRST GRADE[2]

Sample Responses

- Learns to read "three little pigs," but when "three" is replaced by "these" still reads "three"
- Attempts to read "Crest" on a tube of toothpaste, but says "don't know" (knows "toothpaste" from context, recognizes letter *c* and its /k/ sound link, finds conflict between initial sound in *toothpaste*, /t/, and initial sound from word *Crest*, /k/, so knows he or she has no answer).

Alternate Names

Partial alphabetic, rudimentary alphabetic, phonetic cue reading, discrimination net guessing, initial reading or decoding, early alphabetic

Descriptions

- Acts as if letters in a written word are for representing sounds in the spoken form of the word, but each word is read as a known whole word
- Associates letters with corresponding parts of spoken words, but focuses on initial and final positions, overlooking details in the middle
- Asks for help with an unidentified word by saying letter names
- Uses some GPC and letter-name knowledge to differentiate among words in sight vocabulary, including high-interest words (such as names), easily imaged words (for example, colors or action verbs), and high-frequency grammatical function words (such as *what, who,* or *was*), even if much of the rest of the words recognized depend on rare GPCs or are exceptions that the reader does not know about
- Learns one-to-one GPCs conditioned by surrounding structure (for example, *b* for /b/ but not *c* for both /s/ and /k/); sometimes uses them to recognize words

- Can use analogy to known words to identify new ones, if analogy is cued or prompted to words that are so familiar that they are represented in memory with letter details specified
- Follows text with finger as others read aloud (finger-point reading)
- Makes reading errors that are plausible based on combined context and partial letter-sound cues; makes more errors in the middle of words than in the beginning or ending of words; errors are related to inexperience with left-to-right orientation for sequential decoding (such as *was/saw*).

Other Word-Identification-Related Proficiency

Phonemic awareness: undertakes analytic, synthetic, or identity tasks for sounds in all positions in a word

Letter knowledge: recognizes and makes upper- and lowercase for all letters, knows at least one sound link for many letters

Spelling: estimates letter match for sequentially encountered phonemes in spoken words based on the sound of the letter name and some GPCs (DiStefano and Hagerty, 1985; Gentry, 1982; and Graves, 1983; about spelling and reading relations, see Frith, 1985; and Treiman and Kessler, 2003).

Variability and Transitions

GPC learning varies in relation to sound values in letter names; the easiest are those for letters whose names begin with the consonants that are the conventionally associated sounds for them, for example, *d* named /diy/ but not *f* named /ef/ (Henderson, 1981; Read, 1971; Treiman, 1993; Ehri, 1983; and Treiman, Sotak, and Bowman, 2001).

Word learning varies, too, according to whether the phonemes in the word match the phonemes in the names of the letters used in the word; words with long vowel sounds, *b, d, f, j, k, l, m, n, p, r, s, t, v, z,* soft *c* as /s/, and *g* as /j/ are learned early compared to other words, especially those with consonant digraphs (such as *sh, wh, th*) or those with long vowels spelled with digraphs (such as *boat, bead*) or silent *e* (as in *gate*) (McBride-Chang, 1999; Treiman, Tincoff, Rodriguez, Mouzaki, and Francis, 1998). Children who are very much younger and who do not otherwise use alphabetic cues learn to use them if they can take advantage of sounds in the letter names that match the initial sounds of the words being taught (Treiman and Rodriguez, 1999), but children do not learn to take advantage of other letter-sound links until later in their reading learning (Treiman, Sotak, and Bowman, 2001; Bowman and Treiman, 2002). Reading and spelling can proceed separately even for the same words; some visually distinctive words can be read but not spelled and some words with simple GPCs can be spelled but not read (Bradley and Bryant, 1979).

FIRST GRADE[3]

Sample Responses

- Reads *three* and *these* more accurately but maybe more slowly than in kindergarten
- Reads *says* as if it rhymes with *ways* rather than with *Pez*.

Alternate Names

Full alphabetic, spelling sound, cipher reading, alphabetic, sequential decoding, controlled, glued to print.

Descriptions

- Focuses attention on all letters in all positions of the words in a text
- Learns to phonologically recode (sound out) words, grapheme by grapheme, from left to right, blending, and retrieving spoken word form from memory
- Learns and uses GPCs even in multisyllabic words and even when GPCs involve more than one grapheme, are not bi-unique, or are conditioned by surrounding letters or morphology (for example, the *augh* in *caught;* the *c* in *cat* and *city;* and the *ed* in *walked* and *wanted*)
- Attempts to read words never before seen and whose meanings are unknown
- Asks for help with a word by providing pronunciation if meaning is at issue, but letters if pronunciation is at issue
- Relearns words that had been learned earlier as whole-sight words, phonologically recoding and reading them more slowly, using GPCs as far as each word allows, thus using fewer widely applicable cues to replace the wide array of graphemic cues needed to distinguish each item before
- Practices reading connected text, increases rate of reading, increases size of sight vocabulary, relying more on subword level details
- Reads new words by analogy to sight words in memory (no longer needs cue or prompt; subword details available in written text for target word and subword details for potential source words in memory can be matched)
- Makes errors by overapplying GPCs and analogies

Other Word-Identification-Related Proficiency

Phonemic awareness: responds to analytic, synthetic, and identity questions about phonemes in any position in a word; some interference from word spelling (for example, *mix* said to have three rather than four phonemes)

Spelling: estimated spellings represent all phonemes in a word, influenced by GPCs and orthographic patterns from reading practice and from conventional spelling lessons; ease of learning conventional spellings related to reliance on GPC patterns; nonletter forms or scribbles rare even in playful renditions of extended texts.

Variability and Transitions

Some words, especially those with irregular grapheme-phoneme links, continue to be processed by making use of partial letter-sound to guide memory searches for a likely word, the common strategy for an earlier period (Goulandris and Snowling, 1995).

A process begins that comes to full flower in the later period, the *self-teaching* mechanism (Share 1995, 1999; Share and Stanovich, 1995). As the student phonologically recodes a word, she or he not only reads the word so the passage can be understood, but, at the same time, sets features of the written form of the word in memory alongside a phonological representation familiar from speaking and listening. Each time the word (or a part of it) is met, phonological recoding is easier, quicker, and more assured than the previous time. After being encountered some number of times,[4] the word is processed without laborious focus on each separate grapheme-phoneme link and the processing provides familiarity with links among the graphemes (in other words, the letters, the orthographic information). Eventually word recognition seems to be based on the lexical unit instead of depending on left-to-right letter-to-sound processing: the word joins the child's sight vocabulary; thanks to self-teaching, phonological recoding works itself out of a job, except for the relatively rare occasions when proficient readers encounter an unfamiliar word. Some first-graders will experience more self-teaching and be further along in reading development than others because of this variation. From school to school, from child to child, and from word to word, the opportunities for self-teaching vary on at least two dimensions (beyond whether the words contain taught GPCs, that is, are decodable). First, the amount of practice (print exposure) with words from different domains and styles varies in the population, even in the early years (Cunningham and Stanovich, 1990, 1993). Second, some first-graders are taught with books that have a very heavy cognitive load, with many new words presented and seldom repeated. Johnston (2000) found that even the most proficient first-grade readers learn less than a fifth of the words that are present only once in their text; classmates who did not start out reading as well fared even worse with these unique words. Yet, over the years and in the face of considerable emphasis on text reform, children's readers show increasing cognitive load (Hiebert, 2002; Hiebert, Martin, and Menon, 2005; compare Juel and Roper-Schneider, 1985, Juel and Solso, 1981). Higher cognitive load does not support self-teaching, and first-graders at all levels of achievement have a better chance when texts are provided that lessen the cognitive load (see, for instance, Menon and Hiebert, forthcoming).

SECOND GRADE AND BEYOND [5]

Sample Responses

- Reads *coincide,* when part of the word is covered but, when shown the rest of the letters, switches stress and vowel to appropriately read *coincidental*

- Also reads strings as letter names (abbreviations like *UN*), letter sounds (acronyms like *NCLB* read like *Nicklebee*), or unconventional symbol-sound links (*l8r* and *r8*)

- Reads emoticons :-) and :-& via symbol-meaning links as *happy* and *tongue-tied.*

Alternate Names

Consolidated alphabetic, orthographic, hierarchical decoding, confirmation, fluency, ungluing from print, automatic.

Descriptions

- Learns and uses GPCs that show the conditional influence graphemes exercise on other graphemes, sometimes retrospectively, sometimes at a distance, not just contiguously and sequentially (such as *mutt, mute*) and within multisyllabic words (for instance, *hit, hitting, Hittite*)

- Learns and uses orthographic subword-blended units larger than graphemes for onsets and rimes, including consonant clusters and high-frequency rimes that also stand alone as words (for example, *at, in, all*) and for morphological inflections (such as *ed, ing, er, est*) and morphological derivations (prefixes, suffixes, roots)

- Uses orthographic units for decoding and self-teaching new words including multisyllabic words, sometimes via partial word analogies

- Continues to use strategies learned earlier and continues to self-teach new words creating an ever larger sight vocabulary

- Larger-sized units decrease the number of units in a word that need processing, so displays ease, accuracy, and speed increase, even with novel words in text.

Variability and Transitions

Words with more frequent orthographic patterns are read more accurately than words with unfamiliar patterns, even if the words compared have the same individual grapheme-phoneme links but in a different order (Treiman, Goswami, and Bruck, 1990).

Successful phonological recodings of a potential orthographic unit lead to facility with processing it orthographically (Share and Stanovich, 1995). Hence, both print exposure and success with the use of GPCs account for variation among people in the development of orthographic processing. Proficiency at identifying multisyllabic words varies with the reader's comprehension of the surrounding text and the richness of the reader's spoken vocabulary as well as the sight vocabulary for reading.

Even within one reading session and with one text, readers switch strategies for word identification depending on the reader's purpose, on the reader's familiarity with the topic and domain, and on the vocabulary and structural features of the text. Some sections or words are subject to deliberate and detailed phonological recoding; other parts are processed orthographically with automaticity; some parts are skimmed while others are skipped altogether.

Notes

1. Byrne, 1992; Byrne and Fielding-Barnsley, 1995; Chall, 1983; Ehri, 1999, 1994, 1995; Ehri and Sweet, 1991; Ehri and Wilce, 1985; Frith, 1985; Gough and Hillinger, 1980; Gough, Juel, and Roper-Schneider, 1983; Homer and Olson, 1999; Juel, 1991; Lomax and McGee, 1987; Marsh, Friedman, Welch, and Desberg, 1981; Masonheimer, Drum, and Ehri, 1984; Morris, 1993; Seymour and Elder, 1986; Share and Gur, 1999; Spear-Swerling and Sternberg, 1997.

2. Chall, 1983; Ehri, 1991, 1994, 1997a, 1995, 1998, 2002; Ehri and Wilce, 1985, 1987a, 1987b; Goswami 1986, 1988; Laing and Hulme, 1999; Marsh, Friedman, Welch, and Desberg, 1981; Metsala, 1999; Spear-Swerling and Sternberg, 1997; Stahl and Murray, 1998; Vellutino, 1979.

3. Chall, 1983; Ehri, 1995, 1999; Ehri and Robbins, 1992; Ehri and Wilce, 1985, 1987a, 1987b; Juel, 1991; Frith, 1985; Gough and Hillinger, 1980; Gough, Juel, and Roper-Schneider, 1983; Marsh, Friedman, Welch, and Desberg, 1981; Spear-Swerling and Sternberg, 1997.

4. Some say as many as twenty, but Reitsma (1983a) says that sometimes four times is enough.

5. Bryant, Nunes, and Bindman, 1997; Chall, 1983; Ehri, 1991, 1994, 1995, 1998, 1999; Ehri and Wilce, 1985; Frith, 1985; Laxon, Coltheart, and Keating, 1988; Leslie and Calhoun, 1995; Marsh, Friedman, Welch, and Desberg, 1981; Juel, 1983; Share, 1995, 1999; Spear-Swerling and Sternberg, 1997; Treiman, Goswami, and Bruck, 1990; Venezky, 1970; Venezky and Johnson, 1973; Wagner, Torgesen, Rashotte, and others, 1997.

REFERENCES

Adams, M. J. (1990). *Beginning to read: Thinking and learning about print.* Cambridge, MA: MIT Press.

Afflerbach, P. A., and VanSledright, B. (2001). Hath! doth! what! The challenges middle school students face when they read innovative history text. *Journal of Adolescent and Adult Literacy, 44,* 696–707.

Agee, J. (2000). *Theory, identity, and practice: A study of two high school English teachers' literature instruction.* Report No. 13003. Albany, NY: National Research Center on English Learning & Achievement.

Alexander, K., and Entwisle, D. (1996). Schools and children at risk. In A. Booth and J. Dunn (Eds.), *Family-school links: How do they affect educational outcomes?* Mahwah, NJ: Lawrence Erlbaum Associates.

Alexander, P. (2002). Profiling the struggling adolescent reader: A new perspective on an enduring problem. *Adolescent Literacy: Research Informing Practice.* Retrieved June 14, 2005, from www.nifl.gov/partnershipforreading/adolescent/summary.html.

Alexander, P., and Jetton, T. L. (2000). Learning from text: A multidimensional and developmental perspective. In M. L. Kamil, P. B. Mosenthal, P. D. Pearson, and R. Barr (Eds.), *Handbook of reading research, Vol. III* (pp. 285–310). Mahwah, NJ: Lawrence Erlbaum Associates.

Alfassi, M. (1998). Reading for meaning: The efficacy of reciprocal teaching in fostering reading comprehension in high school remedial reading classes. *American Educational Research Journal, 35*(2), 309–332.

Allen, B. A., de Villiers, J. G., and François, S. (2002). Deficit or difference: African American children's linguistic paths towards a theory of mind. In M. Almgren, A. Barrena, M. J. Ezeizabarrena, I. Idiazabal, and B. MacWhinney (Eds.), *Research on child language acquisition: Proceedings of the 8th Conference of the International Association for the Study of Child Language* (pp. 1006–1014). Somerville, MA: Cascadilla Press.

Allen, J. (1999). *Words, words, words.* Portland, ME: Stenhouse Publishers.

Allington, R. L. (1983). Fluency: The neglected reading goal. *The Reading Teacher, 37,* 556–561.

Allington, R. L., and McGill-Franzen, A. (2003). The impact of summer setback on the reading achievement gap. *Phi Delta Kappan, 85*(1), 68–75.

Alvermann, D. E. (2001). *Effective literacy instruction for adolescents.* Chicago: National Reading Conference.

Alvermann, D. E. (2004). Multiliteracies and self-questioning in the service of science learning. In W. Saul (Ed.), *Crossing borders.* Newark, DE: International Reading Association and National Science Teachers Association.

Alvermann, D. E., and Hagood, M. C. (2000). Fandom and critical media literacy. *Journal of Adolescent & Adult Literacy, 43*(5), 436–446.

Alvermann, D. E., and Phelps, S. (1998). *Content reading and literacy.* Boston: Allyn & Bacon.

Alvermann, D. E., O'Brien, D. G., and Dillon, D. R. (1990). What teachers do when they say they're having discussions of content area reading assignments: A qualitative analysis. *Reading Research Quarterly, 25,* 296–322.

Alvermann, D. E., Qian, G., and Hynd, C. E. (1995). Effects of interactive discussion and text type on learning counterintuitive science concepts. *Journal of Educational Research, 88,* 146–154.

Alvermann, D. E., Hagood, M. C., Heron, A. H., Hughes, P., Williams, K. B., and Jun, Y. (2000). *After-school media clubs for reluctant adolescent readers* (Final report to the Spencer Foundation, Grant #199900278). Chicago: Spencer Foundation.

Alvermann, D. E., Young, J. P., Weaver, D., Hinchman, K. A., Moore, D. W., Phelps, S. F., and others (1996). Middle and high school students' perceptions of how they experience text-based discussions: A multicase study. *Reading Research Quarterly, 31,* 244–267.

American Educational Research Association. (1999). *Standards of Educational and Psychological Testing.* Washington, D.C.: Author.

American Federation of Teachers, National Council on Measurement in Education, and National Education Association. (1990). *Standards for teacher competence in educational assessment of students.* Retrieved May 15, 2005, from www.unl.edu/buros/article3.html.

Anders, P. (2002). Secondary reading programs: A story of what was. In D. Schallert, C. Fairbanks, J. Worthy, B. Maloch, and J. Hoffman (Eds.), *51st yearbook of the National Reading Conference.* Oak Creek, WI: National Reading Conference.

Anders, P., Hoffman, J., and Duffy, G. (2000). Teaching teachers to teach reading: Paradigm shifts, persistent problems, and challenges. In M. L. Kamil, P. B. Mosenthal, P. D. Pearson, and R. Barr (Eds.). *Handbook of reading research, Vol. III* (pp. 721–744). Mahwah, NJ: Lawrence Erlbaum Associates.

Anderson, R. C., Armbruster, B. B., and Roe, M. (1989). *A modest proposal for improving the education of reading teachers.* Technical Report No. 487. Urbana: University of Illinois at Urbana-Champaign, Center for the Study of Reading.

Anderson, R. C., Hiebert, E. H., Scott, J. A., and Wilkinson, I.A.G. (l985). *Becoming a nation of readers: The report of the commission on reading.* Washington, DC: The National Institute of Education, U.S. Department of Education.

Anderson, V., and Roit, M. (1993). Planning and implementing collaborative strategy instruction for delayed readers in grades 6–10. *The Elementary School Journal, 94,* 121–137.

Anderson, V., Chan, C., and Henne, R. (1995). The effects of strategy instruction on the literacy models and performance of reading and writing delayed middle school students. In K. A. Hinchman and D. J. Leu (Eds.), *Perspectives on literacy research and practice: 44th yearbook of the National Reading Conference* (pp. 180–189). Chicago: National Reading Conference.

Anglin, J. M. (1993). Vocabulary development: A morphological analysis. *Monographs of the Society for Research in Child Development, 58*(10), Serial #238.

Anthony, J. L., Lonigan, C. J., Driscoll, K., Phillips, B. M., and Burgess, S. R. (2003). Phonological sensitivity: A quasi-parallel progression of word structure units and cognitive operations. *Reading Research Quarterly, 38*(4), 470–487.

Applebee, A. N., Langer, J. A., Nystrand, M., and Gamoran, A. (2003). Discussion-based approaches to developing understanding: Classroom instruction and student performance in middle and high school English. *American Educational Research Journal, 40*(3), 685–730.

Archibald, J. (Ed.). (1995). *Phonological acquisition and phonological theory.* Mahwah: NJ: Lawrence Erlbaum Associates.

Armbruster, B. B., and Anderson, T. H. (1984). Structures of explanations in history textbooks, or so what if Governor Stanford missed the spike and hit the rail? *Journal of Curriculum Studies, 16*(2), 181–194.

Armbruster, B. B., and Anderson, T. H. (1985). Frames: Structures for informative text. In D. H. Jonassen (Ed.), *The technology of text* (Vol. 2, pp. 90–104). Englewood Cliffs, NJ: Educational Technology Publications.

Arthur, J., and Phillips, R. (Eds.). (2000). *Issues in history teaching.* London: Routledge.

Ashkenazi, O., and Ravid, D. (1998). Children's understanding of linguistic humor: An aspect of metalinguistic awareness. *Current Psychology of Cognition, 17,* 367–387.

Au, K. (1997). Ownership, literacy achievement, and students of diverse cultural backgrounds. In J. T. Guthrie and A. Wigfield (Eds.), *Reading engagement: Motivating readers through integrated instruction* (pp. 168–182). Newark, DE: International Reading Association.

August, D., and Hakuta, K. (1997). *Improving schooling for language-minority children: A research agenda.* Washington, DC: National Academies Press.

Baker, L., and Wigfield, A. (1999). Dimensions of children's motivation for reading and their relations to reading activity and reading achievement. *Reading Research Quarterly, 34,* 452–477.

Baker, L., Afflerbach, P., and Reinking, D. (Eds.). (1996). *Developing engaged readers in school and home communitie*s. Mahwah, NJ: Lawrence Erlbaum Associates.

Baker, L., Dreher, M. J., and Guthrie, J. T. (Eds.). (2000). *Engaging young readers: Promoting achievement and motivation.* New York: Guilford.

Baker, S., Gersten, R., and Graham, S. (2003). Teaching expressive writing to students with learning disabilities: Research-based applications and examples. *Journal of Learning Disabilities, 36*(2), 109–123.

Baldwin, R. S., and Coady, J. M. (1978). Psycholinguistic approaches to a theory of punctuation. *Journal of Reading Behaviour, 10,* 363–376.

Ball, A. F. (1992). Cultural preferences and the expository writing of African-American adolescents. *Written Communication, 9*(4), 501–532.

Ball, A. F. (1995). Text design patterns in the writing of urban African-American students: Teaching to the strengths of students in multicultural settings. *Urban Education, 30,* 253–289.

Ball, A. F., and Farr, M. (2003). Language varieties, culture and teaching the English language arts. In J. Flood, D. Lapp, J. Squire, and J. Jensen (Eds.), *Handbook of research on teaching the English language arts* (pp. 435–445). Mahwah, NJ: Lawrence Erlbaum Associates.

Ball, D. L. (2000). Bridging practices: Intertwining content and pedagogy in teaching and learning to teach. *Journal of Teacher Education, 51*(3), 241–247.

Ball, D. L., and RAND Mathematics Study Panel. (2002). *Research and development program in mathematics education.* (Draft final report.) Santa Monica, CA: RAND.

Ball, D. L., Phelps, G., Rowan, B., and Schilling, S. (2003). *Measuring teachers' content knowledge for teaching reading: Elementary reading release items.* Ann Arbor, MI: Study of Instructional Improvement.

Ballenger, C. (1999). *Teaching other people's children: Literacy and learning in a bilingual classroom.* New York: Teachers College Press.

Banaji, M., and Bhaskar, R. (2000). Implicit stereotypes and memory: The bounded rationality of social beliefs. In D. L. Schacter and E. Scarry (Eds.), *Memory, brain, and belief* (pp. 139–175). Cambridge, MA: Harvard University Press.

Baranes, R., Perry, M., and Stigler, J. W. (1989). Activation of real-world knowledge in the solution of word problems. *Cognition and Instruction, 6,* 287–318.

Barca, I. (1998). *Adolescents' ideas about explanatory assessment in history.* College Park, MD: Eric Clearinghouse on Assessment and Evaluation. (Ed 429 116)

Barnes, M. A., Dennis, M., and Haefele-Kalvaitis, J. (1996). The effects of knowledge availability and knowledge accessibility on coherence and elaborative inferencing in children from six to fifteen years of age. *Journal of Experimental Child Psychology, 61*, 216–241.

Baron, J. (1979). Orthographic and word-specific mechanisms in children's reading of words. *Child Development, 50*, 60–72.

Barone, D. (1990). The written responses of young children: Beyond comprehension to story understanding. *The New Advocate, 2*(1), 49–56.

Barr, R. (1975). The effect of instruction on pupil reading strategies. *Reading Research Quarterly, 10*, 555–582.

Barry, A. L. (2002). Reading strategies teachers say they use. *Journal of Adolescent and Adult Literacy, 26*(2), 132–141.

Bates, E., Thal, D., Finlay, B., and Clancy, B. (forthcoming). Early language development and its neural correlates. In F. Boller and J. Grafman (Series Eds.) and I. Rapin and S. Segalowitz (Vol. Eds.), *Handbook of neuropsychology, Vol. 7: Child neurology* (2nd ed). Amsterdam: Elsevier.

Baumann, J. F., and Kameenui, E. J. (1991). Research on vocabulary instruction: Ode to Voltaire. In J. Flood, J. M. Jensen, D. Lapp, and J. R. Squire (Eds.), *Handbook on teaching the English language arts* (pp. 604–632). New York: Macmillan.

Baumann, J. F., Edwards, E. C., Font, G., Tereshinski, C. A., Kameenui, E. J., and Olejnik, S. (2002). Teaching morphemic and contextual analysis to fifth-grade students. *Reading Research Quarterly, 37*(2), 150–176.

Beal, C. R. (1990). Development of knowledge about the role of inference in text comprehension. *Child Development, 61*(4), 1011–1023.

Beal, C. R., and Flavell, J. H. (1984). Development of the ability to distinguish communicative intention and literal message meaning. *Child Development, 55*, 920–928.

Bean, R. M., Cassidy, J., Grumet, J. E., and Shelton, D. S. (2002). What do reading specialists do? Results from a national survey. *The Reading Teacher, 55*(8), 736–744.

Bean, T. W. (2001). An update on reading in the content areas: Social constructivist dimension. *Reading Online, 4*(11). Retrieved June 20, 2005, from www.readingonline.org/articles/handbook/bean

Bear, D. R., Invernizzi, M., Templeton, S. R., and Johnston, F. (2003). *Words their way: Word study for phonics, vocabulary, and spelling instruction.* Englewood Cliffs, NJ: Prentice Hall.

Beck, I. L. (1981). Reading problems and instructional practices. In G. Mackinnon and T. Waller (Eds.), *Reading research: Advances in theory and practice* (Vol. 2, pp. 55–95). New York: Academic Press.

Beck, I., and McKeown, M. (1991). Conditions of vocabulary acquisition. In R. Barr, M. Kamil, P. Mosenthal, and P. D. Pearson (Eds.), *Handbook of reading research* (Vol. 2, pp. 789–814). New York: Longman.

Beck, I. L., and McKeown, M. G. (2001). Text Talk: Capturing the benefits of reading-aloud experiences for young children. *The Reading Teacher, 55*(1), 10–20.

Beck, I. L., McKeown, M. G., and Gromoll, E. W. (1989). Learning from social studies texts. *Cognition and Instruction, 6*(2), 99–158.

Beck, I. L., McKeown, M. G., and Kucan, L. (2002). *Bringing words to life: Robust vocabulary instruction.* New York: Guilford.

Beck, I. L., McKeown, M. G., Hamilton, R. L., and Kucan, L. (1997). *Questioning the author: An approach for enhancing student engagement with text.* Newark, DE: International Reading Association.

Beck, I. L., McKeown, M. G., Omanson, R. C., and Pople, M. T. (1984). Improving the comprehensibility of stories: The effects of revisions that improve coherence. *Reading Research Quarterly, 19,* 263–277.

Beck, I. L., McKeown, M. G., Sandora, C., and Worthy, J. (1996). Questioning the author: A yearlong classroom implementation to engage students with text. *Elementary School Journal, 96*(4), 385–414.

Bell, L. C., and Perfetti, C. A. (1994). Reading skill: Some adult comparisons. *Journal of Educational Psychology, 86,* 244–255.

Bergen, D., and Mauer, D. (2000). Symbolic play, phonological awareness, and literacy skills at three age levels. In K. A. Roskos and J. F. Christie (Eds.), *Play and literacy in early childhood* (pp. 45–62). Mahwah, NJ: Lawrence Erlbaum Associates.

Berko, J. (1958). The child's learning of English morphology. *Word, 14,* 150–177.

Berkowitz, S. (1986). Effects of instruction in text organization on sixth-grade students' memory for expository reading. *Reading Research Quarterly, 21,* 161–178.

Berliner, D. C. (1988). *The development of expertise in pedagogy.* New Orleans: American Association of Colleges for Teacher Education.

Bernardt, D., and Stemberger, J. (1997). *Handbook of phonological development: From the perspective of constraint-based nonlinear phonology.* San Diego: Academic Press.

Bernhardt, E., Destino, T., Kamil, M., and Rodriguez-Munoz, M. (1995). Assessing science knowledge in an English/Spanish bilingual elementary school. *Cognosos, 4,* 4–6.

Berninger, V. W., Abbott, R. D., Billingsley, F., and Nagy, W. (2001). Processes underlying timing and fluency of reading: Efficiency, automaticity, coordination, and morphological awareness. In M. Wolf (Ed.), *Time, fluency, and dyslexia.* Timonium, MD: York Press.

Berninger, V., Abbott, R., Brooksher, R., Lemos, Z., Ogier, S., Zook, D., and Mostafapour, E. (2000). A connectionist approach to making the predictability of English orthography explicit to at-risk beginning readers: Evidence for alternative, effective strategies. *Developmental Neuropsychology, 17*(2), 241–271.

Bertram, R., Laine, M., and Virkkala, M. M. (2000). The role of derivational morphology in vocabulary acquisition: Get by with a little help from my morpheme friends. *Scandinavian Journal of Psychology, 41*(4), 287–296.

Bialystok, E. (1986a). Children's concept of word. *Journal of Psycholinguistic Research, 15,* 13–22.

Bialystok, E. (1986b). Factors in the growth of linguistic awareness. *Child Development, 57,* 498–510.

Biber, D. (1988). *Variation across speech and writing.* Cambridge, UK: Cambridge University Press.

Biber, D., Johansson, S., Leech, G., Conrad, S. and Finegan, E. (1999). *Longman grammar of spoken and written English.* London: Longman.

Biemiller, A. (1970). The development of the use of graphic contextual information as children learn to read. *Reading Research Quarterly, 6,* 75–96.

Biemiller, A. (1999). *Language and reading success.* Newton Upper Falls, MA: Brookline Books.

Biemiller, A., and Shany, M. T. (1995). Assisted reading practice: Effects on performance for poor readers in grades 3 and 4. *Reading Research Quarterly, 30*(3), 382–395.

Blachman, B. A., Tangel, D. M., Ball, E. W., Black, R., and McGraw, C. K. (1999). Developing phonological awareness and word recognition skills: A two-year intervention with low-income, inner-city children. *Reading and Writing, 11*(3), 239–273.

Blachowicz, C., and Fisher, P. (2000). Vocabulary instruction. In M. Kamil, P. Mosenthal, P. D. Pearson, and R. Barr (Eds.), *Handbook of reading research* (Vol. 3, pp. 503–523). Mahwah, NJ: Lawrence Erlbaum Associates.

Blachowicz, C., and Ogle, D. 2001. *Reading comprehension.* New York: Guilford.

Black, J., Wagner, M., Cameto, R., Hebbeler, R., and Newman, L. (1993). *Summary of findings: The national longitudinal transition study.* Menlo Park, CA: SRI International.

Black, P., and William, D. (1998). Inside the black box. *Phi Delta Kappan, 80*(2), 139–147.

Blackmore, A. M., and Pratt, C. (1997). Grammatical awareness and reading in grade 1 children. *Merrill-Palmer Quarterly, 43,* 567–590.

Blackmore, A. M., Pratt, C., and Dewsbury, A. (1995). The use of props in a syntactic awareness task. *Journal of Child Language, 22,* 405–422.

Blake, R., and Cutler, C. (2003). AAE and variation in teachers' attitudes: A question of school philosophy? *Linguistics and Education, 14,* 163–194.

Blischak, D. M. (1995). Thomas the writer: Case study of a child with severe physical, speech and visual impairments. *Language, Speech, and Hearing Services in Schools, 26,* 11–20.

Block, C. C., and Pressley, M. (Eds.). (2002). *Comprehension instruction: Research-based best practices.* New York: Guilford.

Block, C. C., Oakar, M., and Hurt, N. (2002). The expertise of literacy teachers: A continuum from preschool to grade 5. *Reading Research Quarterly, 37*(2), 178–206.

Bloom, L. (1998). Language acquisition in its developmental context. In W. Damon (Series Ed.), D. Kuhn, and R. S. Siegler (Vol. Ed.), *Handbook of child psychology, vol. 2, cognition, perception, and language* (5th ed.) (pp. 309–370). New York: Wiley.

Bloom, P. (2000). *How children learn the meanings of words (learning, development and conceptual change).* Cambridge, MA: MIT Press.

Bond, G. L., Tinker, M. A., Wasson, B. B., and Wasson, J. B. (1984). *Reading difficulties: Their diagnosis and correction* (5th ed.). Paramus, NJ: Prentice Hall.

Borasi, R., and Siegel, M. (2000). *Reading counts: Expanding the role of reading in mathematics classrooms.* Columbia University: Teachers College Press.

Borko, H., and Putnam, R. T. (1997). Learning to teach. In D. C. Berliner and R. Calfee (Eds.), *Handbook of educational psychology.* New York: Macmillan.

Bos, C., Mather, N., Dickson, S., Podhajski, B., and Chard, D. (2001). Perceptions and knowledge of preservice and inservice educators about early reading instruction. *Annals of Dyslexia, 51,* 97–120.

Bowers, P. G. (1993). Text reading and rereading: Determinants of fluency beyond word recognition. *Journal of Reading Behavior, 25,* 133–153.

Bowman, M., and Treiman, R. (2002). Relating print and speech: The effect of letter names and word position on reading and spelling performance. *Journal of Experimental Child Psychology, 82,* 305–340.

Bradley, L., and Bryant, P. (1979). Independence of reading and spelling in backward and normal readers. *Developmental Medicine and Child Neurology, 21,* 504–514.

Brady, S., and Moats, L. (May 1997). *Summary of position paper, informed instruction for reading success: Foundations for teacher preparation.* Baltimore, MD: Orton Dyslexia Society.

Bransford, J. D., and Johnson, M. K. (1972). Contextual prerequisites for understanding: Some investigations of comprehension and recall. *Journal of Verbal Learning and Verbal Behavior, 11,* 717–726.

Bransford, J., Brown, A., and Cocking, R. (Eds.). (1999). *How people learn: Brain, mind, experience, and school.* Washington, DC: National Academy Press.

Brennan, A., Bridge, C., and Winograd, P. (1986). The effects of structural variation on children's recall of basal reader stories. *Reading Research Quarterly, 21,* 91–104.

Breznitz, Z. (1997). Reading rate acceleration: Developmental aspects. *Journal of Genetic Psychology, 158,* 427–443.

Britt, M. A., Rouet, J. F., Georgi, M. A., and Perfetti, C. A. (1994). Learning from history texts: From causal analysis to argument models. In G. Leinhardt, I. L. Beck, and C. Stainton (Eds.), *Teaching and learning in history* (pp. 47–84). Hillsdale, NJ: Lawrence Erlbaum Associates.

Britzman, D. P. (2003). *Practice makes practice: A critical study of learning to teach* (Rev. ed.). Albany, NY: SUNY Press.

Brophy, J. E., and Good, T. (1986). Teacher behavior and student achievement. In M. C. Wittrock (Ed.), *Handbook of research on teaching* (3rd ed., pp. 328–375). New York: Macmillan.

Brown, A. L. (1997). Transforming schools into communities of thinking and learning about serious matters. *American Psychologist, 52*(4), 399–414.

Brown, A. L., Palincsar, A. S., and Armbruster, B. B. (1984). Instructing comprehension-fostering activities in interactive learning situations. In H. Mandl, N. L. Stein, and T. Trabasso (Eds.), *Learning and comprehension of text* (pp. 255–286). Mahwah, NJ: Lawrence Erlbaum Associates.

Brown, G., and Yule, G. (1983). *Discourse Analysis.* Cambridge, UK: Cambridge University Press.

Brown, P., and Levinson, S. C. (1987). *Politeness: Some universals in language usage.* Cambridge, UK: Cambridge University Press.

Brown, R. (2002). Straddling two worlds: Self-directed comprehension instruction for middle schoolers. In C. Collins Block and M. Pressley (Eds.), *Comprehension instruction: Research-based best practices* (pp. 337–350) New York: Guilford Press.

Brown, R., Pressley, M., VanMeter, P., and Schuder, T. (1996). A quasi-experimental validation of transactional strategies instruction with low-achieving second grade readers. *Journal of Educational Psychology, 88,* 18–37.

Brozo, W. G., and Simpson, M. L. (1999). *Readers, teachers, learners: Expanding literacy across content areas.* Des Moines, IA: Merrill Prentice Hall.

Bryant, P., Nunes, T., and Bindman, M. (1997). Chldren's understanding of the connection between grammar and spelling. Linguistic knowledge and learning to read and spell. In B. Blachman (Ed.), *Foundations of reading acquisition* (pp. 219–240). Mahwah, NJ: Lawrence Erlbaum Associates.

Bryant, P., Nunes, T, and Bindman, M. (2000). The relations between children's linguistic awareness and spelling: The case of the apostrophe. *Reading and Writing 12*(3), 253–276.

Bryk, A. S, and Raudenbush, S. W. (2002). *Hierarchical linear models: Applications and data analysis methods* (2nd ed.). Thousand Oaks, CA: Sage.

Buehl, D. (2001). *Classroom strategies for interactive Learning* (2nd ed.). Newark, DE: International Reading Association.

Bulgren, J. A., and Scanlon, D. (1998). Instructional routines and learning strategies that promote understanding of content area concepts. *Journal of Adolescent and Adult Literacy, 41*(4), 292–302.

Bulgren, J. A., Deshler, D. D., Schumaker, J. F., and Lenz, B. K. (2000). The use and effectiveness of analogical instruction in diverse secondary content classrooms. *Journal of Educational Psychology, 92*(3), 426–441.

Burling, R. (1971). Talking to teachers about social dialects. *Language Learning, 21*(2), 221–234.

Burns, M. S., Snow, C. E., and Griffin, P. (Eds.). (1999). *Starting out right: A guide to promoting children's reading success.* Washington DC: National Academy Press.

Bybee, J. L. (1995). Regular morphology and the lexicon. *Language and cognitive processes, 10,* 425–455.

Byrne, B. (1992). Studies in the acquisition procedure: Rationale, hypotheses, and data. In P. B. Gough, L. C. Ehri, and R. Treiman (Eds.), *Reading acquisition* (pp. 1–34). Mahwah, NJ: Lawrence Erlbaum Associates.

Byrne, B., and Fielding-Barnsley, R. (1995). Evaluation of a program to teach phenomic awareness to young children. A 2- and 3-year follow up and a new preschool trial. *Journal of Educational Psychology, 87*(3), 488–503.

Byrne, B., Fielding-Barnsley, R., and Ashley, L. (2000). Effects of preschool phoneme identity training after six years: Outcome level distinguished from rate of response. *Journal of Educational Psychology, 92,* 659–667.

Cacciari, C., and Levorato, M. C. (1989). How children understand idioms in discourse. *Journal of Child Language, 16,* 387–405.

Cain, K. (1999). Ways of reading: How knowledge and use of strategies are related to reading comprehension. *British Journal of Developmental Psychology, 17*, 295–312.

Cain, K., and Oakhill, J. V. (1999). Inference making ability and its relation to comprehension failure. *Reading and Writing, 11*, 489–503.

Cain, K., and Oakhill, J. V. (2004). Reading comprehension difficulties. In P. E. Bryant and T. Nunes (Eds.), *Handbook of Children's Literacy*. Dordrect: Kluwer.

Cain, K., Oakhill, J. V., and Bryant, P. E. (2000). Investigating the causes of reading comprehension failure: The comprehension-age match design. *Reading and Writing, 12*, 31–40.

Cain, K., Oakhill, J. V., Barnes, M. A., and Bryant, P. E. (2001). Comprehension skill, inference making ability and their relation to knowledge. *Memory and Cognition, 29*, 850–859.

Camilli, G., Vargas, S., and Yurecko, M. (2003). Teaching children to read: The fragile link between science and federal education policy. *Education Policy Analysis Archives, 11*(15). Retrieved May 15, 2005, from epaa.asu.edu/epaa/v11n15/.

Cappella, E., and Weinstein, R. (2001). Turning around reading achievement: Predictors of high school students' academic resilience. *Journal of Educational Psychology, 93*(4), 758–771.

Carlisle, J. F. (1995). Morphological awareness and early reading achievement. In L. Feldman (Ed.), *Morphological aspects of language processing*. Hillsdale, NJ: Lawrence Erlbaum Associates.

Carlisle, J., and Nomanbhoy, D. (1993). Phonological and morphological awareness in first graders. *Applied Psycholinguistics, 14*, 177–195.

Carlo, M. S., August, D., McLaughlin, B., Snow, C. E., Dressler, C., Lippman, D. N., and others. (2004). Closing the gap: Addressing the vocabulary needs of English-language learners in bilingual and mainstream classrooms. *Reading Research Quarterly, 39*(2), 188–215.

Carnicelli, T. (2001). *Words work: Activities for developing vocabulary, style, and critical thinking*. Portsmouth, NH: Heinemann.

Carnine, L., Carnine, D., and Gersten, R. (1984). Analysis of oral reading errors made by economically disadvantaged students taught with a synthetic phonics approach. *Reading Research Quarterly, 19*, 343–356.

Carpenter, B. (1998). *Type-logical semantics*. Cambridge, MA: MIT Press.

Carr, J. F., and Harris, D. E. (2001). *Succeeding with standards: Linking curriculum, assessment and action planning*. Alexandria, VA: Association for Supervision and Curriculum Development.

Carr, S. C., and Thompson, B. (1996). The effects of prior knowledge and schema activation strategies on the inferential reading comprehension of children with and without learning disabilities. *Learning Disability Quarterly, 19*, 48–61.

Carraher, T. N., Carraher, D. W., and Schliemann, A. D. (1987). Written and oral mathematics. *Journal for Research in Mathematics Education, 18*, 83–97.

Carver, R. P., and Hoffman, J. V. (1981). Effect of practice through repeated reading on gain in reading ability using a computer-based instructional system. *Reading Research Quarterly, 16*(3), 374–390.

Caswell, L. J., and Duke, N. K. (1998). Non-narrative as a catalyst for literacy development. *Language Arts, 75,* 108–117.

Catts, H. W. (1989). Defining dyslexia as a developmental language disorder. *Annals of Dyslexia, 39,* 50–64.

Catts, H. W., and Kamhi, A. G. (1998). *Language and reading disabilities.* Upper Saddle River, NJ: Pearson Education.

Chafe, W. L. (1982). Integration and involvement in speaking, writing and oral literature. In D. Tannen (Ed.), *Spoken and written language: Exploring orality and literacy* (pp. 35–53). Norwood, NJ: Ablex.

Chall, J. (1983). *Stages of reading development.* New York: McGraw-Hill.

Chall, J. S., Jacobs, V. A., and Baldwin, L. E. (1990). *The reading crisis: Why poor children fall behind.* Cambridge, MA.: Harvard University Press.

Champion, T. (1998). "Tell me somethin' good": A description of narrative structures among African-American children. *Linguistics and Education, 9*(3), 251–286.

Charity, A. H., Scarborough, H. S., and Griffin, D. M. (2004). Familiarity with school English in African American children and its relation to early reading achievement. *Child Development, 75*(5), 1340–1356.

Chierchia, G., and McConnell-Ginet, S. (2000). *Meaning and grammar: Introduction to semantics.* Cambridge, MA: MIT Press.

Chikalanga, I. W. (1993). Exploring inferencing ability of ESL readers. *Reading in a Foreign Language, 10*(1), 931–952.

Chomsky, C. (1969). *Acquisition of syntax in children from 5–10.* Cambridge, MA: MIT Press.

Chomsky, C. (1970a). Reading, writing, and phonology. *Harvard Educational Review, 40,* 287–309.

Chomsky, C. (1970b). Invented spelling in the open classroom. *Word, 27,* 499–518.

Chomsky, C. (1972). Stages in language development and reading exposure. *Harvard Educational Review, 42,* 1–33.

Chomsky, C. (1978). When you still can't read in third grade. After decoding, what? In S. J. Samuels (Ed.), *What research has to say about reading instruction* (pp. 13–30). Newark, DE: International Reading Association.

Chomsky, N., and Halle, M. (1968). *The sound patterns of English.* New York: Harper & Row.

Christenbury, L. (1994). *Making the journey: Being and becoming a teacher of language arts.* Upper Montclair, NJ: Boynton/Cook Heinemann.

Christoph, J. N., and Nystrand, M. (2001). *Taking risks, negotiating relationships: One teacher's transition towards a dialogic classroom.* Report No.14003. Albany, NY: National Research Center on English Learning & Achievement.

Clark, E. V. (1993). *The lexicon in acquisition.* Cambridge, UK: Cambridge University Press.

Clarke, J., Martell, K., and Willey, C. (1994, March-April). Sequencing graphic organizers to guide historical research. *The Social Studies, 70–75.*

Clay, M. M. (1993). *An observation survey of early literacy achievement.* Portsmouth, NH: Heinemann.

Coltheart, M. (1978). Lexical access in simple reading tasks. In G. Underwood (Ed.), *Strategies of information processing.* London: Academic Press.

Coltheart, M. (2000). Dual routes from print to speech and dual routes from print to meaning: Some theoretical issues. In A. Kennedy, R. Radach, J. Pynte, and D. Heller (Eds.), *Reading as a perceptual process.* Oxford: Elsevier.

Coltheart, M., Rastle, K., Perry, C., Langdon, R., and Ziegler, J. (2001). DRC: A dual route cascaded model of visual word recognition and reading aloud. *Psychological Review, 108,* 204–256.

Cook, V. (2004) *The English writing system.* London: Arnold.

Cooper, J. D., and Kiger, N. (2001). *Literacy assessment.* New York: Houghton Mifflin.

Cornoldi, C., and Oakhill, J. (Eds.). (1996). *Reading comprehension difficulties: Processes and intervention.* Mahwah, NJ: Lawrence Earlbaum Associates.

Cote, N., Goldman, S. R., and Saul, E. U. (1998). Students making sense of informational text: Relations between processing and representation. *Discourse-Processes, 25,* 1–53.

Council for Exceptional Children. (2002). *CEC response to the president's commission issues report on special education.* Retrieved May 15, 2005, from www.cec.sped.org/pp/legupd071202.html.

Craig, H. K., and Washington, J. A. (1994). The complex syntax skills of poor, urban African American preschoolers at school entry. *Language Speech and Hearing Services in Schools, 25,* 181–190.

Cullinan, B. E. (2000) Independent reading and school achievement. *School Library Media Research Online* 3. Retrieved June 14, 2005, from www.ala.org/ala/aasl/aaslpubsandjournals/slmrb/slmrcontents/volume32000/independent.htm.

Cunningham, A. E., and Stanovich, K. E. (1990). Tracking the unique effects of print exposure in children: Associations with vocabulary, general knowledge and spelling. *Journal of Educational Psychology, 83,* 264–274.

Cunningham, A. E., and Stanovich, K. E. (1993). Children's literacy environments and early word recognition subskills. *Reading and Writing, 5,* 193–204.

Cunningham, A. E., and Stanovich, K. E. (1997). Early reading acquisition and its relation to reading experience and ability 10 years later. *Developmental Psychology, 33,* 934–935.

Cunningham, A. E., Perry, K. E., Stanovich, K. E., Stanovich, P. J., and Chappell, M. (2001, June). *Is teachers' knowledge of important declarative knowledge of reading well calibrated?* Paper presented at the annual meeting of the Society for the Scientific Study of Reading, Boulder, Colorado.

Cunningham, P. M. (1976). Teachers' correction responses to Black-dialect miscues which are non-meaning-changing. *Reading Research Quarterly, 12,* 637–653.

Cunningham, P. M. (1998). The multisyllabic-word dilemma: Helping students build meaning, spell, and read "big" words. *Reading and Writing Quarterly, 14,* 189–218.

Curtis, M. E. (1980). Development of components of reading skill. *Journal of Educational Psychology, 72,* 656–669.

Curtis, M. E. (2002). Adolescent reading: A synthesis of research. *Adolescent Literacy: Research Informing Practice.* Retrieved May 15, 2005, from http://216.26.160.105/conf/nichd/synthesis.asp.

Cutler, A. (1989). Auditory lexical access: Where do we start? In W. Marslen-Wilson (Ed.), *Lexical representation and process* (pp. 342–356). Cambridge, MA: MIT Press.

Dahl, P. (1974). *An experimental program for teaching high speed word recognition and comprehension skills* (Final report project #3–1154). Washington, DC: National Institute of Education.

Daneman, M., and Carpenter, P. A. (1980). Individual differences in working memory and reading. *Journal of Verbal Learning and Verbal Behavior, 19,* 450–466.

Daneman, M., and Carpenter, P. A. (1983). Individual differences in integrating information between and within sentences. *Journal of Experimental Psychology: Learning, Memory, and Cognition, 9,* 561–584.

Darling-Hammond, L. (1996). What matters most: A competent teacher for every child. *Phi Delta Kappan, 78*(3), 193–200.

Darling-Hammond, L. (1997). *Doing what matters most: Investing in teacher quality.* Kutztown, PA: National Commission on Teaching and America's Future.

Darling-Hammond, L. (1999). *Teacher quality and student achievement: A review of state policy evidence.* Seattle, WA: Center for the Study of Teaching and Policy.

Darling-Hammond, L., and Youngs, P. (2002). Defining "highly qualified teachers": What does "scientifically based research" actually tell us? *Educational Researcher, 31,* 13–25.

Darling-Hammond, L., Chung, R., and Frelow, F. (2002). Variation in teacher preparation: How well do different pathways prepare teachers to teach? *Journal of Teacher Education, 53* (4).

Darling-Hammond, L., Bransford, J., LePage, P., Hammerness, K., and Duffy, H. (2005). *Preparing teachers for a changing world: What teachers should learn and be able to do.* San Francisco: Jossey-Bass.

DeBoer, J. J. (1959). Grammar in language teaching. *Elementary English, 36,* 413–421.

Deci, E. L., Koestner, R., and Ryan, R. M. (1999). A meta-analytic review of experiments examining the effects of extrinsic rewards on intrinsic motivation. *Psychological Bulletin, 125,* 627–668.

Delpit, L. (1986). Skills and other dilemmas of a progressive Black educator. *Harvard Educational Review, 56,* 379–385.

Delpit, L. (1988). The silenced dialogue: Power and pedagogy in educating other people's children. *Harvard Education Review, 58*(3), 280–298.

Delpit, L. (1995). *Other people's children: Cultural conflict in the classroom.* New York: The New Press.

Demott, E., and Gombert, J. E. (1996). Phonological awareness as a predictor of recoding skills and syntactic awareness as a predictor of comprehension skills. *British Journal of Educational Psychology, 66,* 315–332.

Dennis, G., and Walter, E. (1995). The effects of repeated read-alouds on story comprehension as assessed through story retellings. *Reading Improvement, 32,* 140–153.

Derwing, B. L., Smith, M. L., and Wiebe, G. E. (1995). On the role of spelling in morpheme recognition: Experimental studies with children and adults. In L. B. Feldman (Ed.), *Morphological aspects of language processing* (pp. 3–27). Mahwah, NJ: Lawrence Erlbaum Associates.

Designs for Change (1998). *What makes these schools stand out: Chicago elementary schools with a seven-year trend of improved reading achievement.* Chicago, IL: Author. Retrieved June 19, 2005, from www.designsforchange.org/pdfs/SOScomplete.pdf.

Dickinson, D., and Tabors, P. (2001). *Beginning literacy with language.* Baltimore, MD: Brookes.

Dickson, S. V., Simmons, D. C., and Kameenui, E. J. (1995). *Text organization: Curricular and instructional implications for diverse learners.* Eugene, OR: National Center to Improve the Tools of Educators.

Dillon, D. R., O'Brien, D. G., and Volkman, M. (2001). Reading, writing, and talking to get work done in biology. In E. B. Moje and D. G. O'Brien (Eds.), *Constructions of literacy: Studies of teaching and learning in and out of secondary schools.* Mahwah, NJ: Lawrence Erlbaum Associates.

DiStefano, P., and Hagerty, P. J. (1985). Teaching spelling at the elementary level: A realistic approach. *The Reading Teacher, 38,* 373–377.

DiStefano, P., and Killion, J. (1984). Assessing writing skills through a process approach. *English Education, 16*(4), 203–207.

Dole, J. A., Duffy, G. G., Roehler, L. R., and Pearson, P. D. (1991). Moving from the old to the new: Research on reading comprehension instruction. *Review of Educational Research, 61*(2), 239–264.

Donahue, D. M. (2000). Experimenting with texts: New science teachers' experience and practice as readers and teachers of reading. *Journal of Adolescent and Adult Literacy, 43*(8), 728–739.

Donovan, C. A., and Smolkin, L. B. (2001). Genre and other factors influencing teachers' book selection for science instruction. *Reading Research Quarterly, 36*(4), 412–440.

Donovan, M. S. and Cross, C. (2002). *Minority students in special and gifted education.* Washington, DC: National Academies Press.

Dowhower, S. L. (1991). Speaking of prosody: Fluency's unattended bedfellow. *Theory in Practice, 30,* 158–164.

Duke, N. K. (2000). 3.6 minutes per day: The scarcity of informational texts in first grade. *Reading Research Quarterly, 35,* 202–224. Also available as CIERA Report #1–007. (1999). *The scarcity of informational texts in first grade.* Ann Arbor, MI: CIERA.

Duke, N. K., and Kays, J. (1998). "Can I say 'Once upon a time'?" Kindergarten children developing knowledge of information book language. *Early Childhood Research Quarterly, 13,* 295–318.

Duke, N. K., and Pearson, P. D. (2002). Effective practices for developing reading comprehension. In A. E. Farstup and S. J. Samuels (Eds.), *What research has to say about reading instruction* (pp. 205–242). Newark, DE: International Reading Association.

Duke, N. K., Bennett-Armistead, S., and Roberts, E. M. (2003). Bridging the gap between learning to read and reading to learn. In D. M. Barone and L. M. Morrow (Eds.), *Literacy and young children: Research-based practices* (pp. 226–242). New York: Guilford.

Duncan, L. G., Seymour, P.H.K., and Hill, S. (2000). A small to large unit progression in metaphonological awareness and reading? *The Quarterly Journal of Experimental Psychology (Section A), 53,* 1081–1104.

Durkin, D. (1978). What classroom observations reveal about reading comprehension instruction. *Reading Research Quarterly, 14*(4), 481–533.

Duthie, C. (1996). *True stories: Nonfiction literacy in the primary classroom.* York, ME: Stenhouse.

Dweck, C. (2000). *Self-theories: Their role in motivation, personality, and development.* Philadelphia, PA: Psychology Press.

Education Trust. (2001). *Youth at the crossroads: Facing high school and beyond.* Washington, DC: Author.

Edwards, P. A. (1994). Connecting African-American families and youth to the school's reading program: Its meaning for school and community literacy. In V. L. Gadsden and D. Wagner (Eds.), *Literacy among African-American youth: Issues in learning, teaching, and schooling* (pp.263–281). Cresskill, NJ: Hampton Press.

Egan, K. (1993). Narrative and learning: A voyage of implications. *Linguistics and Education, 5,* 119–126.

Ehri, L. (1983). Summaries and a critique of five studies related to letter-name knowledge and learning to read. In L. Gentile, M. Kamil, and J. Blanchard (Eds.), *Reading Research Revisited* (pp. 131–153). Columbus, OH: C. E. Merrill.

Ehri, L. (1991). Development of the ability to read words. In R. Barr, M. Kamil, P. Mosenthal, and P. Pearson (Eds.), *Handbook of reading research, Vol. II* (pp. 383–417). New York: Longman.

Ehri, L. (1994). Development of the ability to read words: Update. In R. Ruddell, M. Ruddell, and H. Singer (Eds.), *Theoretical models and processes of reading* (pp. 323–358). Newark, DE: International Reading Association.

Ehri, L. (1995). Phases of development in learning to read words by sight. *Journal of Research in Reading, 18*(2), 116–125.

Ehri, L. (1997a). Sight word reading in normal readers and dyslexics. In B. Blachman (Ed.), *Foundations of reading acquisition and dyslexia* (pp. 163–189). Mahwah, NJ: Lawrence Erlbaum Associates.

Ehri, L. (1997b). Learning to read and learning to spell are one and the same, almost. In C. A. Perfetti, L. Rieben, and M. Fayol (Eds.), *Learning to spell: Research, theory, and practice across languages* (pp. 237–269). Mahwah, NJ: Lawrence Erlbaum Associates.

Ehri, L. (1998). Grapheme-phoneme knowledge is essential for learning to read words in English. In L. C. Ehri and J. L. Metsala (Eds.), *Word recognition in beginning literacy* (pp. 3–40). Mahwah, NJ: Lawrence Erlbaum Associates.

Ehri, L. (1999). Phases of development in learning to read words. In J. Oakhill and R. Beard (Eds.), *Reading development and the teaching of reading: A psychological perspective* (pp. 79–108). Malden, MA: Blackwell.

Ehri, L. (2002). Phases of acquisition in learning to read words, and implications for teaching. In R. Stainthorp and P. Tomlinson (Eds.), *Learning and teaching reading* (pp. 7–28). Leicester, UK: The British Psychological Society.

Ehri, L., and Robbins, C. (1992). Beginners need some decoding skill to read words by analogy. *Reading Research Quarterly, 27*, 12–26.

Ehri, L., and Snowling, M. (2004). Developmental variation in word recognition. In B. Shulman, K. Apel, B. Ehren, E. Silliman, and C. Stone (Eds.), *Handbook of language and literacy development and disorders.* New York: Guilford.

Ehri, L. C., and Sweet, J. (1991). Fingerpoint-reading of memorized text: What enables beginners to process the print? *Reading Research Quarterly, 26*(4), 442–462.

Ehri, L., and Wilce, L. (1985). Movement into reading: Is the first stage of printed word learning visual or phonetic? *Reading Research Quarterly, 20*, 163–179.

Ehri, L., and Wilce, L. (1987a). Cipher versus cue reading: An experiment in decoding acquisition. *Journal of Educational Psychology, 79*, 3–13.

Ehri, L., and Wilce, L. (1987b). Does learning to spell help beginners learn to read words? *Reading Research Quarterly, 22*, 47–65.

Ehri, L. C., Nunes, S., Willows, D, Schuster, B., Yaghoub-Zadeh, Z., and Shanahan, T. (2001). Phonemic awareness instruction helps children to read: Evidence from the National Reading Panel's meta-analysis. *Reading Research Quarterly, 3*, 250–257.

Ehrlich, M. F., and Remond, M. (1997). Skilled and less skilled comprehenders: French children's processing of anaphoric devices in written texts. *British Journal of Developmental Psychology, 15*, 291–309.

Ehrlich, M. F., Remond, M., and Tardieu, H. (1999). Processing of anaphoric devices in young skilled and less skilled comprehenders: Differences in metacognitive monitoring. *Reading and Writing, 11*, 29–63.

Elbro, C., Nielsen, I., and Petersen, D. K. (1994). Dyslexia in adults: Evidence for deficits in non-word reading and in the phonological representation of lexical items. *Annals of Dyslexia, 44*, 205–226.

Elley, W. B. (1991). Acquiring literacy in a second language: The effect of book-based programs. *Language Learning, 41*(3), 375–411.

Elliot, J. A., and Hewison, J. (1994). Comprehension and interest in home reading. *British Journal of Educational Psychology, 64*, 203–220.

Ellis, N. (1997). Interactions in the development of reading and spelling: Stages, strategies, and exchange of knowledge. In C. A. Perfetti, L. Rieben, and M. Fayol (Eds.), *Learning to spell: Research, theory, and practice across languages.* Mahwah, NJ: Lawrence Erlbaum Associates.

Emig, J. (1981). Non-magical thinking: Presenting writing developmentally in schools. In C. Frederickson and J. Dominic (Eds.), *Writing: The nature, development, and teaching of written communication* (Vol. 2, pp. 21–30). Mahwah, NJ: Lawrence Erlbaum Associates.

Englert, C. S., Mariage, T. V., Garmon, M. A., and Tarrant, K. L. (1998). Accelerating reading progress in Early Literacy Project classrooms: Three exploratory studies. *Remedial and Special Education, 19,* 142–159.

Entwisle, D. R., and Alexander, K. L. (1988). Factors affecting achievement test scores and marks of black and white first graders. *The Elementary School Journal, 88,* 449–471.

Ericson, B. (Ed.). (2001). *Teaching reading in high school English classes.* Urbana, IL: National Council of Teachers of English.

Erikson, K. A., and Koppenhaver, D. A. (1997). Integrated communication and literacy instruction for a child with multiple disabilities. *Focus on Autism and Other Developmental Disabilities, 12,* 142–152.

Feiman-Nemser, S. (1983). *Learning to teach* (Report No. IRT-OP-64). Lansing, MI: The Institute for Research on Teaching.

Feiman-Nemser, S. (2001). From preparation to practice: Designing a continuum to strengthen and sustain teaching. *Teachers College Record, 103*(6), 1013–1055.

Ferguson, R. (1991). Paying for public education: New evidence on how and why money matters. *Harvard Journal on Legislation, 28*(Summer), 465–498.

Ferreiro, E. (1991). Psychological and epistemological problems on written representation of language. In M. Carretero, M. Pope, R. Simons, and J. Pozo (Eds.), *Learning and instruction: European research in an international context* (Vol. 3, pp. 157–173). Oxford, UK: Pergamon Press.

Ferreiro, E., and Teberosky, A. (1982). *Literacy before schooling.* Exeter, NH: Heinemann.

Fillmore, L. W., and Snow, C. E. (2002). What teachers need to know about language. In C. T. Adger, C. E. Snow, and D. Christian (Eds.), *What teachers need to know about language* (pp. 7–54). McHenry, IL: Delta Systems.

Fischer, U. (1994). Learning words from context and dictionaries: An experimental comparison. *Applied Psycholinguistics, 15*(4), 551–574.

Fletcher, J. M., Shaywitz, S. E., Shankweiler, D. P., Katz, L. Liberman, I. Y., Stuebing, K. K., and others. (1994). Cognitive profiles of reading disability: Comparisons of discrepancy and low achievement definitions. *Journal of Educational Psychology, 86*(1), 6–23.

Flexer, C. (1999). *Facilitating hearing and listening in young children.* San Diego: Singular Publishing Group.

Flexer, C. (2002). Using sound-field amplification to teach phonemic awareness to preschoolers. *The Hearing Journal, 55,* 10–21.

Flexner, A., and Pritchett, H. S. (1910). *Medical education in the United States and Canada: A report to the Carnegie Foundation for the Advancement of Teaching.* New York: Carnegie Foundation for the Advancement of Teaching.

Foorman, B. R. (1995). Practiced connections of orthographic and phonological processing. In V. W. Berninger (Ed.), *The varieties of orthographic knowledge, Vol. II: Relationships to phonology, reading and writing* (pp. 377–418). Boston: Kluwer.

Foorman, B. R., Perfetti, C., Seidenberg, M., and Francis, D. J. (2001, April). *What kind of text is a decodable text?* Paper presented at the annual meeting of the American Educational Research Association, Seattle.

Foorman, B. R., Francis, D. J., Davidson, K. C., Harm, M. W., and Griffin, J. (2002, April). *Variation in text features in six grade 1 basal reading programs.* Paper presented at the annual meeting of the American Educational Research Association, New Orleans.

Ford, D. J., Palincsar, A. S., and Magnusson, S. J. (2002, April). *The role of text in the development of fourth-graders' understandings of the nature of scientific activity.* Paper presented at the Annual Conference of the American Educational Research Association, New Orleans.

Fowler, A. E., and Liberman, I. Y. (1995). The role of phonology and orthography in morphological awareness. In L. B. Feldman (Ed.), *Morphological aspects of language processing* (pp. 157–188). Mahwah, NJ: Lawrence Erlbaum Associates.

Frazier, L. (1995). Issues of representation in psycholinguistics. In J. L. Miller and P. D. Eimas (Eds.), *Speech, language and communication.* New York: Academic Press.

Freebody, P., and Anderson, R. C. (1983). Effects on text comprehension of differing proportions and locations of difficult vocabulary. *Journal of Reading Behavior, 15*(3), 19–39.

Frith, U. (1985). Beneath the surface of developmental dyslexia. In K. Patterson, J. Marshall, and M. Coltheart (Eds.), *Surface dyslexia: Neuropsychological and cognitive studies of phonological reading* (pp. 301–330). Mahwah, NJ: Lawrence Erlbaum Associates.

Fuchs, L. S., Fuchs, D., Hosp, M. K., and Jenkins, J. (2001). Oral reading fluency as an indicator of reading competence: A theoretical, empirical, and historical analysis. *Scientific Studies of Reading, 5*(3), 239–256.

Fujiura, G. T., and Yamaki, K. (2000). Trends in demography of childhood poverty and disability. *Exceptional Children, 66,* 187–199.

Fullan, M. (2002). *Leading in a culture of change.* Toronto: University of Toronto, OISE.

Fuller, E. (1999). *Does teacher certification matter? A comparison of elementary TAAS performance in 1997 between schools with high and low percentages of certified teachers.* Unpublished report. Austin: University of Texas, Charles A. Dana Center.

Gadda, G. (1995). Language change in the history of English: Implications for teachers. In D. B. Durkin (Ed.), *Language issues: Readings for teachers* (pp. 262–273). White Plains, NY: Longman.

Galda, L., and Beach, R. (2001). Response to literature as a cultural activity. *Reading Research Quarterly, 36*(1), 64–73.

Gambrell, L., and Almasi, J. F. (1996). *Lively discussions! Fostering engaged reading.* Newark, DE: International Reading Association.

Gambrell, L., Morrow, L. M., Neuman, S. B., and Pressley, M. (1999). *Best practices in literacy instruction.* New York: Guilford.

Garcia, G. E., and Pearson, P. D. (1991). *Literacy assessment in a diverse society* (No. 525). Urbana-Champaign, IL: Univeristy of Illinois at Urbana-Champaign Center for the Study of Reading.

Garner, J. K., and Bochna, C. R. (2002, April). *Transfer of a listening comprehension strategy to independent reading activity in first graders.* Paper presented at the meeting of the American Educational Research Association, New Orleans.

Garton, A., and Pratt, C. (1998). *Learning to be literate: The development of spoken and written language* (2nd ed.). Oxford: Blackwell.

Garvey, C. (1984). *Children's talk.* Cambridge, MA: Harvard University Press.

Gasden, V., and Wagner, D. (1995). *Literacy among African-American youth: Issues in learning, teaching and schooling.* Cresskill, NJ: Hampton Press.

Gathercole, S. E., Service, E., Hitch, G. J., Adams, A., and Martin, A. J. (1999). Phonological short-term memory and vocabulary development: Further evidence on the nature of the relationship. *Applied Cognitive Psychology, 13*, 65–77.

Gaultney, J. F. (1995). The effect of prior knowledge and metacognition on the acquisition of a reading comprehension strategy. *Journal of Experimental Child Psychology, 59*(1), 142–163.

Gaux, C., and Gombert, J. E. (1999). Implicit and explicit syntactic knowledge and reading in pre-adolescents. *British Journal of Developmental Psychology, 17*, 169–188.

Gee, J. P. (1999). *An introduction to discourse analysis: theory and method.* New York: Routledge.

Gentry, J. R. (1982). An analysis of developmental spelling in GNYS AT WRK. *The Reading Teacher, 36*, 192–200.

Gernsbacher, M. A. (1997). Coherence cues mapping during comprehension. In J. Costermans and M. Fayol (Eds.), *Processing interclausal relationships: Studies in the production and comprehension of text* (pp. 3–21). Mahwah, NJ: Lawrence Erlbaum Associates.

Gill, J. T. (1992). The relationship between word recognition and spelling. In S. Templeton and D. R. Bear (Eds.), *Development of orthographic knowledge and the foundations of literacy: A memorial Festschrift for Edmund H. Henderson* (pp. 79–104). Mahwah, NJ: Lawrence Erlbaum Associates.

Glazer, S. M. (1998). *Assessment is instruction: Reading, writing, spelling, and phonics for all learners.* Norwood, MA: Christopher-Gordon.

Gleason, J. B. (Ed.). (2001). *The development of language* (5th ed.). Boston: Allyn & Bacon.

Gleitman, L., and Landau, B. (1994). *The acquisition of the lexicon.* Cambridge, MA: MIT Press.

Goldenberg, C. (1993). Instructional conversations: Promoting comprehension through discussion. *The Reading Teacher, 46*(4), 316–326.

Goldenberg, C. N., and Gallimore, R. (1995). Immigrant Latino parents' values and beliefs about their children's education: Continuities and discontinuities across cultures and generations. In P. Pintrich and M. Maehr (Eds.), *Advances in motivation and achievement* (Vol. 9, pp. 183–228). Greenwich, CT: JAI Press.

Golish, T., and Caughlin, J. (2002). "I'd rather not talk about it": Adolescents' and young adults' use of topic avoidance in stepfamilies. *Journal of Applied Communication Research, 30*(1), 78–106.

Gombert, J. E. (1992). *Metalinguistic development.* New York: Harvester Wheatsheaf.

Goodman, Y., and Goodman, D. (2000). "I hate 'postrophes": Issues of dialect and reading proficiency. In J. K. Peyton, P. Griffin, W. Wolfram, and R. Fasold (Eds.), *Language in action: New studies of language in society* (pp. 408–435). Cresskill, NJ: Hampton Press.

Goswami, U. (1986). Children's use of analogy in learning to read: A developmental study. *Journal of Experimental Child Psychology, 42,* 73–83.

Goswami, U. (1988). Orthographic analogies and reading development. *Quarterly Journal of Experimental Psychology, 40,* 239–268.

Goswami, U. (1999). Phonological development and reading by analogy: Epilinguistic and metalinguistic issues. In J. Oakhill and R. Beard (Eds.), *Reading development and the teaching of reading: A psychological perspective.* Malden, MA: Blackwell.

Goswami, U., and East, M. (2000). Rhyme and analogy in beginning reading: Conceptual and methodological issues. *Applied Psycholinguistics, 21,* 63–93.

Goswami, U., and Mead, F. (1992). Onset and rime awareness and analogies in reading. *Reading Research Quarterly, 27,* 152–162.

Gottardo, A., Stanovich, K. E., and Siegel, L. S. (1996). The relationships between phonological sensitivity, syntactic processing, and verbal working memory in the reading performance of third-grade children. *Journal of Experimental Child Psychology, 63,* 563–582.

Gough, P. B., and Hillinger, M. L. (1980). Learning to read: An unnatural act. *Bulletin of the Orton Society, 20,* 179–196.

Gough, P. B., Hoover, W. A., and Peterson, C. L. (1996). Some observations on a simple view of reading. In C. Cornoldi and J. Oakhill (Eds.), *Reading comprehension difficulties* (pp. 1–13). Mahwah, NJ: Lawrence Erlbaum Associates.

Gough, P., Juel C., and Roper-Schneider, D. (1983). A two-stage model of initial reading acquisition. In J. Niles and L. Harris (Eds.), *Searches for meaning in reading/language processing and instruction* (pp. 207–211). Rochester, NY: National Reading Conference.

Goulandris, N., and Snowling, M. J. (1995). Assessing reading skills. In E. Funnell and M. Stuart (Eds.), *Learning to read: Psychology and the classroom.* Oxford: Blackwell.

Graesser, A. C., and Bertus, E. L. (1998). The construction of causal inferences while reading expository texts on science and technology. *Scientific Studies of Reading, 2,* 247–269.

Graesser, A. C., Millis, K. K., and Zwan, R. A. (1997). Discourse comprehension. *Annual Review of Psychology, 48,* 163–189.

Graesser, A. C., Singer, M., and Trabasso, T. (1994). Constructing inferences during narrative text comprehension. *Psychological Review, 101*(3), 371–395.

Graesser, A. C., Kassler, M. A., Kreuz, R. J., and McLain-Allen, B. (1998). Verification of statements about story worlds that deviate from normal conceptions of time: What is true about Einstein's dreams. *Cognitive Psychology, 35,* 246–301.

Graf, R., and Torrey, J. W. (1966). Perception of phrase structure in written language. *Proceedings of the Annual Convention of the American Psychological Association, 74,* 83–84.

Graves, D. H. (1983). *Writing: Teachers and children at work.* Exeter, NH: Heinemann Educational Books.

Graves, M. (2000). A vocabulary program to complement and bolster a middle-grade comprehension program. In B. M. Taylor, M. F. Graves, and P. van den Boek (Eds.), *Reading for meaning: Fostering comprehension in the middle grades* (pp. 116–135). New York: Teachers College Press.

Graves, M. F., and Slater, W. H. (1996). Vocabulary instruction in content areas. In D. Lapp, J. Flood, and N. Farnan (Eds.), *Content area reading and learning instructional strategies* (2nd ed., pp. 261–275). Boston: Allyn & Bacon.

Green, G. M. (1981). Competence for implicit text analysis: Literary style discrimination in five-year-olds. *University of Illinois at Urbana-Champaign Linguistics, 11*(1), 39–56.

Greene, J. P. (1997). A meta-analysis of the Rossell and Baker review of bilingual education research. *Bilingual Research Journal, 21,* 103–122.

Greenleaf, C. (2004). An inquiry into how experienced readers of literature read a novel: A reading process analysis using *The God of Small Things* by Arundhati Roy. In professional development materials for National Institutes in Reading Apprenticeship, 2004. Oakland, CA: Strategic Literacy Initiative/WestEd.

Greenleaf, C. L., and Schoenbach, R. (2004). Building capacity for the responsive teaching of reading in the academic disciplines: Strategic inquiry designs for middle and high school teachers' professional development. In D. Strickland and M. L. Kamil (Eds.), *Improving reading achievement through professional development.* Norwood, MA: Christopher-Gordon.

Greenleaf, C., Brown, W., and Litman, C. (2004). Apprenticing urban youth to science literacy. In D. Strickland and D. Alvermann (Eds.), *Bridging the gap: Improving literacy learning for preadolescent and adolescent learners in grades 4–12.* New York: Teachers College Press.

Greenleaf, C. L., Schoenbach, R., Cziko, C., and Mueller, F. L. (2001). Apprenticing adolescent readers to academic literacy. *Harvard Educational Review, 71*(1), 79–129.

Greenwald, A. G., and Banaji, M. R. (1995). Implicit social cognition: Attitudes, self-esteem, and stereotypes. *Psychological Review, 102*(1), 4–27.

Greenwald, A. G., McGhee, D. E., and Schwartz, J.L.K. (1998). Measuring individual differences in implicit cognition: The implicit association test. *Journal of Personality and Social Psychology, 74,* 1464–1480.

Gregory, E. (Ed.). (1997). *One child, many worlds: Early learning in multicultural communities.* Language and Literacy Series. Williston, VT: Teachers College Press.

Griffin, P. (2000). Collaboration in school: "I (don't) know" answers and questions. In J. Peyton, P. Griffin, W. Wolfram, and R. Fasold, *Language in action: New studies of language in society* (pp. 472–491). Cresskill, NJ: Hampton Press.

Grigg, W. S., Daane, M. C., Jin, Y., and Campbell, J. R. (2002). *The nation's report card: Reading 2002.* Washington, DC: National Center for Education Statistics.

Gunn, B. K., Simmons, D. C., and Kameenui, E. J. (1998). Emergent literacy: Synthesis of the research. In D. C. Simmons (Ed.), *What reading research tells us about children with diverse learning needs: The bases and basics* (pp. 19–50). Mahwah, NJ: Lawrence Erlbaum Associates.

Gustafson, W. N. (1998). Content analysis in a history class. *Social Studies, 89*(1), 39–44.

Guthrie, J. T., and Alvermann, D. (Eds.). (1999). *Engagement in reading: Processes, practices, and policy implications.* New York: Teachers College Press.

Guthrie, J. T., and Knowles, K. (2001). Promoting reading motivation. In L. Verhoeven and C. Snow (Eds.), *Literacy and motivation: Reading engagement in individuals and groups* (pp. 159–176). Mahwah, NJ: Lawrence Erlbaum Associates.

Guthrie, J. T., and Wigfield, A. (2000). Engagement and motivation in reading. In M. L. Kamil, P. B. Mosenthal, P. D. Pearson, and R. Barr (Eds.), *Handbook of reading research, Vol. III* (pp. 403–422). Mahwah, NJ: Lawrence Erlbaum Associates.

Guthrie, J. T., Alao, S., and Rinehart, J. M. (1997). Engagement in reading for young adolescents. *Journal of Adolescent and Adult Literacy, 40*(6), 438–446.

Guthrie, J. T., Wigfield, A., and Perencevich, K. C. (Eds.). (2004). *Motivating reading comprehension: Concept-oriented reading instruction.* Maywah, NJ: Lawrence Erlbaum Associates.

Guthrie, J., Wigfield, A., and VonSecker, C. (2000). Effects of integrated instruction on motivation and strategy use in reading. *Journal of Educational Psychology, 92,* 331–341.

Guthrie, J. T., McGough, K., Bennett, L., and Rice, M. E. (1996). Concept-oriented reading instruction: An integrated curriculum to develop motivations and strategies for reading. In L. Baker, P. Afflerbach, and D. Reinking (Eds.), *Developing engaged readers in school and home community* (pp. 165–190). Mahwah, NJ: Lawrence Erlbaum Associates.

Guthrie, J. T., Schafer, W., Wang, Y. Y., and Afflerbach, P. (1995). Relationships of instruction to amount of reading: An exploration of social, cognitive and instructional connections. *Reading Research Quarterly, 30*(1), 8–25.

Guthrie, J. T., VanMeter, P., Hancock, G. R., Alao, S., Anderson, E., and McCann, A. (1998). Does concept-oriented reading instruction increase strategy use and conceptual learning from text? *Journal of Educational Psychology, 90*, 261–278.

Guthrie, J., VanMeter, P., McCann, A., Wigfield, A., Bennett, L., Poundstone, C., and others. (1996). Growth of literacy engagement: Changes in motivations and strategies during concept-oriented reading instruction. *Reading Research Quarterly, 31*, 306–325.

Gutiérrez, K. D., Baquedano-López, P., and Tejeda, C. (1999). Rethinking diversity: Hybridity and hybrid language practices in the third space. *Mind, Culture, and Activity: An International Journal, 6*(4), 286–303.

Hacker, D. J., Dunlosky, J., and Graesser, A. C. (Eds.). (1998*). Metacognition in educational theory and practice.* Mahwah, NJ: Lawrence Erlbaum Associates.

Hale, G. (2000, Summer). *Summary compilation of secondary science teachers' reading processes after completing an inquiry into their reading of a challenging science text.* Westerbeke Ranch, Sonoma, CA: WestEd.

Hall, R.M.R., and Hall, B. D. (1965, January). *The child's learning of noun modification.* Paper read at Linguistic Society of America meeting, Chicago.

Halliday, M.A.K., and Hasan, R. (1976). *Cohesion in English.* New York: Longman.

Hannahs, S. J., and Young-Scholten, M. (Eds.). (1998). *Generative studies in the acquisition of phonology.* Amsterdam: Benjamins.

Hapgood, S., MacLean, F., and Palincsar, A. (2000). *Guided inquiry: Supporting the young child's engagement with informational text.* International Reading Association presentation. Retrieved June 15, 2005, from http://www.ciera.org/library/presos/2000/2000-IRA/palinscar/palinscar-ira-2000.pdf.

Harker, W. J. (1994). Plain sense and poetic significance: Tenth-grade readers reading two poems. *Poetics, 22*, 199–218.

Harm, M. W., and Seidenberg, M. S. (1999). Phonology, reading acquisition, and dyslexia: Insights from connectionist models. *Psychological Review, 106*(3), 491–528.

Harmon, J., Hedrick, W., Martinez, M., Perez, B., Keehn, S., Fine, J. C., and others. (2001). Features of excellence of reading teacher preparation programs. In J. V. Hoffman, D. L. Schallert, C. M. Fairbanks, J. Worthy, and B. Maloch (Eds.), *50th yearbook of the National Reading Conference* (pp. 262–274). Chicago: National Reading Conference.

Harp, B., and Brewer, J. (2000). Assessing reading and writing in the early years. In D. S. Strickland and L. M. Morrow (Eds.), *Beginning reading and writing* (pp. 154–167). New York: Teachers College Press and the International Reading Association.

Harris, P. L. (2002). What do children learn from testimony? In P. Carruthers, M. Siegal, and S. Stich (Eds.), *The cognitive basis of science.* Cambridge, UK: Cambridge University Press.

Harris, R. J. (1962). *An experimental inquiry into the functions and value of formal grammar in the teaching of written English to children aged twelve to fourteen.* Unpublished doctoral dissertation, University of London.

Hart, B., and Risley, T. R. (1995). *Meaningful differences in the everyday experience of young American children.* Baltimore: Paul H. Brookes.

Hatch, E., and Brown, C. 1996. *Vocabulary, semantics and language education.* Cambridge, UK: Cambridge University Press.

Haycock, K. (1998). Good teaching matters: How well-qualified teachers can close the gap. *Thinking K-16: A Publication of the Education Trust, 3,* 1–14.

Heap, B. (1991). Evaluating the effects of an LA course. In C. James and P. Garrett (Eds.), *Language awareness in the classroom* (pp. 247–253). London: Longman.

Heath, S. B. (1983). *Ways with words: Language, life, and work in communities and classrooms.* New York: Cambridge University Press.

Heath, S. B. (1998). Working through language. In S. Hoyle and C. T. Adger (Eds.), *Kids talk: Strategic language use in later childhood* (pp. 217–240). New York: Oxford University Press.

Heath, S. B. (1999). Dimensions of language development. In A. S. Masten (Ed.), *Cultural processes of child development: The Minnesota Symposia on Child Psychology* (*Vol. 29,* pp. 59–76). Mahweh, NJ: Lawrence Erlbaum Associates.

Heckelman, R. G. (1986). N.I.M. revisited. *Academic Therapy, 21,* 411–420.

Henderson, E. H. (1981). *Learning to read and spell: The child's knowledge of words.* DeKalb, IL: Northern Illinois Press.

Henderson, E. H. (1985). *Teaching spelling.* Boston: Houghton Mifflin.

Henderson, E. H., and Templeton, S. (1986). A developmental perspective of formal spelling instruction through alphabet, pattern, and meaning. *Elementary School Journal, 86,* 305–316.

Henry, M. (1988). Beyond phonics: Integrated decoding and spelling instruction based on word origin and structure. *Annals of Dyslexia, 38,* 258–275.

Henry, M. (1989). Children's word structure knowledge: Implications for decoding and spelling instruction. *Reading and Writing: An Interdisciplinary Journal, 2,* 135–152.

Henry, M. (1993). Morphological structure: Latin and Greek roots and affixes as upper grade code strategies. *Reading and Writing: An Interdisciplinary Journal, 5*(2), 227–241.

Henry, M. (1996). *Words: Integrated decoding and spelling instruction based on word origin and word structure.* Austin, TX: Pro-Ed.

Hess, R. D., and Holloway, S. (1984). Family and school as educational institutions. In R. D. Parke (Ed.), *Review of child development research, 7: The family.* Chicago: Chicago University Press.

Heubert, J., and Hauser, R. (1999). *High stakes: Testing for tracking, promotion, and graduation*. Washington, DC: National Academy Press.

Hickmann, M. (2002). *Children's discourse: Person, space and time across languages* (Cambridge Studies in Linguistics 98). Cambridge, UK: Cambridge University Press.

Hickmann, M., and Hendriks, H. (1999). Cohesion and anaphora in children's narratives: A comparison of English, French, German, and Mandarin Chinese. *Journal of Child Language, 26,* 419–452.

Hicks, D. (Ed.). (1996). *Discourse, learning, and schooling.* New York: Cambridge University Press.

Hiebert, E. H. (2002). Standards, assessment, and text difficulty. In A. E. Farstrup and S. J. Samuels (Eds.), *What research has to say about reading instruction* (3rd ed., pp. 337–369). Newark, DE: International Reading Association.

Hiebert, E. H., Martin, L. A., and Menon, S. (2005). Are there alternatives in reading textbooks? An examination of three beginning reading programs. *Reading Writing Quarterly 21*(1), 7–32.

Hiebert, E. H., Pearson, P. D., Taylor, B. M., Richardson, V., and Paris, S. G. (1998). *Every child a reader.* Ann Arbor, MI: Center for the Improvement of Early Reading Achievement.

Hiebert, J., and Stigler, J. W. (2000). A proposal for improving classroom teaching: Lessons from the TIMSS Video Study. *Elementary School Journal, 101,* 3–20.

Hill, R. L., and Murray, W. S. (2000). Commas and spaces: Effects of punctuation on eye-movements and sentence parsing. In A. Kennedy, R. Radach, D. Heller, and J. Pynte (Eds.), *Reading as a perceptual process* (pp. 565–590). Oxford: Elsevier Science.

Hillocks, G. Jr. (1986). *Research on written composition: New directions for teaching.* Urbana, IL: National Council of Teachers of English.

Hillocks, G. Jr., and Smith, M. W. (1991). Grammar and usage. In J. Flood, J. M. Jensen, D. Lapp, and J. R. Squire (Eds.), *Handbook of research on teaching the English language arts* (pp. 591–603). New York: Macmillan.

Hoffman, J. (1987). Rethinking the role of oral reading. *Elementary School Journal, 87,* 367–373.

Hoffman, J., and Pearson, P. D. (2000). Reading teacher education in the next millennium: What your grandmother's teacher didn't know that your granddaughter's teacher should. *Reading Research Quarterly, 35*(1), 28–44.

Hoffman, J. V., Roller, C. M., Maloch, B., Sailors, M., Beretvas, N., and the National Commission on Excellence in Elementary Teacher Preparation for Reading Instruction. (2003). *Prepared to make a difference: Final report of the National Commission on Excellence in Elementary Teacher Preparation for Reading Instruction.* Newark, DE: The International Reading Association.

Hoffman, J., McCarthey, S. J., Abbott, J., Christian, C., Corman, L., Curry, C., and others. (1994). So what's new in the new basals? A focus on first grade. *Journal of Reading Behavior, 26,* 47–74.

Hogan, K. (1999). Thinking aloud together: A test of an intervention to foster students' collaborative scientific reasoning. *Journal of Research in Science Teaching, 36*(10), 1085–1109.

Holme, R. (2004). *Mind, metaphor and language teaching.* New York: Palgrave Macmillan.

Holmes Group, Inc. (1986). *Tomorrow's teacher: A report of the Holmes Group.* East Lansing, MI: The Holmes Group, Inc. (ED 270 454).

Holt-Reynolds, D. (1992). Personal history-based beliefs as relevant prior knowledge in coursework: Can we practice what we teach? *American Educational Research Journal, 29*, 325–349.

Homer, B. D., and Olson, D. R. (1999). The role of literacy in children's concept of words. *Written Language and Literacy, 2*(1), 113–140.

Hoyle, S., and Adger, C. T. (Eds.). (1998). *Kids talk: Strategic language use in later childhood.* New York: Oxford University Press.

Hudson, R. (1995). *Word meaning.* London: Routledge.

Hudson, R. (2001). Grammar teaching and writing skills: The research evidence. *Syntax in the Schools, 17*(1), 1–6.

Hudson, T. (1983). Correspondences and numerical differences between disjoint sets. *Child Development, 54*, 84–90.

Huffman, L. E. (1998). Spotlighting specifics by combining focus questions with K-W-L. *Journal of Adolescent & Adult Literacy, 41*(6), 470–472.

Hughes, J. E., Packard, B. W., and Pearson, P. D. (2000). Pre-service teachers' experiences using hypermedia and video to learn about literacy instruction. *Journal of Literacy Research, 32*(4), 599–630.

Hughes, M., and Searle, D. (1997). *The violent e and other tricky sounds: Learning to spell from kindergarten through grade 6.* York, ME: Stenhouse.

Hulit, L. M., and Howard, M. R. (2002). *Born to talk: An introduction to speech and language development* (3rd ed.). Boston: Allyn & Bacon.

Hunt, K. (1965). *Grammatical structures written at three grade levels.* Champaign, IL: National Council of Teachers of English.

Hunt, K. (1970). Syntactic maturity in school children and adults. *Monographs of the Society for Research in Child Development, 35,*(1), 1–67.

Hunt, K. (1977). Early blooming and late blooming syntactic structures. In C. R. Cooper and L. Odell (Eds.), *Evaluating writing: Describing, measuring, judging* (pp. 91–106). Urbana, IL: National Council of Teachers of English.

Hyon, S., and Sulzby, E. (1994). African American kindergarteners' spoken narratives: Topic associating and topic-centered styles. *Linguistics and Education, 6*(2), 121–152.

Individuals with disabilities education act amendments of 1997. (1997). (P.L. 105–17). 20 U.S.C. 1400 et seq. (*Congressional Record* 1997).

International Reading Association. (2000). *Excellent reading teachers: A position statement of the International Reading Association.* Newark, DE: International Reading Association. Retrieved June 19, 2005, from www.reading.org/downloads/positions/ps1041_excellent.pdf.

International Reading Association. (2003). *Standards for reading professionals—revised 2003.* Newark, DE: International Reading Association.

International Reading Association and National Association for the Education of Young Children. (1998). Learning to read and write: Developmentally appropriate practices for young children. *The Reading Teacher, 52,* 193–216.

Interstate New Teacher Assessment and Support Consortium. (1992). *Model standards for beginning teacher licensing and development: A resource for state dialogue.* Washington, DC: Council of Chief State School Officers.

Jackendoff, R. (1990). *Semantic structures.* Cambridge, MA: MIT Press.

Jacobs, J., Lanza, S., Osgood, D., Eccles, J., and Wigfield, A. (2002). Changes in children's self-competence and values: Gender and domain differences across grades one through twelve. *Child Development, 73,* 509–527.

James, S. L. (1990). *Normal language acquisition.* Boston: Little, Brown.

Jimenez, R. (2000). Literacy and identity development of Latina/o students. *American Educational Research Journal, 37*(4), 971–1000.

Johnson, D., and Pearson, P. D. (1978). *Teaching reading vocabulary.* New York: Holt, Rinehart and Winston.

Johnson-Laird, P. N. (1983). *Mental models.* Cambridge, UK: Cambridge University Press.

Johnston, F. R. (2000). Word learning in predictable text. *Journal of Educational Psychology, 92,* 248–255.

Joubert, S. A., and Lecours, A. R. (1999). A study of the interaction between lexical and sublexical reading routes. *Brain & Cognition, 40,* 150–153.

Juel, C. (1983). The development and use of mediated word identification. *Reading Research Quarterly, 18,* 306–327.

Juel, C. (1988). Learning to read and write: A longitudinal study of fifty-four children from first through fourth grade. *Journal of Educational Psychology, 80,* 437–447.

Juel, C. (1991). Beginning reading. In R. Barr, M. Kamil, P. Mosenthal, and P. Pearson (Eds.), *Handbook of reading research, Vol. II* (pp. 759–788). New York: Longman.

Juel, C., and Minden-Cupp, C. (2000). One down and 80,000 to go: Word recognition instruction in the primary grades. *The Reading Teacher, 53*(4), 332–335.

Juel, C., and Roper-Schneider, D. (1985). The influence of basal readers on first-grade reading. *Reading Research Quarterly, 20*(2), 134–152.

Juel, C., and Solso, R. L. (1981). The role of orthographic redundancy, versatility and spelling-sound correspondences in word identification. In M. L. Kamil (Ed.), *Directions in reading: Research and instruction* (30th yearbook of the National Reading Conference, pp. 74–92). Rochester, NY: National Reading Conference.

Juel, C., Biancarosa, G., Coker, D., and Deffes, R. (2003, April). Walking with Rosie: A cautionary tale of early reading instruction. *American Educator, 60*(7), 12–18.

Jusczyk, P. W. (1997). *The discovery of spoken language.* Cambridge, MA: MIT Press.

Just, M. A., and Carpenter, P. A. (1987). *The psychology of reading and language comprehension.* Newton, MA: Allyn & Bacon.

Justice, L. M., and Ezell, H. K. (2001). Word and print awareness in 4-year-old children. *Child Language Teaching and Therapy, 17*(3), 207–225.

Kameenui, E., and Simmons, D. (Eds.). (2001). Special issue on fluency. *Scientific Studies of Reading, 5.*

Kameenui, E. J., Simmons, D. C., Good, R. H., and Harn, B. A. (2001). The use of fluency-based measures in early identification and evaluation of intervention efficacy in schools. In M. Wolf (Ed.), *Time, fluency, and dyslexia.* Timonium, MD: York Press.

Kamil, M. L., and Lane, D. (1997, March). *A classroom study of the efficacy of using information text for first-grade reading instruction.* Paper presented at the annual meeting of the American Educational Research Association, Chicago.

Kanstoroom, M., and Finn, C. E. (1999). The teachers we need and how to get more of them: A manifesto. In M. Kanstoroom and C. E. Finn (Eds.), *Better teachers, better schools.* Washington, DC: Fordham Foundation.

Karmiloff-Smith, A. (1992). *Beyond modularity: A developmental perspective of cognitive science.* Cambridge: MIT Press.

Karmiloff-Smith, A., Grant, J., Sims, K., Jones, M.-C., and Cuckle, P. (1996). Rethinking metalinguistic awareness: Representing and accessing knowledge about what counts as a word. *Cognition, 58,* 197–219.

Katims, D. (2000). Literacy instruction for people with mental retardation: Historical highlights and contemporary analysis. *Education and Training in Mental Retardation and Development Disabilities, 53,* 3–15.

Keenan, J. M. (2002). The psychology of inferences. In N. Smelser and P. Baltes (Eds.), *International Encyclopedia of the Social & Behavioral Sciences, 11,* 7432–7435. Amsterdam: Pergamon.

Keene, E. O., and Zimmermann, S. (1997). *Mosaic of thought: Teaching comprehension in a reader's workshop.* Portsmouth, NH: Heinemann.

Kelly, M. H., Morris, J., and Verrekia, L. (1998). Orthographic cues to lexical stress: Effects on naming and lexical decision. *Memory and Cognition, 26,* 822–832.

Kelter, S., and Kaup, B. (1998). Language is a surrogate for experience. *Abeitspapier 1/1998.* Berlin: Technical University of Berlin.

Kessler, B., and Treiman, R. (2001). Relationships between sounds and letters in English monosyllables. *Journal of Memory and Language, 44,* 592–617.

King, A. (1994). Guiding knowledge construction in the classroom: Effects of teaching children how to question and how to explain. *American Educational Research Journal, 31*(2), 338–368.

Kintsch, W. (1998). *Comprehension: A paradigm for cognition.* New York: Cambridge University Press.

Klein, L., Johnson, J. F., and Ragland, M. (1997). *Successful Texas schoolwide programs: Research study results.* Austin, TX: Charles A. Dana Center, University of Texas at Austin.

Kliewer, C., and Biklen, D. (2001). "School's not really a place for reading": A research synthesis of the literate lives of students with severe disabilities. *The Journal of the Association for Persons with Severe Handicaps, 26*(1), 1–12.

Kliewer, C., and Landis, D. (1999). Individualizing literacy instruction for young children with moderate to severe disabilities. *Exceptional Children, 66*(1), 85–100.

Koedinger, K. R., and Nathan, M. J. (2004). The real story behind story problems: Effects of representations on quantitative reasoning. *The Journal of the Learning Sciences, 13*(2), 129–164.

Koppenhaver, D. A., and Yoder, D. E. (1993). Classroom literacy instruction for children with severe speech and physical impairment (SSPI): What is and what might be. *Topics in Language Disorders, 13,* 1–15.

Koretz, D. (2002). Limitations in the use of achievement tests as measures of educators' productivity. In E. Hanushek, J. Heckman, and D. Neal (Eds.), *Designing incentives to promote human capital,* a special issue of the *Journal of Human Resources, 37*(4), 752–777.

Krashen, S. (1993). *The power of reading: Insights from the research.* Englewood, CO: Libraries Unlimited.

Krashen, S. (2001). More smoke and mirrors: A critique of the National Reading Panel report on fluency. *Phi Delta Kappan, 83,* 119–123.

Kucan, L., and Beck, I. L. (1997). Thinking aloud and reading comprehension research: Inquiry, instruction, and social interaction. *Review of Educational Research, 67,* 271–299.

Kuczaj, S. A., and Barrett, M. D. (Eds.). (1986). *The development of word meaning.* New York: Springer-Verlag.

Kuhn, D. (1993). Science argument: Implications for teaching and learning scientific thinking. *Science Education, 77*(3), 319–337.

Kuhn, M. R., and Stahl, S. A. (1998). Teaching children to learn word meanings from context: A synthesis and some questions. *Journal of Literacy Research, 30,* 120–138.

Kuhn, M. R., and Stahl, S. A. (2003). Fluency: A review of developmental and remedial practices. *Journal of Educational Psychology, 95*(1), 3–21.

LaBerge, D., and Samuels, S. J. (1974). Toward a theory of automatic information processing in reading. *Cognitive Psychology, 6,* 293–323.

Labov, W. (1981). Speech actions and reactions in personal narrative. In D. Tannen (Ed.), *Analyzing discourse: Text and talk* (pp. 217–247). Georgetown University Round Table. Washington, DC: Georgetown University Press.

Labov, W., and Waletzky, J. (1967). Narrative analysis. In J. Helm (Ed.), *Essays on the verbal and visual arts* (pp. 12–44). Seattle: University of Washington Press.

Labov, W., Ash, S., and Boberg, C. (2002). *Atlas of North American English: Phonetics, phonology and sound change.* New York: Mouton de Gruyter.

Laczko-Kerr, I., and Berliner, D. C. (2002, September 6). The effectiveness of "Teach for America" and other under-certified teachers on student academic achievement: A case of harmful public policy. *Education Policy Analysis Archives, 10*(37). Retrieved January 10, 2003, from epaa.asu.edu/epaa/v10n37/.

Laing, E., and Hulme, C. (1999). Phonological and semantic processes influence beginning readers' ability to learn to read words. *Journal of Experimental Child Psychology, 73*(3), 183–207.

Lakoff, G., and Johnson, M. (1980). *Metaphors we live by.* Chicago: University of Chicago Press.

Lakoff, G., and Johnson, M. (1999). *Philosophy in the flesh: The embodied mind and its challenge to Western thought.* New York: Basic Books.

Langer, J. A. (1990). The process of understanding: Reading for literary and informative purposes. *Research in the Teaching of English, 24*(3), 229–257.

Langer, J. A. (1991, reprinted 2000). *Literary understanding and literature instruction* (Report Series 2.11). Albany, NY: National Research Center on English Learning & Achievement.

Langer, J. A. (1998). Beating the odds: Critical components boost student performance. *English Update: A Newsletter from The Center on English Learning and Achievement, Fall,* 1–8.

Langer, J. A. (2001). Beating the odds: Teaching middle and high school students to read and write well. *American Educational Research Journal, 38*(4), 837–880.

Langer, J. A. (2002). *Effective literacy instruction: Building successful reading and writing programs.* Urbana, IL: National Council of Teachers of English.

Langer, J. A., and Close, E. (2001). *Improving literary understanding through classroom conversation.* Albany, NY: National Research Center on English Learning & Achievement. [Also available online at cela.albany.edu/env.pdf.]

Langer, J. A., Close, E., Angelis, J., and Preller, P. (2000). *Teaching middle and high school students to read and write well: Six features of effective instruction.* Albany, NY: National Research Center on English Learning & Achievement.

Lappin, S. (Ed.). (1996). *The handbook of contemporary semantics.* Oxford: Blackwell.

Lasky, K. (1981). *The night journey.* New York: Puffin.

LAS-O (2000). *Language Assessment Scales—Oral.* Monterey, CA: CTB-MacMillan/McGraw-Hill.

Laufer, B., and Nation, P. (1999). A vocabulary size test of controlled productive ability. *Language Testing 16,* 33–51.

Laxon, V., Coltheart, V., and Keating, C. (1988). Children find friendly words friendly too: Words with many orthographic neighbours are easier to read and spell. *British Journal of Educational Psychology, 58,* 103–119.

Leap, W. (1993). *American Indian English.* Salt Lake City: University of Utah Press.

Learning First Alliance. (1998). *Every child reading: An action plan.* Washington, DC: Learning First Alliance.

Learning First Alliance. (2000). *Every child reading: A professional development guide.* Washington, DC: Learning First Alliance.

Lederer, R. (1987). *Anguished English: An anthology of accidental assaults upon our language.* New York: Wyrick and Company.

Lee, C. D. (1992). Literacy, cultural diversity, and instruction. *Education and Urban Society, 24*(2), 279–291.

Lee, C. D. (1995a). A culturally based cognitive apprenticeship: Teaching African American high school students skills in literary interpretation. *Reading Research Quarterly, 30(*4), 608–631.

Lee, C. D. (1995b). Signifying as a scaffold for literary interpretation. *Journal of Black Psychology, 21*(4), 357–381.

Lee, C. D. (1997). Bridging home and school literacies: A model of culturally responsive teaching. In J. Flood, S. B. Heath, and D. Lapp (Eds.), *A handbook for literacy educators: Research on teaching the communicative and visual arts* (pp. 330–341). New York: Macmillan.

Lee, C. D. (2000). Signifying in the zone of proximal development. In C. D. Lee and P. Smagorinsky (Eds.), *Vygotskian perspectives on literacy research: Constructing meaning through collabative inquiry.* New York: Cambridge University Press.

Lee, C. D. (2001). Is October Brown Chinese? A cultural modeling activity system for underachieving students. *American Educational Research Journal, 38*(1), 97–141.

Lee, C. D., Rosenfeld, E., Mendenhall, R., Rivers, A., and Tynes, B. (2003). Cultural modeling as a frame for narrative analysis. In C. L. Daiute and C. Lightfoot (Eds.), *Narrative analysis: Studying the development of individuals in society.* Thousand Oaks, CA: Sage.

Lee, M. (2004, April). *Promoting historical inquiry using secondary sources: Exploring the promise and possibilities in new genres of historical writing.* Paper presented at the annual meeting of American Educational Research Association, San Diego.

Lehrer, A., and Kittay, E. (Eds.). (1992). *Frames, fields, and contrasts: New essays in semantics and lexical organization.* Mahwah, NJ: Lawrence Erlbaum Associates.

Leinhardt, G. (1994). History: A time to be mindful. In G. Leinhardt, I. L. Beck, and C. Stainton (Eds.), *Teaching and learning in history.* Mahwah, NJ: Lawrence Erlbaum Associates.

Leinhardt, G. (2000). Lessons on teaching and learning in history from Paul's pen. In P. N. Stearns, P. Seixas, and S. Wineburg (Eds.), *Knowing, teaching, and learning history: National and international perspectives* (pp. 223–245). New York: New York University Press.

Lenski, S., Wham, M. A., and Johns, J. (1999). *Reading and learning strategies for middle and high school students.* Dubuque, IA: Kendall/Hunt.

Leslie, L., and Calhoon, A. (1995). Factors affecting children's reading of rimes: Reading ability, word frequency, and rime-neighborhood size. *Journal of Educational Psychology, 87,* 576–586.

Levin, B., and Hovav, M. R. (1998). Morphology and lexical semantics. In A. Spencer and A. M. Zwicky (Eds.), *The handbook of morphology* (pp. 248–271). Oxford: Blackwell.

Levin, B., and Pinker, S. (Eds.). (1991). *Lexical and conceptual semantics.* Oxford: Blackwell.

Levinson, S. C. (1983). *Pragmatics.* Cambridge, UK: Cambridge University Press.

Levy, B. A., Abello, B., and Lysynchuk, L. (1997). Transfer from word training to reading in context: Gains in fluency and comprehension. *Learning Disability Quarterly, 20,* 173–188.

Lewis, C. (2000, April). *Lesson study: The core of Japanese professional development.* Paper presented at the Annual Meeting of the American Educational Research Association, New Orleans.

Lewis, C. (2002). Everywhere I looked: Levers and pendulums. *Journal of Staff Development, 23*(3), 59–65.

Lewis, D., and Windsor, J. (1996). Children's analysis of derivational suffix meanings. *Journal of Speech and Hearing Research, 39,* 209–216.

Lewis, L., Parsad, N., Carey, N., Bartfai, N., Farris, E., and Smerdon, B. (1999). *Teacher quality: A report on the preparation and qualifications of public school teachers.* Washington, DC: U.S. Department of Education, National Center for Education Statistics.

Liberman, I. Y., Rubin, H., Duques, S., and Carlisle, J. (1985). Linguistic abilities and spelling proficiency in kindergartners and adult poor spellers. In J. Kavanagh and D. Gray (Eds.), *Biobehavioral measures of dyslexia.* Parkton, MD: York Press.

Loban, W. (1963). *The language of elementary school children: A study of the use and control of language and the relations among speaking, reading, writing, and listening.* Champaign, IL: National Council of Teachers of English.

Loban, W. (1966). *Problems in oral English: Kindergarten through grade nine.* Champaign, IL: National Council of Teachers of English.

Loban, W. (1976). *Language development: Kindergarten through grade twelve.* Urbana, IL: National Council of Teachers of English.

Löbner, S. (2002). *Understanding semantics.* London: Arnold.

Lomax, R., and McGee, L. (1987). Young children's concepts about print and reading: Toward a model of word reading acquisition. *Reading Research Quarterly, 22,* 237–256.

Lortie, D. (1975). *Schoolteacher: A sociological study.* Chicago: University of Chicago Press.

Luria, A. R. (1976–1977). The development of writing in the child. *Soviet Psychology, 12*(2), 65–114.

Lyon, G. R. (1995). Toward a definition of dyslexia. *Annals of Dyslexia, 45,* 3–30.

MacWhinney, B. (Ed.). (1999). *The emergence of language.* Mahweh, NJ: Lawrence Erlbaum Associates.

Malone, R., and McLaughlin, T. F. (1997). The effects of reciprocal peer tutoring with a group contingency on quiz performance in vocabulary with 7th- and 8th-grade students. *Behavioral Interventions, 12,* 27–40.

Maltz, D., and Borker, R. (1982). A cultural approach to male-female miscommunication. In J. Gumperz (Ed.), *Language and social identity.* Cambridge, UK: Cambridge University Press.

Mannes, S. M., and Kintsch, W. (1987). Knowledge organization and text organization. *Cognition and Instruction, 4,* 91–115.

Marcus, G. F. (1996). Why do children say "breaked"? *Current Directions in Psychological Science, 5*(3), 81–85.

Marsh, G., Desberg, P., and Cooper, J. (1977). Developmental changes in reading. *Journal of Reading Behavior, 21*(9), 391–394.

Marsh, G., Friedman, M. P., Welch, V., and Desberg, P. (1981). A cognitive-developmental theory of reading acquisition. In T. G. Waler and G. E. MacKinnon (Eds.), *Reading research: Advances in theory and practice.* London: Academic Press.

Marslen-Wilson, W. D. (1999). Abstractness and combination: The morphemic lexicon. In S. Garrod and M. Pickering (Eds.), *Language processing* (pp. 101–119). East Sussex, England: Psychology Press.

Marslen-Wilson, W. D., and Tyler, L. K. (1998). Rules, representations, and the English past tense. *Trends in Cognitive Sciences, 2*(11), 428–435.

Marslen-Wilson, W. D., and Warren, P. (1994). Levels of perceptual representation and process in lexical access: Words, phonemes, and features. *Psychological Review, 101,* 653–675.

Mason, J., and Allen, J. B. (1986). A review of emergent literacy with implications for research and practice in reading. *Review of Research in Education, 13,* 3–47.

Masonheimer, P. E., Drum, P. A., and Ehri, L. C. (1984). Does environmental print identification lead children into word reading? *Journal of Reading Behavior, 16,* 257–272.

McBride-Chang, C. (1999). The ABC's of the ABC's: The development of letter-name and letter-sound knowledge. *Merrill-Palmer Quarterly, 45,* 285–308.

McCutchen, D., and Berninger, V. (1999). Those who know, teach well: Helping teachers master literacy-related subject matter knowledge. *Learning Disabilities Research and Practice, 14*(4), 215–226.

McCutchen, D., Harry, D. R., Cunningham, A. E., Cox, S., Sidman, S., and Covill, A. E. (2002). Reading teachers' knowledge of children's literature and English phonology. *Annals of Dyslexia, 52,* 207–228.

McCutchen, D., Abbott, R. D., Green, L. B., Beretvas, S. N., Cox, S., Potter, N. S., and others. (2002). Beginning literacy: Links among teacher knowledge, teacher practice, and student learning. *Journal of Learning Disabilities, 35*(1), 69–86.

McDonnell, L. M., McLaughlin, M. J., and Morison, P. (1997). *Educating one and all: Students with disabilities and standards-based reform.* Washington, DC: National Academy Press.

McGee, L. M., and Lomax, R. G. (1990). On combining apples and oranges: A response to Stahl and Miller. *Review of Educational Research, 60*(1), 133–140.

McInerny, D., and Vanetten, S. (Eds.). (2001). *Research on sociocultural influences on motivation and learning.* Greenwich, CT: Information Age.

McKenna, M. C., Kear, D. J., and Ellsworth, R. A. (1995). Children's attitudes toward reading: A national survey. *Reading Research Quarterly, 30,* 934–956.

McKeown, M. G. (1993). Creating effective definitions for young word learners. *Reading Research Quarterly, 28*(1), 17–31.

McKeown, M. G., and Beck, I. L. (1994). Making sense of accounts of history: Why young students don't and how they might. In G. Leinhardt, I. L. Beck, and C. Stainton (Eds.), *Teaching and learning in history* (pp. 1–26). Hillsdale, NJ: Lawrence Erlbaum Associates.

McKeown, M. G., Beck, I. L., Omanson, R. C., and Pople, M. T. (1985). Some effects of the nature and frequency of vocabulary instruction on the knowledge of use of words. *Reading and Research Quarterly, 20,* 522–535.

McKoon, G., and Ratcliff, R. (1992). Inference during reading. *Psychological Review, 99,* 440–466.

McLaughlin, M., and Allen, M. B. (2002). *Guided comprehension: A teaching model for grades 3–8.* Newark, DE: International Reading Association.

McLeod, S., van Doorn, J., and Reed, V. A. (2001). Normal acquisition of consonant clusters. *American Journal of Speech-Language Pathology, 10,* 99–110.

McMahon, S., and Raphael, T. (Eds.). (1997). *The book club connection.* New York: Teachers College Press.

McMillan, J. H. (2000). Fundamental assessment principles for teachers and school administrators. *Practical Assessment, Research & Evaluation, 7*(8). Retrieved January 21, 2005, from http://pareonline.net/getvn.asp?v = 7&n = 8.

McMillan, J. H. (2001). Essential assessment concepts for teachers and administrators. In T. R. Guskey and R. J. Marzano (Eds.), *Experts in assessment series.* Thousand Oaks, CA: Corwin Press.

McNamara, D. S., Kintsch, E., Songer, N. B., and Kintsch, W. (1996). Are good texts always better? Interactions of text coherence, background knowledge, and levels of understanding in learning from text. *Cognition and Instruction, 14*(1), 1–43.

McQuillan, J. (1997). The effects of incentives on reading. *Reading Research and Instruction, 36*(2), 111–125.

Meece, J. L., and Miller, S. D. (1999). Changes in elementary school children's achievement goals for reading and writing: Results of a longitudinal and an intervention study. *Scientific Studies of Reading, 3*(3), 207–229.

Mehler, J., Dommergues, J. Y., Frauenfelder, U., and Segui, J. (1981). The syllable's role in speech segmentation. *Journal of Verbal Learning and Verbal Behavior, 20,* 298–305.

Mellor, B., and Patterson, A. (2000). *Investigating texts: Analyzing fiction and nonfiction in high school.* Urbana, IL: National Council of Teachers of English.

Menon, S., and Hiebert, E. H. (forthcoming). A comparison of first-graders' reading acquisition with little books or literature anthologies. *Reading Research Quarterly.*

Menyuk, P. (1963). A preliminary evaluation of grammatical capacity in children. *Journal of Verbal Learning and Verbal Behavior, 2,* 429–439.

Menyuk, P. (1964). Syntactic rules used by children from preschool through first grade. *Child Development, 35,* 533–546.

Menyuk, P. (1988). *Language development: Knowledge and use.* Glenview, IL: Scott, Foresman and Company.

Metsala, J. L. (1999). Young children's phonological awareness and nonword repetition as a function of vocabulary development. *Journal of Educational Psychology, 91,* 3–19.

Metsala, J. L., and Walley, A. C. (1998). Spoken vocabulary growth and the segmental restructuring of lexical representations: Precursors to phonemic awareness and early reading ability. In J. L. Metsala and L. C. Ehri (Eds.), *Word recognition in beginning literacy* (pp. 89–120). Mahwah, NJ: Lawrence Erlbaum Associates.

Meyer, M. S., and Felton, R. H. (1999). Repeated reading to enhance fluency: Old approaches and new directions. *Annals of Dyslexia, 49,* 283–306.

Miller, G. A., and Gildea, P. (1987). How children learn words. *Scientific American, 257*(3), 94–99.

Mitchell, M. (1993). Situational interest: Its multifaceted structure in the secondary school mathematics classroom. *Journal of Educational Psychology, 85,* 424–436.

Mitchell, R. (1999). Examining student work. *Journal of Staff Development, 20*(3), 32–33.

Moats, L. C. (1994). The missing foundation in teacher education: Knowledge of the structure of spoken and written language. *Annals of Dyslexia, 44,* 81–102.

Moats, L. C. (1999). *Teaching reading IS rocket science: What expert teachers of reading should know and be able to do.* Washington, DC: American Federation of Teachers. (Item No. 372).

Moats, L. C. (2000). *Speech to print: Language essentials for teachers.* Baltimore: Brooks.

Moats, L. C., and Foorman, B. R. (2003). Measuring teachers' content knowledge of language and reading. *Annals of Dyslexia, 53*(3), 23–45.

Moats, L. C., and Lyon, G. R. (1996). Wanted: Teachers with knowledge of language. *Topics in Learning Disorders, 16*(2), 73–86.

Moats, L. C., and Smith, C. (1992). Derivational morphology: Why it should be included in assessment and instruction. *Language, Speech, and Hearing in the Schools, 23,* 312–319.

Mody, M., Studdert-Kennedy, M., and Brady, S. (1997). Speech perception deficits in poor readers: Auditory processing or phonological coding? *Journal of Experimental Child Psychology, 64*(2), 199–231.

Moir, E. (n.d.). *Putting new teachers at the center.* Santa Cruz, CA: New Teacher Center. Retrieved June 14, 2005, from www.newteachercenter.org/ti_article3.php.

Moje, E. B., and O'Brien, D. G. (Eds.). (2001). *Constructions of literacy: Studies of teaching and learning in and out of secondary schools.* Mahwah, NJ: Lawrence Erlbaum Associates.

Moje, E. B., Dillon, D. R., and O'Brien, D. G. (2000). Re-examining the roles of the learner, the text, and the context in secondary literacy. *Journal of Educational Research, 93*, 165–180.

Moje, E., Young, J. P., Readence, J., and Moore, D. (2000). Remembering adolescent literacy for new times: Perennial and millennial issues. *Journal of Adolescent and Adult Literacy, 43*(5), 400–410.

Moje, E. B., Ciechanowski, K. M., Kramer, K., Ellis, L., Carrillo, R., and Collazo, T. (2003). Working toward third space in content area literacy: An examination of everyday funds of knowledge and discourse. *Reading Research Quarterly, 39*(1), 38–70.

Moll, L. C., Amanti, C., Neff, D., and Gonzalez, N. (1992). Funds of knowledge for teaching: Using a qualitative approach to connect homes and classrooms. *Theory into Practice, 21*, 132–141.

Monaghan, E. J. (1983). *A common heritage: Noah Webster's blue-back speller.* Hamden, CT: Archon.

Montgomery, M. (2000). *Ways of reading: Advanced reading skills for students of English literature.* New York: Routledge.

Moore, D. W., Bean, T. W., Birdyshaw, D., Rycik, J. A. (1999). *Adolescent literacy: A position statement for the Commission on Adolescent Literacy.* Newark, DE: International Reading Association.

Morris, D. (1993). The relationship between children's concept of word in text and phoneme awareness in learning to read: A longitudinal study. *Research in the Teaching of English, 27*, 133–154.

Morrow, L. M., Pressley, M., Smith, J. K., and Smith, M. (1997). The effect of a literature-based program integrated into literacy and science instruction with children from diverse backgrounds. *Reading Research Quarterly, 32*(1), 55–76.

Moss, B., and Newton, E. (1998, December). *An examination of the informational text genre in recent basal readers.* Paper presented at the National Reading Conference, Austin, Texas.

Moss, H. E., and Gaskell, G. (1999). Lexical semantic processing during speech. In M. Pickering and S. Garrod (Eds.), *Lexical processing.* Sussex: Psychology Press.

Mufwene, S., Rickford, J., Bailey, G., and Baugh, J. (1998). *African-American English: Structure, history and use.* New York: Routledge.

Murphy, P. K., and Alexander, P. A. (2002). What counts? The predictive power of subject-matter knowledge, strategic processing, and interest in domain-specific performance. *Journal of Experimental Education, 70*, 197–214.

Muter, V., Snowling, M. J., and Taylor, S. (1994). Orthographic analogies and phonological awareness: Their role and significance in early reading development. *Journal of Child Psychology and Psychiatry, 35*, 293–310.

Nagy, W. E., and Anderson, R. C. (1984). How many words are there in printed school English? *Reading Research Quarterly, 19,* 304–330.

Nagy, W. E., and Herman, P. A. (1987). Breadth and depth of vocabulary knowledge: Implications for acquisition and instruction. In M. G. McKeown and M. E. Curtis (Eds.), *The nature of vocabulary acquisition* (pp. 19–36). Hillsdale, N.J.: Lawrence Erlbaum Associates.

Nagy, W. E., and Scott, J. A. (2000). Vocabulary processes. In M. L. Kamil, P. B. Mosenthal, P. D. Pearson, and R. Barr (Eds.), *Handbook of reading research, Vol. III.* Mahwah, NJ: Lawrence Erlbaum Associates.

Nagy, W. E., Anderson, R. C., and Herman, P. A. (1987). Learning word meanings from context during normal reading. *American Educational Research Journal, 24*(2), 237–270.

Nathanson, J. H. (2001). *The condition of education: 2000 in brief.* Washington, DC: National Center for Education Statistics.

Nation, K., Allen, R., and Hulme C. (2001). The limitations of orthographic analogy in early reading development: Performance on the clue word task depends upon phonological priming and elementary decoding skill, not the use of orthographic analogy. *Journal of Experimental Child Psychology, 80,* 75–94.

National Board for Professional Teaching Standards. (n.d.). *Standards and national board certification: Standards.* Arlington, VA: Author. Retrieved May 26, 2003, from www.nbpts.org/standards/stds.cfm.

National Commission on Excellence in Elementary Teacher Preparation for Reading Instruction. (2003). *Prepared to make a difference: Research evidence on how some of America's best college programs prepare teachers of reading.* Newark, DE: International Reading Association.

National Commission on Teaching and America's Future. (1996). *What matters most: Teaching for America's future.* New York: Author.

National Council on Measurement in Education. (1995). *Code of professional responsibilities in educational measurement.* Washington, DC: Author.

National Literacy Trust, and Hertrich, J. (2004). *Secondary literacy: Key extracts from a survey HMI* (Her Majesty's Inspectorate of Education). London: National Literacy Trust. Also available online at www.literacytrust.org.uk/database/secondary.

National Reading Panel. (2000). *Report of the National Reading Panel: Teaching children to read: An evidence-based assessment of the scientific research literature on reading and its implications for reading instruction.* Washington, DC: National Institute of Child Health and Human Development. Retrieved June 25, 2005, from www.nichd.nih.gov/publications/nrp.

National Research Council and the Committee on Increasing High School Students' Engagement and Motivation to Learn. (2004). *Engaging schools: Fostering high school students' motivation to learn.* Washington, DC: The National Academies Press.

Nelson, N., and Calfee, R. C. (Eds.). (1998). The reading-writing connection viewed historically. In N. Nelson and R. C. Calfee (Eds.), *Ninety-Seventh Yearbook of the National Society for the Study of Education, Part II*. Chicago: University of Chicago Press.

Nesbit, C. R., and Rogers, C. A. (1997). Using cooperative learning to improve reading and writing in science. *Reading and Writing Quarterly, 13*(1), 53–70.

Neuman, S., and Dickinson, D. (Eds.). (2001). *Handbook for research in early literacy*. New York: Guilford.

Neuman, S. B., and Roskos, K. (1993). Access to print for children of poverty: Differential effects of adult mediation and literacy-enriched play settings on environmental and functional print tasks. *American Educational Research Journal, 30*, 95–122.

Nicoladis, E., and Genesee, F. (1997). Language development in preschool bilingual children. *Journal of Speech Language Pathology and Audiology, 21*, 258–270.

Nieto, S. (2000). *Puerto Rican students in U.S. schools*. Mahwah, NJ: Lawrence Erlbaum Associates.

Ninio, A., and Snow, C. E. (1996). *Pragmatic development*. Boulder: Westview.

Ninio, A., and Snow, C. E. (1999). The development of pragmatics: Learning to use language appropriately. In T. Bhatia and W. Ritchie (Eds.), *Handbook of child language acquisition* (pp. 347–383). New York: Academic Press.

Nippold, M. (1988). *Later language development*. Boston: Little, Brown.

Nippold, M., and Sullivan, M. P. (1987). Verbal and perceptual analogical reasoning and proportional metaphor comprehension in young children. *Journal of Speech and Hearing Research, 30*, 367–376.

Nippold, M., Uhden, L., and Schwarz, I. (1997). Proverb explanation through the lifespan: A study of adolescence and adults. *Journal of Speech, Language, and Hearing Research, 40*, 245–253.

Norris, S. P., and Phillips, L. M. (1994). Interpreting pragmatic meaning when reading popular reports of science. *Journal of Research in Science Teaching, 31*(9), 947–967.

North Carolina State Department of Public Instruction. (1999). Classroom assessment: Linking instruction and assessment. *Eric Document Reproduction Services No. ED429112*.

Nunes, T., Bryant, P., and Bindman, M. (1997). Morphological spelling strategies: Developmental stages and processes. *Developmental Psychology, 33*, 637–649.

Nystrand, M. (1997). *Opening dialogue: Understanding the dynamics of language and learning in the English classroom*. New York: Teachers College Press.

Nystrand, M., and Gamoran, A. (1997). The big picture: The language of learning in dozens of English lessons. In M. Nystrand (Ed.), *Opening dialogue: Understanding the dynamics of language and learning in the English classroom*. New York: Teachers College Press.

Nystrand, M., Wu, L. L., Gamoran, A., Zeiser, S., and Long, D. A. (2003). Questions in time: Investigating the structure and dynamics of unfolding classroom discourse. *Discourse Processes, 35*(2), 135–198.

Oakhill, J., and Beard, R. (Eds.) (1999). *Reading development and the teaching of reading: A psychological perspective.* Malden, MA: Blackwell.

Oakhill, J., and Cain, K. (2004). The development of comprehension skills. In P. E. Bryant and T. Nunes (Eds.), *Handbook of children's literacy* (pp. 155–180). Dordrect: Kluwer.

Oakhill, J., Cain, K., and Bryant, P. E. (2003). The dissociation of single-word reading and text comprehension: Evidence from component skills. *Language and Cognitive Processes 18*, 443–468.

Oakhill, J. V., Cain, K., and Yuill, N. M. (1998). Individual differences in children's comprehension skill: Towards an integrated model. In C. Hulme and R. M. Joshi (Eds.), *Reading and spelling: Development and disorder.* Mahwah, NJ: Lawrence Erlbaum Associates.

Oakhill, J. V., Hartt, J., and Samols, D. (1996, August 12–16). *Comprehension monitoring and working memory in good and poor comprehenders.* Paper presented at the XIVth Biennial ISSBD Conference, Quebec City.

Oakhill, J. V., Yuill, N., and Parkin, A. (1996). On the nature of the difference between skilled and less-skilled comprehenders. *Journal of Research in Reading, 9,* 80–91.

O'Brien, D. G., Dillon, D. R., Wellinski, S. A., Springs, R., and Stith, D. (1997). *Engaging "at-risk" high school students.* Athens, GA: National Reading Research Center.

Ochs, E. (1979). Planned and unplanned discourse. In T. Givón (Ed.), *Discourse and syntax* (pp. 51–80). New York: Academic Press.

O'Donnell, R. C., Griffin, W. J., and Norris, R. C. (1967). *Syntax of kindergarten and elementary school children; A transformational analysis.* Champaign, IL: National Council of Teachers of English.

Office of Policy and Planning. (1995). *Prospects: The Congressionally mandated study of educational growth and opportunity, first annual report.* Washington, DC: U.S. Department of Education.

Ogle, D. M. (1986). K-W-L: A teaching model that develops active reading of expository text. *Reading Teacher, 39,* 564–570.

O'Hare, F. (1973). *Sentence combining: Improving student writing without formal grammar instruction.* Urbana, IL: National Council of Teachers of English.

Olson, C. B. (2002). *The reading/writing connection: Strategies for teaching and learning in the secondary classroom.* Boston: Allyn & Bacon.

Olson, D. (1999, March 11). *The written word: Inaugural lecture as university professor.* University of Toronto. Retrieved June 14, 2005, from http://lsn.oise.utoronto.ca/Bruce/Rliteracy/Spring99.nsf/pages/olson/.

Olson, D., Torrance, N., and Hildyard, A. (Eds.). (1985). *Literacy, language, and learning.* Cambridge, UK: Cambridge University Press.

Osborne, J. F. (2002). Science without literacy: A ship without a sail? *Cambridge Journal of Education, 32*(2), 203–215.

Osborne, J. F., Simon, S., and Erduran, S. (2002, September). *Enhancing the quality of argumentation in school science.* Paper presented at an international conference titled "Ontological, epistemological, linguistic and pedagogical considerations of language and science literacy: Empowering research and informing instruction." University of Victoria, British Columbia.

Ostrowski, S. (2000). *How English is taught and learned in four exemplary middle and high school classrooms.* Report No. 13002. Albany, NY: National Research Center on English Learning & Achievement.

Owens, R. (2001). *Language development: An introduction.* Boston: Allyn & Bacon.

Palincsar, A. S. (2001, May). *Text, talk, and experience: Providing supportive contexts for inquiry-based science instruction in the elementary grades.* A paper presented at the annual meeting of the International Reading Association.

Palincsar, A. S., and Brown, A. L. (1984). Reciprocal teaching of comprehension fostering and comprehension-monitoring activities. *Cognition and Instruction, 1*(2), 117–175.

Palincsar, A. S., and Brown, A. L. (1986). Interactive teaching to promote independent learning from text. *The Reading Teacher, 39,* 771–777.

Palincsar, A., and Magnusson, S. (2001). The interplay of first-hand and second-hand investigations to model and support the development of scientific knowledge and reasoning. In S. Carver and D. Klahr (Eds.), *Cognition and instruction: Twenty-five years of progress.* Mahwah, NJ: Lawrence Erlbaum Associates.

Pany, D., Jenkins, J. R., and Schreck, J. (1982). Vocabulary instruction: Effects on word knowledge and reading comprehension. *Learning Disability Quarterly, 5,* 202–215.

Papandropoulou, I., and Sinclair, H. (1974). What is a word? An experimental study of children's ideas on grammar. *Human development, 17,* 240–258.

Pappas, C. C. (1993). Is narrative "primary"? Some insights from kindergartners' pretend readings of stories and information books. *Journal of Reading Behavior, 25,* 97–129.

Pappas, C. C., and Barry, A. (1997). Scaffolding urban students' initiations: Transactions in reading information books in the read aloud curriculum. In N. J. Karolides (Ed.), *Reader response in elementary classrooms: Quest and discovery* (pp. 215–236). Mahwah, NJ: Lawrence Erlbaum Associates.

Paris, A. H., and Paris, S. G. (2003). Assessing narrative comprehension in young children. *Reading Research Quarterly, 38,* 36–76.

Paris, S. G. (2001). *How can I assess children's early reading achievement?* Ann Arbor: Center for the Improvement of Early Reading Achievement.

Paris, S. G., and Jacobs, J. E. (1984). The benefits of informed instruction for children's reading awareness and comprehension skills. *Child Development, 55,* 2083–2093.

Parish, P. (1979). *Amelia Bedelia and the surprise shower.* New York: HarperTrophy.

Paxton, R. J. (1999). A deafening silence: History textbooks and the students who read them. *Review of Educational Research, 69*(3), 315–339.

Pearson, P. D., and Fielding, L. (1991). Comprehension instruction. In R. Barr, M. L. Kamil, P. B. Mosenthal, and P. D. Pearson (Eds.), *Handbook of reading research: Vol. II* (pp. 815–860). White Plains, NY: Longman.

Pearson, P. D., and Johnson, D. D. (1978). *Teaching reading comprehension.* New York: Holt, Rinehart and Winston.

Perfetti, C. A. (1985). *Reading ability.* New York: Oxford University Press.

Perfetti, C. A. (1992). The representation problem in reading acquisition. In P. B. Gough, L. C. Ehri, and R. Treiman (Eds.), *Reading acquisition* (pp. 145–174). Mahwah, NJ: Lawrence Erlbaum Associates.

Perfetti, C. A., and Zhang, S. (1995). Very early phonological activation in Chinese reading. *Journal of Experimental Psychology: Learning, Memory, and Cognition, 21,* 24–33.

Perfetti, C., Fayol, M., and Rieben, L. (Eds.). (1997). *Learning to spell.* Mahwah, NJ: Lawrence Erlbaum Associates.

Perry, N. E., and VandeKamp, K. O. (2000). Creating classroom contexts that support young children's development of self-regulated learning. *International Journal of Educational Research, 33,* 821–843.

Perry, N. E., VandeKamp, K. O., Mercer, L. K., and Nordby, C. J. (2002). Investigating teacher-student interactions that foster self-regulated learning. *Educational Psychologist, 37,* 5–15.

Peterson, C. (1990). The who, when, and where of early narratives. *Journal of Child Language, 17,* 433–455.

Peterson, C. L., Caverly, D. C., Nicholson, S. A., O'Neal, S., and Cusenbary, S. (2000). *Building reading proficiency at the secondary level: A guide to resources.* Austin: Southwest Educational Development Laboratory. Retrieved May 15, 2005, from www.sedl.org/pubs/reading16.

Phelps, G., and Schilling, S. (2003). *Developing measures of the content knowledge that it takes to teach reading.* Ann Arbor, MI: Study of Instructional Improvement.

Phelps, G., and Schilling, S. (forthcoming). Developing measures of content knowledge for teaching reading. *Elementary School Journal.*

Pierce, P. L., and McWilliam, P. J. (1993). Emerging literacy and children with severe speech and physical impairments (SSPI): Issues and possible intervention strategies. *Topics in Language Disorders, 13*(2), 47–57.

Pinkard, N. (2001). *Lyric reader: Creating intrinsically motivating and culturally responsive reading environments.* Retrieved May 15, 2005, from www.ciera.org/library/reports/inquiry-1/1–013/1–013.pdf.

Pinker, S. (1999). *Words and rules: The ingredients of language.* New York: Basic Books.

Pintrich, P. R. (1999). The role of motivation in promoting and sustaining self-regulated learning. *International Journal of Educational Research, 31,* 459–470.

Plaut, D. C., and Kello, C. T. (1999). The interplay of speech comprehension and production in phonological development: A forward modeling approach. In B. MacWhinney (Ed.), *The emergence of language* (pp. 381–415). Mahweh, NJ: Lawrence Erlbaum Associates.

Plaut, D. C., McClelland, J. L., Seidenberg, M. S., and Patterson, K. (1996). Understanding normal and impaired word reading: Computational principles in quasi-regular domains. *Psychological Review, 103,* 56–115.

Poole, M. E., and Field, T. W. (1976). A comparison of oral and written code elaboration. *Language and Speech, 19*, 305–311.

Porter, A. C., Youngs, P., and Odden, A. (2001). Advances in teacher assessments and their uses. In V. Richardson (Ed.), *Handbook of reading research.* (4th ed.). Washington, DC: American Educational Research Association.

Porter-O'Donnell, C. (2004). Beyond the yellow highlighter: Teaching annotation skills to improve reading comprehension. *English Journal, 93*(5), 82–89.

Pressley, M. (1995). More about the development of self-regulation: Complex, long-term, and thoroughly social. *Educational Psychologist, 30*, 207–212.

Pressley, M. (1998). Comprehension strategies instruction. In J. Osborn and F. Lehr (Eds.), *Literacy for all: Issues in teaching and learning* (pp. 113–133). New York: Guilford.

Pressley, M. (2000a). *Comprehension instruction: What makes sense now, what might make sense soon.* Retrieved May 15, 2005, from www.readingonline.org/articles/handbook/pressley.

Pressley, M. (2000b). What should comprehension instruction be instruction of? In M. L. Kamil, P. B. Mosenthal, P. D. Pearson, and R. Barr (Eds.) *Handbook of reading research, Vol. III* (pp. 545–562). Mahwah, NJ: Lawrence Erlbaum Associates.

Pressley, M., and Wharton-McDonald, R. (1997). Skilled comprehension and its development through instruction. *School Psychology Review, 26*, 448–466.

Pressley, M., Rankin, J., and Yokoi, L. (1996). A survey of instructional practices of primary teachers nominated as effective in promoting literacy. *Elementary School Journal, 96*, 363–384.

Pressley, M., Allington, R., Wharton-McDonald, R., Block, C. C., and Morrow, L. M. (2001). *Learning to read: Lessons from exemplary first grades.* New York: Guilford.

Pressley, M., Dolezal, S. E., Raphael, L. M., Mohan, L., Roehrig, A. D., and Bogner, K. (2003). *Motivating primary-grade students.* New York: Guilford.

Pressley, M., Wood, E., Woloshyn, V. E., Martin, V., King, A., and Menke, D. (1992). Encouraging mindful use of prior knowledge: Attempting to construct explanatory answers facilitates learning. *Educational Psychologist, 27*, 91–110.

Pressley, M., Wharton-McDonald, R., Allington, R., Block, C. C., Morrow, L., Tracey, D., and others. (2001). A study of effective first-grade literacy instruction. *Scientific Studies of Reading, 5*, 35–58.

Pugach, M. C., & Johnson, L. J. (1989). Prereferral interventions: Progress, problems, and challenges. *Exceptional Children, 56*(3), 217–226.

Pugach, M. C., and Warger, C. L. (1996). Challenges for the special education-curriculum reform partnership. In M. C. Pugach and C. L. Warger (Eds.), *Curriculum trends, special education, and reform: Refocusing the conversation. Special education series* (pp. 227–252). New York: Teachers College Press.

Pungello, E. P., Kupersmidt, J. B., Burchinal, M. R., and Patterson, C. J. (1996). Environmental risk factors and children's achievement from middle childhood to early adolescence. *Developmental Psychology, 32*(4), 755–767.

Purcell-Gates, V. (1988). Lexical and syntactic knowledge of written narrative held by well-read-to kindergartners and second graders. *Research in the Teaching of English, 22*, 128–160.

Purcell-Gates, V. (1996). Stories, coupons, and the TV guide: Relationships between home literacy experiences and emergent literacy knowledge. *Reading Research Quarterly, 31*, 406–428.

Purcell-Gates, V., and Duke, N. K. (2001, August). *Explicit explanation/teaching of informational text genres: A model for research.* Paper presented at Crossing Borders: Connecting Science and Literacy conference, sponsored by the National Science Foundation, Baltimore.

Rack, J. P., Snowling, M. J., and Olson, R. K. (1992). The nonword reading deficit and developmental dyslexia: A review. *Reading Research Quarterly, 27*, 28–53.

Rashotte, C. A., and Torgesen, J. K. (1985). Repeated reading and reading fluency in learning-disabled children. *Reading Research Quarterly, 20*, 180–188.

Rastle, K., and Coltheart, M. (2000). Lexical and nonlexical print-to-sound translation of disyllabic words and nonwords. *Journal of Memory and Language, 42*, 342–364.

Ravid, D., and Gillis, S. (2002). Teachers' perception of spelling patterns and children's spelling errors: A cross-linguistic perspective. In M. Neef, A. Neijt, and R. Sproat (Eds.), *The relation of writing to spoken language* (pp. 71–95). Tübingen, Germany: Niemeyer Verlag.

Rayner, K., Foorman, B. F., Perfetti, C. A., Pesetsky, D., and Seidenberg, M. S. (2001). How psychological science informs the teaching of reading. *Psychological Science in the Public Interest, 2*(2), 30–74.

Read, C. (1971). Preschool children's knowledge of English phonology. *Harvard Educational Review, 14*, 1–34.

Read, C. (1975). *Children's categorizations of speech sounds in English.* Urbana, IL: National Council of Teachers of English.

Reeve, J., Bolt, E., and Cai, Y. (1999). Autonomy-supportive teachers: How they teach and motivate students. *Journal of Educational Psychology, 91*(3), 537–548.

Reich, P. A. (1986). *Language development.* Englewood Cliffs, NJ: Prentice-Hall.

Reitsma, P. (1983a). Printed word learning in beginning readers. *Journal of Experimental Child Psychology, 36*, 321–339.

Reitsma, P. (1983b). Word-specific knowledge in beginning reading. *Journal of Research in Reading, 6*, 41–55.

Reitsma, P. (1988). Reading practice for beginners: Effects of guided reading, reading-while-listening, and independent reading with computer-based speech feedback. *Reading Research Quarterly, 23*, 219–235.

Rex, L. A., and McEachen, D. (1999). "If anything is odd, inappropriate, confusing, or boring, it's probably important": The emergence of inclusive academic literacy through English classroom discussion practices. *Research in the Teaching of English, 34*, 65–129.

Reyes, P., Scribner, J. D., and Paredes Scribner, A. (Eds.). (1999). *Lessons from high-performing Hispanic schools: Creating learning communities.* New York: Teachers College Press.

Richgels, D. J. (1995). Invented spelling ability and printed word learning in kindergarten. *Reading Research Quarterly, 30,* 96–109.

Ritchie, W., and Bhatia, T. (Ed.). (1998). *Handbook of child language acquisition.* San Diego: Academic Press.

Rittle-Johnson, B., and Siegler, R. S. (1999). Learning to spell: Variability, choice, and change in children's strategy use. *Child Development, 70,* 332–348.

Roberts, B. (1992). The evolution of the young child's concept of word as a unit of spoken and written language. *Reading Research Quarterly, 27*(2), 125–138.

Roehler, R. L., and Cantlon, D. J. (1997). Scaffolding: A powerful tool in social constructivist classrooms. In K. Hogan and M. Pressley (Eds.), *Scaffolding student learning: Instructional approaches and issues* (pp. 6–42). Cambridge, MA: Brookline.

Roller, C. M. (Ed.). (2001). *Learning to teach reading: Setting the research agenda.* Newark, DE: International Reading Association.

Romaine, S. (1984). *The language of children and adolescents: The acquisition of communicative competence.* Oxford: Blackwell.

Rosenholtz, S. J., and Simpson, C. (1990). Workplace conditions and the rise and fall of teachers' commitment. *Sociology of Education, 63*(4), 241–257.

Rosenshine, B., and Meister, C. (1994). Reciprocal teaching: A review of the research. *Review of Educational Research, 64*(4), 479–530.

Rosenshine, B., Meister, C., and Chapman, S. (1996). Teaching students to generate questions: A review of the intervention studies. *Review of Educational Research, 66,* 181–221.

Rothstein, R. (2004). *Class and schools: Using social, economic, and educational reform to close the Black-White achievement gap.* Washington, DC: Economic Policy Institute.

Rouet, J.-F., Britt, M. A., Mason, R. A., and Perfetti, C. A. (1996). Using multiple sources of evidence to reason about history. *Journal of Educational Psychology, 88,* 478–493.

Rowell, P. M., and Ebbers, M. (2002). *An uncertain role for literacy in elementary school science.* Electronic publication: retrieved May 15, 2005, from www.aare.edu.au/02pap/row02074.htm. ISSN 1324–9339 (row02074). Brisbane: Australian Association for Research in Education.

Rubin, H., Rotella, T., Schwartz, L., and Bernstein, S. (1991). The effect of phonological analysis training on naming performance. *Reading & Writing: An Interdisciplinary Journal, 3,* 1–10.

Ruddell, M. (2001). *Teaching content reading and writing* (3rd ed.). New York: Wiley.

Ruddell, M. R., and Shearer, B. A. (2002). "Extraordinary," "tremendous," "magnificent": Middle school at-risk students become avid word learners with Vocabulary Self-Collection Strategy (VSS). *Journal of Adolescent & Adult Literacy, 45,* 352–363.

Rueda, R., MacGillivray, L., Monzo, L., and Arzubiaga, A. (2001). Engaged reading: A multi-level approach to considering sociocultural factors with diverse learners. In D. McInerny and S. Vanetten (Eds.), *Research on sociocultural influences on motivation and learning* (pp. 233–264). Greenwich, CT: Information Age.

Ryan, R., and Deci, E. (2000a). Self-determination theory and the facilitation of intrinsic motivation, social development, and well-being. *American Psychologist, 55,* 68–78.

Ryan, R., and Deci, E. (2000b). When rewards compete with nature: The undermining of intrinsic motivation and self-regulation. In C. Sansone and J. Harachiewicz (Eds.), *Intrinsic and extrinsic motivation: The search for the optimal motivation and performance* (pp. 13–54). San Diego: Academic Press.

Saeed, J. I. (2003). *Semantics* (2nd ed.). Oxford and Cambridge, MA: Blackwell.

Samuels, S. J. (1979). The method of repeated readings. *The Reading Teacher, 32,* 403–408.

Samuels, S. J. (1985). Automaticity and repeated reading. In J. Osborn, P. T. Wilson, and R. C. Anderson (Eds.), *Reading education: Foundations for a literate America.* Lexington, MA: Lexington Books.

Samuels, S. J., Schermer, N., and Reinking, D. (1992). Reading fluency: Techniques for making decoding automatic. In S. J. Samuels and A.E. Farstrup (Eds.), *What Research Has to Say About Reading Instruction.* Newark, DE: International Reading Association.

Scarborough, H. S. (1998). Early identification of children at risk for reading disabilities: Phonological awareness and some other promising predictors. In B. K. Shapiro, P. J. Accardo, and A. J. Capute (Eds.), *Specific reading disability: A view of the spectrum* (pp. 75–119). Timonium, MD: York Press.

Scarborough, H. S. (2001). Connecting early language and literacy to later reading (dis)abilities: Evidence, theory, and practice. In S. Neuman and D. Dickinson (Eds.), *Handbook for research in early literacy* (pp. 97–110). New York: Guilford.

Scarborough, H. S., Ehri, L. C., Olson, R. K., and Fowler, A. E. (1998). The fate of phonemic awareness beyond the elementary school years. *Scientific Studies of Reading, 2*(2), 115–142.

Schiefele, U. (1999). Interest and learning from text. *Scientific Studies of Reading, 3*(3), 257–279.

Schloss, P. J., Alexander, N., Hornig, E., Parker, K., and Wright, B. (1993). Teaching meal preparation vocabulary and procedures to individuals with mental retardation. *Teaching Exceptional Children, 25*(3), 7–12.

Schmidt, P. (1995). Working and playing with others: Cultural conflict in a kindergarten literacy program. *The Reading Teacher, 48,* 404–412.

Schoenbach, R., Braunger, J., Greenleaf, C., and Litman, C. (2003). Apprenticing adolescents to reading in subject area classrooms. *Phi Delta Kappan, 85*(2), 133–138.

Schoenbach, R., Greenleaf, C., Cziko, C., and Hurwitz, L. (1999). *Reading for understanding: A guide to improving reading in middle and high school classrooms.* San Francisco: Jossey-Bass.

Scholes, R. J. (1999). *A linguistic approach to reading and writing.* Lewiston, NY: Edwin Mellen Press.

Scholes, R. J., and Willis, B. J. (1987). Language and literacy. *Journal of Literary Semantics, 16*(1), 3–11.

Scholes, R. J., and Willis, B. J. (1990). Prosodic and syntactic functions of punctuation: A contribution to the study of orality and literacy. *Interchange, 21*(3), 13–20.

Schreiber, P. A. (1987). Prosody and structure in children's syntactic processing. In R. Horowitz and S. J. Samuels (Eds.), *Comprehending oral and written language* (pp. 243–270). New York: Academic Press.

Schunk, D. H., and Rice, J. M. (1993). Strategy fading and progress feedback: Effects on self-efficacy and comprehension among students receiving remedial reading services. *Journal of Special Education, 27,* 257–276.

Schwanenflugel, P. J., Stahl, S. A., and McFalls, E. L. (1997). *Partial word knowledge and vocabulary growth during reading comprehension* (Research Report No. 76). Athens: University of Georgia, National Reading Research Center.

Schwenk, M. A., and Danks, J. H. (1974). A developmental study of the pragmatic communication rule for prenominal adjective ordering. *Memory and Cognition, 2,* 149–152.

Scott, J. A., and Nagy, W. E. (1997). Understanding the definitions of unfamiliar verbs. *Reading Research Quarterly 32*(2), 184–200.

Seidenberg, M. S., and McClelland, J. L. (1989). A distributed, developmental model of word recognition and naming. *Psychological Review, 96,* 523–568.

Seigneuric, A., Ehrlich, M.-F., Oakhill, J. V., and Yuill, N. M. (2000). Working memory resources and children's reading comprehension. *Reading and Writing, 13,* 81–103.

Serpell, R. (1997). Literacy connections between school and home: How should we evaluate them? *Journal of Literacy Research, 29*(4), 587–616.

Seymour, H. N., and Roeper, T. (1999). Grammatical acquisition of African American English. In O. Taylor, and L. Leonard (Eds.), *Speech and language in North America* (pp. 109–153). San Diego, CA: Singular Press.

Seymour, H., Roeper, T., de Villiers, J., and de Villiers, P. (2003). *Diagnostic evaluation of language variation (DELV) criterion-referenced.* San Antonio, TX: Psychological Corp.

Seymour, P.H.K. (1997). Foundations of orthographic development. In C. A. Perfetti, L. Rieben, and M. Fayol (Eds.), *Learning to spell: Research, theory, and practice across languages.* Mahway, NJ: Lawrence Erlbaum Associates.

Seymour, P.H.K., and Elder, L. (1986) Beginning reading without phonology. *Cognitive Neuropsychology, 3*(1), 1–36.

Seymour, P.H.K., Duncan, L. G., and Bolik, F. M. (1999). Rhymes and phonemes in the common unit task: Replications and implications for beginning reading. *Journal of Research in Reading, 22,* 113–130.

Shankweiler, D., Lundquist, E., Dreyer, L. G., and Dickinson, C. C. (1996). Reading and spelling difficulties in high school students: Causes and consequences. *Reading and Writing: An Interdisciplinary Journal, 8,* 267–294.

Share, D. L. (1995). Phonological recoding and self-teaching: Sine qua non of reading acquisition. *Cognition, 55,* 151–218.

Share, D. L. (1999). Phonological recoding and orthographic learning: A direct test of the self-teaching hypothesis. *Journal of Experimental Child Psychology, 72,* 95–129.

Share, D. L., and Gur, T. (1999). How reading begins: A study of preschoolers' print identification strategies. *Cognition and Instruction, 17,* 177–213.

Share, D. L., and Stanovich, K. E. (1995). Cognitive processes in early reading development: Accommodating individual differences into a model of acquisition. *Issues in Education: Contributions from Educational Psychology, 1,* 1–57.

Shearer, B. A., Ruddell, M. R., and Vogt, M. E. (2001). Successful middle school reading intervention: Negotiated strategies and individual choice. In J. V. Hoffman, D. L. Schallert, C. M. Fairbanks, J. Worthy, and B. Maloch (Eds.), *50th Yearbook of the National Reading Conference.* Chicago: National Reading Conference.

Shefelbine, J., and Calhoun, J. (1991). Variability in approaches to identifying polysyllabic words: A descriptive study of sixth graders with highly, moderately, and poorly developed syllabication strategies. In J. Zutell and S. McCormick (Eds.), *Learner factors/teacher factors: Issues in literacy research and instruction, 40th yearbook of the National Reading Conference* (pp. 169–177). Chicago: The National Reading Conference, Inc.

Shibatani, M., and Thompson, S. (Eds.). (1995). *Essays in semantics and pragmatics.* Amsterdam: John Benjamins.

Shulman, L. (1986). Those who understand: Knowledge growth in teaching. *Educational Researcher, 15*(2), 4–14.

Shulman, L. (1987). Knowledge and teaching: Foundations of the new reform. *Harvard Educational Review, 57,* 1–22.

Siegal, M., Borasi, R., and Fonzi, J. (1998). Supporting students' mathematical inquiries through reading. *Journal for Research in Mathematics Education, 29*(4), 378–413.

Siegler, R. S. (1996). *Emerging minds: The process of change in children's thinking.* New York: Oxford University Press.

Silvén, M., Niemi, P., and Voeten, M.J.M. (2002). Do maternal interaction and early language predict phonological awareness in 3- to 4-year olds? *Cognitive Development, 17,* 1133–1155.

Simon, S., Erduran, S., Osborne, J. (2002, April). *Enhancing the quality of argumentation in school science.* Paper presented at the Annual Meeting of the National Association for Research in Science Teaching, April 7–10, 2002, New Orleans.

Simpson, G. B. (1995). Context and the processing of ambiguous words. In M. A. Gernsbacher (Ed.), *Handbook of Psycholinguistics* (pp. 359–374). San Diego: Academic Press.

Singer, M., Harkness, D., and Stewart, S. T. (1997). Constructing inferences in expository text comprehension. *Discourse Processes, 24,* 199–228.

Slobin, D. I. (1978). A case study of early language awareness. In A. Sinclair, R. J. Jarvella, and W.J.M. Levelt (Eds.), *The child's conception of language.* Berlin; New York: Springer-Verlag.

Slobin, D. I., Gerhardt, J., Kyratzis, A., and Guo, J. (Eds.). (1996). *Social interaction, social context, and language: Essays in honor of Susan Ervin-Tripp.* Mahwah, NJ: Lawrence Erlbaum Associates.

Smitherman, G. (1994). The Blacker the berry, the sweeter the juice: African American student writers and the NAEP. In A. H. Dyson and C. Genishi (Eds.), *The need for story: Cultural diversity in classroom and community.* Urbana, IL: National Council of Teachers of English.

Smolensky, P. (1996). On the comprehension/production dilemma in child language. *Linguistic Inquiry, 27,* 720–731.

Smolkin, L. B., and Donovan, C. A. (2001). Comprehension acquisition and information book read alouds in a first grade classroom. *Elementary School Journal, 102,* 97–122.

Smolkin, L. B., and Donovan, C. A. (2002). "Oh, excellent, excellent question!": Developmental differences and comprehension acquisition. In C. C. Block and M. Pressley (Eds.), *Comprehension instruction: Research-based best practices* (pp. 140–157). New York: Guilford.

Smolkin, L. B., and Donovan, C. A. (2003). Supporting comprehension acquisition for emerging and struggling readers: The interactive information book read-aloud. *Exceptionality, 11*(1), 25–38.

Snow, C. E. (1983). Literacy and language: Relationships during the preschool years. *Harvard Educational Review, 53*(2), 165–189.

Snow, C. E. (1991). The theoretical basis for relationships between language and literacy in development. *Journal of Research in Childhood Education, 6*(1), 5–10.

Snow, C. E. (2002). *Reading for understanding: Toward an R&D program in reading comprehension.* Santa Monica, CA: RAND.

Snow, C. E. (2003). Assessment of reading comprehension: Researchers and practitioners helping themselves and each other. In A. Sweet and C. E. Snow (Eds.), *Rethinking reading comprehension* (pp. 192–206). New York: Guilford.

Snow, C. E., and Sweet, A. P. (2003). Reading for comprehension. In A. P. Sweet and C. E. Snow (Eds.), *Rethinking reading comprehension* (pp. 1–11). New York: Guilford.

Snow, C. E., Burns, M. S., and Griffin, P. (Eds.). (1998). *Preventing reading difficulties in young children.* Washington, DC: National Academy Press.

Snow, C. E., Pan, B., Imbens-Bailey, A., and Herman, J. (1996). Learning how to say what one means: A longitudinal study of children's speech act use. *Social Development, 5,* 56–84.

Soto, G. (1997). *Buried Onions.* New York: HarperCollins.

Spear-Swerling, L., and Sternberg, R. (1997). *Off track: When poor readers become labelled learning disabled.* Boulder, CO: Westview.

Spencer, A., and Zwicky, A. M. (1998). *The handbook of morphology.* Oxford: Blackwell.

Sperling, R. A., Walls, R. T., and Hill, L. A. (2000). Early relationships among self-regulatory constructs: Theory of mind and preschool children's problem solving. *Child Study Journal, 30*(4), 233–252.

Spinelli, J. (1990). *Maniac magee.* New York: Little Brown.

Spinillo, A. G., and Pinto, G. (1994). Children's narrative under different conditions: A comparative study. *British Journal of Developmental Psychology, 12,* 177–194.

Spires, H. A., and Donley, J. (1998). Prior knowledge activation: Inducing engagement with informational texts. *Journal of Educational Psychology, 90*(2), 249–260.

Stahl, S. A. (1991). Beyond the instrumentalist hypothesis: Some relationships between word meanings and comprehension. In P. Schwanenflugel (Ed.), *The psychology of word meanings* (pp. 157–178). Hillsdale, NJ: Lawrence Erlbaum Associates.

Stahl, S. A. (2002, November). *Fluency: Instruction and assessment.* Presentation at the Focus on Fluency Forum, November 2002, San Francisco.

Stahl, S. A. (2003). Words are learned incrementally over multiple exposures. *American Educator,* Spring. Retrieved June 14, 2005, from www.d261.k12.id.us/ NewCurriculum/Parent%20Information/Reading%20Articles/ Words%20are%20learned.pdf.

Stahl, S. A., and Fairbanks, M. (1986). The effects of vocabulary instruction: A model-based meta-analysis. *Review of Educational Research, 56*(1), 72–110.

Stahl, S. A., and Kapinus, B. A. (1991). Possible sentences: Predicting word meanings to teach content area vocabulary. *Reading Teacher, 45*(1), 36–43.

Stahl, S. A., and Miller, P. D. (1989). Whole language and language experience approaches for beginning reading: A quantitative research synthesis. *Review of Educational Research, 59*(1), 87–116.

Stahl, S. A., and Murray, B. A. (1998). Issues involved in defining phonological awareness and its relation to early reading. In J. Metsala and L. C. Ehri (Eds.), *Word recognition in beginning literacy* (pp. 65–87). Mahwah, NJ: Lawrence Erlbaum Associates.

Stahl, S., Heubach, K., and Cramond, B. (1997). *Fluency-oriented reading instruction.* Athens, GA: National Reading Research Center, U.S. Department of Education Office of Educational Research and Improvement Educational Resources Information Center.

Stahl, S. A., Hynd, C. R., Britton, B., K., McNish, M. M., and Bosquet, D. (1996). What happens when students read multiple source documents in history? *Reading Research Quarterly, 31,* 430–456. Retrieved May 15, 2005, from curry.edschool.virginia.edu/ go/clic/nrrc/hist_r45.html.

Stanovich, K. E., and Cunningham, A. E. (1992). Studying the consequences of literacy within a literate society: The cognitive correlates of print exposure. *Memory and Cognition, 20,* 51–86.

Stanovich, K. E., and Siegel, L. S. (1994). Phenotypic performance profiles of children with reading disabilities: A regression-based test of the phonological-core variable-difference model. *Journal of Educational Psychology, 86,* 24–53.

Stanovich, P. J., and Stanovich, K. E. (2003, May). *Using research and reason in education: How teachers can use scientifically based research to make curricular and instructional decisions.* Portsmouth, NH: RMC Research Corporation. Retrieved May 15, 2005, from www.nifl.gov/partnershipforreading/publications/html/stanovich.

State Board for Educator Certification and National Evaluation Systems. (2003). *Texas examinations of educator standards preparation manual: 131 English language arts and reading 8–12.* Austin, TX: Author. Also available online at www.excet.nesinc.com/prepmanuals/PDFs/TExES_fld131_prepmanual.pdf.

Stearns, P. N., Seixas, P., and Wineburg, S. (Eds.). (2000). *Knowing, teaching, and learning history: National and international perspectives.* New York: New York University Press.

Steinhauer, K., and Friederici, A. D. (2001). Prosodic boundaries, comma rules, and brain responses: The closure positive shift in ERPs as a universal marker for prosodic phrasing in listeners and readers. *Journal of Psycholinguistic Research, 30*(3), 267–295.

Sternberg, R. J. (1987). Most vocabulary is learned from context. In M. G. McKeown and M. E. Curtis (Eds.), *The nature of vocabulary acquisition* (pp. 89–106). Mahwah, NJ: Lawrence Erlbaum Associates.

Stevens, R. J., Madden, N. A., Slavin, R. E., and Farnish, A. M. (1987). Cooperative integrated reading and composition: Two field experiments. *Reading Research Quarterly, 22*(4), 433–454.

Sticht, T. G. (1976). Comprehending reading at work. In M. Just and P. Carpenter (Eds.), *Cognitive Processes in Comprehension.* Hillsdale, NJ: Lawrence Erlbaum Associates.

Sticht, T. G. (2002, January). *Teaching reading with adults.* Retrieved May 15, 2005, from www.nald.ca/fulltext/sticht/jan02/teach.pdf.

Sticht, T. G., and James, J. H. (1984). Listening and reading. In P. Pearson, R. Barr, M. Kamil, and P. Mosenthal (Eds.), *Handbook of reading research, Vol. I* (pp. 293–317). New York: Longman.

Stiggins, R. J. (2001). *Student-involved classroom assessment.* Upper Saddle River, NJ: Prentice Hall.

Stigler, J., and Hiebert, J. (1999). *The teaching gap: Best ideal from the world's teachers for improving education in the classroom.* New York: The Free Press.

Stipek, D. (2002). *Motivation to learn: Integrating theory and practice* (4th ed.). Boston: Allyn & Bacon.

Stipek, D., Feller, R., Daniels, D., and Milburn, S. (1995). Effects of different instructional approaches on young children's achievement and motivation. *Child Development, 66,* 209–221.

Strickland, D. S. (1998). Educating African American children: Finding a better way. In M. F. Opitz (Ed.), *Literacy instruction for culturally and linguistically diverse students* (pp. 71–80). Newark, DE: International Reading Association.

Strickland, D. S., and Taylor, D. (1989). Family storybook reading: Implications for children, families, and curriculum. In D. S. Strickland and L. M. Morrow (Eds.), *Emerging literacy: Young children learn to read and write* (pp. 27–34). Newark, DE: International Reading Association.

Strickland, D. S., Snow, C. E., Griffin, P., Burns, M. S., and McNamara, P. (2002). *Preparing our teachers: Opportunities for better reading instruction.* Washington, DC: National Academy Press.

Stringfield, S. (1994). Outlier studies of school effectiveness. In B.C.D. Reynolds, P. Nesselrodt, E. Stringfield, and C. Teddlie (Eds.), *Advances in school effectiveness research*. Oxford: Pergamon.

Stothard, S., and Hulme, C. (1992). Reading comprehension difficulties: The role of language comprehension and working memory. *Reading and Writing, 4,* 245–256.

Stothard, S., and Hulme, C. (1996). A comparison of reading comprehension and decoding difficulties in children. In C. Cornoldi and J. V. Oakhill (Eds.), *Reading comprehension difficulties: Processes and remediation*. Mahwah, NJ: Lawrence Erlbaum Associates.

Stuart, M., and Coltheart, M. (1988). Does reading develop in a sequence of stages? *Cognition, 30,* 139–181.

Stuebing, K. K., Fletcher, J. M., LeDoux, J. M., Jyon, G. R., Shaywitz, S. E., and Shaywitz, B. A. (2002). Validity of IQ-discrepancy classifications of reading disabilities: A meta-analysis. *American Educational Research Journal, 39,* 469–518.

Sulzby, E., and Teale, W. (1991). Emergent literacy. In R. Barr, M. L. Kamil, P. B. Mosenthal, and P. D. Pearson (Eds.), *Handbook of reading research, Vol. II* (pp. 727–757). New York: Longman.

Sulzby, E., Barnhart, J., and Hieshima, J. (1989). Forms of writing and rereading from writing: A preliminary report. In J. Mason (Ed.), *Reading and writing connections* (pp. 31–63). Needham Heights, MA: Allyn & Bacon.

Tannen, D. (1982). Oral and literate strategies in spoken and written narratives. *Language, 58,* 1–21.

Swanson, H. L., Mink, J., and Bocian, K. M. (1999). Cognitive processing deficits in poor readers with symptoms of reading disabilities and ADDHD more alike than different? *Journal of Educational Psychology, 91*(2), 321–333.

Sweet, R. W. (2004). The big picture: Where we are and how we got here. In P. McCardle and V. Chhabra (Eds.), *The voice of evidence in reading research* (pp. 13–44). Baltimore, MD: Brookes.

Tangel, D. M., and Blachman, B. A. (1995). Effect of phoneme awareness instruction on the invented spelling of first-grade children: A one-year follow-up. *Journal of Reading Behavior, 27*(2), 153–185.

Tannen, D. (1982). The oral/literate continuum in discourse. In D. Tannen (Ed.), *Spoken and written language: Exploring orality and literacy* (pp. 1–16). Norwood, NJ: Ablex.

Tannen, D. (1990). *You just don't understand: Women and men in conversation.* New York: William Morrow.

Tannen, D. (1996). *Gender and discourse.* New York: Oxford University Press.

Taylor, B. M. (1985). Improving middle-grade students' reading and writing of expository text. *Journal of Educational Research, 79*(2), 119–125.

Taylor, B. M., and Beach, R. W. (1984). Effects of text structure instruction on middle-grade students' comprehension and production of expository text. *Reading Research Quarterly, 19*(2), 134–146.

Taylor, B. M., and Graves, M. F. (2000). *Reading for meaning: Fostering comprehension in the middle grades.* New York: International Reading Association and Teachers College Press.

Taylor, B. M., and Pearson, P. D. (Eds.). (2002). *Teaching reading: Effective schools, accomplished teachers.* Mahwah, NJ: Lawrence Erlbaum Associates.

Taylor, B. M., Pressley, M. P., and Pearson, P. D. (2002). Research-supported characteristics of teachers and schools that promote reading achievement. In B. M. Taylor and P. D. Pearson (Eds.), *Teaching reading: Effective schools, accomplished teachers* (pp. 361–374). Mahwah, NJ: Lawrence Erlbaum Associates.

Taylor, B. M., Pearson, P. D., Clark, K. F., and Walpole, S. (1999). Effective schools/accomplished teachers. *Reading Teacher, 53*(2), 156–159.

Taylor, B. M., Pearson, P. D., Clark, K., and Walpole, S. (2000). *Beating the odds in teaching all students to read: Lessons from effective schools and accomplished teachers.* Ann Arbor, MI: University of Michigan, Center for the Improvement of Early Reading Achievement.

Taylor, B. M., Pearson, P. D., Peterson, D. S., and Rodriguez, M. C. (2003). Reading growth in high-poverty classrooms: The influence of teacher practices that encourage cognitive engagement in literacy learning. *Elementary School Journal, 104*(1), 3–28.

Taylor, B. M., Critchley, C., Paulsen, K., MacDonald, K., and Miron, H. (Forthcoming). *Learning to teach an early reading intervention program through internet-supported professional development.* Edina, MN: Web Education Company.

Taylor, D. (1986). Creating family story: "Matthew! We're going to have a ride!" In W. H. Teale and E. Sulzby (Eds.), *Emergent literacy: Writing and reading* (pp. 139–155). Norwood, NJ: Ablex.

Taylor, L. (1999). Personalizing classroom instruction to account for motivational and developmental differences. *Reading & Writing Quarterly, 15*(2), 255–276.

Teachscape. (n.d.) *Teachscape literacy program.* New York: Author. Retrieved May 15, 2005, from http://ts2.teachscape.com/html/ts/public/.

Templeton, S. (1989). Tacit and explicit knowledge of derivational morphology: Foundations for a unified approach to spelling and vocabulary development in the intermediate grades and beyond. *Reading Psychology, 10,* 233–253.

Templeton, S., and Bear, D. (Eds.) (1992). *Development of orthographic knowledge and the foundations of literacy: A memorial Festschrift for Edmund H. Henderson.* Mahwah, NJ: Lawrence Erlbaum Associates.

Templeton, S., and Morris, D. (2000). Reconceptualizing spelling development and instruction. In M. L. Kamil, P. B. Mosenthal, P. D. Pearson, and R. Barr (Eds.), *Handbook of reading research, Vol. III.* Mahwah, NJ: Lawrence Erlbaum Associates.

Thomas, W. P., and Collier, V. P. (2002). *A national study of school effectiveness for language minority students' long-term academic achievement final report.* Santa Cruz, CA: Center for Research on Education, Diversity and Excellence. Retrieved May 15, 2005, from www.crede.ucsc.edu/research/llaa/1.1_final.html.

Thompson, R., Mixon, G., and Serpell, R. (1996). Engaging minority students in reading: Focus on the urban learner. In L. Baker, P. Afflerbach, and D. Reinking (Eds.), *Developing engaged readers in school and home communities* (pp. 43–63). Mahwah, NJ: Lawrence Erlbaum Associates.

Tierney, R. J., and Shanahan, T. (1991). Research on the reading-writing relationship: Interaction, transactions and outcomes. In R. Barr, M. L. Kamil, P. Mosenthal, and P. D. Pearson (Eds.), *Handbook of reading research, Vol. II.* New York: Longman.

Tierney, R. J., Carter, M. A., and Desai, L. E. (1991). *Portfolio assessment in the reading writing classroom.* Norwood, MA: Christopher-Gordon.

Tierney, R. J., Clark, C., Fenner, L., Herter, R. J., Simpson, C. S., and Wiser, B. (1998). Portfolios: Assumptions, tensions, and possibilities. *Reading Research Quarterly, 33,* 434–469.

Tinkham, T. (1993). The effect of semantic clustering on the learning of second language vocabulary. *System, 21*(3), 371–380.

Tolchinsky-Landsmann, L., and Levin, I. (1985). Writing in kindergarteners: An age related analysis. *Applied Psycholinguistics, 6,* 319–339.

Tomasello, M. (2000). Do young children have adult syntactic competence? *Cognition, 74,* 209–253.

Tomasello, M., and Bates, E. (Eds.). (2001). *Language development: The essential readings.* Oxford: Blackwell.

Tomlinson, D. (1994). Errors in the research into the effectiveness of grammar teaching. *English in Education, 28,* 2–26.

Torgesen, J., Rashotte, C., and Alexander, A. (2001). The prevention and remediation of reading fluency problems. In M. Wolf (Ed.), *Dyslexia, fluency, and the brain.* Timonium, MD: York Press.

Torgesen, J. K., Wagner, R. K., Rashotte, C. A., Rose, E., Lindamood, P., Conway, J., and Garvan, C. (1999). Preventing reading failure in your children with phonological processing disabilities: Group and individual responses to instruction. *Journal of Educational Psychology, 91,* 579–594.

Tosteson, D., Adelstein, S., and Carver, S. (1994). *New pathways in medical education: Learning to learn at Harvard Medical School.* Cambridge, MA: Harvard University Press.

Tower, C. (2002). "It's a snake, you guys!": The power of text characteristics on children's responses to information books. *Research in The Teaching of English, 27*(1), 55–86.

Treiman, R. (1993). *Beginning to spell: A study of first-grade children.* New York: Oxford University Press.

Treiman, R., and Cassar, M. (1996). Effects of morphology on children's spelling of final consonant clusters. *Journal of Experimental Child Psychology, 63,* 141–170.

Treiman, R., and Cassar, M. (1997). Can children and adults focus on sound as opposed to spelling in a phoneme counting task? *Developmental Psychology, 33,* 771–780.

Treiman, R., and Kessler, B. (2003). The role of letter names in the acquisition of literacy. In R. Kail (Ed.), *Advances in child development and behavior* (Vol. 31, pp. 105–135). San Diego: Academic Press.

Treiman, R., and Rodriguez, K. (1999). Young children use letter names in learning to read words. *Psychological Science, 10,* 334–338.

Treiman, R., Cassar, M., and Zukowski, A. (1994). What types of linguistic information do children use in spelling? The case of flaps. *Child Development, 65,* 1310–1329.

Treiman, R., Goswami, U., and Bruck, M. (1990). Not all nonwords are alike: Implications for reading development and theory. *Memory and Cognition, 18,* 559–567.

Treiman, R., Sotak, L., and Bowman, M. (2001). The role of letter names and letter sounds in connecting print and speech. *Memory and Cognition, 29,* 860–873.

Treiman, R., Tincoff, R., and Richmond-Welty, E. D. (1996). Letter names help children connect print to speech. *Developmental Psychology, 32,* 505–514.

Treiman, R., Zukowski, A., and Richmond-Welty, E. D. (1995). What happened to the "n" of sink? Children's spelling of final consonant clusters. *Cognition, 55,* 1–38.

Treiman, R., Tincoff, R., Rodriguez, K., Mouzaki, A., and Francis, D. J. (1998). The foundations of literacy: learning the sounds of letters. *Child Development, 69*(6), 1524–1540.

Tunmer, W. E., and Hoover, W. A. (1992). Cognitive and linguistic factors in learning to read. In P. Gough, L. Ehri, and R. Treiman (Eds.), *Reading Acquisition* (pp. 175–214). Mahwah, NJ: Lawrence Earlbaum Associates.

Tunmer, W. E., and Hoover, W. A. (1993). Language-related factors as sources of individual differences in the development of word recognition skills. In G. B. Thompson, W. E. Tunmer, and T. Nicholson (Eds.), *Reading acquisition: Book 3. Reading Acquisition Processes* (pp. 123–147). Avon, England: Multilingual Matters.

Turner, J. C. (1995). The influence of classroom contexts on young children's motivation for literacy. *Reading Research Quarterly, 30,* 410–441.

Tyler, A., and Nagy, W. (1989). The acquisition of English derivational morphology. *Memory and Language, 28,* 649–667.

Unsworth, L. (2001). Evaluating the language of different types of explanations in junior high school science texts. *International Journal of Science Education, 23*(6), 585–609.

U.S. Census. (2000). *Profile of selected economic characteristics: 2000.* Washington, DC: U.S. Census Bureau.

U.S. Department of Education. (2002). *Meeting the highly qualified teachers' challenge: The secretary's annual report on teacher quality.* Washington, DC: U.S. Department of Education, Office of Postsecondary Education, Office of Policy Planning and Innovation.

U.S. Department of Education, Office of Special Education and Rehabilitative Services. (2002). *A new era: Revitalizing special education for children and their families.* Washington, DC: Author.

Vacca, R. T. (2005). Let's not minimize the "Big L" in adolescent literacy: A response to Donna Alvermann. In J. Flood and P. L. Anders (Eds.), *Literacy development of students in urban schools: Research and policy.* Newark, DE: International Reading Association.

Vacca, R. T., and Vacca, J.A.L. (1999). *Content area reading: Literacy and learning across the curriculum.* New York: Longman.

Valencia, S. R., and Pearson, P. D. (1991). The development and use of literacy portfolios for students, classes and teachers. *Applied Measurement in Education, 4*(4), 333–346.

Van Bon, W. H., Boksebeld, L. M., Font Freide, T. A., and Van den Hurk, A. J. (1991). A comparison of three methods of reading-while-listening. *Journal of Learning Disabilities, 24,* 471–476.

Van Boxtel, C., van der Linden, J. L., and Kanselaar, G. (2000). The use of textbooks as a tool during collaborative physics learning. *The Journal of Experimental Education, 69*(1), 57–76.

Van Oostendorp, H., and Goldman, S. R. (Eds.). (1999). *The construction of mental representations during reading.* Mahwah, NJ: Lawrence Erlbaum Associates.

Van Orden, G. C. (1987). A ROWS is a ROSE: Spelling, sound, and reading. *Memory & Cognition, 15,* 181–198.

VanSledright, B. (2002). *In search of America's past: Learning to read history in elementary school.* New York: Teachers College Press.

VanSledright, B., and Frankes, L. (2000). Concept and strategic-knowledge development in historical study: A comparative exploration in two fourth-grade classrooms. *Cognition and Instruction, 18*(2), 239–283.

Vellutino, F. R. (1979). *Dyslexia: Theory and research.* Cambridge, MA: MIT Press.

Venezky, R. L. (1970). *The structure of English orthography.* The Hague: Mouton.

Venezky, R. L. (1999). *The American way of spelling: The structure and origins of American English orthography.* New York: Guilford.

Venezky, R. L. (2000). The origins of the present-day chasm between adult literacy needs and school literacy instructions. *Scientific Studies of Reading, 4*(1), 19–39.

Venezky, R. L., and Johnson, D. (1973). Development of two letter-sound patterns in grades one through three. *Journal of Educational Psychology, 64,* 109–115.

Venezky, R. L., and Winfield, L. F. (1979). *Schools that succeed beyond expectations in reading* (No.1). Newark: University of Delaware.

Verhoeven, L., and Snow, C. E. (Eds.). (2001). *Literacy and motivation: Reading engagement in individuals and groups.* Mahwah, NJ: Lawrence Erlbaum Associates.

Visser, T.A.W, and Besner, D. (2001). On the dominance of whole-word knowledge in reading aloud. *Psychonomic Bulletin & Review, 8,* 560–567.

Vogt, M. E. (1997). *Intervention strategies for intermediate and middle school students: Three models (that appear) to work.* Paper presented at the meeting of the Research Institute of the California Reading Association, Anaheim, California.

Vogt, M. E. (1999, December). *Read-2-Succeed: An intervention model for middle and high school students.* Paper presented at the Annual Meeting of the 49th National Reading Conference, Orlando, Florida.

Vogt, M. E., and Shearer, B. A. (2003). *Reading specialists in the real world: A sociocultural view.* Boston: Allyn & Bacon.

Volk, D. (1997). Questions in lessons: Activity settings in the homes and school of two Puerto Rican kindergartners. *Anthropology & Education Quarterly, 28*(1), 22–49.

Voss, J., and Carretero, M. (2000). Learning and reasoning in history. *International Review of History Education* (Vol. 2). London: Woburn Press.

Wagner, R., and Torgesen, J. K. (1987). The nature of phonological processing and its causal role in the acquisition of reading skills. *Psychological Bulletin, 101*(2), 192–212.

Wagner, R., Torgesen, J., Rashotte, C., and others. (1997). Changing relationships between phonological processing abilities and word-level reading as children develop from beginning to skilled readers: A longitudinal study. *Developmental Psychology, 33,* 468–479.

Walberg, H. J., and Tsai, S. (1984). Reading achievement and diminishing returns to time. *Journal of Educational Psychology, 76*(3), 442–451.

Waring, R. (1997). The negative effects of learning words in semantic sets: A replication. *System, 25*(2), 61–74.

Washington, J. A. (1996). Issues in assessing language abilities in African American children. In A. G. Kamhi, K. E. Pollock, and J. L. Harris (Eds.), *Communication development and disorders in African American children: Research, assessment, and intervention.* Baltimore, MD: Brookes.

Washington, J. A., and Craig, H. K. (1998). Socioeconomic status and gender influences on children's dialectal variations. *Journal of Speech, Language & Hearing Research, 41,* 618–626.

Washington, J. A., and Craig, H. K. (2002). Morphosyntactic forms of African American English used by young children and their caregivers. *Applied Psycholinguistics, 23,* 209–231.

Weaver, C. (1996). *Teaching grammar in context.* Portsmouth, NH: Boynton/Cook.

Weaver, C. (1998). *Lessons to share on teaching grammar in context.* Portsmouth, NH: Heinemann.

Wegner, D. M., and Bargh, J. A. (1998). Control and automaticity in social life. In D. T. Gilbert and S. T. Fiske (Eds.), *The handbook of social psychology, Vol. 2* (4th ed., pp. 446–496). Boston: McGraw-Hill.

Weizman, Z. O., and Snow, C. E. (2001). Lexical input as related to children's vocabulary acquisition: Effects of sophisticated exposure and support for meaning. *Developmental Psychology, 37,* 265–279.

Wenglinsky, H. (2000). *How teaching matters: Bringing the classroom back into discussions of teacher quality.* Princeton, NJ: Educational Testing Service. Retrieved May 2, 2003, from www.ets.org/research/pic/teamat.pdf.

West, J., Denton, K., and Germino-Hausken, G. (2000). *America's kindergartners.* Washington, DC: National Center for Education Statistics.

Wharton-McDonald, R., Pressley, M., and Hampston, J. M. (1998). Outstanding literacy instruction in first grade: Teacher practices and student achievement. *Elementary School Journal, 99,* 101–128.

White, K. R. (1982). The relation between socioeconomic status and academic achievement. *Psychological Bulletin, 91,* 461–481.

Whitehurst, G., and Lonigan, C. (1998). Child development and early literacy. *Child Development, 69*(3), 848–872.

Whitehurst, G. J., Epstein, J. N., Angell, A. C., Payne, A. C., Crone, D. A., and Fischel, J. E. (1994). Outcomes of an emergent literacy intervention in Head Start. *Journal of Educational Psychology, 86,* 542–555.

Whitehurst, G. J., Zevenbergen, A. A., Crone, D. A., Schultz, J. D., Velting, O. N., and Fischel, J. E. (1999). Outcomes of an emergent literacy intervention from Head Start through second grade. *Journal of Educational Psychology, 91,* 261–272.

Wigfield, A., and Guthrie, J. T. (1997). Relations of children's motivation for reading to the amount and breadth of their reading. *Journal of Educational Psychology, 89,* 420–432.

Wiggins, G. (1998). *Educative assessment: Designing assessments to inform and improve student performance.* San Francisco: Jossey-Bass Publishers.

Wiley, J., and Voss, J. F. (1996). The effects of "playing historian" on the learning of history. *Journal of Applied Cognitive Psychology, 10,* 563–572.

Wiley, J., and Voss, J. F. (1999). Constructing arguments from multiple sources: Tasks that promote understanding and not just memory for text. *Journal of Educational Psychology, 91,* 301–311.

Wilhelm, J. D., Baker, T. N., and Dube, J. (2001). *Strategic reading: Guiding students to lifelong literacy 6–12.* Portsmouth, NH: Heinemann.

Williams, J. (1992). Processing polysemous words in context: evidence for interrelated meanings. *Journal of Psycholinguistic Research, 21,* 193–218.

Willig, A. C. (1985). A meta-analysis of selected studies on the effectiveness of bilingual education. *Review of Educational Research, 55,* 269–317.

Wilson, S. M., Floden, R. E., and Ferrini-Mundy, J. (2001). *Teacher preparation research: Current knowledge, gaps, and recommendations.* Seattle: Center for the Study of Teaching and Policy.

Wimmer, H., and Goswami, U. (1994). The influence of orthographic consistency on reading development: Word recognition in English and German children. *Cognition, 51,* 91–103.

Wineburg, S. (1991). On the reading of historical texts: Notes on the breach between school and academy. *American Educational Research Journal, 28,* 495–519.

Wineburg, S. (1992). Probing the depths of students' historical knowledge. *Perspectives of the American Historical Association, 30,* 20–24.

Wineburg, S. (1994). The cognitive representation of historical texts. In G. Leinhardt, I. Beck, and C. Stainton, *Teaching and learning in history* (pp. 85–135). Mahwah, NJ: Lawrence Erlbaum Associates.

Wineburg, S. (1998). Reading Abraham Lincoln: An expert/expert study in historical cognition. *Cognitive Science, 22,* 319–346.

Wineburg, S. (1999). Historical thinking and other unnatural acts. *Phi Delta Kappan, 80*(7), 488–499. Retrieved May 15, 2005, from www.pdkintl.org/kappan/kwin9903.htm.

Wineburg, S. (2003). Teaching the mind good habits. *The Chronicle of Higher Education* (Section: The Chronicle Review), *49*(31), B20.

Winograd, P., and Arrington, H. J. (1999). Best practices in literacy assessment. In L. Gambrell, S. B. Neuman, and M. Pressley (Eds.), *Best practices in literacy instruction* (pp. 210–241). New York: Guilford.

Winsler, A., Diaz, R. M., Espinosa, L., and Rodriguez, J. L. (1999). When learning a second language does not mean losing the first: Bilingual language development in low-income, Spanish-speaking children attending bilingual preschool. *Child Development, 70*(2), 349–362.

Wise, B. W., Ring, J., and Olson, R. K. (1999). Training phonological awareness with and without explicit attention to articulation. *Journal of Experimental Child Psychology, 72*(4), 271–304.

Wolf, M. (Ed.). (2001). *Time, fluency, and dyslexia.* Timonium, MD: York Press.

Wolf, M., and Katzir-Cohen, T. (2001). Reading fluency and its intervention. *Scientific Studies of Reading* (Special Issue on Fluency), *5,* 211–238.

Wolf, M., and Kennedy, R. (2003). How the origins of written language instruct us to teach: A response to Steven Strauss. *Educational Researcher, 32*(2), 26–30.

Wolf, M., and Segal, D. (1992). Reading in the developmental dyslexias. *Topics in Language Disorders, 13*(1), 51–65.

Wolf, M., Bowers, P. G., and Biddle, K. (2000). Naming-speed processes, timing, and reading: A conceptual review. *Journal of Learning Disabilities, 33*(4), 387–407.

Wolf, M., Miller, L., and Donnelly, K. (2000). The retrieval, automaticity, vocabulary elaboration, orthography (RAVE-O): A comprehensive fluency-based reading intervention program. *Journal of Learning Disabilities, 33*(4), 375–386.

Wolf, M., Vellutino, F., and Gleason, J. (1998). Psycholinguistic account of reading. In J. Gleason and N. Ratner (Eds.), *Psycholinguistics.* Fort Worth, TX: Harcourt Brace.

Wolfram, W., and Schilling-Estes, N. (1998). *American English: Dialects and variation.* Oxford: Blackwell.

Wolfram, W., Adger, C. T., and Christian, D. (1999). *Dialects in schools and communities.* Mahwah, NJ: Lawrence Earlbaum Associates.

Wood, K. D., and Nichols, W. D. (2000). Helping struggling learners read and write. In K. D. Wood and T. S. Dickinson (Eds.), *Promoting literacy in grades 4–9* (pp. 233–249). Boston: Allyn & Bacon.

Wysocki, K., and Jenkins, J. (1987). Deriving word meanings through morphological generalization. *Reading Research Quarterly, 22*, 66–81.

Yaden, D. B., and Tardibuono, J. M. (2004). The emergent writing development of urban Latino preschoolers: Developmental perspectives and instructional environments for second-language learners. *Reading & Writing Quarterly, 20*(1), 29–61.

Yopp, R. H., and Yopp, H. K. (2000). Sharing informational text with young children. *The Reading Teacher, 53*, 410–423.

Young, A., Bowers, P., and MacKinnon, G. (1996). Effects of prosodic modeling and repeated reading on poor readers' fluency and comprehension. *Applied Psycholinguistics, 17*, 59–84.

Young, K. M., and Leinhardt, G. (1998). Writing from primary documents: A way of knowing in history. *Written Communication, 15*(1), 25–68.

Yuill, N., and Joscelyne, T. (1988). Effects of organisational cues and strategies on good and poor comprehenders' story understanding. *Journal of Educational Psychology, 80*, 152–158.

Yuill, N., and Oakhill, J. (1988). Effects of inference awareness training on poor reading comprehension. *Journal of Applied Cognitive Psychology, 2*, 33–45.

Yuill, N., and Oakhill, J. (1991). *Children's problems in text comprehension: An experimental investigation.* Cambridge, UK: Cambridge University Press.

Yuill, N. M., Oakhill, J. V., and Parkin, A. J. (1989). Working memory, comprehension ability and the resolution of text anomaly. *British Journal of Psychology, 80*, 351–361.

Zamuner, T. S. (2003). *Input-based phonological acquisition.* New York: Routledge.

Zarnowski, M. (1995). Learning history with informational books: A social studies educator's perspective. *The New Advocate, 8*, 183–196.

Zutell, J., and Rasinski, T. (1989). Reading and spelling connections in third and fifth grade students. *Reading Psychology, 10*, 137–155.

Zwaan, R. A., and Radvansky, G. A. (1998). Situation models in language comprehension and memory. *Psychological Bulletin, 123*, 162–185.

NAME INDEX

SUBJECT INDEX

CPSIA information can be obtained at www.ICGtesting.com
Printed in the USA
BVOW01n2232170914

367267BV00009B/15/P